Beyond 1848

Interpretations of the Modern Chicano Historical Experience

Michael R. Ornelas
*Chicano Studies Department
San Diego Mesa College*

KENDALL/HUNT PUBLISHING COMPANY
4050 Westmark Drive   Dubuque, Iowa 52002

CREDITS

"The Psycho-Historical and Socioeconomic Development of the Chicano Community in the United States" by Rodolfo Alvarez is from *Social Science Quarterly* 53:4, pp. 920-942; by permission of the author and the University of Texas Press. All rights retained by the University of Texas Press.

"The U.S. Courts and the Treaty" is from *The Treaty of Guadalupe Hidalgo* by Richard Griswold del Castillo. Copyright © 1990 by the University of Oklahoma Press. Reprinted by permission.

"The Lost Land" and "Aztlan Rediscovered" are from *The Lost Land: The Chicano Image of the Southwest* by John R. Chavez. Copyright © 1984 by the University of New Mexico Press. Reprinted by permission.

"Race and Class in a Southwestern City: The Mexican Community of Tucson" by Thomas E. Sheridan is from *The Renato Rosaldo Lecture Series Monograph*, Mexican American Studies & Research Center, University of Arizona, Tucson, 1988. Reprinted by permission of the author.

"Las Gorras Blancas: A Secret Gathering of Fence Cutters" is from *Mexicano Resistance in the Southwest* by Robert Rosenbaum. Copyright © by Robert Rosenbaum. Reprinted by permission of the author.

"An Essay on Understanding the Work Experience of Mexicans in Southern California, 1900-1939" by Douglas Monroy is from *Aztlan, International Journal of the Social Sciences and the Arts*, Volume 12, No. 1, 1981. Reprinted by permission of the author.

"Responses to Mexican Immigration, 1910-1930" by Ricardo Romo is reprinted with permission from the author.

"Closing America's Back Door" is from *Unwanted Mexican Americans in the Great Depression: Repatriation Pressure, 1929-1939* by Abraham Hoffman. Copyright © 1974 The Arizona Board of Regents. Reprinted by permission of the University of Arizona Press.

"Luisa Moreno and the 1939 Congress of Mexican and Spanish Speaking People" by Albert Camarillo is reprinted by permission of the author.

"The Mexican-American Mind" by Richard A. Garcia is from *History, Culture & Society: Chicano Studies in the 1980's*, edited by Mario T. Garcia and Francisco Lomeli. Reprinted by permission of Richard A. Garcia and Bilingual Press/Editorial Bilingue.

"Mexican American Labor and the Left: The Asociación Nacional México-Americana, 1949-1954" is from *The Chicano Struggle: Analyses of Past and Present Efforts* by Mario T. Garcia. Copyright 1984 by Bilingual Press/Editorial Bilingue. Reprinted by permission.

"Latinos and the 'New Immigrants'" by Richard Griswold del Castillo is reprinted with permission from the author.

COVER
Photos courtesy of Ralph Sánchez, Jr. and César A. González.

Copyright © 1993, 1999 by Kendall/Hunt Publishing Company

ISBN 0-7872-5691-9

All rights reserved. No part of this publication may be reproduced, stored in a retrieval system, or transmitted, in any form or by any means, electronic, mechanical, photocopying, recording, or otherwise, without the prior written permission of the copyright owner.

Printed in the United States of America
10   9   8   7   6   5   4   3

This book is dedicated to
César A. González-T.
"el profe"

crystal

Beyond 1848, Second Edition
Contents

vii	Preface

I
1848-1900

3	The Psycho-Historical and Socioeconomic Development of the Chicano Community in the United States Rodolfo Alvarez
27	The Treaty of Guadalupe Hidalgo, Selected Articles
31	The Protocol of Querétaro
33	The U.S. Courts and the Treaty Richard Griswold del Castillo
49	The Lost Land John R. Chávez
71	Race and Class in a Southwestern City: The Mexican Community of Tucson, 1854-1941 Thomas E. Sheridan
91	Las Gorras Blancas: A Secret Gathering of Fence Cutters Robert J. Rosenbaum
109	Nuestra Plataforma Las Gorras Blancas

II
Since 1900

113	An Essay on Understanding the Work Experience of Mexicans in Southern California, 1900-1939 Douglas Monroy
125	Responses to Mexican Immigration, 1910-1930 Ricardo Romo
149	Closing America's Back Door Abraham Hoffman
163	Luisa Moreno and the 1939 Congress of Mexican and Spanish Speaking People Albert Camarillo
181	The Mexican American Mind Richard A. García
191	Mexican American Labor and the Left: The Asociación Nacional México-Americana, 1949-1954 Mario T. García
213	Aztlán Rediscovered John R. Chávez
245	Latinos and the "New Immigrants," Since 1975 Richard Griswold del Castillo
269	Key Terms and Discussion Questions
301	Index
309	The Contributors

Preface

Beyond 1848 is a collection of interpretive essays with a special focus on the Chicano historical experience since 1848. The end of the Mexican American War and the tough negotiations resulting in the Treaty of Guadalupe Hidalgo defined, at least in legal terms, the incorporation of former Mexican territories and the first generation of Mexican-born United States citizens. Promising to include these new Americans on an equal basis with their other fully entitled American citizens, the treaty had little moral or legal influence on officials or institutions that participated in undermining it.
Each of the selections within this book introduces students to a particular aspect of the Chicano historical experience since this pivotal time in the history of the two nations.

In the 1840s and 1850s Mexico's former citizens were blindly plunged into a new and alien cultural, political and social world. The protections guaranteed between two former enemy nations left the victor, the United States, with the moral and legal obligation to establish mechanisms to ensure their full and equal inclusion into the political life of the country. But the original 120,000 inhabitants of the newly acquired territories faced tremendous unanticipated pressures to preserve their culture, political voice and economic base. For the most part, the next twenty years would set in motion forces which would shape a new subordinate status. These new American citizens came to occupy a position not much better than that of the American Indian, but free from slavery. The United States would ultimately fail to incorporate the new citizens "to the enjoyment of all the rights of citizenship according to the principles of the Constitution."

Beyond 1848 offers interpretations of this modern historical experience since the middle of the nineteenth century. Section I includes the nineteenth century experience from the signing of the Treaty of Guadalupe Hidalgo to about 1900. We witness historic struggles over land, the legal exclusion of Mexicans from sharing in the economic resources of the territories and the eventual subordination of the new American citizens. This was the outcome, to varying degrees, in the four major areas of the Southwest: California, New Mexico, Arizona and Texas. And this is the creation experience for the first generation, but similar patters would continue long into the twentieth century.

Beyond 1848

Section II offers interpretations of the historical experience since then. It includes patterns of early twentieth century migrations and immigrations into the American Southwest, accommodation strategies by native-born and immigrant Mexicans, the formation of ethnic-based organizations responsive to their needs, patterns of residential and labor specialization, and patterns of racial segregation and discrimination not unlike that which was faced by other ethnic minority groups in the United States. What emerges is that each generation, from the original inhabitants to the current Chicano generation, has embraced strategies to create new responses and implememented new visions of their place in American society.

Since this important time, Chicanos continue to reside in the same area which the United States acquired through war and treaty. But now their numbers and influence continue to grow to unprecedented levels throughout the Southwest. And like their predecessors, they are trying to unmake their former status and create whole new ones. This struggle continues into the present, in the midst of California's revitalized anti-immigrant attitude and legislation that demonstrates a growing intolerance toward ethnic minority people.

I would like to extend thanks to a number of people who helpful in the making of this second edition of *Beyond 1848*. First and foremost I would like to extend my sincere appreciation to my wife and friend, Eva, for her great assistance in the preparation of this book. I would also like to thank César A. González-T. and Ralph Sánchez for the use of their photos. Richard Lou also deserves my appreciation for his helpful assistance in the preparation of the photos. Janice Samuells, Lenny Behnke and Joyce Blum of Kendall/Hunt also deserve my thanks for their support and encouragement. Without them, this collection would not have been possible.

Michael R. Ornelas
San Diego, California
mornelas@sdccd.cc.ca.us

I
1848-1900

Photo courtesy of Ralph Sánchez, Jr.

Rodolfo Alvarez' interpretive essay on the Chicano historical experience traces the development of the community through four generational phases. Chicanos, Alvarez argues, are products of two conquests of the distant past. Their presence in the Southwest following the Treaty of Guadalupe Hidalgo is the product of the more recent Mexican American war. Since that time, the Chicano experience has entered into four phases: the Creation, Migrant, Mexican American and Chicano. Each has had a unique impact on the socioeconomic and political evolution of the Chicano community. Chicanos have also evolved individually identifiable self-identities based upon their generational experience. Each reflect their historical experience and their mode of self-perception.

The Psycho-Historical and Socioeconomic Development of the Chicano Community in the United States

Rodolfo Alvarez

The closest approximation to objective knowledge can be gained from the confrontation of honestly different perspectives that subsume the same or related sets of facts. What is presented in this paper is a marshalling of historical fact from a perspective not traditionally taken into account in scholarly discourse on Mexican Americans. The objective is to confront the reality of Mexican American society as we have experienced it and from that basis to generate hypotheses for future multi-disciplinary research in this area. For this purpose we identify four historical periods and describe the climate of opinion within the generation of Mexican Americans that numerically dominates the period. What I mean by a "generation" is that a critical number of persons, in a broad but delimited age group, had more or less the same socialization, experiences because they lived at a particular time under more or less the same constraints imposed by a dominant United States society. Each generation reflects a different state of collective consciousness concerning its relationship to the larger society; psycho-historical differences related to, if not induced by, the economic system.

We begin our analysis with the assertion that, *as a people,* Mexican Americans are a creation of the imperial conquest of one nation by another through military force. Our people were thrown into a new set of circumstances, and began to evolve new modes of thought and action in order to survive, making Mexican American culture different from the culture of Mexicans in Mexico. Because we live in different circumstances we have evolved different cultural modes; just as we are neither identical to "Anglos" in the United States nor to Mexicans in Mexico, we, nevertheless, incorporate into our own ethos much from both societies. This is because we respond to problems of existence that confront us in unique ways, distinct from the way in which Anglos and Mexicans experience them.

How, then, did we pass from being a sovereign people into a state of being compatriots with the newly arrived Anglo settlers, coming mostly from the southern United States, and, finally, into the condition of becoming a conquered people-a charter minority on our own land?

The coming of the Spaniards to Mexico began the development of a mestizo people which has come to be the largest category of Mexican society. The mestizo is the embodiment of biological, cultural and social heterogeneity. This sector of Mexican society was already numerically ascendant by the time Mexico gained its independence from Spain. Sovereign Mexico continued more or less the identical colonization patterns that had been developed by Spain by sending a cadre of soldiers, missionaries, and settlers to establish a mission and presidio where Indians were brought in and "Christianized." Once the Indians were socialized to the peculiar mixture of Indian and Hispanic western cultural patterns which constituted the mestizo adaptation to the locale, they were granted tracts of land, which they cultivated to support themselves in trade with the central settlement, and through that, with the larger society with its center in Mexico City. As the settlement grew and prospered, new outposts were developed further and further out into the provinces. Thus, Mexican society, like the Spanish society before it, was after *land* and *souls* in its development of the territories over which it held sovereignty. The Indian quickly was subjugated into the lowest stratum of society to do the heaviest and most undesirable work at the least cost possible-although biologically "pure," but fully acculturated Indians frequently entered the dominant mestizo society. They also tended to marry settlers coming north from central Mexico to seek their fortunes. Light and dark skinned alike were "Mexican."

What is of historic significance here is that in the early 1800's, particularly on the land now called Texas, this imperialistic system came into direct conflict with another; that sponsored by England which resulted in the creation of the United States of America. Both systems set out aggressively to induce the economic development of the area. However, while the Hispanic system sought economic development through the acquisition of *land* and *souls*, the Anglo system that had been established on the northern Atlantic seaboard was one of acquiring *land, but not souls.* An Indian could not have been elected president of the United States as Don Benito Juarez was in Mexico. Rather, the Indian was "pushed back" as the European settlement progressed. He had to be either manifestly cooperative in getting out of the way (and later into reservations), or be exterminated. The new society in the United States was, therefore, a great deal more homogeneous than in Mexico since it was fundamentally a European adaptation to the new land and not in any way a mixture of Indian and European elements.

It should be said here, without wanting to overemphasize, that there is some evidence from correspondence between Thomas Jefferson and James Monroe that these and other key figures in the United States had intended to take the Southwest long before U.S. settlers started moving into Texas. Insofar as the stage was not yet set for this final move, the coming of United States citizens into Texas was a case study in peaceful cooperation between peoples with fundamentally different ideological perspectives. The Anglo settlers initially and publicly made the minimal necessary assertions of loyalty to Mexico-despite the fact that they did not live up to the letter of the settlement contracts which called for them to become Mexican citizens and Roman Catholic.

This cooperative experience lasted until approximately 1830-35. During this time Texas was being rapidly settled by Mexicans moving north ("rapidly," considering their form of colonization). Also, some Europeans, a few of them Roman Catholic, arrived in Galveston and settled throughout the territory. Others, in a stream that was ultimately to become the majority, came from the southern region of the United States. I call this the cooperative experience because there is historical evidence that all of these people, regardless of their point of origin, cooperated relatively well with each other. The frontier was sufficiently rugged that all needed each other's help and ideas in order to survive. Because everyone was given title to generous amounts of land, there was no struggle over land, which was the capital that they all sought. This period may be characterized as one in which every group could, apparently, optimize accomplishment of its objectives. The Mexican government needed to settle the area to secure its claim over the land and to reap the economic gain from its productivity; the settlers, whatever their origin (Indian, mestizo, European, or Anglo) came to develop their own personal economic assets. Because the country was so biologically and culturally heterogeneous, the question of how to develop a stable functioning society was crucial, once the break with Spain had been accomplished. During this period, some Anglo filibustering (insurrectionist activity in a foreign country) did take place. However, there is evidence that other Anglo groups were instrumental in helping to put these activities down. The *general* tone of the times was that of inter-cultural cooperation. Each group learned from the others as they applied their resources to the economic development of the area.

Somewhere around 1835 began what I call the "revolutionary experience." This was a revolutionary experience, in the usual sense of the term, only toward the end of this phase, as was perhaps inevitable given widespread territorial ambitions in the United States (subsequently labeled "manifest destiny" by historians of the period). The conflict was exacerbated by an ideological struggle within Mexican society between federalists and centralists. These political philosophies, while based to a considerable degree on economic self-interest of the partisans of either faction, also embodied widely divergent views on the nature of man himself.

The centralists were for administrative control over all Mexican territory by the governing elite in Mexico City. The federalists, on the other hand, were idealists trying to implement in Mexico the noble political principles of the rights of man as enunciated by the United States Constitution (after which the federalist constitution of 1824 was modeled) and by French political theorists of the Enlightenment. They were for egalitarianism in practice within a culturally and racially heterogeneous society, and not only in principle within a relatively racially and culturally homogeneous society, as in the United States. The centralists were skeptical of the possibility of self-government by a heterogeneous population, the major proportion of whom they considered inferior culturally, especially so because a poor country, such as Mexico, could not invest sufficient resources to educate the masses, who were mostly Indian.

It appeared to the majority of settlers in Texas-Mexicans, as well as others-that federalism would provide the best economic outcome for them. The province of Texas became a stronghold of federalism, and the majority decided to remain loyal to the federalist Mexican constitution of 1824. Santa Anna by this time had switched his ideological stance from federalism to centralism and had taken control of the central government in Mexico City. His reaction to events in Texas was to send troops to discipline the dissident province. However, the poorly professionalized army acted badly in Texas and alienated much of the populace by the unnecessary spilling of blood. The fact that many of these settlers came from the slave holding South probably did not make relations with Mexicans, whom they considered inferior, easier. Heightened sentiment led to hostile actions and a revolution was started. The upshot was that Santa Anna personally came to command the army that was to put down the revolution and was himself defeated. Once the chief executive and the army of the sovereign country of Mexico were defeated, there was no real pressure for the dissident province to remain a loyal entity within the mother country-even though many of the settlers had set out originally simply to attain a federalist rather than a centralist government in Mexico. Furthermore, when the fighting broke out, adventurers and fortune seekers poured from the United States into Texas to participate in the fight. Evidence that these people, as well as their friends and relatives who remained behind, had a great sense of their "manifest destiny" to acquire more land for the United States, is abundant and is illustrated by the fact that from as far away as Cincinnati, Ohio, came contributions of cannons and supplies as soon as it appeared that separating Texas from Mexico was a possibility. Once hostilities began and these people began to pour in, the federalists loyal to Mexico were outnumbered and full-blown independence from Mexico was declared. When Santa Anna was ultimately defeated, it was still not clear that Mexico would be incapable of reassembling an army and returning to discipline the dissident province. The extreme biological and cultural heterogeneity which characterized Mexico then (as it does today) was one of the bases of Mexico's difficulty in self-government. The depth of Mexico's internal disarray became apparent soon enough. Texas was absorbed into the United States, provoking armed conflict with Mexico. If Mexico had not been able to discipline Texas, it certainly was no match for the well-trained and well equipped U.S. Army backed by a *relatively* homogeneous society. By 1848 Mexico had lost approximately 50 percent of its territory. It appears that perhaps Santa Anna may have personally profited by Mexico's disarray. With the signing of the Treaty of Guadalupe-Hidalgo, the Mexican American people were created *as a people:* Mexican by birth, language and culture; United States citizens by the might of arms.

The Creation Generation

Following incorporation of the Southwest into the United States in the mid-1800's there developed the experience of economic subjugation, followed by race and ethnic prejudice:

Mexico ... simply had to accept the best deal possible under the circumstances of military defeat; that deal meant that Mexico lost any respect it might have had in the eyes of the Mexicans living on the lands annexed by the United States. This rapid change must, certainly have given them a different social-psychological view of self that they had prior to the break. The break and annexation meant that they were now citizens of the United States, but surely they could not have changed their language and culture overnight merely because their lands were now the sovereign property of the United States; thus they maintained their "Mexicanness." Because their cultural ties were to Mexico, they were, in effect, "Mexicans" in the United States. As the number of "Americans" in the region increased, "Mexicans" became an ever smaller proportion of the population. They were ... a minority. They thought, spoke, dressed, acted, and had all of the anatomical characteristics of the defeated Mexicans. In fact, were they not still "Mexicans" from the point of view of "Americans" even though they were United States citizens by virtue of the military defeat and treaties that gave sovereignty to the United States. For all of these reasons and more, the "Mexican" minority could be viewed as the deviants onto whom all manner of aggressions could be displaced whenever the Calvinistic desire for material acquisition was in the least frustrated.

It is the psycho-historical experience of a rapid and clear break with the culture of the parent country, and subsequent subjugation against the will of the particular population under analysis-all of this taking place on what the indigenous population considered to be its "own" land-that makes the experience of Mexican Americans different from all other ethnic populations that migrated to this country in the nineteenth and twentieth centuries.

All of the factors necessary for the development of race prejudice against Mexicans, now Mexican Americans, were present after 1836 in Texas. Any bloody war will engender very deeply felt animosity between contending factions. Furthermore, in order to kill, without feelings of remorse, it may be necessary to define the enemy as being sub-human and worthy of being killed. In the case of the fight between centralist and federalist forces in Texas it should be noted that the centralist army was almost exclusively Mexican, having been recruited deep in Mexico and brought north by Santa Anna. The federalist forces in the province of Texas, on the other hand, were a mixture of Mexican, European, and U.S. settlers. However, once the centralist forces were defeated, the hatred toward them, that had now become a hatred of Mexico and Mexicans, could easily be displaced onto settlers who in every respect could be said to be Mexicans, even though they had been federalists and had fought for Texas independence.

Second, since most of the settlers in Texas who came from the United States were from the slave holding South, the idea of racial inferiority was not unknown to them and could easily be used to explain the hostile emotions they held toward the Mexicans, against whom they had just fought a winning fight.

A third factor making for the development of intense race prejudice against Mexican Americans was economic. Once Texas became independent it left the door open wide for massive migration from the United States. Title to the land had already been parceled out under Mexican sovereignty. Through legal and extra-legal means, the land was taken away from those provincial Mexicans, who as Texans had cooperated to try to give the province a measure of autonomy. These were the betrayed people, betrayed by their fellow Texans, once Texas became fully autonomous. By 1900 even those provincial Mexicans who had owned large tracts of land and who had held commanding social positions in Texas and throughout southwestern society had been reduced to a landless, subservient wage-earner class-with the advent of a new English language legal system, masses of English speaking land hungry migrants, and strong anti-Mexican feelings-both by force of arms and through legal transactions backed up by force of arms. Furthermore, it was the importation of race prejudice that created an impenetrable caste boundary between the dominant provincials of northern European background and the provincial Mexicans. Once race prejudice was imported and accepted on a broad scale as an adequate explanation and justification for the lower caste condition of local "Mexicans," these attitudes could spread rapidly into the rest of the Southwest, when the United States acquired a large proportion of northern Mexico. The experience of socioeconomic and political subjugation was repeated throughout the Southwest, with some variations for peculiar circumstances in specific areas, New Mexico in particular. Many of the distinctly Mexican American attitudes throughout the country today stem from the subjugation experience of this period.

The Migrant Generation

By socioeconomic as well as political subservience of the Mexican American throughout the Southwest was well established. At the same time, the United States population was slowly becoming urbanized and was increasing very rapidly in size. Instead of small farms and ranches that provided income for one family, agriculture was increasingly conducted on very large farms in order to grow massive quantities of food profitably. Despite the growing mechanization during this period (after 1900 and before World War II), the large farms and ranches of the Southwest required massive manual labor at certain periods in the growing season. Cheap Mexican labor was inexpensive and required much less care than the machines that were only then coming on the farms.

To provide the massive agricultural labor needed, recruiters were sent deep into Mexico to spread the word of higher wages on the large farms in the United States. Coincidently with this "pull," political upheavals in Mexico created a population "push." The resulting huge waves of migrants coming north to work the fields give the name "Migrant Generation" to this period. Until the 1920's the migrant stream flowed north predominantly through Texas (where racial attitudes were imposed) and then beyond Texas to spread out over the agricultural region of the Great Lakes and western United States. It was not until after World War II that the migrant flow began to come predominantly through California. These people have been called "immigrants" by social scientists and by policy makers because they moved from one sovereign country to another. However true their "immigrant" status might have been legally, they were not immigrants either sociologically or culturally because of the peculiar psycho-historical experience of Mexican Americans in the Southwest prior to 1900. Even those who eventually settled around the Great Lakes and later in the Northwest usually lived for a period of time in the Southwest where they were socialized into the cultural mode of the period.

There are at least four reasons why Mexicans arriving after 1900 but before World War II should be sociologically viewed as "migrants" who simply expanded the number of people who had more or less the same consciousness of lower caste status as those Mexican Americans who were here prior to 1900. First, the post-1900 waves of Mexican nationals coming into the United States did not come into a fresh social situation where they were meeting the host society for the first time. They did not arrive with the "freedom" to define themselves in the new society in accordance with their own wishes and aspirations. Not only were they denied the social-psychological process of "role taking" among the established higher status occupations, but demands and impositions of the dominant society were such that neither could they experiment with the process of "role making"; i.e., the creation of alternative but equal-status occupations. They did not arrive with the "freedom" that comes from having one's self-image and self-esteem determined almost exclusively from one's presentation-of-self to strangers, where these strangers have no prior experience with which to question or invalidate the social claims being made by the performance. Immigrants from other lands arrived in the United States, and their place in the social hierarchy was, in a sense, freshly negotiated according to what the group as a whole could do here. The social situation that the post-1900 waves of Mexicans entering the United States encountered was very different from that of immigrants from other lands. Their experience upon entering the United States was predefined by the well established social position of pre-1900 Mexican Americans as a conquered people (politically, socially, culturally, economically, and in every other respect). They came to occupy the category closest to simple beasts of burden in the expanding regional economy.

The people coming from Mexico, in very large numbers after 1900, viewed themselves and were viewed by the dominant host society as the "same" as those Mexican Americans who had been living on the land long before, during, and after the psycho-historical experience described above as resulting in the "Creation

Generation." Before they came they knew they would find, and when they arrived they did find, a large, indigenous population with whom they had language, kinship, customs, and all manner of other genetic, social, cultural, and psychological aspects in common. The very interesting and highly peculiar circumstance in the case of the post-1900 migrant from Mexico is that he left a lower *class* status in Mexico to enter a lower *caste* status in the United States without being aware of it. The reasons he was unaware of it are multiple, reflecting the great network of characteristics in common with the people already here. The fact is that the vast majority of Mexican Americans never realized they were in a caste, as opposed to a class, category because they never tried to escape in any substantial numbers. The permeability of normative boundaries need never be an issue, so long as no one attempts to traverse them. Until World War II there existed a state of pluralistic ignorance between those few individuals and groups of Mexican Americans who tried to escape the caste and the majority of relatively unaware members of the Mexican American population. The state of development of mass communications probably prevented widespread knowledge across the Southwest of the many isolated incidents that took place during this period. When a critical proportion of Mexican Americans began to earn enough money to pay for their children's education and began to expect services that they saw non-Mexican American members of the society enjoying, they found out that they were not viewed just simply as members of a less affluent class, but, rather, as members of a despised caste. This was the critical test. If they had achieved skills and affluence in Mexico, race and ethnicity would have been no barrier to personal mobility into a higher socioeconomic class. It was the attempt to permeate the normative boundaries and the subsequent reaction by the larger society that brought out in the open the way they were perceived by the dominant host society. During the period designated as the "Migrant Generation," there were many isolated instances of great conflict between groups of Mexican Americans trying to alter their lower caste status, but they were locally overpowered, and a general state of acquiescence became the state of collective consciousness.

    A second factor that characterized post-1900 incoming Mexicans as migrants rather than immigrants is that the land they came to was virtually identical to the land they left. Today there is a sharp contrast between the terrain north and south of the border because of mechanization and irrigation for large scale industrialized farming on the United States side, and the same old water-starved flatland on the Mexican side. However, in the early period when the great waves of migrants came, the land was sufficiently similar to what they had left behind that it did not require a cognitive reorientation for them.

The fact that the land they came to was very similar, physically, to the land they left behind is very important because it had been part of Mexico. Thus, the post-1900 migrant from Mexico to the United States was not leaving land to which he had a deep identity-giving psychological relationship and going off to another, very different "foreign" land, to which he needed to develop another sort of identity giving relation. The Irish immigrant, for example, experienced a great discontinuity between the land of origin and the land of destination. Furthermore, the nation-state and the culture identified with the land to which he was going had never been part of the nation-state and culture he was leaving behind. When the Irish immigrant left "Ireland" to go to "America," there surely must have been a very clear psychic understanding that he was leaving behind a land to which he had a very special relationship that made him an "Irishman." The post-1900 migrant from Mexico need not have noticed any change. He was simply moving from one part of his identity-giving land to another. The work he was to perform on the land of destination was identical to the work he performed on the land of origin.

A third set of factors that distinguished the Migrant Generation from immigrants from other countries involves the physical nature of the border that they had to cross to come into the United States. Over large distances the border between the United States and Mexico was never more than an imaginary line. Even in that part of Texas separated from Mexico by the Rio Grande, the natural obstacles are minimal. During much of the year people could simply walk across, and certainly at other times they could cross the river as any other river might be crossed. The amount of time that it takes to cross the border also affects the degree of anticipatory socialization that the person can engage in prior to arrival at his point of destination. The Irish immigrant spent the better part of two weeks crossing an enormous physical obstacle, the Atlantic Ocean. The great physical boundary separating his land of origin from his land of destination could not escape his notice. The time it took to traverse that boundary afforded the immigrant the opportunity gradually, but profoundly, to engage in serious contemplation that allowed him to significantly "disassociate" his identity from one nation-state and its culture and to engage in more or less effective anticipatory socialization for his new identity and new life in another nation-state and its culture. The point here is that the nature of the physical border (its overpowering size) and the time it took to traverse it made it virtually impossible for the immigrant not to be deeply conscious of the fact that he was entering a new society and therefore, a new place within the structure of that society. This was not the case with the Mexican migrant.

A fourth set of factors distinguishing Mexicans of the Migrant Generation from immigrants from other countries is the nature of their activity in coming to this country. There is undoubtedly a significant psychic impact deriving from the degree to which the individual is a free and autonomous agent in determining the course of his own behavior. The greater the degree to which the individual perceives himself as self-determining, the less his behavior will precipitate a change of his already established identity. Conversely, the more the individual perceives (and his perceptions are validated) that his behavior is significantly determined by others, the greater will be the impact of that realization on his identity. The Irish immigrant, for example, had significant others affecting his behavior in such a way that he could not avoid considering the identity that he was rejecting and the one he was assuming. He had to ask for official permission to leave his country of origin, be physically conveyed across an ocean to enter a country he had had to obtain official permission to enter. Those actions forced him to consider his purpose in making the crossing, and whether he was prepared to abandon one identity for the other; whether he was prepared to pay the psychic price. The Mexican migrants, on the other hand, were "active agents," more or less in control of their own movement. They did not, in the early 1900's, have to ask anyone for permission to leave one country to enter the other. If they made their own personal decision to go, they simply went. There was no official transaction that in any way impinged on their collective self-identity. It took seven minutes to cross a river. The significance of the decision to swim or use the bridge is analogous to the modern-day decision either to walk downtown or to pay for a taxi-hardly an identity-making decision. It was not until the mid-1930's that the border was "closed," that is, when an official transaction was required to cross the border. By this time, however, such an enormous number of people had already crossed, and the Mexican American population, within the lower caste existing in the southwestern United States, was so large that it did not matter in terms of the conceptual argument. The later migrant waves simply inflated the lower caste and took on its psychic orientation (i.e., its collective state of consciousness), despite the fact that by the official transaction they were made conscious that they were now in the sovereign territory of another nation-state. This was so because all other factors still applied, and, in addition, the impact of the large population into which they moved was overwhelming.

The post-1900 migrants came mainly to Texas and California. There they assumed the already established lower caste position we have described, as a consequence of the prior established social structure. Socio-psychologically, the migrants, too, were a conquered people, both because their land of origin had been conquered by the United States and because the Mexican Americans, with whom they were completely commingled, had been treated as a lower caste of conquered people inside the now expanded version of the United States. As such, they were powerless appendages of the regional economy. Their manual labor was essential to the agricultural development of the area. But whenever the business cycle took a turn for the worse, they were easily forced to go back to Mexico; they were forcibly deported. Their United-States-born children were deported right along with the parents. The deportation of Mexican Americans-United States citizens-was not uncommon, since to the U.S. Border Patrol, U.S. Immigration Service ("Migra"), and the Texas Rangers there frequently seemed little or not difference between Mexican Americans and Mexican nationals; they were all simply "Mexican."

There is for Mexican Americans a very bitter irony in all of this. The irony is that the post-1900 migrants and the pre-1900 lower caste citizens of Mexican descent learned to live more or less comfortably with all of this largely because of their frame of reference. Both constantly compared themselves to Mexican citizens in Mexico. That they should have Mexico as their cultural frame of reference is understandable. The irony is, however, that they never compared themselves to other minority groups in this country, possibly because of geographic isolation. The price the Mexican American had to pay in exchange for higher wages received for stoop labor in the fields and for lower status work in the cities was a pervasive, universal subjugation into a lower caste that came about silently and engulfed him, long before he became aware of it. He became aware of his lower caste, economically powerless position only when he (or his children) tried to break out of the caste and was forced to remain in it. By that time it was too late. He had learned to enjoy a higher wage than he would have had in Mexico and to accept a degrading lower caste position. His lower socioeconomic position in the United States was never salient in his mind.

The Mexican American Generation

Starting somewhere around the time of the Second World War, and increasing in importance up to the war in Vietnam, there has developed another state of collective consciousness which I call the "Mexican American Generation." This generation increasingly has turned its sense of cultural loyalty to the United States. As members of this generation were achieving maturity, they began to ask their parents:

What did Mexico ever do for you? You were poor and unwanted there. Your exodus reduced the unemployment rate and welfare problems that powerful economic elements in Mexico would have had to contend with, so they were happy to see you leave. You remained culturally loyal to the memory of Mexico, and you had dreams of returning to spend your dollars there. You sent money back to your family relations who remained in Mexico. Both of these acts of cultural loyalty on your part simply improved Mexico's dollar balance of payment. And what did Mexico do for you except help labor contractors and unscrupulous southwestern officials to further exploit you? I am an "American" who happens to be of Mexican descent. I am going to participate fully in this society because, like descendants of people from so many other lands, I was born here, and my country will guarantee me all the rights and protections of a free and loyal citizen.

    What the members of the Mexican American generation did not realize was that, relative to the larger society, they were still just as economically dependent and powerless to affect the course of their own progress as the members of the older Migrant Generation. If the Migrant Generation had Mexicans in Mexico as their socioeconomic reference, the Mexican American Generation, in similar fashion, did not effectively compare its own achievements to those of the larger society, but to the achievements of the Migrant Generation. This comparison was a happy one for the Mexican American Generation. They could see that they were economically better off than their parents had ever been. They could see that they had achieved a few years of schooling while their parents had achieved virtually none.

    What the Mexican American Generation did not realize was that their slight improvement in education, income, political efficacy, and social acceptance was an accomplishment only by virtue of comparison to the Migrant Generation which started with nothing. The Mexican American Generation was far behind the black population as the black population was behind the Anglo on every measure of social achievement; i.e., years of education achieved, political efficacy, annual income per family, etc. But these comparisons were rarely made during this period when Mexican Americans changed from being a predominantly rural population employed in agricultural stoop labor to an urban population employed predominantly in unskilled service occupations. Today, for example, approximately 83 percent of the Mexican American population lives in cities, even though in most instances the mass media still portrays Mexican Americans as rural stoop laborers. This was the period when the first relatively effective community protective organizations began to be formed. The organizing documents are so painfully patriotic as to demonstrate the conceptualized ambitions of the membership rather than their actual living experience.

The change of Mexican Americans from a rural to an urban population was precipitated by the rapid industrialization of agriculture that was brought about initially by the production requirements of World War II (and the simultaneous manpower drain required for the military) and was subsequently sustained and enhanced by the scientific and technological revolution that followed the war. Agriculture had increasingly been organized around big farms since 1900 in order to meet the demands of an expanding population. The massive production required by World War II, in the absence of Mexican American labor-since the Mexican American population participated disproportionately in the war-led to the increasingly rapid conversion of agriculture to resemble the industrialized factory. During the initial phases of the war, much stoop labor was imported from Mexico, but later this became less necessary because machines increasingly were filling the need for all but the most delicate agricultural picking jobs. The entire economic system reached the highest development of the ideals of industrialized society. Perhaps more money and somewhat better working conditions were to be found in cities, but that was not because of any gains on the part of Mexican Americans; it was rather because of the nature of urban living and industrial production of the post-World War II era of United States capitalism. Compared to the majority, the Mexican American did not have sufficient understanding of the nature of the society in which he lived and its economic system to even know that he was being treated unfairly. To the extent that he became conscious of his economically disadvantaged position, he was powerless to do anything about it.

At this point it is fair to ask: If the Mexican American Generation was so poorly educated, how did it ever get the training, skills, and general awareness of things to be able to move in large numbers from the fields to the cities and survive? Here, we have to introduce another statement about socioeconomic dependency. About the time of World War II when industrialization was beginning to be felt out in the fields, a substantial proportion of the Migrant Generation was nearing old age. Older people began to move to the cities to do the lighter work that was available there. At the same time, the young people were being moved into the war effort, young men to the military and young women to work in the war production industries and the skills and technical competency that young Mexican Americans acquired in the military were directly transferable to industrial employment in the cities after the war ended.

Finally, the fact that they fought and saw their military friends and neighbors die in defense of the United States led Mexican Americans generally not to question their relative status in the economy and their lack of control over it. Little did they realize that everyone else was also experiencing both a real and an inflationary increase in economic standing; that other groups were experiencing a faster rate of economic increase because of their more effective direct participation in bringing it about. The Mexican American was only experiencing a kind of upward coasting with the general economy and was not directly influencing his own economic betterment. As a group, Mexican Americans remained at the bottom of the socioeconomic ladder.

Many Mexican Americans attempted to escape their caste-like status by leaving the Southwest to seek employment in the industrial centers of the mid-western Great Lakes region and in the cities of the Northwest. Others went to California. A high degree of industrialization and a very heterogeneous population (religiously, ethnically, and politically) have always been the factors that attenuated discrimination against Mexican Americans in California. In fact, it is in California (and of course in the Midwest to a smaller extent) that the Mexican American first began to have the characteristics of a lower *class* population on a massive scale, as opposed to the lower *caste* experience. Of course, among the southwestern states on a smaller but widespread scale, the state of New Mexico seems to have come to a condition of class as compared to caste emphasis in a prolonged, gradual manner. This was perhaps due to the fact that the experience of the Migrant Generation never took place as intensely in New Mexico. The post-1900 immigrants came in large numbers to Texas early in the period and to California later (circa W.W. II). However, New Mexico was essentially bypassed by the Migrant Generation. Furthermore, in New Mexico the experience of the Creation Generation was neither as severe nor as complete as it was in Texas and California. In New Mexico the Creation Generation experience did take place, but so-called Hispanos managed to retain some degree of political and economic control since they represented such a large percentage of the population- even with, or in spite of, all the extensive land swindles by invading Anglos. Interestingly, the fact that the Mexicans in middle and northern New Mexico were never fully subjugated into a lower caste position is reflected in the linguistic labels they use to identify themselves. It may be argued that in order to differentiate themselves from those who had been subjugated into a lower caste, the so-called Hispanos in New Mexico started calling themselves Spanish Americans some time around the First World War, despite the fact that their anatomical features were those of Mexican mestizaje and did not resemble Spaniards. At that time, their previous geographic isolation began to be ended by large numbers of Anglos from Texas who came to settle in the southeastern part of the state of New Mexico. The Texans brought with them their generalized hatred of Mexicans and their view of them as lower caste untouchables. Thus, out of self-protection, New Mexicans started to call themselves Spanish Americans and to insist that they could trace their racial and ethnic origins to the original Spanish settlements in the area. The linguistic ruse worked so well that Mexican Americans in New Mexico came to believe their own rhetoric. The point to be made here is that this linguistic device was used by a large and isolated population that had not been fully subjugated into a lower caste to maintain in New Mexico the semblance of a class position. It is in New Mexico more than in any of the other southwestern states that Mexican Americans have participated in the society as people who have had the freedom and possibility of social mobility to become members of various social classes. They did this, however, at the price of altering their identity to make themselves acceptable to stronger economic, if not political, interests in the state. Today, however, the younger members of the post-World War II period are developing a new consciousness even in New Mexico. It is the current high school and college age offspring of the so-called Spanish Americans who are using the term Chicano and who are demanding documentation for the presumed historic culture links to Spain. What they are finding-the greater links to Mexican and to Indian culture-is beginning to have an effect on their parents, many of whom are beginning to view themselves as Mexican Americans with some measure of pride.

Some of the tensions within the Mexican American community during this period of time could be explained in terms of the generalized attempt to be more like "Anglo" citizens. Those people who were themselves born in the United States had greater legitimation for their claims of loyalty to the United States and for their psychic sense of security on the land. They in fact would, in various disingenuous ways, disassociate themselves from those whose claim to belonging could not be as well established; even parents or family elders who were born in Mexico and came over during the period described as the Migrant Generation would be viewed as somehow less legitimate. In the cities a slight distinction was made between the older Mexican Americans who now held stable working class and small entrepreneurial positions as compared to newly arrived migrants from Mexico who entered the urban unskilled labor pool. This, of course, increased the insecurity and decreased the willingness to engage in collective action among the members of the Migrant Generation. They were in a particularly insecure position psychically, economically, and in almost every other regard. They were rejected and mistreated by the dominant Anglo population and rebuffed (as somehow deserving of that mistreatment) by their offspring.

The Mexican American Generation purchased a sense of psychic "security" at a very heavy price. They managed to establish their claims as bona fide citizens of the United States in the eyes of only one of the social psychologically relevant populations: themselves. The dominant Anglo population never ceased to view them as part of the "inferior" general population of Mexican Americans. The Migrant Generation never fully believed that their offspring would be able to become "Anglos" in any but the most foolhardy dreams of aspiring youth. They had a very apt concept for what they saw in the younger person wanting to become an Anglo facsimile: "Mosca en leche!" The Mexican American who so vehemently proclaimed his United States citizenship and his equality with all citizens never realized that all of the comparisons by which he evaluated progress were faulty. Because of his psychic identification with the superordinate Anglo, he abandoned his own language and culture and considered himself personally superior to the economically subordinate Migrant Generation. The fact that he could see that he was somewhat better off educationally and economically than the Migrant Generation led the Mexican American of this period to believe himself assimilated and accepted into the larger society. He did not fully realize that his self-perceived affluence and privileges existed only in comparison to the vast majority of Mexican Americans. He did not realize that for the same amount of native ability, education, personal motivation and actual performance, his Anglo counterpart was much more highly rewarded than he. He never made the observation that even when he achieved a higher education, he still remained at the bottom of the ladder in whatever area of economic endeavor he might be employed. Individuals, sometimes with the help of protective organizations, did bring some legal action against personal cases of discrimination. But despite a growing psychic security as citizens of the United States, they did not make effective collective comparisons. The greater security that the Mexican American Generation achieved was a falsely based sense of self-worth. To be sure, because a sizable proportion of the population managed to exist for several decades with a sense of self-worth, they could give birth to what will be called the Chicano Generation in the next section of this paper. However much the Mexican American Generation may have been discriminated against educationally and especially economically, they did achieve enough leisure and economic surplus so that their offspring did not begin from a hopeless disadvantage at birth. This extra measure of protection was perhaps the greatest indicator that the Mexican American Generation was now part of a class and not a caste system.

The Chicano Generation

In the late 1960's a new consciousness began to make itself felt among Mexican Americans. By this time the population was solidly urban and well entrenched as an indisputable part of the country's working underclass. Migration from Mexico had slowed and was predominantly to urban centers in the United States. Theories of racial inferiority were dying, not without some sophisticated revivals, to be sure, but in general the country was beginning to accept the capacity of human populations given equal opportunities and resources. Moreover, despite the ups and downs of the market-place, it was becoming clear to all that both technological sophistication and economic potential existed in sufficient abundance to eradicate abject poverty in the United States. These conditions had not existed in the Southwest with regard to the Mexican American population since that historical period immediately preceding the Creation Generation.

The Chicano Generation is now comparing its fortunes with those of the dominant majority as well as with the fortunes of other minorities within the United States. This represents an awareness of our citizenship in a pluralistic society. It is perhaps early to be writing the history of the Chicano Generation, but already it is clear that we have gone through an initial phase and are now in a second phase. The first phase consisted of the realization that citizenship bestows upon those who can claim it many rights and protections traditionally denied to Mexican Americans. The second phase, only now achieving widespread penetration into the population's consciousness, is that citizenship also entails obligations and duties, which we have traditionally not been in a position to perform. These two perspectives are rapidly colliding with each other. The general mental health of the Chicano community is being severely buffeted by the change in comparative focus and the relative current inability to achieve measurable success according to the new standards.

The parameters of the Mexican American population had been slowly changing, until by the mid-1960's the bulk of the post-World War II baby boom had reached draftable age and now faced the prospect of military service in the war in Vietnam. As a cohort, these young Mexican Americans were the most affluent and socio-politically liberated ever. The bulk were the sons and daughters of urban working class parents. However, a small proportion were the offspring of small businessmen;

and an even smaller proportion were the offspring of minor bureaucratic officials, semi-professionals, and professionals. Especially in these latter types of families, a strong sense of the benefits of educational certification and of the rights of citizenship had been developed. When the bulk of this cohort of young people reached draftable age, which is also the age when young people generally enter college, they made some extremely interesting and shocking discoveries, on which they were able to act because they had the leisure and resources to permit self-analysis and self-determining action.

Despite the fact that the Mexican American population has the highest school dropout rate of any ethnic population in the country, by the mid-1960's a larger proportion than ever before were finishing high school. These young people then faced three major alternative courses of action, all of them unsatisfactory. One course was to enter an urban industrial labor force for which they were ill-prepared because a high school education is no longer as useful as in previous generations. And even for those positions for which a high school education is sufficient, they were ill-prepared because the high schools located in their neighborhoods were so inadequate compared to those in Anglo neighborhoods. Moreover, persistent racial discrimination made it difficult to aspire to any but lower working class positions. Another course of action, which a disproportionate number of young men took, was to go into military service as a way to travel, gain salable skills, and assert one's citizenship, as so many Mexican Americans had done in the previous generation. But unlike the Mexican American going into the military of World War II, the young Chicano of the mid-1960's went into a highly professionalized military, the technical skills for which he found difficult to acquire because of his inadequate high school preparation. So instead of acquiring skills for the modern technical society into which he would eventually be released, he disproportionately joined the ranks of the foot soldier and was disproportionately on the war casualty list. A third course of action open to the young Mexican American leaving high school in the mid-1960's was to make application for and enter college. This alternative was unsatisfactory because colleges and universities were not prepared to accept more than the occasional few-and then only those who would be willing to abandon their ethnicity. Refusal to admit was, of course, based on assertions of incapacity or lack of preparation. The former has racist underpinings, while the latter is class biased since poverty and the inferior schools in which Chicano youth were concentrated did not permit adequate preparation for college and eventual middle class certification.

No matter which course of action the bulk of the young people took they disproportionately faced dismal futures. The larger society in which this ethnic minority exists had become so technical, bureaucratized, and professionalized-in short, so *middle class*-that the strictly lower working class potential of the bulk of the Mexican American population was irrelevant to it. Faced with the prospect of almost total economic marginality, the Chicano Generation was the first generation since the Creation Generation to confront the prospect of large-scale failure-of, in effect, losing ground, of psychically accomplishing less than the Mexican American Generation. The low-skill, labor intensive society into which the Mexican American Generation had established a firm, but strictly lower working class status, was disappearing. The United States was now predominantly professionalized and middle class, with increasingly fewer labor-intensive requirements. It is in this relatively more limited context that the Chicano Generation came to have relatively higher aspirations.

With higher aspirations than any previous generation, with the prospect of a severe psychic decline compared to its parent generation, and now, because of its greater affluence and exposure, it had to compare itself to its youth counterpart in the dominant society. The broader exposure comes from many sources, including television and greater schooling in schools that, however inferior, were better than those to which prior generations were even minimally exposed. The Chicano Generation very painfully began to ask of what value its United States citizenship was going to be. At this time a significantly large proportion of the black population of this country "revolted." That may well have been the spark that ignited the Chicano movement. The Mexican American Generation had asserted its United States citizenship with great pride, asserting a relationship between economic success and their complete "Angloization" which was now shown to be false. The Chicano Generation came to realize that it was even more acculturated than the previous generation, yet it did not have any realistic prospects of escaping its virtually complete lower and workingclass status. Its new consciousness came into being at a time when the Chicano Generation could hardly find any older role models with certified middle class status. Comparatively, for example, out of a population of twenty-four million there are 2,200 black persons who have earned Ph.D. degrees in all disciplines combined. Among the eight million (approximately) Mexican Americans there are only 60 who have earned Ph.D. degrees, when a similar level of disadvantage would lead us to expect approximately 730. The number of Ph.D.'s in a population is used here as a sort of barometric indicator of the level and quality of technically trained and certified leadership available to a population within a predominantly middle class society. This is so because one can guess at the ratio of lawyers and doctors as well as master and bachelor degrees for each Ph.D. Thus, the Mexican American population which began to enter colleges and universities in noticeable numbers only as late as the mid-1960's is almost completely lacking in certification for middle class status.

Another indication of the lack of certified leadership that is self-consciously concerned with the welfare of the community is the lack of institutions of higher learning of, for, and by Chicanos. There are over 100 black institutions of higher learning (both privately and publicly supported, including colleges, universities, law schools and medical schools). As recently as five years ago there were no such institutions for Chicanos. Now there are a handful of schools that either have been created *ad hoc* or where a significant number of Chicanos have moved into administrative positions due to pressures from large Chicano student enrollments. The point here is that however inadequate the black schools may have been, compared to "white" schools, they provided the institutional foci within which a broad sector of the black population has been trained and certified for middle class status since prior to 1900. Mexican Americans could neither get into institutions of the dominant society, nor did we have our own alternate institutions. Thus, the difficulty of acquiring broad scale consciousness of the condition of our people is apparent, as is the insecure ethnic identification of the early few who entered "white" institutions.

The Chicano Generation has experienced the pain of social rejection in essentially the same fashion (in the abstract) that it was experienced by the Creation Generation. That is, having been ideologically prepared to expect egalitarian co-participation in the society in which it exists, it had instead been confronted with the practical fact of exclusion from the benefits of the society. Because it can no longer compare itself to its immediate predecessors (no matter what the quantity or quality of accomplishments of the Mexican American Generation), it has to compare itself to other groups in the larger society. Relative to them it is more disadvantaged than any other ethnic group, except the American Indian with whom it has much in common both culturally and biologically. Every new demographic analysis gives the Chicano Generation more evidence of relative deprivation, which leads to the rise of a psychic sense of betrayal by the egalitarian ideology of the United States not unlike that experienced by the Creation Generation. Members of the Chicano Generation are therefore saying to the previous generation:

So you are a loyal "American," willing to die for your country in the last three or four wars; what did your country ever do for you? If you are such an American, how come your country gives you less education even than other disadvantaged minorities, permits you only low status occupations, allows you to become a disproportionately large part of casualties in war, and socially rejects you from the most prestigious circles? As for me, I am a Chicano, I am rooted in this land, I am the creation of a unique psychohistorical experience. I trace part of my identity to Mexican culture and part to United States culture, but most importantly my identity is tied up with those contested lands called Aztlan. My most valid claim to existential reality is not the false pride and unrequited loyalty of either the Migrant Generation or the Mexican American Generation. Rather, I trace my beginnings to the original contest over the lands of Aztlan, to the more valid psycho-historical experience of the Creation Generation. I have a right to intermarriage if it suits me, to economic achievement at all societal levels, and to my own measure of political self-determination within this society. I have a unique psycho-historical experience that I have a right to know about and to cultivate as part of my distinctive cultural heritage.

The concerns of the Chicano Generation are those which predominantly plague the middle class: sufficient leisure and affluence to contemplate the individual's origin and potential future, sufficient education and affluence to make it at least possible for the individual to have a noticeable impact on the course of his life's achievements, but not so rich an inheritance that the individual's prominence is society is virtually assured. The Chicano Generation is the first sizable cohort in our history to come to the widespread realization that we can have a considerable measure of self-determination within the confines of this pluralistic society. Yet we are only at the threshold of this era and have hardly begun to legitimate our claims to effective self-determination, i.e., acquisition of professional- technical certification as well as establishment of relatively independent wealth. Our capacity to secure middle class entry for a sizable proportion of our population is threatened on two major fronts.

First, we are threatened by our redundancy or obsolescence at the bottom of the social structure. This has two dimensions: we cannot earn enough money to support a United States standard of living on laborer's wages; even if we were willing to do the few remaining back-breaking jobs, there would not be enough work to go around because these are being automated, and the few that are around will be taken over by cheap Mexican labor from Mexico, unless we organize factory and farm workers effectively. Thus, in a sense, the economic bottom of out community is falling away.

Second, we are threatened because just as the middle class sector of the larger society is getting ready to acknowledge our capacities and our right to full participation, we find that the major proportion of our population does not have the necessary credentials for entry-i.e., college, graduate and professional degrees. When large corporate organizations attempt to comply with federal equal employment regulations concerning the Spanish speaking population, they do not care whether the person they hire comes from a family that has been in the United States since 1828 or whether the person arrived yesterday from Mexico or some other Latin American country. The irony is that as discrimination disappears or is minimized, those who have historically suffered the most from it continue to suffer its after affects. This is so because as multi-national corporations have begun their training programs throughout Latin America, and especially in Mexico, a new technically skilled and educated middle class has been greatly expanded in those countries. Many of these persons begin to question why they should perform jobs in their home country at the going depressed salaries when they could come to the United States and receive higher salaries for the same work and participate in a generally higher standard of living. This, in effect, is part of the brain drain experienced by these countries from the point of view of their economy. From the point of view of the Chicano community, however, we experience it as being cut off at the pass. That is, just as the decline of prejudice and the increase in demand for middle class type positions might pull us up into the secure middle class, a new influx of people from another country comes into the United States economy above us. Because it would cost corporations more to develop Chicanos for these positions, and because we do not have a sufficiently aware and sufficiently powerful Chicano middle class to fight for the selection of Chicanos, and because of federal regulations which only call for Spanish surname people to fill jobs, without regard to place of origin, it is conceivable that the bulk of our population might become relegated into relatively unskilled working class positions. Thus, the plight of the urban Chicano in the 1970's is not only technically complicated (how do you acquire middle class expertise with working class resources), but psychically complex (how do you relate to urban middle class immigrants from Spanish speaking countries and to rapidly organizing rural Mexican Americans) at a time when the general economy of the United States appears to be in a state of contraction, making competition for positions severe. Unless we can deal creatively with these trends, we will remain at the bottom of the social structure. This, in spite of outmoded social theories that postulated that each wave of new immigrants would push the previous wave up in the socioeconomic structure.

The introspectiveness of the Chicano generation is leading to new insights. The psycho-historical links of the Chicano Generation with the Creation Generation are primarily those of collective support against a common diffuse and everywhere present danger. The threat of cultural extinction has led the Chicano to deep introspection as to what distinguishes him both from Mexicans in Mexico and from "Anglos" in the United States. This introspection has led to a deep appreciation for the positive aspects of each culture and a creative use of our inheritance in facing the future. The fight for self-definition is leading to a reanalysis of culture. For example, Anglo research has defined "machismo" as unidimensional male dominance, whereas, its multi-dimensional original meaning placed heavier emphases on personal dignity and personal sacrifice on behalf of the collectivity-i.e., family or community. This concern for the collectivity comes through again in the emphasis placed on "la familia" in activities within a Chicano movement perspective. The fight for professional and middle class certification is the fight for our collectivity to be heard. The objective is to produce enough certified professionals who can articulate and defend our peculiarly distinct culture in such a manner that educational and other institutions of the dominant society will have to be modified. Until we have our certified savants, we will continue to be defined out of existence by outsiders insensitive to the internal dynamic of our own collectivity. The willingness to fight may be what will get us there.

The Treaty of Guadalupe Hidalgo ended the Mexican American War of 1846-1848 and defined the terms of peace. Article V culminated United States expansionistic schemes on Mexican territory dating back to the early 19th century. It forced Mexico to relinquish sovereignty over its northern frontier zones, today's American Southwest. Ultimately these regions would become the states of California, Arizona, New Mexico, Colorado and Nevada. In addition, portions of the states of Texas, Utah and Wyoming would be absorbed by the United States through Article V. For Mexico, the treaty represented an unprecedented national humiliation highlighted by the loss of approximately fifty percent of its national territory. For the United States, it culminated the successful conclusion of expansion on the North American continent. For the newly incorporated Mexicans who resided in these territories, estimated to be as many as 120,000, Articles VIII, IX and X promised unprecedented property, civil, constitutional, and religious protections. Richard Griswold del Castillo and John Chávez, in later readings, uncover the United States government's failure to honor the letter and spirit of this international treaty.

The Treaty of Guadalupe Hidalgo, Selected Articles

Mexico: February 2, 1848

Treaty of Guadalupe Hidalgo. Treaty of Peace, Friendship, Limits, and Settlement (with additional and secret article which was not ratified), with Map of the United Mexican States and with Plan of the Port of San Diego, signed at Guadalupe Hidalgo February 2, 1848. Originals of the treaty and additional secret article in English and Spanish.

Treaty and additional and secret article submitted to the Senate February 23, 1848. Ratified by the United States March 16, 1848. Ratified by Mexico May 30, 1848. Ratifications exchanged at Querétaro May 30, 1848. Proclaimed July 4, 1848.

Article V.

The Boundary line between the two Republics shall commence in the Gulf of Mexico, three leagues from land, opposite the mouth of the Rio Grande, otherwise called Rio Bravo del Norte, or opposite the mouth of its deepest branch, if it should have more than one branch emptying directly into the sea; from thence, up the middle of that river, following the deepest channel, where it has more than one, to the point where it strikes the southern boundary of New Mexico; thence, westwardly, along the whole southern boundary of New Mexico (which runs north of the town called *Paso*) to its western termination; thence, northward, along the western line of New Mexico, until it intersects the first branch of the River Gila; (or if it should not intersect any branch of that river, then, to the point on the said line nearest to such branch, and thence in a direct line to the same) thence down the middle of the said branch and of the said river, until it empties into the Rio Colorado, following the division line between Upper and Lower California, to the Pacific Ocean.

The southern and western limits of New Mexico, mentioned in this Article, are those laid down in the Map, entitled *"Map of the United Mexican States, as organized and defined by various acts of the Congress of said Republic, and constructed according to the best authorities. Revised Edition. Published at New York in 1847 by J. Disturnell:"* of which Map a Copy is added to this Treaty, bearing the signatures and seals of the Undersigned Plenipotentiaries. And, in order to preclude all difficulty in tracing upon the ground the limit separating Upper from Lower California, it is agreed that the said limit shall consist of a straight line, drawn from the middle of the Rio Gila, where it unites with the Colorado, to a point on the coast of the Pacific Ocean, distant one marine league due south of the southernmost point of the Port of San Diego, according to the plan of said port, made in the 1782, by Don Juan Pantoja, second-sailing master of the Spanish fleet, and published at Madrid in the year 1802, in the Atlas to the voyage of the schooners *Sutil* and *Mexicana*: of which plan a copy is hereunto added, signed and sealed by the respective plenipotentiaries.

In order to designate the Boundary line with due precision, upon authoritative maps, and to establish upon the ground landmarks which shall show the limits of both Republics, as described in the present Article, the two Governments shall each appoint a Commissioner and a Surveyor, who, before the expiration of one year from the date of the exchange of ratifications of this treaty, shall meet at the Port of San Diego, and proceed to run and mark the said boundary in its whole course, to the mouth of the Rio Bravo del Norte. They shall keep journals and make out plans of their operations; and the result, agreed upon by them, shall be deemed a part of this Treaty, and shall have the same force as if it were inserted therein. The two Governments will amicably agree regarding what may be necessary to these persons, and also as to their respective escorts, should such be necessary.

The Boundary line established by this Article shall be religiously respected by each of the two Republics, and no change shall ever be made therein, except by the express and free content of both nations, lawfully given by the General Government of each, in conformity with its own constitution.

Article VIII.

Mexicans now established in territories previously belonging to Mexico, and which remain for the future within the limits of the United States, as defined by the present treaty, shall be free to continue where they now reside, or to remove at any time to the Mexican Republic, retaining the property which they possess in the said territories, or disposing thereof, and removing the proceeds wherever they please; without their being subjected, on this account, to any contribution, tax or charge whatever.

Those who shall prefer to remain in said territories, may either retain the title and rights of Mexican citizens, or acquire those of citizens of the United States. But they shall be under the obligation to make their election within one year from the date of the exchange of ratifications of this treaty: and those who shall remain in the said territories, after the expiration of that year, without having declared their intention to retain the character of Mexicans, shall be considered to have elected to become citizens of the United States.

In the said territories, property of every kind, now belonging to Mexicans, not established there, shall be inviolably respected. The present owners, the heirs of these, and all Mexicans who may hereafter acquire said property by contract, shall enjoy with respect to it, guaranties equally ample as if the same belonged to citizens of the United States.

Article IX.

The Mexicans who, in the territories aforesaid, shall not preserve the character of the citizens of the Mexican Republic, conformably with what is stipulated in the preceding article, shall be incorporated into the Union of the United States and be admitted, at the proper time (to be judged of by the Congress of the United States) to the enjoyment of all the rights of citizens of the United States according to the principles of the Constitution; and in the mean time shall be maintained and protected in the free enjoyment of their liberty and property, and secured in the free exercise of their religion without restriction.

Article X.
(prior to its omission by the United States Senate)

All grants of land made by the Mexican Government or by the competent authorities, in territories previously appertaining to Mexico, and remaining for the future within the limits of the United States, shall be respected as valid, to the same extent that the same grants would be valid, if the said territories had remained within the limits of Mexico. But the grantees of land in Texas, put in possession thereof, who, by the reason of circumstances of the country since the beginning of the troubles between Texas and the Mexican Government, may have been prevented from fulfilling all the conditions of their grants, shall be under the obligation to fulfill the said conditions within the periods limited in the same respectively; such periods to be now counted from the date of the exchange of ratifications of this treaty: in the default of which the said grants shall not be obligatory upon the State of Texas, in virtue of the stipulations contained in this Article.

The foregoing stipulation in regard to grantees of land in Texas, is extended to all grantees of land in the territories aforesaid, elsewhere than in Texas, put in possession under such grants; and, in default of the fulfillment of the conditions of any such grant, within the new period, which, as is above stipulated, begins with the day of the exchange of ratifications of this treaty, the same shall be null and void.

The Mexican Government declares that no grant whatever of lands in Texas has been made since the second day of March one thousand eight hundred and thirty six; and that no grant whatever of lands in any of the territories aforesaid has been made since the thirteenth day of May one thousand eight hundred and forty-six.

After United States Senate ratification of the Treaty of Guadalupe Hidalgo Mexican and American commissioners met to discuss and explain changes and omissions to the treaty. Of particular interest to Mexican officials was the alteration of Article IX and the omission of Article X. The Protocol of Querétaro, originally an oral explanation, was subsequently placed into written form and submitted to Mexican commissioners. Apparently satisfied that these changes would not result in subsequent denials of the intent of the articles, the Mexican commissioners accepted what came to be known as the Protocol of Querétaro.

The Protocol of Querétaro
May 26, 1848

PROTOCOL

In the city of Querétaro on the twenty sixth of the month of May eighteen hundred and forty-eight at a conference between Their Excellencies Nathan Clifford and Ambrose H. Sevier Commissioners of the United States of America, with full powers from their Government to make to the Mexican Republic suitable explanations in regard to the amendments which the Senate and the Government of the said United States have made in the treaty of peace, friendship, limits and definitive settlement between the two Republics, signed in Guadalupe Hidalgo, on the second day of February of the present year, and His Excellency Don Luis de la Rosa, Minister of Foreign Affairs of the Republic of Mexico, it was agreed, after adequate conversation respecting the changes alluded to, to record in the present protocol the following explanations which Their aforesaid Excellencies the Commissioners gave in the name of their Government and in fulfillment of the Commission conferred upon them near the Mexican Republic.

FIRST.

The American Government by suppressing the IXth article of the Treaty of Guadalupe and substituting the III. article of the Treaty of Louisiana did not intend to diminish in any way what was agreed upon by the aforesaid article IXth in favor of the inhabitants of the territories ceded by Mexico. Its understanding that all of that agreement is contained in the IIId article of the Treaty of Louisiana. In consequence, all the privileges and guarantees, civil, political, and religious, which would have been possessed by the inhabitants of the ceded territories, if the IXth article of the Treaty had been retained, will be enjoyed by them without any difference under the article which had been substituted.

SECOND.

The American Government by suppressing the Xth article of the Treaty of Guadalupe did not in any way intend to annul the grants of lands made by Mexico in the ceded territories. These grants. notwithstanding the suppression of the article of the Treaty, preserve the legal value which they may possess; and the grantees may cause their legitimate titles to be acknowledged before the American tribunals.

Conformably to the law of the United States, legitimate titles to every description of the property personal and real, existing in the ceded territories, are those which were legitimate titles under the Mexican law in California and New Mexico up to the 13th of May 1.846, and in Texas up to the 2d March 1.836.

THIRD.

The Government of the United States by suppressing the concluding paragraph of the article XIIth of the Treaty, did not intend to deprive the Mexican Republic of the free and unrestrained faculty of ceding, conveying or transferring at any time (as it may judge best) the sum of twelve millions of dollars which the same Government of the United States is to deliver in the places designated by the amended article.

And these explanations having been accepted by the minister of Foreign Affairs of the Mexican Republic, he declared in name of his Government that with the understanding conveyed by them, the same Government would proceed to ratify the Treaty of Guadalupe as modified by the Senate and Government of the United States. In testimony of which their Excellencies the aforesaid Commissioners and the Minister have signed and sealed in quintuplicate the present protocol.

Richard Griswold del Castillo's article discusses the ways in which the federal and state courts have interpreted provisions of the Treaty of Guadalupe Hidalgo since 1848. As Griswold reveals, most of the decisions handed down by the courts resulted in the erosion of rights originally guaranteed through this international treaty. Of particular importance is how Griswold links changes in interpretations with changes in United States political history.

The U.S. Courts and the Treaty
Richard Griswold del Castillo

If the treaty was violated by this general statute enacted for the purpose of ascertaining the validity of claims derived from the Mexican government, it was a matter of international concern, which the two states must determine by treaty or by other such means.
Barker v. Harvey (1901)

Conquest gives a title which the courts of the conqueror cannot deny, whatever the private or speculative opinion of individual may be.
Chief Justice Marshall
United States v. Alcea Band of Tillamoks (1946)

When it was promulgated by President James K. Polk on July 4, 1848, the Treaty of Guadalupe Hidalgo achieved the status of a law of the United States. Since its ratification more than two hundred federal, state, and district court decisions have interpreted the treaty, expanding and changing the meaning of the original treaty.

A review of selected U.S. court cases shows that Anglo American land corporations and the state and federal governments were the primary beneficiaries of the legal system's interpretation of the Treaty of Guadalupe Hidalgo.[1] Although some Indians and Hispanics lodged lawsuits citing the treaty guarantees, the vast majority of them were unsuccessful in their efforts.

The U.S. courts' interpretation of the treaty roughly paralleled the political history of the United States. The Civil War and Reconstruction period was one of great expansion in civil and political rights in American jurisprudence with the ratification of the 13th, 14th, and 15th amendments, abolishing slavery, defining citizenship, and expanding the electoral franchise. The period after Reconstruction until the early 1930s was largely one of conservative politics, with the exception of a progressive reform movement in the first two decades of the twentieth century. Juridical settlements mirrored a society caught up in a struggle for wealth and preoccupied with the supremacy of the white race. Examples of this conservative trend include *Plessy v. Ferguson*, which affirmed segregation in public facilities; *In re Debs*, which undercut labor unions; and *United States v. E. C. Knight Co.*, which vitiated anti-trust legislation. Since 1930, there has been periodic resurgence and decline of liberal and conservative political philosophies. During this period the U.S. Supreme Court lost its liberal majority and became more balanced politically, and neither political party has enjoyed a monopoly of both the legislature and the presidency.

The U.S. Supreme Court decided almost half the major cases interpreting the Treaty of Guadalupe Hidalgo. The political evolution of the Court influenced how the justices regarded the treaty. Prior to the Civil War, the Supreme Court had been concerned primarily with the nation-state relationship and the preservation of the union. During the tenure of Chief Justice Taney, the Court sought ways to avoid a civil war over the issue of slavery and sectionalism. The sanctity of property was foremost in their reasoning. For example, when they rendered their famous *Dred Scott* opinion in 1857, they stated that Congress had no power to exclude slaves as property from the territories.

After the Civil War the Court turned to the relationship between government and private business and tended to favor the latter. Many Supreme Court decisions opposed the government's attempts to regulate or restrain the excesses of capitalism. Not surprisingly, in the decades following Reconstruction, the Court opposed interpretations of the Treaty of Guadalupe Hidalgo that might hinder the growth of the American economy in the Southwest.

The Supreme Court changed its views in 1937 when it abandoned its opposition to government programs that challenged private business. Increasingly thereafter the Court adopted a more balanced opinion of the role of government in the economy.[2] After World War II the Court was more inclined to concentrate on the relationship of the individual to the government, and specifically on civil rights.

The court cases decided by district, territorial, and state supreme courts usually reflected the pressures of regional interests and local concerns. Most cases came from courts in California and dealt with the issue of property rights, a concern emerging out of that state's growing population pressures on natural resources. Court cases coming from Arizona and New Mexico focused on Indian- and tribal-rights questions as well as challenges to Hispano community grants. Cases decided in Texas reflected a recognition of the Mexican common-law traditions in that state but only those that did not conflict with Anglo-American rule.

1848-1889

In the first period of juridical interpretation, federal and state courts issued judgments that tended to interpret the treaty liberally. Generally the courts bolstered the status of the treaty as a document confirming and protecting rights. On the subject of property rights, the courts sought to clarify the meaning of the language in Article VIII and the Protocol of Querétaro. In 1850 the California Supreme Court ruled that an inchoate title (i.e., not clearly a legal Mexican title) was protected by the treaty and that its legitimacy could be affected or questioned only by the federal government. This construction went far beyond the implied guarantees in the stricken Article X and the Protocol of Querétaro. Even landholders lacking clear titles would be protected until the grants could be examined by the U.S. courts.[3] Sixteen years later, in *Mintern v. Bower et al.*, the California court further expanded this concept to include perfected land grants. In that case the court decided "that perfect titles to lands which existed at the date of the treaty of Guadalupe Hidalgo in Mexicans then established in California, were guaranteed and secured to such persons not only by the law of nations, but also by the stipulations of that treaty."[4] This meant that those individuals who held perfect titles need not submit them before the Board Of Land Commissioners established in 1851 to validate titles. This position, which recognized the primacy of federal treaty obligation over congressional legislation, guided California until it was overturned in the federal case of *Botiller v. Dominguez* in 1889.

Other court findings also interpreted the Treaty of Guadalupe Hidalgo liberally. In *United States v. Reading* (1855) the Supreme Court ruled that the treaty protected the property rights of a Mexican citizen who had fought in the U.S. Army against Mexico at the very time his land grant was pending certification by the Mexican government. Because of the treaty's protection, the Court ruled that his military action did not result in a forfeit of land rights. In *Palmer v. United States* (1857), the Court argued that the dates given in the Protocol of Querétaro were not limiting and that in New Mexico and California legitimate titles might have been made by Mexican officials after May 13, 1846. In *Townsend et al. v. Greeley* (1866) the Court held that town or community grants as well as private ones were protected by the treaty.

In other rulings the Court interpreted the treaty to legitimize the transfer of Mexican law to the conquered Southwest. In *United States v. Moreno* (1863), the Supreme Court affirmed that the treaty protected land grants that were legitimate under Mexican law; in 1884 the Court ruled that treaty stipulations did not invalidate the powers of local officials, acting under Mexican law, to make legitimate land grants prior to the implementation of American laws, and in *Philips v. Mound City* the Court advanced the position that the treaty also protected partitions and divisions of land made under Mexican law prior to July 4, 1848.[6]

In this period the implications of the treaty for the civil rights of former Mexican citizens were also a concern of the courts. In the 1870 *De la Guerra* case, the California court interpreted the treaty as confirming U.S. citizenship for Mexicans. In New Mexico the presence of a large group of Hispanicized Pueblo Indians complicated the issue of citizenship. The territorial government in New Mexico did not give Indians citizenship, but in 1869 the New Mexico Supreme Court ruled that by virtue of the treaty, the Pueblo Indians were citizens of the territory and of the United States. In *United States v. Lucero* the justices analyzed the treaty extensively to support this view. After reviewing Article 9, Justice Watts, writing for the court, stated: "This court, under this section of the treaty of Guadalupe Hidalgo, does not consider it proper to assent to the withdrawal of eight thousand citizens of New Mexico from the operation of the law, made to secure and maintain them in their liberty and property, and consign their liberty and property to a system of laws and trade made for wandering savages."[7] The justices thus proposed that the Pueblo Indians were not tribal Indians subject to laws administered by the Department of Indian Affairs. This interpretation regarding the treaty status of the Pueblo Indians was reaffirmed by the New Mexico Supreme Court in 1874 but reversed in 1940.[8]

A narrower view of the meaning of the treaty in this period was largely limited to the question of the application of the treaty to Texas. In 1856 the Supreme Court heard a case involving a land-grant claim in Texas that sought remedy under the treaty. In *McKinney v. Saviego* the Court decided that the treaty did not apply to Texas lands. Justice Campbell, writing for the Court, summarized Article VIII in the treaty and asked: "To what territories did the high contracting parties refer to in this article? We think it clear that they did not refer to any portion of the acknowledged limits of Texas." The Court argued that Texas had been recognized by the U. S. government as an independent country and had been annexed as a state prior to the Mexican War. Therefore, the Treaty of Guadalupe applied only to those territories annexed by the United States in 1848. This interpretation was sustained by several subsequent decisions, and it stands as law today.[9]

1889-1930

A liberal view of the meaning of the Treaty of Guadalupe Hidalgo prevailed in the period prior to the landmark judgment of *Botiller v. Dominguez* in 1889. This case inaugurated a decidedly conservative attitude regarding the extent to which the treaty was important in protecting the property of the former Mexican citizens. The most far-reaching impact of the *Botiller* case was summarized in the statement written by Justice Miller for the Court.

> If the treaty was violated by this general statute (the Land Law of 1851), enacted for the purpose of ascertaining the validity of claims derived from the Mexican government, it was a matter of international concern, which the two states must determine by treaty or by such other means as enables one state to enforce upon another the obligations of a treaty. This court, in cases like the present, has no power to set itself up as the instrumentality for enforcing the provisions of a treaty with a

foreign nation which the government of the United States, as a sovereign power, chooses to disregard.[10]

In *Botiller v. Dominguez* the Supreme Court held that the sovereign laws of the United States took precedence over international treaties. This appeared to be in direct contradiction of the Constitution, which (in Article VI, Section 2 and Article III, Section 2, Clause I) gave treaties the same status as the Constitution. The Supreme Court's decision, some argued, sanctioned the confiscation of property and violated the due process provision of the Constitution. Nevertheless the case became an important precedent guiding the Court in its future interpretation of conflicts between treaty obligations and domestic laws.[11] The judgment in *Botiller* declared that the American courts had no responsibility to hear cases involving violations of the Treaty of Guadalupe Hidalgo. To resolve conflicts arising over the treaty there was no recourse but to international diplomatic negotiation.

Eventually the *Botiller* case was cited as a basis for denying lands to the California Mission Indians, who had legal title to their ancestral lands under Mexican law but had not filed their title before the Land Commission as stipulated in the 1851 law. For the Court the right of the government to provide "reasonable means for determining the validity of all titles within the ceded territory" superseded the inhabitant's treaty rights.[12]

Just as the *Botiller* decree became a rule of law in subsequent years, the courts continually reconfirmed the right of Congress and the courts to implement the treaty through laws "to ascertain the legitimacy of title." If these implementing laws ran counter to the protections of the treaty, the congressional laws would take precedence. This principle was affirmed in *California Powderworks v. Davis* (1894), in *United States v. Sandoval et al.* (1897), and in *Arisa v. New Mexico and Arizona Railroad* (1899).[13]

The courts also interpreted the treaty so that it would be more restrictive as to the land rights claimed by former Mexican citizens and those who had acquired their lands. The Supreme Court determined that the treaty "did not increase rights" and that "no duty rests on this government to recognize the validity of a grant to any area of greater extent than was recognized by the government of Mexico."[14] This in itself might have been a reasonable assertion but it hinged on the government's view of the scope of legitimate Mexican laws, and increasingly the courts took a narrow view. One question that arose was whether Mexican landholders would be protected from squatters and speculators during the time it took for the U.S. courts to determine the validity of their Mexican titles. In 1901, in *Lockhart v. Johnson*, the Supreme Court ruled that neither Articles VIII or IX gave such protection. In this case a portion of the Cañada de Cochiti land-grant in New Mexico had been purchased from the U.S. government by a mining company while the grant was pending action by the Surveyor General's Office. An American who had purchased the original grant argued that the mining company's occupancy had violated the Treaty of Guadalupe Hidalgo. Justice Peckham stated for the Supreme Court: "(T)here are no words in the treaty with Mexico expressly withdrawing from sale all lands within claimed limits of a Mexican grant, and we do not think there is any language in the treaty which implies a reservation of any kind."[15]

This 1901 doctrine, that the treaty did not protect land claims from public sale, differed from the long-standing policy of the General Land Office, which had interpreted the treaty to mean that "all lands embraced within the Mexican and Spanish grants were placed in a state of reservation for the ascertainment of rights claimed under said grant."[16] In California the courts also ruled that the treaty would not provide special protection for Mexicans who owned property. In 1913 the California State Supreme Court argued that "the treaty of Guadalupe Hidalgo requires only that the rights of Mexican grantees in their property shall be equal to that of citizens of the United States." And in 1930 it ruled that the treaty did not bind the government to follow the Spanish or Mexican statute of limitations with regard to land or water rights.[17]

Article X in the original treaty, which was stricken out by the U.S. Senate, was not part of the official document proclaimed as law in 1848. Among other things Article X had specified that "all grants of land made by the Mexican government . . . shall be respected as valid, to the same extent that the same grants would be valid, if the said territories had remained within the limits of Mexico." The striking of this article emerged as a point of law for the courts and became a basis for rejecting land claims.

In *Interstate Land Co. v. Maxwell Land Co.* (1891) the U.S. Supreme Court rejected the assertion that a grant was invalid because it had been declared so by a Mexican law prior to 1848. After analyzing the circumstances surrounding the removal of Article X by the Senate, including President Polk's message to Congress, the Court stated that "this claim was one of the class which was expressly refused to be recognized by the treaty" (more accurately by the absence of Article X).[18] In another case, *Cessna v. United States et al.* in 1898, the Supreme Court interpreted the absence of Article X to rule against a New Mexican land claimant whose grant had been rejected by the Court of Private Land Claims. Accordingly, "when the U.S. received this territory under the Treaty of Guadalupe Hidalgo, they refused to recognize as still valid and enforceable all grants which had been assumed to be made prior thereto by the Mexican authorities. Article X, as proposed by the commissioners, was rejected by this government."[19]

Thus the absence of Article X, with its specific guarantees of due process after 1848 under Mexican law provided a basis for the courts to restrict further the meaning of the treaty. The Protocol of Querétaro, which had been drafted to assure the Mexican government that the spirit of Article X would be retained, was not a matter for future juridical consideration.

The U.S. Courts and the Treaty

The final area of conservative interpretation of the treaty in the period 1889-1930 was in Indian affairs. Three cases illustrate the trend. In 1897 the Supreme Court construed the treaty so as to benefit the government and undercut historic understandings between Mexican and Indian communities in New Mexico. The pueblo of Zia claimed proprietory and grazing rights in northern New Mexico by virtue of their use of land with the agreement of the Mexican settlers. The Court, however, ruled that, by ceding Mexican lands to the public domain the treaty provided the basis for revoking these prior concessions as well as for denying any claims of land ownership on the part of the Indians.

The Court also moved to question any extension of citizenship rights to Indians. In an 1869 judgment the New Mexican territorial court ruled that the treaty conferred U.S. citizenship on Pueblo Indians. In a 1913 case the Supreme Court stated that "it remains an open question whether they have become citizens of the U.S." Also, "we need not determine it now, because citizenship is not in itself an obstacle to the exercise by Congress of its power to enact laws for the benefit and protection of tribal Indians as dependent peoples."[20] The next year the Court ruled that the California Indians had not been given citizenship by the Treaty of Guadalupe Hidalgo. Chief Justice White attacked the argument that the California Indians were entitled to citizenship by virtue of the treaty as "so devoid of merit as not in any real sense to involve the construction of the treaty." A later court arrived at similar conclusions regarding the status of the Pueblo Indians in New Mexico.[21]

Although the bulk of court constructions of the treaty from 1880 to 1930 were based on a conservative reading of the document, there were a few cases in which the courts expanded its meaning. Despite earlier indications by the U.S. Supreme Court, in *McKinney v. Saviego*, that the treaty would not apply to Texas, the Texas Supreme Court made a series of rulings that validated the treaty as applying to certain regions of the state. In *Texas Mexican Railroad v. Locke*, the Texas Supreme Court ruled that Mexicans holding valid titles on March 2, 1836, and continuing to hold them until July 4, 1848, "were protected in them by Article 8 of the Treaty of Guadalupe Hidalgo." In a 1914 verdict the same court ruled that the treaty had the "force of law in Texas," and this same principle was affirmed by at least two other Texas rulings.[22] In these decisions the Texas Supreme Court asserted the right of the state to incorporate the treaty into its local laws even though the U.S. Supreme Court refused to do so with respect to the national law. One basis for this difference of interpretation was that in Texas the treaty was being invoked to preserve the rights of property owners who had purchased the lands of former Mexican title holders.

In a similar vein the treaty became the weapon in a struggle between the state and the federal government over the use of the Rio Grande. In 1897 commercial interests in New Mexico sought to construct a dam near Las Cruces to divert water for irrigation projects.

The federal government sued the private company, charging that, among other things, the dam would violate Article VII of the Treaty of Guadalupe Hidalgo, which had stated that "the navigation of the Gila and of the Bravo [Rio Grande] . . . shall be free and common to the vessels and citizens of both countries, and neither shall, without the consent of the other, construct any work that may impede or interrupt, in whole or in part, the exercise of this right." Although it did not address the international question directly, the Supreme Court did find that "if the proposed dam and appropriation of the waters of the Rio Grande constitute a breach of treaty obligations or of international duty to Mexico, they also constitute an equal injury and wrong to the people of the United States."[23] The U.S. government was concerned for the rights of the people of the El Paso region to the water and was using the treaty to buttress their position. The result was that the Supreme Court found in favor of the U.S. government and the project was halted. A subsequent lawsuit, in 1902, reconfirmed this opinion. Finally, in 1914, after securing an agreement with Mexico through an international treaty, the federal government undertook the project, constructing the Elephant Butte Dam.[24]

1930 TO THE PRESENT

The Great Depression, which began in 1929, marked the beginning of a liberal political response that lasted well into the 1960s. Conservative reaction to the social and economic policies of the Democrats occurred during the 1950s, 1970s, and 1980s. Thus the political environment surrounding the juridical interpretation of the treaty became more polarized. Neither strict nor liberal interpretations predominated. Increasingly the treaty became a tool for advancing the interests of various interest groups. Various governmental agencies used the treaty with mixed success to enlarge their powers. Corporate interests sought to interpret the treaty to bolster their positions. Native Americans, mobilized by the New Deal and Vietnam War eras, sought redress for past injustices. Mexican Americans began to use the treaty as a weapon to reclaim lands and rights.

The treaty became part of the struggle between the federal government and the western states. As early as 1922 the states of the Colorado River basin had agreed to a division of the waters of that great river system, and in the early 1930s the federal government neared completion of the Hoover Dam project. In 1931 the federal government successfully asserted its control of the nonnavigable sections of the Colorado River in *United States v. Utah*, citing the Treaty of Guadalupe Hidalgo as a basis for its claim against the rights of the states. The treaty provided the legal basis for federal control of dam projects on the river. Similarly, in this same period, the federal government used the treaty to justify its rights to the California tidelands.[25] In the 1960s the federal government sued the gulf states of Louisiana, Alabama, Florida, and Texas in an attempt to control oil-rich lands beyond the three-mile limit. The states of Texas and Florida cited the treaties that had settled their international boundaries to successfully retain control of lands beyond three miles off shore. The state of Texas cited Article V of the treaty, which stipulated that the Texas-Mexico boundary would begin "three leagues from land opposite the mouth of the Rio Grande." The Florida treaty with Spain contained similar language. Since a league was approximately two miles, both states could claim a six-mile limit. Using this same wording in the treaty, the Mexican government had, since 1936, asserted a three-league offshore limit on its gulf coast. Consequently the Supreme Court found in favor of Texas and Florida but against the other states citing the Treaty of Guadalupe Hidalgo as a major basis for its decision.[26]

Corporate interests have also had some success in using the treaty to their benefit. In 1940 in *Chadwick et al. v. Campbell* the Circuit Court of Appeals for New Mexico gave a lengthy interpretation of the treaty in deciding a corporate struggle over land containing valuable oil and gas leases. Campbell, representing one group of investors, successfully sued Chadwick and the trustees of the Sevilleta de la Joya grant, who controlled 215,000 acres in Socorro County. The trustees had lost title to the lands following nonpayment of taxes. Chadwick argued that the treaty guaranteed protection of Mexican land grants. The court ruled that the treaty did not exempt Mexican landholders from taxes but that "under the Treaty of Guadalupe Hidalgo, private rights of property within the ceded territory were unaffected by the change in sovereignty.[27] In *Summa Corporation v. California* (1984.) an investment corporation successfully challenged an attempt by the State of California to declare their lands part of the public domain. The corporation persuaded the court that the treaty had been legitimately implemented in the actions of the California Land Commission. The court ruled that the corporation's land rights derived from Congress's interpretation of the treaty in law.[28] This was the same argument employed by the federal government in earlier periods to justify its appropriation of the public domain.

During this period (1930 to the present), Native Americans seeking redress for the loss of their tribal lands and liberties used the treaty as one of many treaties that courts might consider. On the whole their efforts were frustrated. Most judicial decisions were against the Indians' rights and in favor of a limited interpretation of the treaty.

In *Tenorio v. Tenorio* (1940) the New Mexico Supreme Court echoed an earlier suggestion of the federal court that the Treaty of Guadalupe Hidalgo did not embrace Pueblo Indians. This judgment reversed an earlier territorial court position in the *Lucero* case, which had applied the treaty to the Pueblo peoples. In 1945 the Supreme Court also ruled that the treaty could not be used to give support to the land claims of the Shoshonean Indians, many of whom had lived within the Mexican Cession in Utah, Nevada, and California. The courts also rejected California Indian claims, refusing to agree that the treaty was a substantive basis for a fiduciary duty towards these people. In *Pitt River Tribe et al. v. United States* (1973) two members of this California tribe sued the government to recover the true value of lands that had been settled in a financial agreement in 1964. The court rejected their appeal, which had been based largely on the treaty.[29]

Two of the most significant interpretations of the Treaty of Guadalupe Hidalgo as it affected American Indians were made in April and May of 1986. They represented both a victory and a defeat for Indian rights.

On January 4, 1985, an officer of the Department of the Interior charged José Abeyta, an Isleta Pueblo Indian, with violating the Bald Eagle Protection Act because he had killed one of these birds to use its feathers in religious ceremonies. Abeyta defended himself before the U.S. District Court in New Mexico, asserting that Indians were protected in the exercise of their religion by Article IX of the Treaty of Guadalupe Hidalgo, which had promised that all Mexican nationals would be "secured in the free exercise of their religion without restriction." The District Court again overruled the 1945 *Tenorio* ruling that the Pueblo Indians were not protected by the Treaty of Guadalupe Hidalgo. Judge Burciaga ruled for the court: "Because the Treaty of Guadalupe Hidalgo afforded protections to the Pueblos, however, it is in this dimension more than a settlement between two hostile nations: it is a living Indian treaty.[30] The court then moved to dismiss the charges against Abeyta based entirely upon the protections of religious liberty contained in the Ist Amendment and the Treaty of Guadalupe Hidalgo. This was a significant finding in that, for the first time, the language of the treaty itself was the primary basis for a legal decision.

One month later, on May 5, 1986, the U.S. Court of Appeals in California decided another case involving Indian rights, specifically the claim of the members of the Chumash tribe to the Santa Barbara, Santa Cruz, and Santa Rosa islands. The Chumash peoples claimed that they had occupied the islands since "time immemorial" and that the Treaty of Guadalupe Hidalgo, by failing to mention the islands as part of the ceded territories, left the tribe in legal possession. The court, in a footnote, issued its opinion of this argument: "While the court generally must assume the factual allegations to be true, it need not assume the truth of the legal conclusions cast in the form of factual allegations."[31] The Indians further argued that if the treaty did apply to them, then "the aboriginal title of the Chumash Indians to the islands came to be recognized by Article VIII and IX of the 1848 Treaty of Guadalupe Hidalgo." The court responded that this argument was "novel and creative but does not appear to have any merit." In rejecting the tribal claims, Judge Fletcher maintained (1) that Indian title to land "derives from their presence on land before the arrival of white settlers" and (2) that the treaty did not convert Indians' claims into recognized titles, because only the Land Commission could do this, and the Chumash had failed to present their claim within the stipulated time limits.

Since the 1930s the treaty has been an instrument most widely used by plaintiffs of non-Mexican origin seeking a variety of remedies. Only a few court cases have been initiated by those whom the treaty was intended to protect. In this period, six court cases citing the treaty directly impinged on the fate of the Mexican-American population. In the 1940s the state of Texas and the Balli family engaged in a series of legal battles over ownership of Padre Island. Alberto Balli had inherited what he thought was a legal Mexican land grant from his family. In 1943 the state of Texas sued the Balli family to recover the land grant, arguing that it had not fulfilled the technical requirements of Mexican statutes. The District Court in Texas found that the Balli family had met most of the requirements of the law and that their rights were protected under the Treaty of Guadalupe Hidalgo. In a series of rulings, the court resoundingly supported Balli against the state. The Texas Supreme Court later affirmed this verdict on appeal. This was a major land-grant victory for Tejanos, and it was based squarely on an interpretation of the treaty. It also was an indication that, notwithstanding previous court decisions exempting Texas from application of the treaty, it was still possible to interpret the document as applying to land-grant cases in that state.[32]

A few years later the courts faced this issue again but ruled in the opposite direction, to divest a Mexican family of its land. In 1946 Amos Amaya and his family, all citizens of Mexico, sued the Texas-based Stanolind Oil and Gas Company to recover lands allegedly taken illegally under the Treaty of Guadalupe Hidalgo. Circuit Court Judge Waller, in his ruling, cited Article VIII of the treaty, specifically that portion requiring the title of Mexican citizens to be inviolably respected: "We regard the phrase as a covenant on the part of the United States to respect from thenceforth any title that Mexicans had, or might thereafter acquire, to property with the region, but not that it would guarantee that those Mexicans would never lose title to persons by foreclosure, sales under execution, trespass, adverse possession, and other non-government acts."[33] Because the Amaya family failed to follow the timetable for land recovery under Texas statutes, the judge sustained the lower court's ruling against recovery of their lands. As he put it, "The provisions of the treaty do not save the Appellants from the fatal effect of the passage of time under the statutes of limitations in the State of Texas."[34]

The issue of the property rights of Mexican citizens reemerged in 1954 during the height of a nationwide campaign to deport or repatriate Mexican immigrants. Robert Galván, a legal Mexican immigrant accused of being a communist, was brought for deportation hearings before the U.S. District Court in Southern California. He in turn filed for a writ of habeas corpus, arguing that his deportation would violate the Treaty of Guadalupe Hidalgo provision protecting the property of Mexican citizens. The court responded that although the treaty was entitled to "juridical obeisance," it did not specify that Mexicans were entitled to remain in the United States to manage their property.[35]

Another Mexican-American land-rights issue came before the court in a series of cases launched by Reies Tijerina and the Alianza Federal de Mercedes Libres in New Mexico. In the 1960s a group of Hispano land-grant claimants led by the charismatic Reies López Tijerina sought to regain their lost community grants. Concurrent with their court battles, the organization sponsored a series of meetings and rallies that eventually erupted in violent confrontations, a take-over of Tierra Amarilla courthouse, shootings, and a statewide manhunt for the leaders of the Alianza. In 1969, with the land-grant struggle still fresh, Tijerina launched another campaign to change the public-school system in New Mexico by forcing reapportionment on local school boards of education and by requiring the teaching of all subjects in both Spanish and English. As in the land-grant wars, Tijerina relied heavily on the legal and moral force of the Treaty of Guadalupe Hidalgo. In a class-action lawsuit on behalf of the "IndioHispano" poor people of New Mexico, Tijerina sued the State Board of Education. On December 4, 1969, the District Court dismissed the suit for a variety of causes, including the court opinion that Tijerina had misinterpreted the scope of the treaty. Tijerina had based his suit for bilingual education on Articles VIII and IX of the treaty, but the court found that the treaty "does not contemplate in any way the administration of public schools. In addition we are not of the opinion that the treaty confers any proprietary right to have the Spanish language and culture preserved and continued in the public schools at public expense."[36] Addressing Tijerina's contention that the rights of poor people were being violated, the court ruled, "This is an unsound position as that treaty has nothing to do with any rights that 'poor' people may have."

Tijerina appealed the District Court ruling to the Supreme Court, and on May 25, 1970, that court also dismissed the appeal. Justice Douglas wrote a dissenting opinion, arguing that although the treaty was not a sound basis for the case, it could be argued on civil rights under the 14th and 15th amendments.[37]

Another land-rights case occurred in 1984, when the Texas Mexican property holders who were members of the Asociación de Reclamantes brought a case before the federal courts. They sought reimbursement for lands taken from them in violation of the treaty. As a result of counterbalancing international claims, the Mexican government had become liable to compensate the heirs of Tejano landholders for their losses. In the 1984 case the Asociación members outlined the damages they sought from the Mexican government. The U.S. Court of Appeals, however, declined to hear the case on the basis that the violation had not occurred within the United States. Of significance, however, was the statement of the judge recognizing that the Tejano landholders had rights that "were explicitly protected by the

Treaty of Guadalupe Hidalgo." This suggested a reversal of the *McKinney v. Saviego* (1856) opinion in which the treaty was interpreted as not being applicable to Texas. U.S. acceptance that the 1941 treaty with Mexico settled the outstanding claims against Mexico appeared to be an admission of the validity of the Tejano land claims under the treaty.[38] This point has not, however, been explicitly tested in the courts.

CONCLUSION

It is difficult to characterize in a few words the direction the American courts have taken in interpreting the Treaty of Guadalupe Hidalgo. The courts have changed their opinions several times on a number of issues, most notably regarding the applicability of the treaty to Texas and the Pueblo Indians. About half of the cases entailing a major interpretation of the treaty have involved Mexican American or Indian litigants. In these cases, defeats outnumbered victories by about two to one. The treaty has been more important in legitimizing the status quo, particularly in justifying federal, state, and corporate ownership of former Spanish and Mexican land grants. About three-fourths of the cases decided since 1848 have been about land-ownership rights, and only a small percentage have been about civil rights under the treaty.[39]

The Treaty of Guadalupe Hidalgo has remained a viable part of the U.S. system of laws, having been interpreted again and again by the federal and state courts. Unfortunately, the treaty has not effectively protected and enlarged the civil and property rights of Mexican Americans. This apparently unfulfilled promise of the treaty fueled a Mexican-American political movement in the 1960s and 1970s that sought to achieve a justice denied them by the American courts.

Notes

1. The procedure followed to analyze United States court cases dealing with the Treaty of Guadalupe Hidalgo was to utilize the on-line computerized reference system called Lexis-Nexis. This system enables a user to access all court cases mentioning a specific treaty or law and to generate paragraphs where the treaty was referenced in the court conclusions. Shephard's Citations were also used to access references to the treaty that did not appear in the Lexis-Nexis system. In this way more than 200 court cases were singled out, along with some detail on the treaty interpretation given by the court. My study was focused on how the court interpreted the treaty, not on how defendants and plaintiffs argued using the treaty. Only direct references to the treaty were the subject of this study, not the hundreds of cases flowing from land-grant litigation where the treaty was not a substantive

concern. Of the 200 cases sampled, only 64 were found to be substantial interpretations of the treaty. My judgment as to what constituted an important interpretation depended both on the length to which the court went in discussing the treaty as well as the importance ascribed to the treaty by the court. Most references to the treaty were minor, where the document was used as a point of reference to make some larger legal argument.

2. Robert McCloskey, *The American Supreme Court* (Chicago and London: University of Chicago Press, 1960), pp. 103-105.

3. *Reynolds v. West* I Cal. 322 (1850).

4. *Mintern v. Bowers et al.* 24 Cal. 644 (1864) at 672.

5. *United States v. Reading* 59 U.S. I (1855); *Palmer v. United States* 65 U.S. 125 (1857); *Townsend et al. v. Greeley* 72 U.S. 326 (1866).

6. *United States v. Moreno* 68 U.S. 400 (1863), *City and County of San Francisco v. Scott* III U.S. 768 (1884); *Phillips v. Mound City* 124 U.S. 605 (1888).

7. *United States v. Lucero* I N.M. 422 (1869) at 441. For California's interpretation see *People v. de la Guerra* 40 CAL 311 (1870).

8. *Tenorio y. Tenorio* 44 N.M. 89 (1940) reversed the *Lucero* decision and ruled that the treaty had not made the Pueblo Indians citizens of the United States and that they were not entitled to the protections of Article VIII and IX.

9. *McKinney v. Saviego* 59 U.S. 365 (1856) at 263. This decision was affirmed at the state level in *The State of Texas v. Gallardo* 135 S.W. 644 (1911).

10. *Botiller v. Dominguez* U.S. 238 (1889).

11. *Horner v. United States* 143 U.S. 570 (1892; *Grant v. Jaramillo* 6 N.M; 313 (1892); 54 S.W. 366 (1898).

12. *Baker et al. v. Harvey* 181 U.S. 481 (1901); *United States v. Title Insurance Co. et al.* 265 U.S. 472 (1924).

13. *California Powderworks v. Davis* 151 US 389 (1894); *United States v. Sandoval et al.* 167 US 278 (1897); *Arisa v. New Mexico and Arizona Railroad* 175 US 76 (1899).

14. *United States v. Greely et al.* 185 US 256 (1901).

15. *Lockhart v. Johnson* 181 US 516 (1901) at 528.

16. Ibid. at 523.

17. *City of Los Angeles v Venice Peninsula Properties et al.* 31 Cal. 3d 288 (1913); *City of San Diego v. Cuyamaca Water Co.* 209 Cal. 105 (1930).

18. *Interstate Land Company v. Maxwell Land Co.* 80 US 460 (1891) at 588.

19. *Cessna v. United States et al.* 169 US 165 (1898) at 186.

20. *Pueblo of Zia v. United States et al.* 168 US 198 (1897); *United States v. Lucero* 1 NM 422 (1869); *United States v. Sandoval* 231 US 28 (1913) at 39, 48.

21. *Apapos et al. v. United States* 233 US 587 (1914); *Tenorio v. Tenorio* 44 NM 89 (1940).

22. *McKinney v. Saviego* 59 US 365 (1856); *Texas Mexican Rail Road v. Locke* 74 Tex. 370 (1889); *State of Texas v. Gallardo et al.* 106 Tex. 274 (1914); *State of Texas v. Sais* 47 Tex. 307 and *Clark v. Hills* 67 Tex. 141.

23. *United States y. Rio Grande Dam and Irrigation Co. et al.* 175 US 690 (1899), at 699, 700.

24. *United States v. Rio Grande Dam and Irrigation Co. et al.* 184 US 416 (1901).

25. *United States v. State of Utah* 238 U.S. 64 (1931); *United States v. O'Donnell* 303 U.S. 501 (1938).

26. *United States v. States of Louisiana et al.* 363 U.S. 1 (1960); For a discussion of the diplomacy surrounding the negotiation of Mexico's off shore limit see 99 *Cong. Rec.* 3623-3624, June 3, 1936.

27. *Chadwick et al. v Campbell* 115 F. 2d 401 (1940).

28. *Summa Corporation v. State of California ex rel. State Lands Commission et al.* 104 S.Ct. 1751 (1984), at 1754.

29. *Tenorio v. Tenorio* 44 N.M. 89 (1940); *Pitt River Tribe et al. v. United States* 485 F. 2d 660 (1973).

30. *United States v. Abeyta* 632 F. Supp. 1301 (1986); at 1301.

31. *United States ex rel. Chunie v. Ringrose* 788 F. 2d 638 (1986).

32. *State of Texas v. Balli* 173 S.W.2d 522 (1943).

33. *Amaya et al. v. Stanolind Oil and Gas Co. et al.* 158.2d 554 (1946).

34. Ibid., at 559.

35. *Application of Robert Galvan for Writ of Habeus Corpus* 127 F. Supp. 392 (1954).

36. *López Tijerina v. Henry* 48 F.R.D. 274 (1969).

37. *Tijerina et al. v. United States* 398 U.S. 922 (1970).

38. See *Treaty on Final Settlement of Certain Claims, United States and Mexico,* 56 Stat. 1347, T.S. No. 980 (Nov. 19, 1941).

39. *Asociacion de Reclamantes et al. v. United Mexican States* 735 F.2d 1517 (1984); See *Treaty on Final Settlement of Certain Claims, United States and Mexico,* 56 Stat. 1347, T.S. No. 980 (Nov. 19, 1941).

In this selection John R. Chávez explores the erosion of the Chicano land base and the subsequent loss of social position. As a result of population pressures, untimely and unfair legislation and immigrants imbued with anti-Mexican hatred, the first generation of Chicanos experienced an unprecedented downward mobility. Chávez also explores early Chicano resistance, as the first generation struggled against the erosion of their economic and political position. Despite these efforts Americanization of the economic and political base of the Southwest was virtually complete by 1900.

The Lost Land
John R. Chávez

We can date to 1848 the modern Chicano image of the Southwest as a lost land. The conquest of the present Southwest severed the region from the control of Mexico City and the local Mexican elites. In some places the Anglo Americans seized complete political power almost immediately after the military conquest, but in other areas, notably New Mexico, the native leadership managed to maintain some influence after the occupation. Command of military power, of course, determined that Anglos would hold the major positions everywhere in the Southwest, but the factor that decisively undermined Mexican political strength was the enormous growth of the Anglo population. We have already seen that the increase of that population in eastern Texas destroyed local Mexican dominance even before the revolution of 1836. *Nuevomexicanos* were more fortunate because they remained a majority in New Mexico well into the twentieth century. In northern California, on the other hand, where the Gold Rush of 1849 resulted in a huge influx of Anglos, *californios* were left powerless almost immediately. Once having lost control of the government, Mexicans soon found themselves losing their economic base to the newcomers. Owing to the quagmire of litigation created by the requirement that Spanish and Mexican land grants be verified, Mexican elites in many parts of the Southwest lost their lands and with them they lost the social position that helped sustain the prestige of Mexican culture in the region.[1] Finding their culture steadily declining with the increasing influence of Anglo society, Mexicans began to see themselves as "*foreigners in their own land,*"[2] a self-image that appeared repeatedly in their writings and that affected their relations with the dominant group for much of the nineteenth century. One result of that alienation was the appearance, in both legend and reality, of the often well-born native hero who, victimized by Anglo society, rebelled against it.[3] Yet, though Mexicans felt themselves increasingly alienated from the Southwest, they continued to see it as their homeland. The fact that Mexico had once embraced the region was still too recent for

Southwest Mexicans to have forgotten; not yet separated from their history in the borderlands, they still recalled their dispossession.

A week before the signing of the Treaty of Guadalupe Hidalgo, gold was discovered in northern California, a discovery that was to cause unprecedented immigration to the area. Although a Mexican ranchman had found gold in southern California in 1842, his find had been too small to attract people from far outside the locality. The discovery of 1842, however, increased the overall population of California from under 10,000 before the North American occupation to over 90,000 by 1850. The U.S. Census of 1850, which excluded Indians, listed 91,635 people in the state, of which approximately 7,500 were native "white" Spanish-speaking Californians. In addition to these *californios* there were about 6,500 other Mexicans who had recently arrived in the gold fields from areas south of the new international boundary.[4] Furthermore, in the first year of the Gold Rush 5,000 South Americans came to California, bringing the total Spanish-speaking population up to roughly 20,000. Despite this increase and the arrival of many foreigners who spoke neither Spanish nor English, by 1850 Anglo-Americans outnumbered the Spanish-speaking three to one. In two years the Latin Americans went from a large majority to a minority.

The *californios* were, needless to say, amazed at the numbers of new arrivals and felt threatened. Mariano Vallejo, a Californio who had long supported annexation to the United States, left a largely unfavorable description of the newcomers, a description which incidentally revealed his own ethnocentric and even racist sentiments:

> *Australia sent us a swarm of bandits . . . The Mormons, lascivious but very industrious people, sent the ship Brooklyn . . . Mexico inundated us with a wave of gamblers . . . Italy sent us musicians . . . (who) lost no time in fraternizing with the keepers of gambling houses . . .*

Although Vallejo emphasized the negative, he did praise those he considered good workers, such as the Mormons and Italian gardeners who became small farmers. He had nothing but praise for the Germans, and he held the Chileans in high regard: "Chile sent us many laborers who were very useful and contributed not a little to the development of the resources of the country." On the other hand, reflecting the extreme prejudice against Asians in nineteenth century California, Vallejo wrote, "I believe that the great Chinese immigration which invaded California in '50, '51, and '52 was very harmful to the moral and material development of the country, . . . the Chinese women, . . . it seems had made it a duty to keep the hospitals always filled with syphilitics." Though this racial slur was vicious, Vallejo saved his most bitter remarks for the non-Mormon, Anglo majority from the rest of the United States:

The Lost Land

> *But all these evils became negligible in comparison with the swollen torrent of shysters who came from Missouri and other states of the Union. No sooner had they arrived than they assumed the title of attorney and began to seek means of depriving the Californians of their farms and other properties.*[6]

At first the population increase was confined to the mining region in the interior of northern California, which permitted *californios* to retain some political control along the coast, especially south of Monterey. Because of this political strength, eight Mexicans participated in the constitutional convention that in 1849 formed the first state government of California; their experience at the convention reflected their people's position in relation to the Anglo American majority. Since the proceedings were conducted in English, the *californio* delegates, finding it necessary to use interpreters in their native country, felt like foreigners; at one point one of the Mexicans became angry when he sensed that an Anglo representative had called him a foreigner. Even though they declined to vote as a block on all matters, in general the *californio* delegates did promote the interests of their people. Realizing that Mexicans were now a minority, the Spanish-speaking representatives engaged in many maneuvers to make the Mexican position under the new regime more secure, but their success was limited.[7]

Since *californios* continued to own most of the land in the proposed state, they feared that the highest taxes would be placed on them. Their representatives gained a concession on this matter when it was decided that assessors would be elected locally, thus permitting Mexicans, in counties where they were numerous, some control over their own taxation. The *californio* delegates also succeeded in having the new constitution require that all laws be translated into Spanish. With regard to the franchise, they confronted the serious threat of racial discrimination when the question of Indian voting rights arose; since some of the Mexican delegates were mestizos, and one was an Indian, they strongly opposed the effort to deny Indians the vote. Despite this resistance, the convention decided that only certain Indians would be allowed to vote and only by direct action of the legislature. Given the large white majority at the convention, this has to regarded as a small victory for the *californios*.[8]

Though the Mexican delegation managed these few successes, the five southern California members failed to achieve perhaps their most important objective, that of separating their area from the north. By creating a territory in the south where they were the majority (and would be until the 1870s),[9] the *californios* of that area hoped to escape domination by the Anglo majority that had settled in the north. To achieve this the *californio* delegates from the south engaged in several complex maneuvers. One was to push for territorial status rather than statehood for all of California, thus keeping the boundaries less rigid and permitting future division. Another was to include within the state, if such it was to be, as much as possible of the land considered at one time or another part of California by Mexico, in other words all of present California and Nevada, and fractions of other present states. By creating such a large state, Mexicans from the southern counties hoped it would eventually become unwieldy and subsequently be divided, possibly leaving the Spanish-speaking in control of southern California. Though these machinations met with no success and were carried out by the Mexican delegation from the south, they revealed the desire all *californios* had for a land where they might retain a measure of independence. This desire did not disappear with the Constitutional Convention of 1849; movements for the division of the state continued for years.[10]

One of the most articulate agitators for such a division, and for other actions beneficial for California's Mexicans, was Francisco Ramírez, editor of *El clamor público*, the Spanish-language newspaper of Los Angeles during the 1850s. Ramírez was a progressive who hoped for full participation of his people in the brilliant future he predicted for California. Despite the unrest caused by the Gold Rush and the threat that the mines might be exhausted, in June of 1855 Ramírez optimistically wrote:

> As great as California's mineral resources are, its livestock and the invaluable products of its agriculture are no less notable ... Adding to these great elements of prosperity, a clear and glossy sky and a healthy climate, it can be said that California is the paradise of America. In regard to natural beauty, the sublime picturesque scenes of lovely Italy and Switzerland do not equal it.

With an increase in the number of respectable citizens, the improvement of highways, and the building of railroads, Ramírez saw California becoming the center for commerce with the Orient, trade which would result in the riches necessary to raise great cities. In this picture we find elements of earlier images of the Southwest: the natural paradise of the Aztecs, the early Spanish land of gold, and the Mexican land of promise. Interestingly, we also find an Anglo vision of prosperous cities built by commerce, especially commerce by rail.[11]

Ramírez drew this optimistic sketch of California in an early issue of his newspaper (published from 1855 through 1859). Though he never doubted the state would reach greatness, he always suspected Mexicans would have little share in the prosperity. By August 1856 he bitterly commented that "the faith that {*californios*} had in the new government that had just established itself on the shores of the Pacific has vanished forever." And he added, "All are convinced that *California is lost to all Spanish-Americans* ..." The more he dealt editorially with issues directly affecting his people, the more publicly pessimistic he became. His early public optimism may be attributed to the knowledge that many of his first subscribers were Anglos, whom he was hesitant to offend; certainly he was privately aware of the abuses Mexicans and other Latin Americans had suffered in California since 1848. In fact Ramírez complained in August 1856, "Despotism, (and) crime have existed here since that day of the discovery of gold. . . . Brute force is the only law that is observed." Unfortunately for Latin Americans much of that brutality and despotism was directed at them.[12]

Because of their proximity to the mines, *californios* were some of the first to reach the gold fields. They were followed by other Mexicans, collectively called Sonorans, who trekked from northern Mexico, across the southern California deserts to the coast, then north to the mines. Chileans and Peruvians found it relatively easy to reach the state by ship directly up the Pacific coast. Because these people arrived early and possessed the rich mining tradition of Spanish America, they were more successful in the gold fields than were the Anglos who were forced to learn from them. As a result, animosity between Anglos and these "foreigners" developed to such a point that the legislature passed the Foreign Miners' Tax Law of 1850, a law whose "avowed purpose," as Josiah Royce sarcastically remarked, "was as far as possible to exclude foreigners from these mines, the God-given property of the American people." When officials attempted to collect the exorbitant tax in Mexican mining settlements, they encountered resistance. Before long, rioting between Anglo and Latin American miners broke out; eventually the Latin Americans were expelled, with many of the Mexicans fleeing to Southern California. The violence of the gold fields, which often amounted to race war, soon spread throughout California; and some Mexicans, chased from their claims, became bandits as a way of getting revenge. Before long almost any crime was blamed on Mexicans, and the lynching of Mexicans became common through much of the third quarter of the nineteenth century.

Interestingly, much of the so-called banditry took on the character of a guerrilla resistance movement. Among the bandits and those who gave them aid were Latin Americans of all types, peons and aristocrats, native *californios* and newcomers. Of the native poor, historian James Miller Guinn commented:

> *a strange metamorphosis took place in the character of the lower classes of the native Californians . . . Before the conquest by the Americans . . . There were no organized bands of outlaws among them . . . The Americans not only took possession of their country and its government, but in many cases despoiled them of their ancestral acres and their personal property. Injustice rankles, and they were often treated by the rougher American elements as aliens and intruders, who had no right in the land of their birth.*[14]

Of the disinherited native elite, Josiah Royce wrote, "those numerous degraded Spanish or half-breed outlaws, the creatures of our injustice, the sons sometimes . . . of the great landowners whom we had robbed, if one remembers how they infested country roads . . . , one sees at length in full how our injustice avenged itself upon us . . ."[15] While many of the California bandits were simply criminals who preyed on all ethnic groups, at least two gained reputations as resistance fighters; these two were the legendary Joaquín Murrieta and Tiburcio Vásquez.

The facts of Joaquín Murrieta's life are obscure; he so successfully concealed his identity from the authorities that they were never quite sure who he was even after they claimed to have killed him in 1853. According to one version of his life, he was a Mexican miner whose claim was jumped by a group of Anglos who had already killed his brother; they knocked him unconscious, raped his wife, then murdered her. Murrieta became an outlaw, swearing to avenge himself on all Anglos.[16] He became a legend during his own life: soon crimes all over California were attributed to his efforts, and other bandits were mistaken for him. Though Anglos regarded him as a curse, Mexicans and other Latin Americans saw him as a hero; long after his exploits, corridos, popular ballads, were sung in praise of him. In one of these, sung in the first person, we find a clear statement of the Mexican's view of himself in relation to the conquered Southwest of the 1850s:

> I came from Hermosillo (Sonora)
> In search of gold and riches;
> With fierceness I defended
> The noble and simple Indian.
> ....
> Now I go out on the roads
> Americans to kill,
> You (who) were the cause
> Of the death of my brother.
> ....
> I am neither gringo nor stranger
> In this land where I walk;
> California is Mexico's
> Because God wished it so;
> And in my serape . . . I carry
> My certificate of baptism.[17]

Clearly the anonymous balladeer, and many of those who repeated the song, refused to acknowledge the presence of the new boundary. This ballad suggests that Mexicans, even those born south of the new border, continued, in opposition to the Anglo conquerors, to identify with the land of the Southwest, and to some extent with the native Indians.

Though Murrieta was a half-mythic character, the motives that supposedly drove him to crime are similar to those of the very real Tiburcio Vásquez, captured in 1876. While Murrieta seems to have been a Sonoran miner, Vásquez belonged to a relatively well-off *californio* family. He became an outlaw because of the repeated insults he and other *californios* suffered when courting their own women in competition with Anglo men; as he put it, "A spirit of hatred and revenge took possession of me. I had numerous fights in defense of what I believed to be my rights and those of my countrymen." Apparently he felt this spirit was widespread because he once claimed he could revolutionize southern California if he had $60,000 to buy arms and recruit men. Indeed the condition of the Spanish-speaking in California was such that many prominent *californio* families were represented among the bandit rebels who roamed the highways in the third quarter of the nineteenth century.[18]

One reason for rebellion of some of the younger members of the elite was the Land Law of 1851. Although, as *El clamor público* noted, "The first occupants of this soil were of Spanish descent (sic)"[19] and were entitled to their property by the Treaty of Guadalupe Hidalgo, the Land Law of 1851 required them to prove ownership of their estates. Anglo squatters, believing in a "right of conquest," had challenged the validity of Spanish and Mexican land grants. Since the boundaries of the original grants were often loosely drawn, the *californios* were soon caught in what seemed endless difficulties: an unfamiliar judicial system conducted in English, unscrupulous lawyers who demanded exorbitant fees often payable only in land, squatters who refused to pay rent until grants were validated, raising money through profitable sales or low-interest loans while claims were being processed, and making land productive without sufficient cash. The Land Law of 1851 together with the *californios'* unfamiliarity with the competitive Anglo economic system eventually led to the loss of their property. (Because the population there was smaller, the process was slower in southern than northern California.)[20]

In the articles of *El clamor público* protesting the land losses and other injustices inflicted on Latin Americans, Francisco Ramírez proposed a variety of possible solutions to these problems. Besides advocating division of the state, which would free southern California from a legislature heavily influenced by squatters, *El clamor público* suggested even more extreme measures. At one point Ramírez helped promote an unsuccessful plan to settle *californios* and other Mexicans in Sonora where they might escape Anglo domination. (He himself left Los Angeles and lived in Sonora between 1860 and 1862.) In one issue an article was published arguing that California be made a protectorate of the European and Latin American nations whose citizens had settled in the state. This was argued on the grounds that California had been "grabbed from Mexico," "that the Hispanic-American and European population, spread throughout the territory, . . . (had) established unchangeable customs," and finally that the United States threatened to "infest" the Pacific region of the world that was the heritage of Latin Americans "emanating originally from the Inca." In a tone of surrender, *El clamor público* once also commented:

> *We are now under the American flag, be it through our own choice or by force, and it is probable that we will remain thus always. We should then accept the events and vicissitudes of our age and familiarize ourselves with the new language, habits, and customs; thus we will not be dominated but equal in everything. This is best for us and our posterity.*

Surely, however, Ramírez never truly agreed with this statement since his more extreme ideas were published after he had written it.[21]

In order to participate fully, especially economically, in California's brilliant future, Ramírez feared Mexicans would have to assimilate, cutting completely their ties with Mexico, the nation which "to insure its independence, and (to insure) that its name did not disappear forever . . . was forced to part with a great portion of its territory," and was forced to leave its northern citizens "strangers in our own country."[22] Though Ramírez and other *californio* progressives fervently believed in economic development, they did not wish to renounce Mexican culture, a renunciation that U.S. society demanded before it would allow them to feel at home in their native country. Even Mariano Vallejo, who had desired annexation to the United States, feeling it would bring prosperity to California, did not give up all ties to Mexico. In 1877 when he went to Mexico City to lobby for a railroad between that capital and his state, he commented,

> *I am an American because the treaty of Guadalupe placed me on the other side of the line dividing the two nations, but I was born a Mexican, my ancestors were Mexicans. . . . I have both Mexican and American children and I desire for my native land all the prosperity and progress enjoyed by the country of some of my children and mine by adoption. The day that Mexico has a railroad which devouring distance unites it with California, commerce and industry will progress.*[23]

Even as Vallejo sought closer ties with Mexico, however, a railroad was being planned from the East to southern California, a railroad that would destroy Mexican dominance in its last major bastion in the state. The boom of the 1880s would bring thousands of Easterners to Los Angeles.

Though they often admired the political ideals and the material advances of the United States, Mexicans throughout the Southwest were at the very least uncomfortable with Anglo civilization because, like Ramírez and Vallejo of California, they saw the damage this civilization was inflicting on their people and their culture. Even those like Vallejo who favored North American rule felt that their property, their way of life, and even their lives were too often threatened. Despite these threats, most Mexicans tried to make the best of their difficult situation. Even in Texas, where relations between Anglos and Mexicans had been hostile since before the Texas Revolution, a San Antonio newspaper, *El bejareño*, found positive things to say about *tejano* life in 1855:

> *As a consequence of one of those changes that are daily observed in the destiny of nations, Texas was violently separated from the Mexican nation. . . . Did this change result in good or evil for the country? The liberty that we enjoy, the wealth and general prosperity, the moderation and fairness of our laws on one side, on the other, the military despotism, the poverty, the edicts, the political convulsions that prevail in Mexico . . . peremptorily answer the question for any intelligent and rational man.*[24]

Yet we do find that at least one thing disturbed *El bejareño*: "The majority (of *tejanos*), we must confess, lacks education, and they frequently pay for this deficiency, finding themselves strangers in the land of their birth . . ." The newspaper clearly saw education, especially education that would teach the ways of the Anglo, as a means toward greater acceptance and participation in the society that had taken possession of Texas. From this we may infer that *El bajereño* saw the retention of Mexican culture as an impediment to success in the new society, as excess clothing merely serving to alienate *tejanos* from the United States. But such was not the case. The newspaper wanted *tejanos* to be able to function comfortably in the new society, but not to abandon the "old ways." We find this attitude clearly evident in a brief description of the schools *El bejareño* desired: "We will always persist in promoting the foundation and stimulation of the *Public Schools* in which, without losing the language of Cervantes, Mexican-Texan children will acquire the national language . . ."[25] Thus, as early as 1855, Southwest Mexicans were calling for an educational system that would teach them English, and by extension other Anglo ways, without depriving them of their own language and culture.

Even though *El bejareño* claimed that life was much better in Texas than in Mexico, many *tejanos* disagreed. Juan Nepomuceno Seguín, one of the *tejanos* whom José Enrique de la Peña had labeled traitors for their support of the Texas Republic, later found life in

Texas so difficult that he left and lived in Mexico for several years. Although he had been a cavalry officer during the Texas Revolution and had served as mayor of San Antonio under the Texas Republic, he was accused by certain envious Anglos of disloyalty. A general in the Mexican Army, in a deliberate attempt to discredit him, had announced that Seguín was actually a loyal citizen of Mexico; using this statement against him, Seguín's Anglo rivals succeeded in destroying him politically. Fearing for his life, Seguín left Texas in 1842 and did not return until 1848, by which time he was no longer a serious threat to his rivals, who by then controlled San Antonio. In his memoirs in 1858, Seguín described his decision to flee Texas: "A victim to the wickedness of a few men, whose imposture was favored by their origin, and recent domination over the country; a foreigner in my native land . . . Crushed by sorrow . . . , I sought for a shelter amongst those against whom I had fought . . ." Though Seguín clearly felt no loyalty to Mexico, he found that being a "Mexican" in Texas was far from comfortable; so true was this that even in 1858 he was writing his memoirs to counter the attacks that were still leveled against him.[26]

Many *tejanos* went to Mexico after the Anglo occupation because, for decades after San Jacinto and Guadalupe Hidalgo, it was simply unsafe in Texas. Bandits from both the United States and Mexico roamed South Texas, making harmonious ethnic relations difficult. Several times, "wars" between Anglos and *tejanos* broke out across the state. Between San Antonio and the Gulf, commercial rivalry between teamsters of the two groups became open conflict in 1857. In 1877 months of interracial violence over rights to salt beds near El Paso ended with the flight of many *tejano* families into Mexico. The Civil War, which found *tejanos* generally opposed to the slave-holding Confederacy, also led to much racial warfare. But the most important episode was the revolt of the Texas equivalent to California's Murrieta and Vásquez--Juan N. Cortina. Cortina was born in the lower Rio Grande Valley into a wealthy Mexican family. In 1859, when a marshal arrested and mistreated a former employee of the family, Cortina shot the officer, declaring war against those Anglos who were persecuting *tejanos*.[27] Cortina sought redress for the ills inflicted on his people and called for armed rebellion against the oppressors: "Mexicans! My part is taken; the voice of revelation whispers to me that to me is entrusted the work of breaking the chains of your slavery . . ."[28]

Indeed Cortina had done his part; for before making this statement he had occupied Brownsville and punished a certain group of Anglos he considered especially cruel. In late 1859 his forces gained much support in the area between Rio Grande City and Brownsville, a distance of a hundred miles. Though he carried the Mexican flag, Cortina attempted neither to regain South Texas for Mexico nor to establish an independent state, but to improve the conditions of his people by threatening Anglos with violence if they failed to respect Mexican rights. During this Texas rebellion from September to December of 1859, Cortina failed to liberate *tejanos*, but he did win several victories over forces sent against him by the governments of both Mexico and Texas. However, he was defeated by U.S. troops at Rio Grande City in December 1859 and fled to Mexico. In 1861 he made one more raid into Texas to avenge several Mexicans who had been killed by Confederates, but was again forced across the border.[29]

After his intrepid but unsuccessful Texas revolt, Cortina spent the rest of his life involved in the maelstrom of Mexico's politics, where he acted as daringly as he had in Texas.[30] Significantly, Cortina had carried on his anti-Anglo activities in the old, Mexican-settled sections of Texas, sections that remained extensions of Mexico. Since these areas contained Mexican majorities, Anglo dominance seemed especially unjust; consequently resistance was stronger and more successful. Like Seguín, Cortina was forced into Mexico after experiencing the problems of being a "Mexican" in Texas, but unlike Seguín, he resisted before he left and briefly continued his fight from Mexico paying little attention to a boundary that to him, as to most Mexicans, was unjust and artificial.

By the 1880s, because of better enforcement on the part of U.S. and Mexican authorities, open conflict along the border had temporarily lessened, yet the life of *tejanos* continued to be difficult. Since they had long been outnumbered, their political power in the state was minimal; even in their enclaves in South and West Texas, the constant pattern of violence and intimidation that had driven many to Mexico prevented those who remained from being sufficiently assertive. Land grant difficulties of the sort experienced in California had occurred in Texas after the revolution, and later *tejanos* lost other property when they were unable to compete effectively in the aggressive Anglo economy. With their political and economic base undermined, *tejanos* made little progress even in such areas as education.[31]

In 1879 we find *El horizonte*, a Corpus Christi newspaper, still asking for the public schools that *El bejareño* had requested in 1855:

> *Mexican children in Corpus Christi are not even foreigners . . . (and yet) innumerable are the Mexican heads of family with their children who have been turned away from the door of the school covered with shame, turned away from where they were going to demand the completion of the faultless obligation (sic) to which they have a right as citizens.*

This lack of education made *tejanos* a "disinherited class" subject to harassment by Anglos merely because "the former (the Mexican) is the son of Guatimoc (*sic*, last emperor of the Aztecs) and the latter are sons of Washington." To remedy this situation *El horizonte*, going beyond the earlier position of *El bejareño*, argued not only that public education be extended to Mexicans but that it be bilingual. Otherwise it would be completely ineffective: "It would be convenient to appoint a professor who speaks English and is Mexican, because otherwise, that is to say, to appoint a teacher who does not know Spanish perfectly, we believe no result would be obtained at all, and the children would do nothing more than waste precious time." *El horizonte* realized that if *tejanos* were ever to live comfortably in Texas, they had to learn the language and ways of the dominant group, but the newspaper did not believe this could be done by ignoring Mexican culture.[32]

While Mexicans in Texas and California by 1850 found themselves and their civilization inundated by Anglo immigrants, the situation in New Mexico, which then included most of Arizona and part of Colorado, was at first different. New Mexico attracted few Anglo immigrants soon after 1848 because it had little gold, less arable land than neighboring areas, problems with the Apaches, and a native Mexican population about ten times that of either Texas or California. In fact, because U.S. troops provided a market for local goods, the initial North American occupation of New Mexico brought a measure of prosperity to the province. This prosperity and the promise of improved defense for the territory even permitted *nuevomexicanos* to expand their areas of settlement so that in the early 1850s the Spanish-speaking were able to found their first permanent towns in present-day southeastern Colorado, an area formerly belonging to but never really occupied by Spain and Mexico. Present day Arizona north of the Gila, also left unsettled by Spain or Mexico, was made part of the U.S. territory of New Mexico after Guadalupe Hidalgo. With the Gadsden Purchase of 1854, a sliver of land, including Tucson and the Mesilla Valley, was added to the territory. The United States thus incorporated another though smaller group of Mexicans within its boundaries; these new residents, especially those in the Tucson area, also benefitted initially from the Anglo-American occupation.[33]

The relationship that Anglos and Mexicans saw between themselves and the geographical space they occupied strongly affected events in the territory of New Mexico from 1848 until statehood was achieved by Arizona and New Mexico in 1912. The division of the huge territory of 1854 into the present day states, the location of the various state capitals, the promotion of public schools, the building of railroads, as well as the writing of constitutions, the adjudication of land claims, and the perpetration of interracial violence were all heavily influenced by the Anglo desire to minimize Mexican control of the area. As Anglos moved into the territory, the problems that were experienced in California and Texas eventually occurred in New Mexico also, becoming severe in the 1880s. By this time, with the Apaches subjected by the military, *nuevomexicanos* had pushed out of their Rio Grande enclaves east into the Texas Panhandle, and also southeast and southwest within present-day New Mexico. However, this expansion ceased when confronted by the movement of Anglo Texans in roughly the opposite directions. The traditional animosity between Texans and Mexicans together with the competition for space led to widespread violence. In the Panhandle a Mexican folk hero of French-Mexican descent, Sostenes l'Archeveque, avenged the murder of his father by killing more than twenty Anglos. Unfortunately, these killings resulted in wholesale retaliations against Mexicans who were forced to retreat into New Mexico, but this retreat did them little good since throughout the territory Mexican sheep herders and Anglo cattlemen constantly fought each other. For example, in southern New Mexico the entrance of Texans caused violent competition for pasture land. As a result, many Mexican families, fleeing Texan terrorism, abandoned their homes and ranches in the Socorro and Doña Ana areas and went to Mexico.[34]

The movement of Anglo cattlemen into New Mexico was followed by a wave of farmers in the mid-1880s, increasing the struggle for land, the best acres of which were usually the legal property of *nuevomexicanos*, the first settlers. As in California, Mexicans gradually lost their property through unfamiliarity with the new legal and economic system so that by the turn of the century four-fifths of the early Spanish and Mexican grants were in Anglo hands. Outraged by their deteriorating situation, *nuevomexicanos* in the 1880s organized several groups of nightriders who vandalized the property of those they held responsible for native losses. In New Mexico an additional factor depriving Mexicans of land rights was a congressional act of 1891 setting aside large tracts as national forest, tracts that had formerly been considered land held in common by ranchers and villagers for grazing purposes. As a result of this act, *nuevomexicanos* were forced to reduce their flocks of sheep, thus cutting the production of wool and causing a depression in the industry. (To this day grazing rights in the national forests are an important issue to Chicanos in New Mexico.) Yet in spite of the loss of land and the dwindling of their economic base, *neuvomexicanos* were able to maintain and have continued to maintain some political power in New Mexico because they have always formed a large percentage of the population. Also, the delay in the arrival of significant numbers of Anglos permitted *nuevomexicanos* to gain some political and economic expertise before the major conflict of the 1880s. Finally, a small number of the elite, who were able to hold on to their economic position, kept a measure of political power and prevented their people from losing all social prestige.[35]

New Mexico then is the one place where Southwest Mexicans succeeded in keeping a modicum of permanent control over their homeland. In fact, partly because Mexicans seemed to have too much power in the northern Rio Grande Valley, Anglos in other parts of the territory constantly tried to escape the rule of Santa Fe by proposing divisions of the huge territory of 1854. (As we have seen, Mexicans had unsuccessfully tried a similar scheme in California, but in that case to escape Anglo dominance.) From as early as 1854, attempts were made to create a territory of Arizona with a boundary running east-west from Texas to California, thus including present southern New Mexico and excluding present northern Arizona. In 1861-62 an invading Southern army actually established such a territory under the Confederacy. Many Mexicans actively opposed the short-lived new government because it derived from Texas, legalized slavery, and specified that English would be the language of the legislature, thus severely limiting Mexican participation.[36]

In 1863, after the Confederate withdrawal, the federal government organized the Arizona territory that would eventually become the state. This new territory was formed and controlled by Anglo businessmen who hoped to build railroads and develop the mineral resources of the area without interference from Santa Fe. Although Mexicans were more numerous than Anglos, and Indians heavily outnumber all the settlers, Anglos were able to make immediate control because of their connections with big business in the East. The small Mexican elite, nominal owners of much land that was often in Indian hands, had some influence but not nearly as much as their counterparts in New Mexico.[37] The separation of the Mexicans in Arizona from their compatriots in New Mexico deprived the former of the protection of Santa Fe; yet since they were still a majority of the settlers in the new territory, they could at least hope to yield more power in the future. This was not true of the many Mexicans who were separated from Santa Fe when they were included within the boundaries of Colorado Territory in 1861.

Unlike the isolated group in and near Tucson, Mexicans in southeastern Colorado lived close to Santa Fe: their separation from that capital by an unnatural boundary weakened them by making them a minority in Colorado rather than part of the majority in New Mexico. The division of the Mexican population in this way permitted Anglos to gain more leverage in Santa Fe by increasing their own percentage of the voters in New Mexico, Though the usual reasons given by Anglos for the new boundary involved slavery and land speculation,[38] this division of the Spanish-speaking at the very least revealed a disregard for, if not a deliberate denial of, the Mexicans' desire to govern themselves in the areas where they lived. Indeed fear of undue Mexican political strength in the Southwest also influenced the placing of capitals in Anglo towns rather than Mexican settlements. Tucson was passed over in favor of Phoenix, and an attempt was made to replace Santa Fe with Albuquerque, where Anglos had settled in large numbers. This followed the pattern set in Texas and

California, where Austin had replaced San Antonio, and Sacramento had replaced Monterey and Los Angeles.

In spite of such geopolitical maneuvers and the support of the military, Anglo-Americans in New Mexico Territory could not completely exclude *nuevomexicanos* from government, simply because the latter made up a vast majority, especially in the first years after the conquest. Consequently, from the beginning the U.S. officials appointed Mexicans, even those who had not cooperated in the conquest, to important positions in the government. Interestingly, one of the results of this policy was to further the cleavage between those *nuevomexicanos* who favored Anglo-American rule and those who opposed it.[39] As time passed, this cleavage developed into one between those who favored "Americanization" and those who wished to retain Mexican culture--a cleavage that persists.

Two of the more noteworthy supporters of Americanization were Miguel Antonio Otero I, New Mexico's delegate to Congress from 1855 to 1861, and his son, Miguel A. Otero II, who served as territorial governor form 1897 to 1906. Though born in New Mexico, the senior Otero attended college in Missouri and New York, entering the legal profession in 1852. His family's business ties with merchants in Missouri oriented him toward acceptance of the customs and political rule of the United States. He married a woman from a prominent Southern family and was a successful businessman, becoming vice president of the Atchison, Topeka & Santa Fe Railroad. According to his son, politically Otero "represented the progressive American element in the Territory. The Otero, Chaves and Armijo families were all for the American Party as against the Mexican Party . . . a powerful anti-American priest-ridden party." The Oteros sided wholeheartedly with the forces of economic development and thus supported the coming of the railroad, which they must have realized would undermine Mexican culture.[40]

In 1882, at the opening of the Montezuma Hotel in Las Vegas, New Mexico, the senior Otero praised the railroad as a civilizer. His rhetoric curiously mingled symbols from the Indian, Mexican, and Anglo traditions of the territory:

> *The Pecos Indians . . . implicitly believed that their mighty but ill-fated emperor, the glorious Montezuma, disappeared from view amid the clouds of their native mountains, that he promised to return . . . that he would come in glory from the east . . . The last remnant of the faithful old tribe has disappeared . . ., but we who will fill their places, have lived to see the return of the mighty chieftain (the train from Chicago later named the Chief and the Super Chief. With power and majesty he comes, with the ancient sun-god from the east, and tonight we hail his coming in the new and splendid halls of the Montezuma!*[41]

In this speech Otero alluded to a southwestern Indian legend, incorporated from the Spaniards and Mexicans who thought the Aztecs had originated in New Mexico a legend that paralleled the Aztec myth of the beneficent god, Quetzalcóatl, who was to return gloriously from exile in the east to rule Mexico City. In 1519 the Aztec emperor Montezuma (confused with Quetzalcóatl in the Southwest) mistook Cortes for the returning god and allowed the Spaniards to seize his palace unopposed. Ironically, Otero was similarly welcoming a conquering god from the east, the beneficent railroad that would help New Mexico.

That other *nuevomexicanos* disagreed is evident from a statement made in 1872 by Francisco Perea, who once ran for office on a platform opposing the building of railroads. "We don't want you damned Yankees in the country," he said, realizing that the trains would bring immigrants from the East; "We can't compete" with you, you will drive us all out, and we shall have no home left us." In 1880 at Cow Creek Hill, railroad construction workers and local Mexicans actually fought a pitched battle because the natives feared the trains would bring invasion of their lands.[42]

During his terms in Congress, Miguel A. Otero I tried to have New Mexico admitted as a state but failed. From the time of the conquest until 1872, both traditional and progressive Mexicans hoped for statehood, the former because it would bring them home rule, the latter because it would mean full acceptance in the Union. Early movements were frustrated not only by the national struggle between the free and slave states but also by the eastern view of New Mexico as a foreign land. The Civil War ended the slavery issue, but the prejudice against "foreign" New Mexico persisted. In 1872 traditional *nuevomexicanos* made a final effort to gain home rule through statehood; they were opposed, according to historian Howard Roberts Lamar, by Anglos in the southern counties who thought New Mexico should wait "until enough Americans were there to balance the Spanish influence effectively."[43] Later, because the Anglo population greatly increased in the late 1870s and the 1880s, *nuevomexicanos* lost interest in statehood. Territorial status then had the advantage of preventing the growing local Anglo population from gaining more political power. In 1889, in an important referendum in which education was a major issue, *nuevomexicanos* as a whole voted against statehood because it seemed untimely to progressives and a definite threat to traditionalists. Progressives, including the younger Otero, thought, because few nonsectarian public schools teaching English and modern democratic (Anglo) ideals existed, that *nuevomexicanos* were unprepared for statehood. Traditionalists, knowing that such schools would be promoted under a new government, voted against statehood because they wanted, at best, schools supported but not administered by the state.[44]

Although the Catholic Church vehemently opposed secular public school education, the issue, as far as Mexicans were concerned, was not simply religious. In 1889 the Archbishop of Santa Fe proposed a system of state supported church schools like that of Quebec, a system that permitted French Canadians to preserve their language and customs as well as religion.[45] In 1884 Archbishop Jean Baptiste Lamy had condemned those Catholics who refused to send their children to Catholic schools (which composed the majority of schools in the territory) because English was not used to the exclusion of Spanish. He had argued that though English was the language of commerce, "we cannot but recommend that they (the schools) neglect not to perfect the children in the knowledge and use of their beautiful native castilian (sic) language, of which they should always show themselves proud . . ." Since the language and customs of *nuevomexicanos* reflected and reinforced their Catholicism, the church sought to preserve much of their culture. To most Mexicans, religion, language, and ethnic identity were inseparable. In 1873, *El clarín mejicano*, a Santa Fe newspaper, had argued that it was practically the sacred duty of Mexicans to subscribe to the paper because it was in Spanish: "Little can be said in favor of the Spanish people of this country . . . who do not wish to support a newspaper written in the language of their parents who gave them birth and taught them the Holy Faith, which . . . is so . . . respected by *nuevomexicanos*." Mexicans saw secular public schools as a threat not only to their religion but to their culture.[46]

By the turn of the century *neuovomexicano* opposition to statehood lessened primarily because the number of Anglos increased to the point where they could draft a constitution and have the territory admitted with a minimum of Mexican help. If *nuevomexicanos* hoped to have any influence on the educational and other policies of the new state, they would have to participate in the statehood movement. The administration of the younger Miguel A. Otero as governor from 1897 to 1906 was instrumental in winning *nuevomexicanos* support for statehood. Otero was born in St. Louis of a Mexican father and an Anglo mother, educated in the East, and raised in close contact with Anglo businessmen and politicians. It is not surprising that on his appointment one Chicago newspaper praised Otero as "thoroughly American in every way."[47]

Although he spoke Spanish, Otero considered his Mexican culture of minor importance. From his lengthy memoirs, we can infer that he saw assimilation of Mexicans into the larger society as an inevitable consequence of progress. To him, the decline of Mexican culture was unimportant as long as *nuevomexicanos* advanced economically and politically with the rest of society. In fact, in his memoirs he regarded antagonism between Anglo and Mexican interests as a thing of the past. He claimed that with increased (Anglo) immigration, new railroads, new industries, and Americanized cities, New Mexico in 1881 "became one of the great territories of the Union" and that "even such old prejudices as the racial discrimination between Americans and Mexicans were gradually wearing off. . . ."[48] Nevertheless, being the first *nuevomexicano* appointed governor, Otero was very popular among Mexicans, and having become an advocate of statehood, he soon had their support by paying special attention to local disputes and by pardoning criminals liberally, two policies that were especially appreciated because they made the Governor appear accessible to the "little man" in the way governors had been during Spanish and Mexican rule. Otero also gained Mexican support by keeping the capital at Santa Fe and by opposing the admission of New Mexico and Arizona as a single state.[49]

Much of the opposition in Congress, and in the East, to New Mexico statehood resulted from the belief that the Spanish-speaking were too powerful in the territory. Consequently, in 1906 an attempt was made to join predominantly Anglo Arizona to New Mexico, thus making Anglos the majority in the new state. This plan, Lamar has commented, appealed to Anglos in New Mexico and progressive *nuevomexicanos*, but most

> *Spanish-Americans in New Mexico did not care to become a minority in a giant state when they could be a majority in a smaller one. Using the same reasoning, the Anglo-American citizens of Arizona were opposed to an increase in the portion of their own Spanish-American minority.*[50]

Although Anglos and progressive Mexicans had enough votes to pass "jointure" in New Mexico, Anglo-Arizonans overwhelmingly rejected the idea in the referendum held in their territory. Even though Otero had opposed jointure, fearing his political machine would lose control in a larger state, his position also served the interest of traditional *nuevomexicanos*. Because jointure was defeated, in 1912 New Mexico was admitted separately to the Union with a constitution heavily influenced by the Spanish-Speaking. Since Mexicans still made up much of the population within the boundaries of the new state, they were able to safeguard their culture, at least in writing, in a number of ways. Among the numerous guarantees were the recognition of Spanish as an official language and the promise of bilingual education.[58]

Although Otero had indirectly helped preserve Mexican culture in the Southwest, the real credit belonged to those who intentionally sought that end. Casimiro Barela, leader of the Spanish-speaking in Colorado for decades, definitely earned such credit. Like his counterparts in New Mexico's legislature and constitutional convention, Barela consciously advanced the interests of his group; he once stated: "When it comes to my people, especially if it concerns discrimination, I abandon my political ideas and dedicate myself to their defense at any time or place." In 1847 Barela was born into a wealthy New Mexico family; in 1867 he migrated to southern Colorado at the head of a

Spanish-speaking colony. Although this area had not been permanently settled by Spain or Mexico, Barela still regarded it as his native land, constantly reminding Anglos: "Mexicans were the legitimate owners of this country which came to them through their inheritance from their ancestors." In defending the rights of his people, he repeatedly based his arguments on the Treaty of Guadalupe Hidalgo, a treaty in which he believed Mexico had desperately sought to protect "her own children, who in their own land, in their own country were to be left like strangers . . . ."[52]

Barela served continuously in Colorado's territorial and state legislatures for over forty years after his first election in 1871, and was also a delegate to the Constitutional Convention in 1875-76. At that convention the major social cleavage was between the Protestant, English-speaking, northern counties. An attempt by Mexicans to have the state support Catholic and other private schools failed miserably; however, Barela succeeded in having laws published in Spanish for at least twenty-five years, and also prevented a knowledge of English from being required of all voters. Barela spent his long career facing the problems that confronted Mexicans throughout the Southwest: land grant disputes, prejudiced courts, gerrymandering, discriminatory election laws, and interracial violence. His success and that of others like him was limited, but because of them Mexican culture in the Southwest lived to be rejuvenated in the twentieth century.[53]

Next to the heavy invasion of Anglo settlers, the most serious attack on Mexican culture in the Southwest during the nineteenth century was the assault on native landowners, an attack that almost uprooted Mexicans from the region. Though the loss of an exploitive elite's huge estates may seem deserved, the loss was also experienced by the common man because the native upper class was replaced by an even more oppressive foreign elite, more oppressive because it had little respect for the culture of the ordinary Mexican who would continue to do much of the heavy labor throughout the Southwest. Outside of New Mexico and Colorado, the loss of land destroyed the native leadership, leaving the average Mexican without representatives in the prestigious positions of society. Without such representation he gradually became alienated from the Southwest and increasingly looked south of the border for cultural reinforcement. Constant and easy communication across the artificial border made thoroughly "Mexican" Mexico seem more of a homeland even to the native whose family had been in the Southwest for generations. The common Mexican began to forget his history, to forget that he was indigenous to the Southwest as well as Mexico, For a time during the twentieth century, this loss of historical memory would obscure the Chicano's image of the Southwest as lost, and of himself as dispossessed.

Beyond 1848

Notes

1. See Robert J. Rosenbaum, *Mexicano Resistance in the Southwest: "The Sacred Right of Self-Preservation,"* The Dan Danciger Publication Series (Austin: University of Texas Press, 1981), pp. 25-35.

2. Pablo de la Guerra, Speech to the California Senate, 1856, quoted in David J.Weber, ed., *Foreigners in Their Native Land: Historical Roots of the Mexican Americans*, with a Foreword by Ramón Eduardo Ruiz (Albuquerque: University of New Mexico Press, 1973), p. vi.

3. Pedro Castillo and Albert Camarillo, eds., *Furia y Muerte: Los Bandidos Chicanos*, Aztlán Publications, Monograph no.4 (Los Angeles: Chicano Studies Center, University of California, 1973), pp. 1-11.

4. *Seventh Census of the United States: 1850*, pp. xxxvii, 972,976, xxxviii, quoted in Richard Lee Nostrand, "The Hispanic-American Borderland: A Regional, Historical Geography" (Ph.D. dissertation, University of California, Los Angeles, 1968), pp. 147-48.

5. Jay Monaghan, *Chile, Peru, and the California Gold Rush of 1849* (Berkeley and Los Angeles: University of California Press, 1973), p. 250; for higher estimates of the Spanish-speaking population, see Arthur F. Corwin, "Early Mexican Labor Migration; A Frontier Sketch, 1848-1900," in *Immigrants-- and Immigrants: Perspectives on Mexican Labor Migration to the United States*, ed. Arthur F. Corwin, Contributions in Economics and Economic History, no. 17 (Westport, Conn.: Greenwood Press, 1978), p. 25; and Juan Gómez-Quiñones,*Development of the Mexican Working Class North of the Rio Bravo: Work and Culture among Laborers and Artisans, 1600-1900*, Popular Series, no.2 (Los Angeles: Chicano Studies Research Center Publications, University of California, 1982), p.16.

6. Mariano Guadalupe Vallejo, "What the Gold Rush Brought to California," quoted in Myrtle M. McKittrick, *Vallejo: Son of California* (Portland, Ore. : Binfords & Mort, 1944), pp. 286-87.

7. Donald E. Hargis, "Native Californians in the Constitutional Convention of 1849," *Historical Society of Southern California Quarterly* 36 (March 1954):5, 9-10.

8. Ibid., pp. 6-8.

9. Matt S. Meier and Feliciano Rivera, *The Chicanos: A History of Mexican Americans*, American Century Series (New York: Farrar, Straus & Giroux, Hill & Wang, 1972), p.82. 10.Hargis, pp. 7-9.

11. *El clamor público* (Los Angeles), 19 June 1855; all translation from this newspaper are my own.

12. Ibid., pp. 6-8.

13. Leonard Pitt, *The Decline of the Californios: A Social History of Spanish-Speaking Californians, 1846-1890* (Berkely and Los Angeles: University of California Press, 1966), pp. 48-68 passim; Josiah Royce, *California: From the Conquest in 1846 to the Second Vigilance Committee in San Francisco, a Study of American Character*, with an Introduction by Robert Glass Cleland (New York: Alfred A. Knopf, Borzoi Books, 1948), pp. 282-85; and Rosenbaum, pp. 58-59.

14. Quoted in Carey McWilliams, *North from Mexico: The Spanish-Speaking People of the United States* (Philadelphia: J. B. Lippincott co., 1949; reprint ed., New York: Greenwood Press, 1968), pp. 129-30.

15. Royce, pp. 385-86.

16. *Joaquín Murieta, the Brigand Chief of California: A Complete History of His Life from the Age of Sixteen to the Time of His Capture and Death in 1853,* with Supplementary Notes by Raymund F.

Wood, Americana Reprints, no 1 (San Francisco: Grabhorn Press, 1932; reprint ed., Fresno, Calif.: Valley Publishers, 1969), pp. 4-5.

17. "Corrido de Joaquín Murrieta," in *Literatura Chicana: Texto y Contexto/Chicano Literature: Text and Context*, ed. Antonia Castañeda Shular, Tomas Ybarra-Frausto, and Joseph Sommers (Englewood Cliffs, N.J.: Prentice-Hall, 1972), p. 66, my translation.

18. "Tiburcio Vasquez: An Interview with the Noted Bandit," in *Foreigners*, Weber, p. 227; Rodolfo Acuña, *Occupied America: A History of Chicanos*, 2nd ed. (New York; Harper & Row, 1981), pp. 113-14; and Pitt, p. 257.

19. *El clamor*, 2 August 1856.

20. Mario Barrera, *Race and Class in the Southwest: A Theory of Racial Inequality* (Notre Dame, Ind.: University of Notre Dame Press, 1979), pp. 21-22; and W(illiam) W(ilcox) Robinson, *Land in California: The Story of Mission Lands, Ranchos, Squatters, Mining Claims, Railroad Grants, Land Scrip, Homesteads*, Chronicles of California (Berkeley and Los Angeles: University of California Press, 1948), pp. 99-109 passim.

21. *El clamor*, 19 June 1855; 16 October, 24 July 1858; and 9 February 1856; for further discussion of the repatriation movement, see Richard Griswold del Castillo *The Los Angeles Barrio, 1850-1890: A Social History* (Berkeley and Los Angeles: University of California Press, 1979), pp. 119-24.

22. *El clamor*, 26 June 1855.

23. *Monitor republicano* (Mexico City), 27 June 1877, quoted in McKittrick, p. 347.

24. *El bejareño* (San Antonio), 7 February 1855, my translation.

25. Ibid.

26. Juan Nepomuceno Seguín, "Personal Memoirs of John N. Seguín . . . ," in *Northern Mexico on the Eve of the United States Invasion: Rare Imprints Concerning California, Arizona, New Mexico and Texas, 1821-1846*, ed. with an Introduction by David J. Weber, The Chicano Heritage (New York Times, Arno Press, 1976), pp. iv, 5-32 passim (of imprint no. 3; pages of each imprint in this volume are numbered separately).

27. Meier and Rivera, pp. 88-93; C[harles] L[eland] Sonnichsen, *The El Paso Salt War [1877]* (El Paso: Carl Hertzog and the Texas Western Press, 1961), pp. 58-59; and Arnoldo de León, *They Called Them Greasers: Anglo Attitudes toward Mexicans in Texas, 1821-1900* (Austin: University of Texas Press, 1983), pp. 82-83, 55-56.

28. Juan Nepomuceno Cortina, "Suffer the Death of Martyrs . . . ," in *Aztlan: An Anthology of Mexican American Literature*, ed. Luis Valdez and Stan Steiner, Marc Corporation Books (New York: Alfred A. Knopf, 1972), p. 115.

29. Charles W. Goldfinch, "Juan N. Cortina 1824-1892: A Re-appraisal," in *Juan N. Cortina: Two Interpretations*, The Mexican American (New York: New York Times, Arno Press, 1974), pp. 42-50 (of Goldfinch article; articles in this volume are numbered separately).

30. Ibid., pp. 51-63.

31. Meir and Rivera, p. 93; and Arnoldo de León, *The Tejano Community, 1836-1900*, with a Contribution by Kenneth L. Stewart (Albuquerque: University of New Mexico Press, 1982), pp. 48-49, 14, 17, 62, 188-89.

32. *El horizonte* (Corpus Christi), 8, 19 November 1879, my translation.

33. Meir and Rivera, p. 97; Richard L. Nostrand, "The Hispano Homeland in 1900," *Annals of the Association of American Geographers* 70 (September 1980): 382; and Howard Roberts Lamar, *The Far*

Southwest, 1846-1912: A Territorial History, Yale Western Americana Series, 12 (New Haven: Yale University Press, 1966), pp. 82, 420-22. 34. McWilliams, pp. 119-21; and Rosenbaum, pp. 95, 97.

35. Meier and Rivera, pp. 104-7; and Rosenbaum, pp. 25-26.

36. Robert W. Larson, *New Mexico's Quest for Statehood, 1846-1912* (Albuquerque: University of New Mexico Press, 1968), pp. 83-86.

37. Lamar, pp. 433-35, 421.

38. Ibid., pp. 219-21.

39. Ibid., pp. 85-86.

40. Miguel Antonio Otero, *My Life on the Frontier,* vol. 1: *1864-1882, Incidents and Characters of the Period When Kansas, Colorado, and New Mexico Were Passing through the Last of Their Wild and Romantic Years* (New Mexico: Press of Pioneers, 1935), pp. 280-86.

41. Ibid., pp. 275-76.

42. McWilliams, p. 119; and Lamar, p. 166.

43. Ibid.

44. Ibid., pp. 186-90; and Miguel Antonio Otero, *My Life on the Frontier,* vol. 2: *1882-1897, Death Knell of a Territory and Birth of a State,* with a Foreword by George P. Hammond (Albuquerque: University of New Mexico Press, 1939), p. 223.

45. *La crónica de Mora* (N. Mex.), 12 September 1889.

46. Archishop Jean Baptiste Lamy, Pastoral Letter, 20 February 1884, MSR12044, quoted by permission of the Henry E. Huntington Library, San Marino, Calif.; and *el clarín mexicano* (Santa Fe), 10 August 1873, my translation.

47. Lamar, pp. 198-99; and *Chicago Times Herald,* 11 June 1897, quoted in Larson, p. 195.

48. Otero, 1882-1897, pp. 1-2.

49. Lamar, pp. 199; and Miguel Antonio Otero, *My Nine Years as Governor of the Territory of New Mexico, 1897-1906,* with a Foreword by Marion Dargan (Albuquerque: University of New Mexico Press, 1940), p. 218.

50. Lamar, pp. 493-94.

51. Ibid., pp. 495-96; and Meier and Rivera, p. 113.

52. José Emilio Fernández, *Cuarenta años de legislador, o biografía del senador Casimiro Barela* (Trinidad, Colo.: n.p., 1911; reprint ed., The Chicano Heritage, New York: New York Times, Arno press, 1976), n. pag., my translation.

53. Ibid.: and Lamar, pp. 292-93.

Thomas E. Sheridan traces the history of Chicanos in southern Arizona and reveals the process of subordination since the late 19th century. Although his study is confined to southern Arizona similar trends leading to subordination were underway in other regions of the Southwest. He elaborates upon patterns of racial and economic subordination, dual processes institutionalized by the middle 20th century. Sheridan also explores Mexican and Chicano resistance "in a variety of ways ranging from political organization to cultural preservation."

Race and Class in a Southwestern City: The Mexican Community of Tucson, 1854-1941

Thomas E. Sheridan

In July, 1892, a prominent Mexican rancher named Ramón Soto wrote a series of influential articles in *El Fronterizo,* Tucson's leading Spanish-language newspaper. In these articles, Soto passionately urged Mexicans in Tucson to set aside their differences and unite into one single politically powerful community. Soto called his vision of Mexican solidarity *la Colonia Hispano-Americana*. He wrote:

> All of us in general believe that this country is the exclusive property of the Americans, any one of whom arriving from New York, San Francisco, or Chicago has the right to be sheriff, judge, councilman, legislator, constable or whatever he wants. Such an American can be Swiss, Irish, German, Italian, Portuguese, or whatever. Always, in the final analysis, he is an American. And ourselves? Are we not Americans by adoption or birth? Of course we are. And as sons of this country, being born here, do we not have an equal or a greater right to formulate and maintain the laws of this land that witnessed our birth than naturalized citizens of European origin? Yes. Nevertheless, the contrary occurs.[1]

In one sense, Ramón Soto's plea for unity was answered less than two years later, when Mexican businessmen, intellectuals, and politicians met to form the *Alianza Hispano-Americana*. One of the primary purposes of the *Alianza* was to protect Mexicans against the rising tide of racism in the United States; at its height, in the 1930s, it was the largest Hispanic mutual-aid society in the nation. On a more fundamental level, however, Soto's dream never really came true. Mexicans in Tucson may have remained a majority of the city's population until the early 1900s, but they never exercised political or economic power in proportion to their actual numbers. *Tucsonenses* found themselves caught up in an increasingly hierarchical society, one that discriminated against them on the basis of class as well as race. Soto blamed Mexican powerlessness on political apathy, but the reality of Mexican subordination in southern Arizona was much more complex. In the following presentation, I want to explore some of the underlying factors--demographic, economic, educational, and political--responsible for that subordination. I also want to suggest a few of the reasons why Soto's vision of a united *Colonia Hispano-Americana* remained just that--a vision and little more. In the process, however, I need to discuss the very nature of southern Arizona society in general, for only then can the particular history of Mexicans in Tucson be understood.

From Sonoran to Territorial Tucson

Tucson was founded in 1775, and for the first eight decades of its existence, it remained the northernmost outpost of Spanish, and later, Mexican Sonora. Its first non-Indian settlers were presidial soldiers and their families. They were tough, resourceful men and women who knew exactly what life was going to be like in the Tucson Basin when they moved up the Santa Cruz River from their former garrison at Tubac. Most of these individuals had grown up in the Sonoran Desert fighting Apaches, forming alliances with neighboring Pimas and Papagos, planting their crops of wheat, corn, beans, and squash along the floodplain of the Santa Cruz itself. In some cases, these families were descendants of pioneers who had first moved into southern Arizona in the early 18th century. Unlike the Anglos who followed them, Tucson's Hispanic pioneers settled the area as seasoned desert dwellers rather than immigrants from a foreign land.

At times, their experience and their endurance were the only qualities that enabled them to survive on the Apache frontier. For most of its history, Sonoran Tucson was a tiny finger of Hispanic society jutting north into harsh and hostile territory. With the exception of Tubac forty miles to the south, the only other Hispanic settlements in southern Arizona were scattered ranches and mines that contracted or disappeared whenever Apache raiding intensified. Contact with the rest of Sonora was sporadic, contact with the Hispanic communities of California and New Mexico almost nonexistent. As a result, Sonoran Tucson never developed into an urban center like Magdalena, Arispe, Hermosillo, or other Sonoran communities to the south. Instead, it remained an isolated frontier garrison of soldiers and the farmers who supported them.

Such isolation came to an end in 1854. Not satisfied with the territory it had won by force during the War with Mexico, the United States dispatched railroad speculator James Gadsden to Mexico City in 1853 to negotiate a further cession of Mexican land. Bankrupt and desperate, Mexican president Santa Anna accepted the offer that transferred the least amount of Mexican soil to the United States--30,000 square miles encompassing southern Arizona and the Mesilla Valley of New Mexico. Sonoran Tucson had survived Apache attacks, Mexican Independence and war with the United States. Suddenly, however, a mere stroke of a pen transformed Tucsonenses from citizens of Sonora into residents of the United States.

Luckily for the Tucsonenses, that transformation was not as traumatic as it was for Mexicans in other areas of the Southwest. In California, for example, Mexicans were overwhelmed by hordes of forty-niners, losing both land and power to the Anglo newcomers as they became a small minority in their native land almost overnight (Pitt 1966; Camarillo 1979; Griswold del Castillo 1979). The situation of Mexicans in Texas was even more desperate, as they were a "race of mongrels" to the victors of the Texas Revolt (Acuña 1981; De León 1982). Tucson, in contrast, did not attract many Anglo immigrants at first. There were no gold fields, no vast tracts of fertile land, no easy access to national and international markets. More to the point, the hostility of the Western and Chiricahua Apaches made life on the Arizona frontier a precarious proposition at best. As a result, Mexicans in Tucson often seemed to assimilate Anglos rather than vice versa in the wake of the Gadsden Purchase.

Nonetheless, the pattern of Anglo dominance and Mexican subordination began to emerge as early as 1860. That year, according to federal census manuscripts, Anglos constituted less than 20 percent of Tucson's total population of 925. However, they possessed 87 percent of the real and personal property in town. Within six years of the Gadsden Purchase, Anglo capital dominated Tucson's economy. Once in control, it never let go.

Part of the reason for this dominance was demographic. Of the 168 Anglos in Tucson in 1860, 159 were adult males, most of whom were in the prime of their lives. Tucson's Mexican population, on the other hand, was much less skewed; its male/female ratio was roughly equal while 37 percent were children fourteen years or younger. In a sense, early territorial Tucson was a dual, almost schizophrenic settlement: a Mexican community organized into families contrasting sharply with a typically frontier population of young aggressive Anglo males. Anglos consequently made up a disproportionate share of Tucson's work force--36 percent. More to the point, they were able to devote their energy and their capital to business enterprises without worrying about the constraints of family life.

But demography alone does not explain Anglo economic ascendancy. One of the most enduring myths about Arizona history is the myth of the rugged individual--the two-fisted, gun-totin' pioneer who wins fame and fortune on the Arizona frontier. Detailed historical research, on the other hand, paints a much different picture. Most of the capital that developed Arizona originated somewhere else. Anglo merchants settling in Tucson often had ties to larger business firms outside of the Arizona territory. Native Tucsonenses, in contrast, had nothing but their Apache-thinned herds of livestock and their small floodplain fields. As a result, most native-born Mexicans did not have the financial resources to successfully compete with the Anglo newcomers.

Most of the prosperous Mexicans in territorial Tucson were in fact immigrants themselves. Estevan Ochoa, partner in one of the biggest freighting companies in the territory, came from Chihuahua. The four Aguirre brothers, who established some of the largest ranches in southern Arizona, were also Chihuahua-born and bred. Leopoldo Carrillo, Tucson's premier urban entrepreneur, and Mariano Samaniego, the town's most successful Mexican politician, migrated from Sonora. Like their Anglo counterparts, these successful Mexican immigrants brought their own capital with them. Most native Tucsonenses, on the other hand, remained tied to a subsistence agrarian economy that was just about dead by the end of the century.

The Southern Pacific Railroad

During the 1860s and 1870s, a number of Mexicans, including Ochoa, Carrillo and Samaniego, were able to compete on a relatively equal footing with the Anglo merchants and freighters in southern Arizona. According to the 1870 federal census, Carrillo was the wealthiest individual, Mexican or Anglo, in Tucson. Five years later, Ochoa became the only Mexican elected mayor of the town following the Gadsden Purchase. Those two decades witnessed the creation of a uniquely bicultural society as Anglos and Mexicans formed partnerships with one another, married into each other's families and, perhaps most importantly, fought the Apaches together. Mexicans continued to be a majority of Tucson's inhabitants, and Spanish served as the *lingua franca* of the southern Arizona frontier. Because of the strength of Mexican society in Tucson, Anglo ascendancy was not as rapid or as brutal as it was in other areas of the Southwest.

But that was before the arrival of the Southern Pacific Railroad. On March 20, 1880, the leading citizens of Tucson turned out to welcome the railroad into town. Charles Crocker, vice-president of the Southern Pacific, proclaimed that Tucson's frontier days were finally over. "From California we will bring you her cereals," he stated, "and from the eastern terminus emigrants to people your valleys and explore your mountains, and to carry both ways your mineral wealth." Crocker was right. The railroad destroyed Tucson's isolation, linking the little community to national and international markets. For the first time in Tucson's history, goods could be shipped in and out cheaply by rail, rather than hauled by pack train or freight wagon. The result was a regional boom in southern Arizona's two major industries, mining and ranching, and an explosion in the economy of scale. Native Tucsonenses had been unable to compete with the immigrant merchants who rode into the area after the Gadsden Purchase. After the arrival of the railroad, no Mexican, immigrant or otherwise, could challenge the great copper or land-and-cattle companies that soon made Arizona a colony of East and West Coast business interests.

One of the most important consequences of this economic revolution was a voracious demand for cheap labor. The railroads needed workers to lay and maintain track. The mining companies needed laborers to dig gold, silver, and especially copper ore. At first, the empire-builders imported Chinese immigrants to perform these jobs. But Anglo and Mexican workers quickly reacted to this threat to their livelihoods by attacking the Chinese and destroying the camps they lived in. Anglo and Mexican newspaper editors soon joined the anti-Oriental crusade, deriding the Chinese as "*chinacates*" or "sons of the Celestial Empire" who stole jobs, spread strange Asiatic diseases, and sent all their money across the sea. In the words of Tucson newspaper *El Fronterizo*, "The Chinaman is a fungus that lives in isolation, sucking the sap of the other plants."[2]

What was happening in Arizona, of course, was the brutal but effective creation of an economic pecking order organized largely along ethnic lines. At the top were the owners and operators of the railroads, the mining corporations, and the land-and-cattle companies. All of these individuals, without exception, were Anglo. In the middle were the small businessmen, ranchers and farmers, most of whom were Anglo, but with a few Mexicans as well. And then, at the bottom, were the men and women who owned no land or businesses but possessed only their own labor to sell.

But even among the working class there were divisions, with Anglos pitted against Mexicans, Mexicans against Native Americans, and everyone against the Chinese. By the end of the 19th century, the ethnic configurations of this pecking order were clear. Anglo workers dominated the relatively good-paying jobs such as railroad engineer or underground miner. Mexicans maintained the tracks, picked the crops, and ran herd on the cattle. The Chinese, on the other hand, had been driven off the railroads and out of the mines. From then on, Mexicans, not Orientals, performed most of the low paying jobs in southern Arizona.

The Subordination of the Mexican Working Class

In Tucson, the establishment of this economic hierarchy was modified in part by the nature of the town's economy, which was commercial rather than extractive. Tucson never became a one-industry town like the mining communities springing up across Arizona, nor did it develop into an agricultural center like Yuma or the Salt River Valley. Consequently, the exploitation of Mexican labor was not quite as stark as it was in other areas. Nonetheless, Tucson's economy still depended upon cheap labor and an abundant labor supply.

No other measure reflects the subordination of the Mexican working class better than the occupational structure of Tucson. By analyzing federal census manuscripts and Tucson city directories, my colleagues and I on the Mexican Heritage Project were able to determine where Mexicans fitted into Tucson's economic hierarchy through time. The results of that analysis reveal that despite major changes in Tucson's economic structure between 1860 and 1940, most Mexicans remained trapped in low-paying, blue-collar jobs. Such occupational stasis contrasts sharply with the significant upward mobility experienced by Anglos during this 80-year period.

Tucson's economy in 1860 was relatively undeveloped, with most members of the work force (77 percent) employed in what today would be called blue-collar occupations. Only seven percent, on the other had, were merchants, traders, or shopkeepers, while a mere five percent were professionals or clerks. In short, most individuals in early territorial Tucson, Anglo or Mexican, worked with their hands.

But even in 1860 there were pronounced differences in the Anglo and Mexican occupational structures. For example, the proportion of Anglo white-collar workers (32 percent) was nearly double that of the Mexicans. Furthermore, 47 percent of the Mexican work force toiled at what could be classified as unskilled jobs, compared to only 27 percent of the Anglos. The disparity between the Mexican and Anglo work forces therefore began soon after Tucson became a part of the United States.

Twenty years later, the year the railroad arrived, the gap between Anglo and Mexican workers had widened. In 1880, the percentage of Anglo white-collar workers increased slightly from 32 to 36 percent. During the same period, the proportion of Anglo unskilled laborers dropped significantly from 27 to 19 percent. Mexicans, on the other hand, registered only a slight gain in the general white-collar category--from 17 to 21 percent--while experiencing a major increase in the proportion of unskilled labor--from 47 to nearly 60 percent. Even before the railroad transformed Tucson's economy, the subordination of the Mexican work force was well under way.

The structural changes triggered by the Southern Pacific increased the economic mobility of both Anglo and Mexican workers during the next two decades. The proportion of Mexican unskilled laborers declined from 60 to 40 percent between 1880 and 1900, while the percentage of skilled workers doubled from nine to 18 percent. Despite these genuine gains, however, it is clear that Mexican upward mobility lagged far behind that of the Anglos in Tucson. At the turn of the century, nearly half of all Anglo members of the work force occupied white-collar positions. Only about one in five Mexicans, by contrast, held such jobs.

The evolution of Tucson's economic structure continued during the first two decades of the 20th century. By 1920, 62 percent of all Anglo workers fell within white-collar categories, compared to 28 percent of all Mexican workers. Meanwhile, the percentage of Anglo unskilled laborers continued to decline--from 12 percent in 1900 to seven percent in 1920. The Mexican unskilled labor sector, on the other hand, remained about the same. Moreover, much of the apparent upward mobility from the blue to the white-collar categories occurred at the lowest levels of the white-collar world, the stratum labeled as "sales/clerical." In 1900, only three percent of the Mexican and seven percent of the Anglo work forces worked as clerks or salesmen. Twenty years later, those figures had jumped to 14 percent among Mexicans and 22 percent among Anglos. As Tucson developed into a commercial center of the Southwest, the city's economy demanded clerks, secretaries and salesmen rather than factory workers or farm laborers.

Meanwhile, Anglos continued to dominate the highest positions in Tucson's economy, occupying 95 percent of the prestigious white-collar jobs such as doctor, lawyer, engineer and government official. Mexican entry into the sales/clerical world did not serve as a stepping stone to the upper echelons of Tucson's economic or political hierarchy.

And even the limited upward mobility of the early 20th century stalled during *la Crisis*--the Great Depression of the 1930s. Between 1920 and 1940, the percentage of Mexican white-collar workers declined slightly from 28 to 27 percent, while the proportion of unskilled Mexican laborers rose from 38 to 41 percent. During that same period, the number of Mexican-owned businesses declined by 18 percent even though the Mexican population jumped from 7,500 to 11,000. Thus, on the eve of World War II, the Mexican community of Tucson was not substantially better off than it had been 80 years earlier. The proportion of Mexican blue-collar workers in 1940 remained essentially the same as it had been in 1860. More to the point, four out of every ten Mexicans continued to labor at low-paying, often temporary, unskilled jobs. Tucson was growing but most of the fruits of that growth were falling into Anglo hands.

The Institutionalized Subordination of Mexicans in Tucson

Part of the disparity between the Mexican and Anglo work forces may have been due to Mexican immigration. It is possible that Mexican residents in Tucson may have enjoyed significant upward mobility from one generation to the next but that the steady flow of Mexicans from south of the border continually replenished the unskilled labor pool. In order to test that hypothesis, researchers would have to chart the occupational movement of particular Mexican families. If sons did tend to secure better jobs than their fathers, then the immigration hypothesis would be vindicated.

In my opinion, however, Mexican immigration alone cannot explain the stubborn persistence of Mexican economic subordination. Between the Gadsden Purchase and World War II, far more Anglos than Mexicans poured into town. Many of those Anglo newcomers may have been better educated than the Mexican immigrants, but they also encountered far fewer impediments--linguistic, economic or political--to their occupational advancement. The major conclusions of my research, in fact, suggest that Tucsonenses, like Mexicans across the Southwest, found themselves in a society that institutionalized their subordination in countless subtle and not-so-subtle ways.

By "institutionalized subordination" I mean subordination woven into the everyday fabric of society. Such subordination is "institutional" in the sense that it is entrenched within and perpetrated by formal organizations such as school systems, political parties, labor unions, businesses, and city, state and national governments. But it also operates on other levels as well, encoded in racial and ethnic stereotypes, reflected by the mass media, latent or overt in most personal transactions between members of the dominant and subordinate groups.

I have carefully chosen the term "institutionalized subordination" rather than "institutionalized discrimination" in order to distinguish between the apartheid-like subjugation of Blacks and Native Americans, which was often legally mandated, and the less overt political and economic subordination of working-class Mexicans. Mexicans were not prohibited from eating in certain restaurants or sitting where they liked in certain theaters in town. Moreover, researchers have yet to uncover any residential covenants that expressly excluded Mexicans from living in certain neighborhoods in Tucson, even though many such covenants banned Orientals, Native Americans, and Blacks. And even though the Operating Brotherhoods of the Southern Pacific did refuse to admit Mexican members, thereby preventing them from holding such jobs as railroad engineer, it is not yet clear whether other businesses overtly barred Mexicans from certain occupations. In Tucson, then, a Mexican Jim Crow system did not exist, at least not on the books.

Ethnic Enclavement

Nevertheless, equality de jure did not ensure equality de facto. Quite the contrary. Nearly every social index available reveals that strong and enduring mechanisms were at work to keep Mexicans in Tucson, especially working-class Mexicans, politically and economically subordinate.

The most visible manifestations of that subordination were the residence patterns of the Mexicans themselves. When Tucson became a part of the United States in 1854, most Tucsonenses lived within the adobe walls of the old presidio in order to protect themselves against Apache raids. Almost immediately, however, a complex process of displacement began as Anglo merchants and artisans settled in and around the presidio while Mexican families moved south. That process accelerated during the next two decades. By 1881, a year after the railroad arrived, most Mexicans in Tucson lived in a roughly rectangular area that began several blocks south of the old presidio and extended as far as 18th Street. The western boundary of this Mexican neighborhood was Main Avenue, the eastern boundary, Stone Avenue.

Meanwhile, the rest of the town was developing according to patterns that still prevail today. The presidial district became the nucleus of Tucson's commercial center, the area where most of the town's major businesses were located. And of those 139 enterprises, Anglos owned 112, or nearly 81 percent. Anglos also occupied most of the downtown residences. At the same time, Anglo households were expanding eastward, drawn by the inexorable pull of the Southern Pacific railroad tracks. According to Tucson historian Don Bufkin, the Southern Pacific "acted like a magnet after 1880, drawing new development east and northeast from the old presidial center."[3]

The geographic dualization of Tucson grew even more pronounced by the turn of the century. Anglos remained in control of the central business district, owning from 70-100 percent of the businesses and residences there. However, by 1900 a second major Anglo neighborhood had developed in the vicinity of the old Military Plaza, where nearly 89 percent of all households were Anglo. Populated in part by employees of the Southern Pacific, this neighborhood soon attracted several of the city's most modern recreational facilities and commercial establishments including the Santa Rita Hotel, the Carnegie Library, and Armory Park.

No other urban development so accurately reflected the priorities of Tucson's city fathers. During the 1880s and 1890s, the most elegant urban oasis in Tucson was Carrillo's Gardens, which was located southwest of the commercial district. As Tucson became more and more of an Anglo town, however, the Gardens withered while eastern neighborhoods bloomed. Geographic distance therefore aggravated the social and economic distances already separating the two major ethnic groups in town.

By 1920, Tucson was essentially cleft in half by ethnic neighborhoods. Anglos continued to dominate the downtown commercial district, but they were also expanding north and east from their base in Armory Park. Health seekers, railroad employees, land speculators, and businessmen mostly turned their backs on the barrios and moved into new neighborhoods on the other side of the Southern Pacific tracks. The march to the Rincons and the Catalinas had begun.

Mexicans, in contrast, kept on moving southward. South Meyer Street--*la calle Meyer*--remained the commercial axis around which the southern barrios turned. But Mexicans were also beginning to settle along the Santa Cruz floodplain, creating semi-rural enclaves on both sides of the ravaged river channel. Furthermore, a major Mexican neighborhood was evolving north of the old presidial district where the Southern Pacific tracks swung north toward Phoenix. This neighborhood--Barrio Anita--soon became a solid working-class district just west of Davis Elementary School and Holy Family Church.

Twenty years later, on the eve of World War II, most of Tucson's modern Mexican barrios had been established. The neighborhoods south of the downtown area persisted as largely Mexican enclaves, even though Blacks and Native Americans were settling in some of the poorer sections. At the same time, Mexican households dominated Tucson's west side, occupying most of the residences in Menlo Park, Kroeger Lane, Barrio Sin Nombre, and the El Río district. Anglos, in contrast, continued to expand north and east.

The reasons for this geographic dualization were complex, involving cultural as well as economic factors. Contrary to stereotype, most Mexican barrios were not slums. Pockets of desperate poverty existed, especially in neighborhoods south of the commercial district such as El Convento, La Meyer, and Barrio Libre. Neighborhoods like Barrio Anita, Millville, El Río, and Menlo Park, on the other hand, were relatively prosperous working-class and middle-class districts. Even the poorer barrios contained large networks of relatives, *compadres*, neighbors, and friends who helped each other weather individual and collective hard times. In most cases barrio life was a positive response to discrimination and subordination. Within them, Mexican society flourished, and many elements of Mexican culture were preserved.

For all their vitality, however, the barrios still symbolized the ethnic enclavement of Mexicans within a larger society dominated by Anglo politicians and Anglo businessmen. Even though many Mexican families would not have left the barrios even if they could have, they were not free to live anywhere in town. First of all, most could not afford to purchase homes in the most exclusive Anglo neighborhoods; the economic subordination of Mexicans therefore restricted their residential options. Secondly, the real estate industry itself may have had a tacit understanding not to sell Mexican families homes in certain areas. Whatever the situation, boundaries of both race and class reinforced each other to concentrate Mexicans on the southern and western sides of town.

Educational Subordination

One of the results of ethnic enclavement was the high concentration of Mexican children in barrio schools. Again, such concentration was not mandated by law as it was in the case of Blacks. And years later, in the 1970s, when Mexican plaintiffs in a lengthy school desegregation case accused Tucson School District One of a wide range of discriminatory practices, the evidence they presented was inconclusive. Tucson Unified School District, on the other hand, commissioned a series of detailed quantitative studies demonstrating considerable levels of integration in supposedly segregated schools. Until more sophisticated studies of the Tucson public school system are undertaken, the available evidence suggests that the high percentage of Mexicans in certain schools was the result of residence patterns rather than school district policies.[4]

But even if the public schools did not intentionally segregate Mexican students, those institutions still were not able to provide Mexican children with equal educational opportunities. As a result, many Mexican pupils fell far below their proper grade levels and eventually dropped out of school. To its credit, the public school system developed a number of programs to rectify the situation, but those programs were not sustained and were not comprehensive enough to surmount the enormous problems they confronted.

One of the problems was economic. As Superintendent C.E. Rose pointed out in the 1920s:

> Several hundred of the Mexican and Indian children each year are taken from school by their parents in order to help with work in the cotton fields. These children are out of school and beyond the jurisdiction of our attendance officers for periods varying from one to three or four months.[5]

When these children returned to Tucson they lagged far behind other students. In such fashion, the children of migrant laborers remained trapped in the same world as their parents, unable to get the education they needed to escape the cotton fields.

The second major problem was linguistic. Again, according to Superintendent Rose:

> The school situation in Tucson is an unusual one in the fact that over 50 percent of the school children as a whole are Spanish-speaking. The 24th St. School (Ochoa) just established this year, is entirely made up of children of foreign blood, Mexican and Indian, who could not speak nor understand a word of English at the opening of the

school year. The Drachman school is 99 percent foreign, the Davis school about 85 percent, the Mansfield about 60 percent, and the Holladay about 30 percent. Beginning English classes have been established in all these schools, and thirteen teachers were employed to do the work of these classes alone.[6]

Those beginning English classes were the notorious 1C courses that gave so many Mexican children their first taste of public education in Tucson. Introduced in 1919, the 1C program became the foundation of the school system's attempt to incorporate Mexican students into the English-speaking world. Not until 1965, in fact, were the 1C classes replaced by more sophisticated programs of bilingual education.

Perhaps the greatest problem of all was the attitudes of the teachers and administrators themselves. To begin with, it is illuminating to note that Superintendent Rose referred to his Mexican and Indian pupils as "foreign," even though many of the Mexican children and nearly all of the Papago ones came from family lines that had resided in Arizona long before the Gadsden Purchase was signed. No other phrasing better captures the cultural arrogance of educators like Rose and his colleagues. During the early 20th century, one of the primary goals of the public school system was the "Americanization" of immigrants to the United States. As Rose himself stated:

> The supervisor and teachers of these children have been persistent in their efforts to get English into the homes and to awaken in the parents an interest to learn English and to learn and to assimilate the high ideals and customs of this country.[7]

Implicit in such a statement is the assumption that "American" ideals and customs are superior to Mexican ones. Prior to World War II, nearly all teachers and administrators in the Tucson public schools were Anglos. And most of these Anglos, no matter how well-intentioned they might have been, carried their derogatory stereotypes of Mexican culture and Mexican children into the classrooms with them.

Nowhere are those stereotypes clearer or more blatant than in a series of master's theses prepared for the University of Arizona's College of Education. At least four such theses written between 1929 and 1946 directly concerned Mexican children in Tucson public schools. Because those theses were approved by the College of Education, they must have reflected widespread attitudes in Arizona educational circles. As such, they constitute a rather damning indictment of Anglo school personnel.

For the purposes of this presentation, I will briefly discuss only two of the theses: Erik Allstrom's "A Program of Social Education for a Mexican Community in the United

States," written in 1929, and Rachel Riggins' "Factors in Social Background which Influence the Mexican Child in School," written in 1946. Together they demonstrate the range of attitudes toward Mexican children among Anglo educators--attitudes ranging from outright racism to sympathetic paternalism. What they lack, however, is any awareness that their own attitudes may have contributed to the problems they sought to address.

Allstrom's thesis begins with the chilling sentence, "There is a Mexican problem in the United States." He then goes on to say, "The people of the United States represent the democratic development of seven hundred years since the Magna Carta. The Mexican is the product of the autocratic individualism of the Latins, plus the pride and exclusiveness of the American Indian" (Allstrom 1929:1-2). What follows is a breathtakingly simplistic analysis of Mexican history and culture, leading Allstrom (1929:4) to conclude that Mexican children are "exceedingly individualistic," lacking in "formal play," preoccupied with "sex thoughts," and "ignorant of the most fundamental social concepts."

Allstrom's solution to the problem was to "socialize" Mexicans in the United States by giving them "an opportunity to understand" the "democratic ideals and practices" of their adopted country. In his own inimitable words:

> This socialization, in my opinion, will best begin with socialized play and supervised reading in the formative years of childhood and adolescence. Play among the Mexicans in the normal Mexican atmosphere is chiefly gambling with cards and dice and on the holidays and Sundays cock fighting and bull fighting at which gambling is a major element. Play as it is known among Anglo-Saxon people is virtually unknown among the Latins. Small children are given over to the care and supervision of servants, who come from the lowest classes both socially and economically, and who are utterly unfit because of lack of knowledge to have the care of any children. These servants fill the minds of the children with filthy stories and with warped ideas of sex, and when the children arrive at the free-play age of Anglo-Saxon childhood they loaf about with nothing to do but discuss sex (Allstrom 1929:17).

It is not hard to imagine what kind of a teacher Allstrom or others like him must have been: racists with little or no understanding of their Mexican pupils. The destructive effect of such attitudes in the classroom must have been immense. Rachel Riggins, on the other hand, was a much more sympathetic observer of Mexican society and culture. A social worker in Tucson during the Depression, Riggins was familiar with the desperate poverty of many Mexican working-class families. She therefore recognized the obstacles many Mexican children faced in their pursuit of an education: poor nutrition, inadequate medical care, cramped and dilapidated housing and the necessity of older children having to quit school in order to work and support their families. As such, her analysis served as a welcome balance to the pseudoscientific nonsense of a man like Allstrom.

Unfortunately, however, Riggins fell into the same trap that has ensnared other, more sophisticated researchers. Foreshadowing the "culture of poverty" school of thought associated with such scholars as Oscar Lewis and Daniel Moynihan, Riggins believed that the economic conditions of the barrios created a cultural milieu that prevented many Mexican children from progressing in school. In her opinion, Mexican students were hampered by a

> mental attitude or mind set which develops rather naturally in such limited homes, retaining the flavor and customs of a culture based on folklore and superstition rather than on scientific knowledge and which tends, therefore, toward vague, mysterious generalization and unquestioning acceptance of ideas rather than careful examination of facts or a desire to prove or disprove them (Riggins 1946:38-39).

The danger in such a viewpoint is that it makes attitudes rather than external conditions the locus of social change. If Mexicans--or, by extension, any other minority in the United States--could just alter the way they thought, or their child-rearing practices, or their patterns of family life--then the rewards of the American Dream would soon be theirs. Such an outlook gives primacy to the consequences of poverty and discrimination rather than to their causes. Moreover, it tends to "blame the victim" for his or her own subordination. What Riggins and others failed to understand was that attitudes change in response to changing social and economic conditions, not vice versa.

No matter how good-hearted an educator like Riggins was, she and people like her undoubtedly conveyed the message that Mexican culture was somehow inferior to "American" culture. Such a message, whether it was blatantly communicated by washing children's mouths out with soap for speaking Spanish in the classroom, or more subtly transmitted through the glorification of "Anglo-Saxon" civilization, must have convinced many Mexican students that they were personally inferior as well. Those feelings of inferiority, combined with very real economic and linguistic disadvantages, deprived many Mexican children of the education they deserved. As one prominent *Tucsonense* later said, "It was a terrible waste of brainpower."[8]

Mexican Resistance in Tucson

So far, I have talked primarily about what happened to Mexicans in Tucson between the Gadsden Purchase and World War II. It is important to realize, however, that Tucsonenses never passively accepted the processes of subordination discussed above. On the contrary, Mexicans actively resisted those processes in a variety of ways ranging from political organization to cultural preservation. Their resistance, in fact, undoubtedly prevented the entrenchment of more overt forms of discrimination afflicting other Mexican populations throughout the Southwest.

One of the primary forms of Mexican resistance was vigorous participation in city and county politics. Contrary to stereotype, Mexicans were not politically apathetic. Instead, they joined both the Democratic and Republican parties in large numbers, supporting Mexican candidates and organizing Mexican political clubs. As a result, Mexican politicians won election to many important offices during the late 19th and early 20th centuries. Mariano Samaniego, for example, served as territorial legislator, county assessor, city councilman, and chairman of the county board of supervisors. He was also chosen as a member of the University of Arizona's first board of regents, a position he was particularly well-qualified for because he was one of the few inhabitants of frontier Tucson, Mexican or Anglo, with a college education. Other successful Mexican politicians included Estevan Ochoa, Joaquín Legarra, Perfecto Elías, and Nabor Pacheco, who served as Pima County Sheriff and Tucson Chief of Police.

But despite those successes, Mexican candidates were frustrated more often than they were rewarded. The number of Mexican elected officials peaked around the turn of the century; in the decades that followed successful candidacies were rare. Between 1904 and 1927, for instance, no Mexican was elected to the Tucson City Council. Tucsonenses like Bernabé Brichta continued to run for office, but they increasingly found that the avenues to political power were closed to all but a handful of the Mexican elite.

One response to the thwarting of Mexican ambitions through conventional political channels was the creation of Mexican organizations, especially the mutual-aid societies, or *mutualistas*. Those mutualistas were part of worldwide phenomenon involving industrialization and the widespread migration of people from the countryside to the cities. As immigrants left traditional networks of support such as extended families or peasant corporate communities, they created new institutions to provide themselves with the security they needed in strange and often hostile environments. Mexican mutual-aid societies sponsored social events, and offered low-cost life and burial insurance to their members. More importantly, they furnished an organizational structure that enabled their members to protest many of the manifestations of discrimination and subordination sweeping across the Southwest.

The largest of these mutualistas in Tucson--indeed, throughout the entire United States and northern Mexico--was the Alianza Hispano-Americana. But the Alianza was joined by other important organizations as well, including the *Sociedad Mutualista Porfirio Díaz*, the *Sociedad Amigos Unidos*, and the most politically active of them all, the *Liga Protectora Latina*, which was founded in Phoenix in 1914. Together, these mutualistas became the most important political instruments of Arizona's Mexican middle-class.

During its heyday, the mutualista movement engaged in a number of important crusades: protecting Mexican nationals from the military draft, protesting derogatory stereotypes of Mexicans in Hollywood movies, campaigning against discriminatory hiring practices in Arizona mines, struggling to win pardons for Mexican prisoners condemned to death in Arizona jails. Organizations like the *Liga* served as forerunners of more activist Mexican organizations such as the League of United Latin American Citizens (LULAC) or the GI Forum, which developed after World War II. Above all, they gave Mexicans an organized voice in Arizona politics at a time when the political climate in Arizona was growing increasingly racist and conservative.

The Politics of Race and Class in Tucson

It is important to note that most mutualistas in Tucson served middle-class rather than working-class interests. At times those interests intersected; the Liga, for example, strongly opposed a series of attempts to exclude Mexicans from running machinery or working underground in the mines. On the other hand, the mutual-aid societies did not appear to take an active role in the organized labor movement, at least not in Tucson. Protesting discriminatory hiring practices or the execution of Mexican convicts was one thing those manifestations of racism affected the status of all Mexicans regardless of class. But the organs of Mexican middle-class opinion were much more ambivalent about basic economic issues such as labor unions and the right to strike.

As early as 1878, for example, the editors of *Las Dos Repúblicas*, Tucson's first Spanish-language newspaper, condemned "workers' societies," contending that they consisted of "idle and depraved people" who wanted "a repetition of the 1792 Revolution in France."[9] Carlos Velasco, founding father of the Alianza Hispano-Americana, echoed those sentiments in a speech given on the Alianza's first anniversary. According to Velasco, one of the organization's major goals was to imbue the Mexican working class with a "hatred of vagrancy" and a "love of work."[10] Such observations stood in stark contrast to the revolutionary rhetoric of the Flores-Magón brothers and other radicals organizing Mexican workers on both sides of the international border.

And Mexican workers did organize, even when they were ignored by Anglo labor unions and opposed by Mexican middle-class intellectuals and businessmen. People familiar with the history of the Mexican Revolution remember the bloody strike in the Cananea copper mines in 1906. Many historians, in fact, consider the Cananea strike to be a precursor of the Revolution itself. But Mexican miners also carried out the first major strike in Arizona--the Clifton strike of 1903. They did so despite the fact that unions like the Western Federation of Miners had largely written Clifton-Morenci off as a "Mexican town."

Even in Tucson, where the economy was commercial rather than industrial, Mexican workers banded together to protest wage cuts and layoffs. Their biggest target, not surprisingly, was the Southern Pacific, the largest employer of Mexican labor in town. In 1920, for example, 27 percent of all Mexican workers worked for the railroad, usually in the shops or section gangs. The following year, when the Southern Pacific threatened to cut their wages by as much as thirty cents an hour, they decided to walk out on strike. *El Tucsonense*, the most important Spanish-language newspaper in Tucson, urged them not to do so, arguing that reduced wages were better than none at all. Eighteen hundred workers disagreed, and in July, 1922, the strike began.[11] The controversy between Mexican railroad workers and a middle-class Mexican newspaper reveals how differences of class often weakened bonds of ethnic identity among Mexicans in Tucson. The Southern Pacific workers, like workers throughout the world, believed that strikes were often necessary to achieve their goals. Mexican businessmen, on the other hand, viewed strikes and organized labor with alarm. First of all, Mexican merchants did not want the wage structure of southern Arizona to rise too sharply; otherwise, their own labor costs would have risen as well. Secondly, they saw strikes as threats to their own economic well-being, even when the strikes were not directed against them. Striking workers, after all, received no paychecks, and no paychecks meant no business in barrio stores. Larger firms could weather widespread strikes or layoffs. Many small, struggling barrio businesses, however, could not. In the final analysis, then, Ramón Soto's vision of a united *Colonia Hispano-Americana* was undercut by the conflicting interests of Mexican workers and Mexican businessmen, making it more of a chimera than a reality.

But even if all Mexicans in Tucson had come together to protest their subordination, the political and economic deck was stacked against them. Prior to World War II, Arizona's economy was dominated by three major extractive industries: mining, ranching, and agriculture. All three of these enterprises--the producers of Arizona's famous "Three C's": copper, cattle, and cotton--converted Arizona's natural resources into raw material to be shipped and processed somewhere else. And like most extractive industries, they depended upon cheap, abundant, often seasonal labor. An attempt to import Chinese workers failed in the late 1800s. Thereafter, Mexicans on both sides of the international border served as the reserve labor supply upon which Arizona's industries drew.

And since the Arizona economy relied upon cheap labor, the major source of that labor had to be subordinated in order to keep labor costs down. The results were differential wage scales for Mexican and Anglo workers, the manipulation of immigration policies to control the flow of Mexicans across the border, and most importantly, the pitting of Mexican and Anglo workers against each other in order to weaken the organized labor movement in general. Ethnic conflict and proximity to Mexico therefore served as two of the most important tools whereby Arizona industries and industries across the southwestern United States, kept workers tractable and wages low.

Moreover, there was no compelling reason to provide those workers with much more than an elementary education. Consequently, little pressure was put upon the public schools to improve their programs and prevent so many Mexican students from dropping out. On the contrary, too much education might have opened other avenues for many workers, thereby threatening the labor supply. In such fashion, derogatory stereotypes about Mexican children were fueled by the need for cheap labor, and even the most gifted of Mexican pupils often found themselves channeled into vocational courses rather than prepared for college and the white-collar world.

It is important to note that the subordination of the Mexican working class in southern Arizona was not the result of any conspiracy masterminded by Phelps-Dodge or the Southern Pacific. On the contrary, it was a much more complex phenomenon, one that developed because of many factors--cultural, political, demographic, and above all, economic--intersecting in the region. Many well-meaning people, even today, do not understand how subtle and pervasive racism really is. They believe that once discriminatory laws are struck down, racism ceases to exist. But what racism really is is a system of attitudes, symbols, and beliefs designed to justify the subordination of one group of people by another. Once rooted in a society, the system becomes extremely difficult to eradicate because it penetrates nearly all aspects of life and thought. Moreover, it operates on unconscious as well as conscious levels, affecting individuals and institutions in ways they often cannot comprehend. Tucson public schools, for example, may not have deliberately segregated Mexican children or intended to offer them inferior educations. Nonetheless, the destructive effects of the attitudes of teachers and administrators themselves must have been incalculable. In a sense, the institutional manifestations of racism are the least insidious because they can be identified and eliminated. It is far more arduous to change the basic assumptions people make about others, especially since many of those assumptions are unconscious and unquestioned.

Above all, racism must be viewed as a cultural construct, not a biological given. And like all such constructs, it is a form of adaptation to changing political and economic realities, the ideological manifestation of a set of historically determined power relationships that change through time. In the Southwest, an aggressive expanding nation dominated by Anglos encountered the sparsely populated frontier of another nation that had not yet recovered from a destructive war for independence. The economic and demographic strength of the one nation collided with the economic and demographic weakness of the other, resulting, not surprisingly, in conquest and colonization. As in all such situations through history and across the world, the conquerors were not honest enough to justify their actions on the grounds that might makes right. They therefore had to develop elaborate rationalizations for the subordination of the people they came to control. It is beyond the scope of this presentation to examine the range of those rationalizations. What I have tried to do here is merely present some of the consequences of race and class in Tucson, consequences that still influence the social, political, and economic life of the community today.

Notes

1. *El Fronterizo*, July 9, 1892. Soto's other two articles appeared in *El Fronterizo* on July 16 and July 23 of the same year.
2. *El Fronterizo*, August 4, 1894.
3. Don Bufkin, "From Mud Village to Modern Metropolis: The Urbanization of Tucson", *Journal of Arizona History* 22:72 (1981).
4. The plaintiffs' case, as well as the studies commissioned by the Tucson Unified School District in defense, is located in the archives of TUSD. The desegregation case is summarized at greater length in Sheridan, 1986.
5. Report of the Superintendent, 1923-24, p. 18. These reports are located in the Special Collections of the University of Arizona's Main Library.
6. Report of the Superintendent, 1920-21, p. 43.
7. Ibid., p. 46.
8. Fred Acosta, quoted in the *Arizona Daily Star*, July 16, 1978.
9. *Las Dos Repúblicas*, August 24, 1878.
10. *El Fronterizo*, January 19, 1895.
11. *El Tucsonense*, October 20, 1921. *El Mosquito*, July 1, 1922.

Bibliography

Acuña, Rodolfo
    1981, *Occupied America: A History of Chicanos*. New York: Harper & Row.

Allstrom, Erik
    1929, A Program of Social Education for a Mexican Community in the United States. Master's thesis, College of Education, University of Arizona.

De León, Arnoldo
    1982, *The Tejano Community, 1836-1900*. Albuquerque: University of New Mexico Press.

Griswold del Castillo, Richard
    1979, *The Los Angeles Barrio, 1850-1900*. Berkeley: University of California Press.

Pitt, Leonard
    1966, *The Decline of the Californios: A Social History of the Spanish-Speaking Californians, 1846-1890*. Berkeley: University of California Press.

Riggins, Rachel
    1946, Factors in Social Background Which Influence the Mexican Child in School. Master's thesis, Department of Education, University of Arizona.

Sheridan, Thomas
    1986, *Los Tucsonenses: The Mexican Community in Tucson, 1854-1941*. The University of Arizona Press.

In March, 1890, Las Gorras Blancas (the White Caps), a secret society of disgruntled native New Mexicans, declared war against outsiders, intelopers, political bossism and land grabbers. They resorted to acts of sabotage against their enemies in an attempt to slow or undue the injustice in their lands. It appears that Las Gorras Blancas enjoyed the sympathies of many of the natives of New Mexico as they formed a commom bond against "los extranjeros" who threatened to change their traditional ways of life forever.

Las Gorras Blancas: A Secret Gathering of Fence Cutters
Robert J. Rosenbaum

Fence cutting was not unique to the *mexicanos* of San Miguel County. The introduction of barbed wire, "the devil's hat-band," to the open ranges of the trans-Mississippi West during the 1880s touched off vicious fence wars from Texas to Oregon; *mexicanos* responded with tactics similar to those used by others in the West threatened by enclosures.[1]

Open-range cattle ranching was the first Anglo enterprise to use the vast, semiarid New Mexico grasslands; its aura of romance and promise of huge profits attracted many Eastern and foreign investors. Profits could be immense because land and water were free. Open-range ranching required a sparse population, a demand for beef in the East, and consensus as to what constituted a "range." Over-grazing, over-production, and bad weather helped burst the open-range cattle bubble by the mid-eighties. Increased population, especially small farmers who took out title under the homestead laws, threatened the cattleman's free use of land and water. Small farmers supported their title with a new invention, cheap but effective wire fencing. Barbed wire ended casual use of the public domain and initiated the transition from cattle ranching to controlled stock raising.[2]

The transition was not smooth. Ranchers attacked homesteaders whose fenced crops cut off their herds from water. Small ranchers attacked large operations possessing the foresight and the capital to enclose land, whether they owned it or not. But by the end of the decade, most ranchers conceded that they needed some kind of title to their grazing land.

The outbreak of fence cutting in San Miguel County fit into the times. New Mexico's grant lands attracted cattlemen who saw an opportunity to acquire title to more land than the General Land Office would allow them from the public domain. The inhabitants on the grants complicated matters. Their residence created precedent for the title that the ranchers sought. But their presence challenged the new holdings. Vague and conflicting Hispanic practices and a tangled body of law and imprecise boundaries opened loopholes for the interlopers. Anglo ranchers, Anglo farmers, and Hispanic opportunists—who read the signs and hoped to take advantage of the new order—put up fences where none had stood before. Las Gorras Blancas struck at the fences and other manifestations of encroachment that threatened their existence.

The World of the White Caps

No one publicly admitted to being a White Cap, and contemporary observers differed in many of their interpretations of the organization. To make sense of the evidence and accusations that survive, it is necessary to begin with the first settlement of the region early in the nineteenth century.

Social Background

In 1794, Lorenzo Marquez and fifty-one others, all heads of families from Santa Fe, petitioned the governor of New Mexico for a tract of land on the Rio Pecos, at the place commonly called El Vado ("the ford"), "where there is room enough, not any for us, . . . but also for everyone in the province not supplied [with enough land to live on]." They described their specific tract at El Vado as bounded "on the north [by] the Rio de la Vaca from the place called the Rancheria to the Agua Caliente, on the South the Canon Blanco, on the east La Cuesta with the little hills of Bernal, and on the west the place commonly called the Gusano:" an area of approximately 315,000 acres. If granted their request, they promised to enclose themselves "in a plaza well fortified with bulwarks and towers, and to exert ourselves to supply all the firearms and ammunition that it may be possible for us to procure."[3]

Their request was granted on November 26, 1794, with the provisions that "the tract aforesaid has to be in common, not only in regard to themselves but also to all settlers who may join them in the future," and that the building of their plaza, the opening of ditches, and all work proper for the common welfare "shall be performed by the community with that union which in their government they must preserve." The last paragraph attests that the boundaries had been walked, that all understood that the pasture and watering places were in common, and that possession had been taken with proper ceremony.

Official occupation took place on March 12, 1803, when the Justice of the Second Note of Santa Fe supervised the equitable division of farming land and the apportionment of both fields and house plots by drawing lots. He also marked out the boundaries of the village of San Miguel del Bado, including a large portion of land downriver "which is necessary for the inhabitants of this town who may require more land to cultivate, which shall be done by the consent of the Justice of said town . . ."[4]

The documents picture a homogeneous body of settlers. House and farm plots were drawn by lot, all work for the common good had to be distributed fairly throughout the community, and all pasture lands and watering holes were free to all. Communal ownership of the bulk of the grant land was the only condition mentioned twice in the grant decree. Despite the humble station of the settlers, they were expected to manage their local affairs "with that union which in their government they must preserve." Concerns of their government included the construction and maintenance of the village, defense, distribution of additional farming land, and, of continual importance, the distribution of irrigation water and the maintenance of the *acequias*.[5] To an Anglo American eye, the grant documents picture a cooperative Hispanic variation on the Jeffersonian image of the sturdy yeoman farmer.

The grant was intended to be open to additional settlement. The petitioners requested land for themselves and for any others who needed enough land to live on. In 1794, fifty-two heads of households received the grant, but in 1803, fifty-eight households participated in the drawing of lots, indicating that this provision was more than just a formality. Others followed, either settling at San Miguel or establishing new villages within the grant's boundaries. As people moved to the region, or as population increase overtaxed the resources of the original tract, the Spanish and Mexican governments made other awards. The Antonchico Grant, a 383,850-acre tract down the Pecos from San Miguel, was given in 1822 to Salvador Tapia et al., settlers migrating from San Miguel del Bado. In 1835, Juan de Dios Maese and others received 496,450 acres called the Las Vegas Grant, centered around a large meadowland on the Gallinas River. It was the ninth tract awarded in the region. By 1845, fourteen awards had been made that supported approximately ten thousand people.[6]

These grants range from the crest of the Sangre de Cristo Mountains to the slope of the Canadian escarpment.[7] Altitude varies from nine thousand feet in the west to three thousand near the Texas panhandle. Streams of varying volume and dependability seam the western portion on a southeastwardly bias, becoming proportionately less frequent the greater the distance from the mountains. Only two rivers cut the entire—the Pecos, rising from the snows of the Sangre de Cristos and carving a deep path as it travels on its southern journey to meet the Rio Grande above Del Rio, and the Canadian, describing an eastward loop en route to the Red River. As one resident observed, "They are not great rivers."[8]

It is varied, broken land with rainfall rarely exceeding sixteen inches annually. Temperature, vegetation, and terrain differ markedly throughout the area, from the rugged mountains on the west, with good stands of timber and sheltered valleys, to the dusty brown-green high plains of scrub pinon, short grass, and rock broken by mesas, isolated hills, canons, and occasional rolling meadows on the east. Streams and waterholes determined the location of settlement everywhere. Except for a few isolated areas, irrigable land was not sufficient to provide a livelihood, and everyone ran some livestock.[9]

Life in San Miguel County, before the railroad aroused the ambitions of Las Vegas, followed a pattern of capricious predictability:[10] capricious because of the uncertainties of health, weather, and hostile Indians, but predictable in the ways that people confronted the chancy business of living. Settlers grouped together in small communities along waterways, tilling what land they could for staples and roaming with their herds or flocks over the hills and eastward toward the Llano Estacado. Village size depended upon the availability of arable land and water; when population threatened these resources, settlers moved on to establish a new village on unoccupied land.

There were differences. The families in one community might be independent farmers, filling their fields and grazing their small herds on the common land, occasionally selling wool or animals for small cash income. In other villages, one or two clans rose above the rest, owning almost all of the livestock and employing most of the village as herders. An entire hamlet might work for one *rico* as wage labor, some occupied a middle ground, herding for a *rico* or a merchant on the partido system, which offered the prospect of independence. A few farmers, fortunate in the quality of land and the amount of water available, produced a surplus and regarded themselves as somehow apart from the *pastores* and vaqueros.[11]

The general pattern was of house lots and fields held in specific ownership and pastureland open to all. Grant boundaries were vague and unimportant, with spheres of use sanctioned by custom. Whether or not a tract was granted to an individual or to a community made little real difference, for wealth and power depended upon the size of herds and the number of people a patron employed, not on exclusive use and title. Before Anglo Americans arrived and demanded that the land be measured and tagged with the name of an owner—an individual, a corporation, or a government—both grant and crown land was used in common by those who could.[12]

A few merchants and traders also participated in this pastoral life. Many hamlets supported small shopkeepers who supplied basic commercial needs. The comanchero trade provided an additional source of income. Until the arrival of Anglo investment and the railroad, Las Vegas was one of three prominent villages in the area, the other two being Antonchico and Puerto de Luna, seats for traders to the Comanches.[13]

Public schools were nonexistent. The Church offered the only available education.. If a village had a priest, he was often the most educated man in the community and served as an intermediary who dealt with the written demands from the outside world. Others in a village might read and write—the storekeeper, if there was one—and they too served as *escribanos* for their neighbors.

Ricos topped the social scale. With large holdings of livestock and often extensive mercantile interests, they claimed descent from the conquistadores and sent their children to private school in Santa Fe and perhaps on to St. Louis University or Notre Dame. Their influence derived from wealth, family, and interest in affairs throughout the territory; they provided territorial legislators and county officials. *Ricos* and local *patrones*—those who employed a number of people in a given area and who, through wealth, family connections, and personality, could exert a great deal of local influence—provided the leadership for the region as a whole.

It would be a mistake to assume that a hegemony of *ricos* and *patrones*, with the aid of the priests, controlled a docile population of *los hombres pobres*. Just as there were gradations within the broad category of rices, so were there differences among *los pobres*. As the case of the San Miguel del Bado Grant demonstrates, the whole adult male population participated in certain group decisions. Of continual importance were theacequias. After their construction, they required yearly cleaning and repair. Equitable distribution of water had to be insured, a touchy problem in a land where lack of water meant starvation.. A *mayordomo de acequia* and a committee responsible for the use of water were elected each year to supervise the irrigation system. The communities chose alcaldes to distribute lands and to adjudicate minor civil and criminal disputes. Cooperative work had to be done, and this too was a part of local government. In some villages, this kind of cooperation planting and harvesting.. As one resident of the San Miguel del Bado Grant described his town:

> *The people of El Cerrito used to elect a conservador each year. He acted as a sort of governor of the village. The people had to do what he told them to. In those times the people would work*

together in planting and harvest time. The conservador would call men to work and could determine which work should be done first. When someone wanted to hire a man he had to come to the conservador. He could determine who could have the job. Always he would select the family that needed work the most. In that way the needy were usually provided for. In case they were not, he could ask the people for money or grain to give the pobres.[14]

Political experience in dealing with crucial local problems was an important element of life for the people clustered in the adobe and stone houses along the streams of San Miguel County. Naturally, a political elite developed among *los pobres*. Leaders could rise because they came from respected families, because they enjoyed more material success than their fellows, because they were adjudged good and wise, or because of personality, influence, or power deriving from the support of a *patron* or *rico*. Just as naturally, factions developed. Rare was the village that was not divided into two groups, usually along family lines.[15]

The political world of the region encompassed a complex network of relationships between factions at each point on the social scale. Support or opposition was determined not by ideology but by the tangible elements of immediate material benefit, by considerations of prestige, or by the more ephemeral factors of admiration or hate. Competition was for power, not for change, a logical situation when there was agreement about the basic structure of life. One student of New Mexican politics observed that if indeed the *jefe politico* dominated New Mexican politics among the Spanish-speaking communities, there were many *jefes* in constant competition for the same constituency.[16] A present resident of Las Vegas expressed the same sentiment more forcefully: "If the *patrones* really controlled so well, why were there so damn many political parties?"[17]

The Anglo Americans shared a region with a people that they did not understand. They saw dirty, ignorant, lazy natives dotting a vast land which, to Anglo American eyes, was unclaimed and unused. Occasionally they could discern a *rico* from among the masses of backward and superstitious *mexicanos*, but they had little conception of the complex patterns of relationships and customs.

It was not an easy situation to comprehend. Isolation characterized the life in each village, but it was an isolation the mobile aspects of a grazing economy and was further broken down by the pattern of settlement which contained many villages in all parts of the region settled by delegations from older villages.[18] Each village on a grant maintained a unique identity, as did each grant, yet there was both conflict and cooperation between villages on the same grant and between grants.[19] This duality between isolation and interaction was enhanced by the coming of the *americanos*. As the Anglos increased in number, the villages tended to withdraw into themselves. Yet the Anglos brought increased opportunities for wage labor and markets, thereby intensifying the mobility and interaction..

Just as there were opposing themes of isolation and interaction, so too were there paradoxical threads of aggression and passivity. When the Anglos arrived, they came to a region of expanding settlement. The Hispanos were still settling and conquering New Mexico, ever-extending their control, when the westward advancing fringes of Anglo America arrived; hardly the behavior of a static culture. But the New Mexican concept of expansion did not include the Anglo's concept of upward mobility or getting ahead. It was expansion along traditional lines, an expansion primarily "to live." Among *los pobres*, the goal was a comfortable existence in their terms. This meant enough land to farm, enough pasture for stock, enough game to hunt, enough wood to burn, and enough material to build. It meant, should the opportunity present itself, wage labor on the railroad, contract freighting or the like, but only to help one live as one ought to live.[20] To the Anglo, such attitudes were backward and slovenly; to *los pobres*, nothing else made any sense.

Politically, the contradictory patterns of autonomy and dependence ran through a social fabric which most Anglos could not unravel. The *mexicanos'* tendency to support members of their upper classes for county and territorial offices, their lack of concern for "political" issues, and the fact that patronage seemed to be the only determinant of their political behavior led Anglos to the conclusion that these were a placid, *patron*-dominated people, politically naive and shot through with corruption. The Anglo did not see the politics of the village and did not understand the areas of autonomy and the mutual obligations and benefits in the seemingly servile system. Neither did the Anglo understand the experience of the people which taught that local affairs were the only ones of importance, that the problems of larger units of government were of no concern, and that unless something offered discernible practical benefit it was of little value. When basic ways of life were as they should be, concern was only for improvement within those ways. When their way of life was threatened, *los pobres* fit neither their servile nor their passive image.

Threat and Response

By the 1880s Las Vegas began to push for territorial leadership, and an atmosphere of boosterism and boom prevailed; land grant speculaffon increased apace. Legislators collaborated to pass laws that would virtually strip *los pobres* of their interest in their grants.[21] Men conspired with the surveyor general of the territory and with land registrars, even on the floors of Congress, to gain title to as many acres as they could.[22]

In a very brief time, things happened that promised fundamentally to change the patterns of life in San Miguel County. Furthermore, the people who had traditionally coped with larger political problems were not defending *los pobres*; they were parffcipaffng in the changes.[23]

San Miguel County's population increased by approximately 3,500, almost all Anglo, in the 1880s, bringing the total to over 24,ooo.[24] Thirty-five hundred people are not many, but if they represent a hundred ranches and a railroad competing for land, water, and timber previously used by others for decades, change is, in fact, great. In addition to usurping land and water, thereby hampering traditional use, these newcomers were hostile and contemptuous in their treatment of the natives, and they were enlisting the *ricos* and *patrones* on their side. In a county in which the *mexicanos* still enjoyed overwhelming numerical superiority, there appeared to be no peaceful recourse. Civil war broke out in April, 1889.

Governor Prince thought that the White Caps consisted almost exclusively of natives of New Mexico of the "ignorant class." A few "active and educated men" arranged the organization, said the governor, and influenced the people with talk that they were being deprived of their rights, using the Las Vegas Grant as a "special illustration." In Prince's view, members joined to protect their "supposed" rights, but the White Caps, once established, were used for "worse purposes." "Worse purposes," in Prince's estimation, included labor agitation, attacks on corporations, politics, and outright banditry.[25] Another observer called them a "lawless mob of several hundred Mexicans" who committed their depredations "upon the plea that the land belongs to the people, and that they are underpaid for their work."[26] Many observers draw a strong correlation between the White Caps and the Knights of Labor: "The White Caps believe that they are backed by the Knights of Labor of the whole United States. To understand this, you must recollect that these are Mexicans; that the Mexicans in New Mexico, with the exception of perhaps five percent, are the most ignorant people on the face of the earth."[27] Not all Anglos viewed Las Gorras Blancas with distaste. Judge O'Brien, writing two months after he dismissed the forty-seven accused fence cutters, told Prince: "To a casual and impartial observer, ignorant of antecedent causes, the so-called outrages are the protests of a simple, pastoral people against the establishment of large landed estates, or baronial feudalism, in their native territory. The term 'White Cap,' when used in any other sense, is, in my opinion, a misnomer."[28]

La Voz del Pueblo, a Spanish-language newspaper published in Las Vegas, constantly defended *las masas de los hombres pobres*, and by implication Los Gorras Blancas, against the "capitalists, monopolists and land grabbers," although the paper never overtly condoned fence cutting. Founded the previous year in Santa Fe by Nestor Montoya, a rising young educated Hispano who sought to end the Santa Fe Ring's domination of the territory, *La Voz* moved to Las Vegas in 1890, when Montoya joined Felix Martinez, another Democrat of similar background and ambitions and of greater financial resources.[29]

All observers agreed that poor *mexicanos* made up the rank and file of Las Gorras Blancas and that land was the major issue. Prince, District Attorney Salazar, and others saw the turbulence as the product of outside agitators duping the native population. Salazar accused Juan Jose Herrera and seven lieutenants of being the instigators and argued that if the leaders were disposed of, the organization would fall apart. He recommended the "strongest measures possible against these people, as the only possible way of putting them to fear, and it is only through fear that they can be persuaded to desist [from] the wholesale destruction of property."[30]

There is a familiar ring to the beleaguered cry that "outsiders" or "evil manipulators" with magical powers caused the unrest, if only because the people were too ignorant to understand their self interest. There was an organization, but to call it an "outside" one is to misunderstand the nature of the issue and the world of the people who fought for it.

Fence cutting and related activities during this period were organized. The number of incidents, their occurrences in a wide geographical area, and the similarity of targets all indicate cooperation. The numbers involved in most attacks or demonstrations exceeded the capabilities of most single villages.[31] Substantial evidence of nocturnal meetings in isolated places attests to communication and planning. The similarity of costume, of technique, and of methods of signaling--using homemade whistles instead of voice commands--also point to organization.[32] Finally, almost all observers, whether hostile or sympathetic, said that a "secret society" was responsible for the fence cutting.

Many identified the Knights of Labor, or at least district organizer Juan Jose Herrera and his brothers, as the organizers. The Herreras the Knights, and *La Voz Del Pueblo* denied this charge, but several factors gave it validity. Herrera had lived for a time in San Miguel County, had left under the cloud of scandalous conduct with a woman, and had joined the Knights of Labor in either Utah or Colorado. The date of his return to San Miguel County is not known, but it is undeniable that he received a commission as district organizer from the Knights of Labor in 1888. He proceeded to establish twenty local assemblies in the county and to begin recruitment in the neighboring counties of Mora and Santa Fe. As Herrera organized his assemblies, Las Gorras Blancas began to ride in the same areas, a coincidence that disturbed several Anglo members of Las Vegas Assembly Number 4636:

> *Just how many Assemblies he has organized, we are not prepared to say, but fence cutting and other depredations are by far too frequent occurrences. We understand that there has [sic] been three Assemblies organized in Santa Fe County and fence cutting has commenced there. Now who these fence cutters or self-called White Caps' are, we are not prepared to say. But the Mexican people who are being organized as K of L are of the poorer class and consequently they are more ignorant, as they have had no advantages of education, there being but very few schools in the Territory. Now we, as members of the K of L would request that no more assemblies be organized or Charters granted to those already organized until the present condition of affairs changes for the better.*[33]

Las Gorras Blancas and the Knights of Labor correspond on three other points. The White Caps' concern about wage scales and job competition, coupled with strike threats, suggests the involvement of people familiar with labor agitation.. The parallel membership between the Knights of Labor and *El Partido del Pueblo Unido* after August, 1890, their support of major White Cap issues, and the coincidence that the strength of all three lay in the same precincts lend additional support to the theory connecting the Knights and the White Caps.[34] The last bit of evidence is the oral tradition about Las Gorras Blancas current in both Las Vegas and the villages on the grants. In this tradition, Las Gorras Blancas and the Knights of Labor are identical: the old people say that Las Gorras Blancas was a nickname, but that they preferred to be called Los Caballeros de Labor.[35]

The Knights of Labor, as led by Juan Jose Herrera, organized or coordinated the fence cutting.. That the organization was not indigenous to New Mexico is undeniable. A national union that had grown out of a league of Philadelphia garment workers, by 1885 under the leadership of Terence V. Powdarly, it encompassed hundreds of thousands of members. The Knights organized people around an ethical substitute for capitalism, and opposition to land speculation and large landowners played a prominent role in their constitution. Although membership was denied only to manipulators of money and corruptors of morals, recruitment was most successful in industries and trades. The many new members in the early 1880s were primarily wage laborers. The strident demands and militant actions of these workers culminated in the Great Southwest Strike of 1885. Powderly could not cope with these tactics and refused to support his own striking members. Defeat by railroad magnate Jay Gould in 1886, coupled with the clamor raised by the Haymarket Riots that same year, sent the national organization on a long slide to decay and irrelevance. As the Knights lost their national impact, the combination of grievances, their stance on land, and Herrera brought them to life in San Miguel County.[36]

District organizer Herrera was no *extranjero*. Herrera had lived outside of New Mexico for a time, but he was a native of New Mexico. He was originally from San Miguel County, and his family still lived there. He did differ from most of *los hombres pobres*: he had traveled, he could read and write, he published a newspaper for a time, and he was involved in a national organization that meant very little to most native New Mexicans. But he understood San Miguel's people and their problems, and he provided a dimension of coordination to their protest that they lacked prior to and after his active years.[37]

Herrera and his lieutenants coordinated; they did not create. They did not make the issues. Fences went up on common land before assemblies of Los Caballeros de Labor spread across the county. These fences dislocated the way of life of the native people, a way of life that had been sanctioned in grant documents and established custom. The dislocation was severe in a marginal land where the loss of grazing privileges brought starvation near.

Herrera did not create the issue; neither did he provide the techniques of protest. *Los pobres* of New Mexico did not seek redress through legislative assemblies or the vote; nothing in their experience taught them that this would be a fruitful course of action.. In their world, peaceful redress of grievances was realized either through judicial arbitration or petitions to the governor.[38] If these avenues failed, only two other choices remained—sullen acceptance or direct action.

Direct action, forceful action, was natural to a culture that remembered a constant hostile Indian threat and placed high emphasis on honor and the stalwart defense of one's rights. Most adults remembered the Comanches who had used the Llano Estacado as a highway between Texas and Mexico. *Comancheros* traded regularly with them, but the commerce did not block out the memory of Indian attacks. Other military memories included the capture of the Texas-Santa Fe expedition near Antonchico in 1841 and the defeat of Sibley's column at Glorieta Pass in 1862.[39] On a personal level, the people of the villages still tell stories and sing corridos about individual triumphs over insulting Texas cowboys, and the phrase mucho hombre—much of a man—punctuates their tales of men who defended their rights with guns.

Feuds between families occurred frequently and are still not uncommon. The village of El Cerrito on the San Miguel Grant was one of the few villages that did not have two political factions in the 1930s. El Cerrito had once had two powerful families, but disagreements over grazing ranges on the common land touched off a feud in the 1880s that drove one family group from the community.[40] Disagreements over communal resources caused many conflicts. For example, the residents of Bado de Juan Pais accused the *mayordomo de acequia* at El Llano of diverting too much water from their common *acequia madre*. Moving quickly, representatives of the aggrieved community set the ditch gate at what they considered to be the proper position, marked it, and left a note for the El Llano *mayordomo* informing him that he would be hanged if anything was changed. The El Llano official complied.[41]

One problem in determining the extent of White Cap activity, a problem recognized by observers at the time, is to separate reported attacks done for personal reasons from those done by Las Gorras Blancas. The large-scale incidents by masked horsemen are easy to identify, but such incidents as isolated murders, stock mutilation, or burning of buildings are less easy to categorize. A Mr. F. LeDuc, whose wellhouse was burned in March, 1890, thought that he was a victim not of the White Caps but of two "troublemakers" from the neighboring village of Los Vigiles.[42] Violence was a part of life for the people of San Miguel County. Juan Jose Herrera brought only a higher degree of efficiency to a people facing a common problem and possessed of common tactics for confrontation.

This is not to say that there was a 100 percent correlation between Los Caballeros de Labor and Las Gorras Blancas. Most probably, Herrera organized his assemblies emphasizing as much as possible the tenet that the land belonged to the people, and then used the assemblies as an institution for careful recruitment of White Cap chapters.[43] Membership could vary. In one village the local leader might be a pillar of the community, the *mayordomo de acequia* for example, while in the next he could be a young, dashing bachelor, a quasi-bandit used to a high-risk life and able to command some respect by his personality or reputation for bravery.[44] Sometimes the entire village supported the movement, sometimes a village might be split, and some villages and areas were never won over by the White Caps. The majority of the members were the poor, but sometimes *patrones*, inspired by outrage at injustices or political opportunism, joined.

Building on a sense of ethnic and class identification that grew stronger in the face of racial slurs and economic threats, Herrera forged a movement out of the traditional materials of Hispanic culture. To *las masas de los hombres pobres*, the issues were clear. Traditional use of land led their list, followed by fair and dignified treatment of wage labor. The two spectres of hunger and change motivated most. Perhaps they hoped that they could drive *los extranjeros* from their land and reunite with Mexico. But they would settle for traditional land tenure and fair treatment of labor.

The White Caps enjoyed some success by the summer of 1890. While they were unable to enlist all of San Miguel's *pobres*, they had gained the tacit support of most. Juries would not convict for fence cutting. Governor Prince could mobilize no popular movement against them. Their actions had temporarily stopped immigration, and the courts seemed to uphold their position.. If they had not beaten the *americanos*, they had at least effected a stalemate. In August, 1890, the movement took a new tack. On the twenty-fifth of the month, the Optic published a call for precincts to organize and send delegates to the county convention of *El Partido del Pueblo Unido*.

Notes

1. Although *mexicanos* were not the only threatened group who destroyed fences, the idea of taking direct action against the obvious cause of problems and the mode of organization used to do so were authentic products of *mexicano* culture.
2. For histories of the Western cattle industry, including the introduction of barbed wire and the loss of the public domain, see Lewis Atherton *The Cattle Kings*; E. E. Dale, *The Range Cattle Industry*, 2nd ed.; Gene Gressley, *Bankers and Cattlemen*; Ernest Staples Osgood, *The Day of the Cattlemen*; Jlames Orin Oliphant, *On the Cattle Ranges of Oregon*; and Webb, *The Great Plains*.
3. "San Miguel del Bado Grant," BLM, Reel 15; Leonard, *Role of the Land Grant*, pp. 167-172; Map 7; and Appendix C.
4. "San Miguel del Bado Grant," BLM, Reel 15.
5. Ibid. An *acequia* is an irrigation ditch. Usually a community dammed a river or stream above the village and constructed an *acequia madre*—main ditch—from which the network of *acequias* to the fields ran.
6. Documents relating to New Mexico land grants are most conveniently found in the BLM microfilm publication of the University of New Mexico Library. Donaldson, "The Public Domain," provides a detailed summary of the situation in New Mexico before the White Cap outbreaks. For a comprehensive analysis of land tenure in northern New Mexico from Oñate to the twentieth century, see Dunbar, "Land Tenure in Northern New Mexico."
7. Beck and Haase, *Historical Atlas of New Mexico*, Maps 2-5.
8. Milton C. Nahm, *Las Vegas and Uncle Joe*, p. 44.

9. One area that could produce a surplus was on the Antonchico Grant just below Antonchico. The *acequia madre* serving the communities from El Llano to Bado de Juan Pais measures twelve miles, waters about 2,100 acres, and is still in use.

10. Sources on the nature of *mexicano* life in the nineteenth century include Leonard, *Role of the Land Grant*; Susan Shelby McGoffln, *Down the Santa Fe Trail*, rev. ed., ed. Stella M. Drumm; Sánchez, *Forgotten People;* Meinig, *Southwest*; Horgan, *Great River*; Gregg, *Commerce on the Prairies*, and interviews in Las Vegas and on the Antonchico Grant.

11. Interview with Tony Márquez, Las Vegas, February 14, 1972. Don Márquez was born and raised at La Loma (formerly El Llano) on the Antonchico Grant, and characterized the attitudes of his relatives.

12. Fabiola C. de Baca, *We Fed Them Cactus*, gives a good description of the life of a ranchero in San Miguel County during the nineteenth century.

13. J. Evetts Haley, "The Comanchero Trade"; Meinig, *Southwest*, p. 33.

14. Quoted in Leonard, *Role of the Land Grant*, p. 185.

15. Leonard points out that El Cerrito, the principal village of his study, was one of these rarities.

16. Holmes, *Politics in New Mexico*, pp. 21-31.

17. Interview with Juan Pena, Las Vegas, February 14, 1972.

18. The Antonchico and Las Vegas Grants were settled by migrants from the San Miguel del Bado Grant. The patterns of settlement are often reflected by place names. For example, the village of San Ignacio, eighteen miles northwest of Las Vegas, was first called Tecoloteños or "natives of Tecolote." T. M. Pearce, ed., *New Mexico Place Names*, pp. 163-164.

19. Conflicts were usually over the use of common resources. El Cerrito's single faction gained its ascendancy by defeating another in a feud that grew out of encroachment on "traditional" grazing areas on the common land. The twelve-mile *acequia madre* between El Llano and Bado de Juan Pais, an example of intervillage cooperation, also created conflicts at times when a village thought that it was not receiving its fair share of water. This tendency toward conflict was also reflected in the chapters of Las Gorras Blancas, who fought each other on occasion in disagreements over which fences to cut. See further discussion of the themes of conflict and cooperaffon later in Chapter 8.

20. Interview with H. H. Mondragón, La Loma, February 18, 1972. Don Mondragón used the phrase that the people "wanted only to live" repeatedly. He went to great pains to explain why the Antonchico Grant had been reduced to one-third its original size, stressing among other things that many people thought that they had "too much land," that leaders of the grant were stealing from the people, and that politicians throughout the territory (and state) had conspired against them. Yet, at the same time that he listed these factors that imply a passivity on the part of most grant residents, he described incident after incident of violent resistance.

21. One such law, passed by the territorial legislature in 1887 and vetoed by Governor Ross, was entitled "An Act Regulating Practices in Cases of Torts . . ." Its purpose was to aid land grant speculators by, in Ross's words, "revolutionizing the rules of evidence." The bill placed the burden of proof on the defendant so that a speculator had only to claim a tract and then sit back, confident that the occupants would have neither the knowledge nor the funds necessary to challenge the claim. Ross's veto concluded that "this Bill is a cunningly devised scheme of robbery and directed mainly to the eviction of the occupants of this class of land grants for the benefit of doubtful claimants." Ross, "Special Message," February 28, 1887, *Terr. of N.M.*, Reel 8.

22. It is arguable that collusion to defraud was the norm rather than the exception in New Mexico during the territorial years. A striking example of the habits of federal officials is the case of Pueblo Indian

Agent Pedro Sánchez and Santa Fe Land Registrar Max Frost. The two obtained nineteen fraudulent homestead entries near Sweetwater in Colfax County, patented in Sánchez's name. As one observer commented: "It must have taken more hands and heads than one to have so thoroughly and handsomely bunched these Homesteads, and to have put them in such solid shape!" Special Agent Paris Folsum to Commissioner of Indian Affairs J. D. C. Atkins, May 18,1885, Int.Dept.,*Appt. Papers*, Reel 10. Westphall, The *Public Domain in New Mexico*, is the basic study of land policy and problems in New Mexico Territory.

23. This was true throughout the territory. Many powerful New Mexican families, like the Lunas and the Oteros of the Rio Abajo, did not attain their eminence until the Anglos provided markets and business opportuniffes. See Espinosa, Chaves, and Ward, *Rio Abajo*. In San Miguel County, almost all the *ricos*—Romero, López, Manzanares—fenced acreage on the grants. Even future advocates of the people like Félix Martínez were guilty of fencing and were visited by the White Caps. See clipping of dispatch to the Chicago *Inter-Ocean*, n.d., *Terr. of N.M.*, Reel 8.

24. *Eleventh Census of the United States.*

25. Governor Prince to Secretary of the Interior John W. Noble, August,1890, Prince Papers.

26. O. D. Barrett, "Report to General Butler," July 26, 1890, *Terr. of N.M.*, Reel 8.

27. Barrett to Butler, July 21, 1890, *Terr. of N.M.*, Reel 8.

28. James O'Brien to Governor Prince, July 30, 1890, Prince Papers.

29. Benjamin H. Reed, *Illustrated History of New Mexico*, pp. 760-761, 767.

30. Miguel Salazar to Governor Prince, July 23, 1890, Prince Papers.

31. Numbers involved in fence cutting incidents ranged from one to more than two hundred. Very few villages in San Miguel County exceeded four hundred in total population (or one hundred total votes cast in any election). Newspaper accounts and letters frequently describe seeing the White Caps ride, and all accounts emphasize two points: the large number of participants and the fact that they came from several villages. One interviewee described witnessing the White Caps ride by his house when he was a boy of fourteen. The column passed two-by-two, and he claimed that while men were still passing his house, the leaders had reached the Pecos River, a distance of not less than three-quarters of a mile. Even allowing for memory's blurring by time, that is an impressive number of men. Other interviewees recounted similar descriptions. Interviews with Don Eduardo Montaño, Don and Doña Antonio Ruiz, Antonchico, February 18, 1972; and Don Francisco Sena, Las Vegas, February 11, 1972.

32. Don Sena described the use of homemade whistles as signaling devices, and others agreed. Don Román Ortega of Antonchico also stated that whistles were used to scare informers: hearing a whistle blow in the darkness outside his house was usually enough to still an informer's tongue; if not, bullets would follow. Interview with Don Román Ortega, February 18, 1972.

33. Ogden et al. to Powderly, August 8,1890, Prince Papers. They date Herrera's commission in 1888 and call it a renewal. Herrera responded to allegations like the above in a letter printed in the *Optic* on April 9, 1890. He admitted that he had left Las Vegas in 1866, but would say no more about the matter as he didn't want to hurt the reputation of an innocent lady. He also denied any connection with the White Caps, although he did acknowledge his connection with the Knights and his support of community rights on the Las Vegas Grant. Robert W. Larson has interviewed several of Herrera's descendants and while they could offer little precise information about the White Cap agitation, they reaffirmed these general assertions. See Larson, "The White Caps of New Mexico."

34. See below, Chapter 9.

35. Interviews with Don H. H. Mondragón, Don Miguel Gonzales, Don George Jarramillo, Don Manual Lucero, and Doña Pedro Lucero, Antonchico Grant, February 15 and 18, 1972. This close correlation between the Knights and the White Caps probably did not hold true to the same extent in other parts of the county, especially in Las Vegas.

36. For a history of the Knights of Labor, see Ware, *The Labor Movement in the United States*; Powderly, *The Path I Trod*; and Weibe, *Search for Order*.

37. Larson, "The White Caps of New Mexico," argues that the "organization of the White Caps was due to the initiative of one man, Juan José Herrera" (p. 175) and concludes: "He acted as a vital link, having apparently been exposed to the rising discontent of Anglo working class people while living away from New Mexico and introducing many of their tactics for bringing about change upon his return" (p. 185). While I agree with Larson that Herrera "acted as a vital link" I disagree with his argument that linkage was between *los pobres* and Anglo labor tactics. With the possible exception of the platform and the wage demands, the tactics were the same as those used by *mexicanos* both before and after the White Cap disturbances, both in New Mexico and elsewhere in the Southwest. Herrera was a "vital link" because he used the Knights to link disaffected communities in common action against a common enemy using well-understood, time-honored tactics. Herrera provided coordination, not innovation, and the distinction is important. For to see Herrera as an innovator is to imply that *mexicanos* were passive and unable to defend themselves, a characterization that runs counter to my understanding of *mexicano* history in the nineteenth century.

38. See Lamar, *Far Southwest*, p. 84.

39. The stipulation about defense in the San Miguel Grant decree indicates the awareness of the problem. The first settlers in the Las Vegas area received a grant in 1823, but Indian attacks drove them from their holdings. See "The Las Vegas Grant," BLM, Reel 15; and Pearce, ed., *New Mexico Place Names*, pp. 12-13 and 85-86. See also Perrigo, *The American Southwest*, pp.152-153 and 231-234.

40. Leonard, *Role of the Land Grant*, pp. 134-135. Don Mondragón also spoke of family feuds that persist into the present.

41. Recounted to me by Don Miguel Gonzales, grandson of the El Llano *mayordomo* and himself the *mayordomo* of the same portion of the *acequia*, now called La Loma.

42. F. LeDuc to Governor Prince, July 22, 1890, Prince Papers.

43. This seems likely because of the variation between membership of the Knights and of Las Gorras Blancas. Charles Siringo, a Pinkerton detective employed by the territory to investigate the Ancheta shooting in 1891 (see below, Chapter 9), thought that the White Caps were involved and joined the Knights to make contact. He reported that although he had gained the confidence of some White Caps, particularly Nicanor Herrera, through the Knights, the two organizations were not identical (Siringo to Governor Prince, April 3,1891, Prince Papers). There was a very close overlap in membership in Siringo's analysis, and his reports also indicate the ethnic identification of the New Mexican Knights: "They are very cautious about taking in new American members" (Siringo to Mr. B. [Bartlett], n.d., Prince Papers)

44. A hypothesis proposed by Tony Marquez of Las Vegas and given further credence by additional interviews. For example, the leader of Las Gorras Blancas at El Llano was Manuel Gonzales, the *mayordomo* of the *acequia* while the leader in Antonchico, two miles up river, was Nicolás Ortega, remembered as a bad, mean man. The El Llano and Antonchico White Caps disagreed as to whether to cut the fence of Candelario Rael, which stood between the two communities, and faced each other with leveled rifles. Interviews with the grandsons of the two leaders, Miguel Gonzales and Román Ortega,

Las Gorras Blancas

February 18, 1872. The latter said that his grandfather won and that the fence was not cut. But Don Eduardo Martínez wrote Governor Prince that Don Rael's fence had been cut. Don Eduardo Martínez to Governor Prince July 9, 1890, Prince Papers.

In March, 1890, copies of this document were found posted on various buildings in Las Vegas, New Mexico and signalled the beginning of Las Gorras Blancas determination to end land grabbing, water and resource monopoly and injustice. In a bold attempt to stop the process of Americanization in New Mexico, the group provided an outlet for disgruntled New Mexicans to combine their energies to protect their traditional way of life.

Nuestra Plataforma
Las Gorras Blancas

Our purpose is to protect the rights and interests of the people in general and especially those of the helpless classes.

We want the Las Vegas Grant settled to the benefit of all concerned, and this we hold is the entire community within the Grant.

We want no 'land grabbers' or obstructionists of any sort to interfere. We will watch them.

We are not down on lawyers as a class, but the usual knavery and unfair treatment of the people must be stopped.

Our judiciary hereafter must understand that we will sustain it only when "Justice' is its watchword

We are down on race issue, and will watch race agitators.

We favor irrigation enterprises, but will fight any scheme that intends to monopolize the supply of water sources to the detriment of residents living on lands watered by the same streams.

The people are suffering from the effects of partisan 'bossism' and these bosses had better quietly hold their peace. The people have been persecuted and hauled about in every which way to satisfy their caprices.

We must have a free ballot and fair court and the will of the Majority shall be respected.

We have no grudge against any person in particular, but we are the enemies of bulldozers and tyrants.

If the old system should continue, death would be a relief to our suffering. And our rights are the least we can pledge.

If the fact that we are law-abiding citizens is questioned, come out to our houses and see the hunger and desolation we are suffering; and 'this' is the result of the deceitful and corrupt methods of 'bossism.'

II
Since 1900

Photo courtesy of Ralph Sánchez, Jr.

Historians Richard Griswold del Castillo, Alberto Camarillo and David Montejano, among others, have uncovered patterns of downward mobility and stagnation for Chicanos during the 19th century. In this study, Douglas Monroy reveals strikingly similar patterns for Mexican immigrants and Chicanos in the early 20th century. He also uncovers patterns of occupational stratification and employment vulnerability inherent in low-wage, labor-intensive industries in southern California during the first decades of the 20th century. In these settings the traditional Mexican family met with new challenges which undermined parental authority and caused generational conflicts.

An Essay on Understanding the Work Experience of Mexicans in Southern California, 1900-1939

Douglas Monroy

Recently Chicano historians have statistically validated what many Mexican workers in Southern California, indeed in all the barrios and colonias of the United States, knew all along: Mexican workers suffered entrapment in dead-end, low paying jobs, under harsh working conditions. The concept of a segmented, stratified, or dual labor market system has helped to illuminate and understand how and why the Mexican work experience became structured in this fashion. A labor force which is segmented into a primary high wage sector and a secondary low wage sector provides the employer class with very real benefits. Certainly, lower wages mean higher profits. The competitive and service sectors of the economy, where profits are much lower than in the industrial, usually monopolized sector, desire low wage employees. Furthermore, by maintaining a divided workforce, employers gain a measure of assurance that workers as a group will not unite against them and threaten their profits or even their class privilege and position. Generally, employers have developed and exacerbated already existing racial and sexual divisions to maintain this profitable labor market. Notable exceptions were the Industrial Workers of the World (IWW) and the Congress of Industrial Organizations (CIO) which successfully united ethnically and racially diverse workers. The use of racially identifiable strike breakers and the encouragement of racist ideologies have typically produced for employers a divided and thereby tractable workforce.[1] Increasingly we are seeing how this situation prevailed among Mexican and Anglo workers in Southern California. We must now proceed to understand the meaning of this work situation for the lives of Mexicans in the United States.

Beyond 1848

The Mexican's Position on the Social Ladder

Between the Anglo conquest of California and 1900, Mexicans in Los Angeles enjoyed little social mobility. Richard Griswold del Castillo has effectively demonstrated how Mexican employment in this period in Los Angeles changed for the better for some, for the worse for others. Some were able to enter into skilled occupations as the local economy expanded and diversified. Others, particularly ranchers, farmers, shopkeepers, and merchants suffered decline which "probably cancelled out these gains for La Raza as a whole." Griswold del Castillo concludes that "During the American era, the Mexican American occupational structure was stagnant, with little opportunity for significant upward mobility."[2]

Albert Camarillo has arrived at similar conclusions in his study of Mexicans in Santa Barbara. For the early 1900s, Castillo shows how "Chicanos remained immobilized within the lowest occupational categories . . ." illustrating "the continuity that existed from the time Chicanos were first incorporated into the labor market during the late nineteenth century." Camarillo finds 64.2 percent of Mexicans working in "low blue collar" jobs in 1910, 68.6 percent in 1920, and 68.3 percent in 1930. In addition, Camarillo cites the California labor commissioner who found working "conditions even worse than reported," and how "so many children (were) in the orchards that the schools were all but depopulated."[3] The exigencies of the labor market also circumscribed education, the heralded vehicle for intergenerational mobility in America.

My investigation of the occupational structure of Mexicans in Los Angeles for the 1930s reflects the same striking trend. Based on marriage records of 1936, we find that 77.5 percent of those younger but probably more settled men worked as unskilled or semi-skilled laborers. Skilled occupations accounted for 9.5 percent of those in this sample and 13.7 percent worked in white collar jobs or had small businesses. The women who worked outside the home in the sample did even worse. A mere 1 percent worked in a skilled trade and 85.4 percent worked in unskilled jobs. In comparison, about 38 percent of Anglo men worked in unskilled and semi-skilled occupations at this time in Los Angeles.

These quantitative studies confirmed that Mexican workers toiled in the lowest paying and harshest jobs. Moreover, the American dream proved futile for them; Mexicans generally did not move up the social ladder nor did their children in the pre-World War II era.[4]

The Work Experience of Mexicans

Hierarchy Within the Strata

Clearly, for Mexicans, job prospects were not good in the periods cited above. "Good," of course, is a relative term. Might certain jobs and employment patterns within the lowest strata have appeared significantly better than others to Mexican workers?

Steadiness and regularity of work appear to be the most important considerations differentiating employment for lower strata Mexican workers. Even within the secondary labor market, Mexican occupations differed significantly with respect to steadiness of work.

Agricultural work was most unstable. In the late 1930s, the Los Angeles County agricultural labor market required a maximum of 7,175 workers in June and a minimum of 2,300 workers in December. In fact, unemployed Mexican agricultural workers from all over the state made Los Angeles their winter home. The depression of 1907-08 first draw attention to this phenomena of winter unemployment of Mexicans who made Los Angeles their off-season headquarters from which they migrated in the spring. Paul Taylor even claimed that "In February, probably 80 percent or more of the Mexican population of the state is found there." This pattern repeated itself throughout the country.[5]

Fruit and vegetable canning, an urban agriculture-related occupation, further demonstrates this situation. In 1928, Mexicans comprised 23.5 percent of those employed in Los Angeles canneries. One cannot imagine a more seasonal industry. Using an index of 100 as the average for the whole year, the monthly average for the three middle years of the 1930s showed a range of from 16.2 and 17.9 workers employed in a December and a January week respectively, to 354.1 workers to one August week for California canneries as a whole. (This compares to rubber workers who deviated only 1.5 above or below the index of 100.) Statewide, 60,000 to 70,000 found late summer jobs in California canneries while only 10,000 to 13,000 did so in winter. Average time of employment amounted to a mere ten to eleven weeks per year.[6]

Cannery workers still managed to live on their meager earnings. With wages averaging $26.64 per week for men and $16.55 per week for women, 75 percent of the women and 50 percent of the men earned less than $300 per year. Cannery workers were not transients; they numbered few out-of-state workers, and average residence in California was a full fifteen years.[7]

One would think that many of these workers found winter work in other industries. They did not. The California Unemployment Reserves Commission of 1937 found that only 1 percent of male cannery workers surveyed found employment outside the canneries and only 10 percent worked the entire year in the canneries. It remains to be determined if Mexicans comprised much of this 10 percent. Fully 70.1 percent of the male cannery workers found only casual or no employment at all; 18.9 percent attended school. For women, cannery work may have been only a supplement to the family income as 61 percent did not work outside the canneries or the home and claimed no desire to do so, although 31.6 percent of those who did desire employment could not find any."[8]

We can see from these statewide figures how a seasonal industry such as canning left many Mexican workers underemployed or unemployed during the winter. Perhaps the Mexicans who comprised 23.5 percent of the cannery workers in Los Angeles did not suffer as grievously as those in the rest of the state because Los Angeles, as a hub for other Southern California agricultural counties, could count on a wider range of products to be canned, thereby tempering the effect of seasonal employment.

Aside from canning, other urban occupations in which Mexicans figured prominently also felt the effects of seasonal employment. Textiles, in which Mexican women comprised three-fourths of the women's clothing workers, was one of the more stable in total employment, though it was a volatile, competitive industry prone to a great deal of turnover. For California as a whole, the industry deviated from the average total employment by only 3.5 percent while the average for seasonal deviation for all of California employment was 2.7 percent. Furniture and cabinet work and woodworking had a seasonal pattern of about 10.5 percent deviation from the norm, but all had considerable unemployment. In the building and construction gangs Mexicans suffered a 12.7 percent deviation from the norm.[9] Importantly, all these figures are for each industry as a whole, and since Mexicans occupied the bottom rung of the employment ladder, we can expect them to have been pushed off the ladder first, pushing these figures upward for the seasonal unemployment rate of Mexican workers.

A trend is obvious for all these seasonal occupations employing large numbers of Mexicans: all the off-seasons occurred in the winter months. A cannery worker could not find winter employment on a construction gang or in a dress shop to carry him or her over for the winter months because it was the off-season there too. When added to the many agricultural workers who wintered in Los Angeles with friends or relatives, this substantial number of unemployed urban laborers in seasonal industry must have produced a substantial amount of surplus laborers in addition to those chronically underemployed or unemployed owing to the Depression.

Some Mexican workers did find steady employment in Los Angeles. For example, 10 percent of Teamster's Local No. 1 were Mexicans who had figured significantly in this important local since the early 1930s. Many Los Angeles cement workers were Mexicans who had been in the union local since it originated. Even in the Hollywood Ornamental Plasterers Local organized in 1928, Mexicans comprised 10 percent of the membership even though they worked at the lowliest jobs. In local packinghouses, many Mexican workers held grimy, but steady and skilled jobs and had the reputation of being "local residents of long standing in the industry." Likewise the business agent of the Lumber and Sawmill Workers Local in 1951 recalled that the Mexican workers were "an old local population which has been in the workforce since the thirties."[10] Clearly unionization did much to insure stability. However, other more informal factors, such as family contacts and informal relationships with employers and foremen, also produced stable employment for some Mexican workers in Los Angeles. Urban and industrial work, while often suffering seasonal variation, was certainly far more steady than agricultural work. Undoubtedly the length of time north of the border contributed to the accumulation of those various factors producing stable work. Camarillo suggests that U.S.-born Mexicans fared better on Santa Barbara's street paving crews than Mexican-born, though by no means as well as Anglo workers.[11] These workers had various skill levels, but they all appear to have achieved a significant measure of stability in their work. This achievement, perhaps a form of social mobility, set some Mexican workers off from the rest, at least as much, I would suggest, as skill levels. The skill categorization gives us a picture of an integral and crucial aspect of the structure of the Mexicano workforce. But this view of the variation in the stability of work gives us an impression of a factor as crucial to the Mexican work experience as labor market segmentation.

This factor of work stability probably figured importantly in status and material differences among Mexican workers in Los Angeles. For example, in El Monte most Mexican workers lived in the deplorable Hick's Camp, but some lived "in comfortable homes . . . where the houses and yards are well kept." These homes were "humble dwellings of four and five rooms, but so infinitely better than the rest." Mexican home ownership was not unusual in Los Angeles in the 1930s. According to a special census of 1933, 18.6 percent of Mexican families in Los Angeles lived in homes they owned as opposed to only 4.8 percent and 8.6 percent for Japanese and Chinese families respectively.[12] Also, a 1933 study of ninety-nine Mexican families found a fairly wide divergence in annual income. Of these families, twenty-one had incomes between $500 and $900, thirty-five between $900 and $1,200, twenty-four between $1,200 and $1,500, and seven over $1,800. For those between $500 and $1,500, the average number of gainful workers per family did not vary significantly--1.43 to 1.34 to 1.58. Those families with incomes over $1,800 had an average of 3.28 gainful workers in the family. The average family net income amounted to $1,204 per year.[13] This wide variation in mean income and home ownership cannot be accounted for by the skill differences of the chief earners alone. The fact that some Mexican workers found steady work explains this wide divergence in annual earnings which in turn brought different families different levels of consumption, home ownership, and physical and psychological security.

Beyond 1848

Moving Up from Agricultural to Industrial Labor

Given the greater stability and higher wages, urban industrial work constituted a step up the social ladder for the Mexican worker within the secondary sector of the labor market. Many urban workers began as agricultural workers in Los Angeles proper or in outlying areas such as Palmdale or San Fernando. Usually recent immigrants went first to the fields and then to better and steadier urban jobs. For example, Manuel Hernández came from Mexico in 1926 to the fields around Los Angeles. Then, in 1934, he and his family moved to a small steel mill community in the city and became an industrial laborer. Similarly, Camarillo finds that recent migrants dominated agricultural work in Santa Barbara. However, even by 1950 the break from agricultural labor was not complete. Women and especially older children from the community in which Manuel Hernández lived would often "go to the fruit" to earn extra money as would whole families in times of strikes at the steel mill. "The walnut season" recalled one Mexican from Santa Barbara who migrated from the city to the field for thirty to forty days, "was the only time of the year us poor people could get a little ahead." [14] Moreover, one finds this pattern repeated in other industrial centers. In the Chicago-Gary region of the Midwest, the same advantages of industrial work drew Mexican workers from the sugar beet fields to the city. In Detroit, the higher wages of the factory attracted Mexicans from agricultural as well as from railroad track labor. [15]

Indeed, the evident desire of Mexican workers for industrial work over agricultural, and the fact that length of residence north of the border related to the achievement of urban work, show that Mexican workers perceived an important and clear-cut difference between different jobs within the secondary labor market. While little social mobility up and out of the low-wage sector occurred until unionization and World War II, Mexican workers' wages, comfort, and status improved relatively and diversified as some found steadier, usually urban jobs. Such mobility, of course, was hardly the end-all. Work continued to be alienating, typically much more so than what Anglo workers experienced.

Understanding the meaning of the structure of work certainly does not complete our task here. People exist in society in relation not only to their factory, but in relation to their families, their neighbors, their enemies, and their gods. These things exist in people's private realms, an area largely closed to historians generally concerned with external circumstances. Yet, to fully understand the meaning of the Mexican work experience, we must see how work affected this private realm.

Discussion of the transition from agricultural to urban industrial labor bares most clearly the connection between the family and work. Though many Mexican workers before World War II had mostly known industrial labor, many had worked in agriculture before they came to the city. The transition affected more than merely their work lives. Agricultural and industrial work patterns have different affects on family structure and patterns of familial interaction. In nonindustrial situations, the family, not the individual family members, is the productive unit. The family produces most of what it consumes. In industrial labor or even in capitalist farming, where private property and the introduction of wage labor replaces more communal forms such as these of Mexico and New Mexico, individuals leave the family in order to earn an industrial wage. Now the family depends on the market for its consumption needs. The transition from the family economy to an individualist economy becomes a mechanism for the breaking down of the organizational strength of the family. The individual, not the family, is the productive unit in industrial labor.

In the transition phase between the family and wage economies, family members commonly pool their individual wages. This practice persisted among Mexican families in the 1930s and after. Previous students of the effect of urbanization on Mexican families have noted the likelihood of a small, steady contribution, such as ten dollars, from older children, sometimes with the understanding that it was for room and board.[16] Industrial work patterns initiated this alteration of the traditional family economy and accelerated its more thorough dissolution after World War II.

Significantly, however, the journey north of the border did not automatically mean individualized labor for Mexicans. In a few areas beginning in the early 1920s, employers realized the greater efficiency they could derive from their employees by engaging whole families. Particularly in the Colorado sugar beet fields, employers hired large families at $23 to $25 per acre to work their allotted fields. In an attempt to discourage the use of labor contractors and gang labor, agricultural employers sought to make each family its own contractor and deal directly with them. Employers also found family labor more stable than solo labor and used family labor in the fields of the Arkansas and South Platte Valleys, Colorado, Wyoming, Idaho, Montana, Nebraska, the Dakotas, Iowa, Minnesota, and Michigan.[17] One does not find evidence of this practice of employing whole families rather than individuals in California. Yet, we still see the continuation, if not actual reinforcement, of the family economy among many agricultural laborers in the United States.

Certainly the fact that Mexican families moved together "following the fruit," reinforced a sense of the family as the economic unit even though they were employed as individuals. The well-known practice of families journeying in their old cars, from crop to crop, up and down the state of California, further demonstrates the structural reinforcement for the family that employment patterns gave to Mexican agricultural wage laborers in California and the rest of the Southwest. These aspects of agricultural, field factory labor maintained or even strengthened a sense of the family as the productive unit. Many Mexicans would bring this experience with them to urban employments.

This transition to industrial labor may even have produced a restrengthening of the family as a form of resistance to the imposition of the new labor system. Oscar Lewis noted an actual increase in family cohesiveness among some rural immigrants in Ciudad México. In general, however, the transition from the family economy weakens the family unit. Rudolfo Anaya in his novels, *Bless Me, Última* and *Heart of Aztlán*, portrays both the weakening of the family and efforts to reaffirm it in the face of individual wage labor. In *Bless Me, Última*, the father leaves the family and their New Mexican land each day to work on highway construction, and three of the sons go into the army. The family, rooted in the land, no longer is the productive unit, and this organizational weakening of the family, to the particular dismay of the mother, ultimately partly dissolves the historical Mexican family. At the same time, the mother struggles to maintain their family, and her efforts save the Luna family from total destruction.[18]

Heart of Aztlán, set in Albuquerque in the 1950s, also portrays the influence that the pressures and expectations of city life and work have on the family. A daughter screams to her father: "It's about time I had something to say about the way things are run around here! I work too! I have my own money! So I will come and go as I want, and nobody will rule me!"[19] The family no longer produced as a unit; now it did not function as a unit.

Corridos also demonstrate both the weakening of old family patterns by urban, industrial labor and the consciousness and understanding of the process:

> Van las muchachas casi encueradas
> y a la tienda llaman estor
> llevan las piernas rete chorreadas
> pero con medias de esas chifón.
> Hasta mi vieja me la han cambiado
> vista de seda rete rabón
> anda pintada como piñata
> y va en las noches al dancin jol.[20]

So lamented a father about the changes in his family.

The pattern of work itself probably affected the patterns of familial interaction and bonding. Secondary market workers often do not have steady shifts at their workplace. Those at the bottom of the labor market structure are most often stuck with swing and graveyard shifts. In interviews conducted in 1949, Los Angeles Mexican housewives expressed the difficulty the odd shifts caused in their households. The pot never seemed to be off the stove and it seemed rare that the whole family sat down together for meals.[21] Now, in industrial labor, families not only did not produce as a unit, but they no longer took their physical sustenance together. In this manner an important agent of familial bonding became lost to recent Mexican immigrants.

The most apparent manifestation of this process of familial dissolution in urbanization is generational conflict. The second generation, influenced by the new, urban, individualist culture, find themselves estranged and isolated from their more traditionalist parents but unable to gain access to the larger society. They must then develop their own social units, a spirit of brotherhood of the peer group, to replace that of the family. This carnalismo often takes the destructive form of gangs. We see, therefore, the importance of the imposition of different work patterns on what are usually deemed "community" problems.

These new patterns also meant a first step towards the freeing of women and children from the patriarchy of the traditional family. However, nothing came along to replace the lost cohesion of the family resulting in gangs and familial conflicts. When women went to work outside the home in "la costura," the canneries, or other similar, unskilled occupations, their economic role changed. Now they had a direct, clear indication of how much they contributed to the family financially. This facilitated greater freedom of activity and more assertiveness in the family for Mexicanas. Such a step was at once positive and disorienting.

Certainly the move, geographically and metaphysically, to the city and urban labor wreaked havoc with the traditional Mexican family. Yet, the tradition was not totally destroyed. Families continued to care for and support its aged members, and family members did not view this endeavor in money equivalents. The "conservative norm" of child care and responsibility of older siblings for the younger, remained strong.[22] Changes in these norms do not appear to have occurred as quickly as economic ones. The family still remains the most important aspect of Mexican life. Because the family offers refuge for its individual members as they venture into a hostile outside world, it will probably remain so. Moreover, the greater power achieved by women through the partial weakening of patriarchy also strengthens them individually and will undoubtedly produce long-term positive results in Mexican communities. Mexicana feminism has its own dynamic and historical roots. Nevertheless, the family's corrosion by urbanization and industrial work patterns cannot be denied.

Conclusion

We see how complex a person's work life is, especially one as onerous and burdensome as that experienced by Mexican workers relegated to the bottom strata of the class. To be sure, the structure must be understood. More importantly, if we are to know the meaning of the Mexican experience in the United States, we must understand the perceptions of that structure and its meaning in the inner realm. From the description of the work lives of Mexicans, one imagines that such experiences must have been morally debilitating. Life and labor confused some into passivity and self-blame. Clemente, the father in *Heart of Aztlán*, cursed the city and blamed himself for ever having come to it.[23]

Just as surely this new life and labor angered others into active resistance; witness the tenacity and solidarity with which Mexicans participated in and led union struggles. Many, if not most, were probably motivated by both sentiments of assertiveness and passivity, supporting their more militant union leaders depending on the time and circumstances. Union organization changed people's private lives because it made possible higher wages, steady work, and for many, the opportunity to move into jobs previously reserved for Anglo workers. Such unionization was not achieved without a struggle. Through such activity many Mexican workers confronted and thereby transcended the structure of the labor market, restructuring their world with tangible gains, a new consciousness, and a new dignity.[24]

Notes

1. Mario Barrera, *Race And Class in the Southwest: A Theory of Racial Inequality* (Notre Dame, Indiana: University of Notre Dame Press, 1979), pp. 174-219, illucidates this and other theories of racial inequality.
2. Richard Griswold del Castillo, *The Los Angeles Barrio, 1850-1890: A Social History* (Berkeley and Los Angeles: The University of California Press, 1979), pp. 51-61.
3. Albert Camarillo, *Chicanos in a Changing Society: From Mexican Pueblos to American Barrios in Santa Barbara and Southern California, 1848-1930* (Cambridge, Massachusetts: Harvard University Press, 1979), pp. 166-74.
4. Douglas Monroy, "Mexican Labor in the Political Economic Development of Los Angeles," forthcoming; for the Anglo and Mexican populations see Faith N. Williams and Alice C. Hanson, *Money Disbursements of Wage Earners and Clerical. Workers in Five Cities in the Pacific Region, 1934-1936: Mexican Families in Los Angeles*, United States Bureau of Labor Statistics Bulletins, no. 639, part 2 (Washington, D.C., 1939), p. 88. This study also corroborates my statistics on the Mexican occupational structure. Mario T. García, "Racial

Dualism in the El Paso Labor Market, 1880-1920," *Aztlán: International Journal of Chicano Studies Research* 6, no. 2 (Summer 1975): pp. 197-218, finds that the same patterns prevailed in El Paso. The 3.3 percent of the women who worked as "sales" or "saleslady" are included in the 13.7 percent who worked in the white collar category. Since sales was a fairly lowly occupation in status and wages, it would probably be better to include them in the unskilled category.

5. State of California, Department of Employment, *Agricultural Activities, Crops, and Labor*, compiled by Ellis S. Coman (Sacramento, 1939); Francis Cahn and Valeska Bary, *Welfare Activity of Federal, State, and Local Governments in California* (Berkeley, 1936), p. 203; Paul S. Taylor, "Mexicans North of the Rio Grande," *The Survey*, vol. 67, no. 3 (May 1, 1931), p. 140; and Norman D. Humphrey, "Employment Patterns of Mexicans in Detroit," *Monthly Labor Review*, vol. 61, no. 5 (November, 1945), p. 913.

6. State of California, Unemployment Reserves Commission, James L. Mathews, Chairman, *A Study of Seasonal Employments in California*, (Sacramento, 1939), pp. 46-51.

7. Ibid., pp. 51-53.

8. Ibid., p. 67.

9. Rose Pesotta, *Bread Upon the Waters* (New York: Dodd, Mead & Company, 1945), pp. 19-20; and State of California, Unemployment Reserves Commission, *A Study of Seasonal Unemployment*, pp. 37 and 86.

10. Scott Greer, "The Participation of Ethnic Minorities in the Labor Unions of Los Angeles County" (Ph.D. diss., University of California, Los Angeles, 1952), pp. 62-3, 69-70, 73, 89, 104.

11. Camarillo, *Chicanos in A Changing Society*, pp. 168-9.

12. Home Missions Council, *A Study of Social and Economic Factors Relating to the Spanish-Speaking People in the United States* (n.p., n.d., probably from the late 1920s), p. 23; and U.S. Bureau of the Census, *Fifteenth Census of the United States, 1930: Population, Special Report on Foreign Born White Families by Country of Birth of Head* (Washington, D.C., 1933), p. 212.

13. Williams and Hanson, *Money Disbursements*, p. 88.

14. Greer, "The Participation of Ethnic Minorities in the Labor Unions of Los Angeles County," pp. 77-78; Alice Bessie Cuep, "A Case Study of the Living Conditions of Thirty-Five Mexican Families of Los Angeles with Special Reference to Mexican Children" (M.A. thesis, University of Southern California, 1921), p. 45; Camarillo, *Chicanos in a Changing Society*, p. 166; and Richard G. Thurston, "Urbanization and Sociocultural Change in a Mexican-American Enclave" (Ph.D. diss., University of California, Los Angeles, 1957), pp. 33, 138.

15. Paul S. Taylor, *Mexican Labor in the United States: Chicago and the Calumet Region* (Berkeley: The University of California Press, 1932), p. 98; and Humphrey, "Employment Patterns of Mexicans in Detroit," p. 918.

16. Rena Blanche Peek, "The Religious and Social Attitudes of the Mexican Girls of the Constituency of the All Nations Foundation in Los Angeles" (Master of Theology thesis, University of Southern California, 1929), pp. 22, 31; and Thurston, "Urbanization and Sociocultural Change," p. 111.

17. Paul Taylor, *Mexican Labor in the United States: The South Platte Valley* (Berkeley, 1929), pp. 134-135, 154; Taylor, "Mexicans North of the Rio Grande," pp. 136-137; and Manuel Gamio, *The Life Story of the Mexican Immigrant* (Chicago: University of Chicago Press, 1931), pp. 145-146.

18. Oscar Lewis, "Urbanization Without Breakdown: A Case Study," *The Scientific Monthly*, vol. 75, no. 1 (July 1952), p. 36; and Rudolfo Anaya, *Bless Me, Última* (Berkeley: Tonatiuh, 1972).

19. Rudolfo Anaya, *Heart of Aztlán* (Berkeley: Editorial Justa, 1976), p. 38.

20. "Corrido Enganchado" in Paul Taylor, *Mexican Labor in the United States, Chicago and the Calumet Region*, pp. VI-VII. Translation: "The girls go about almost naked and call la tienda estor (store)/They go around with dirt streaked legs/But with those stockings of Chiffon,/Even my old woman has changed on me/She wears a bobtailed dress of silk/Goes about painted like a piñata/and goes at night to the dancing hall."

21. Thurston, "Urbanization and Sociocultural Change in a Mexican-American Enclave," p. 33.

22. Ibid., pp. 133-134.

23. Anaya, *Heart of Aztlán*, p. 43.

24. Douglas Monroy, "La Costura en Los Angeles, 1933-1939: The ILGWU and the Politics of Domination," in Magdalena Mora and Adelaida del Castillo, eds., *Mexican Women in the United States: Struggles Past and Present* (Los Angeles: Chicano Studies Research Center, Occasional Paper Number 2, 1980), pp. 171-178; Douglas Monroy, "Anarquismo y Comunismo: Mexican Radicalism and the Communist Party in Los Angeles," forthcoming; and Luis Leobardo Arroyo, "Chicano Participation in Organized Labor: The CIO in Los Angeles, 1938-1950. An Extended Research Note, *Aztlán*, vol. 6, no. 2 (Summer 1975), pp. 277-303.

Exploring push and pull factors of the early 20th century, Ricardo Romo describes Mexican immigration patterns in the context of United States immigration generally. As a result of significant increases in Mexican immigration, particularly during the 1920s, labor-intensive industries of the Southwest continued the growth momentum spurred by World War I. Mexican immigration was not only key to agricultural and industrial growth throughout the Southwest but was preferred above other labor sources. Opposition to Mexican immigration, principally from Restrictionist Leagues and organized labor complicated the free flow of Mexicans to the United States.

Responses to Mexican Immigration, 1910-1930
Ricardo Romo

One of the most striking and persistent phenomena of the Southwest in the 20th century has been immigration from México. Although well under way at the turn of the century, this immigration had its first major impetus during the period 1910-1930. In 1900, perhaps 100,000 persons of Mexican descent or birth lived in the United States; by 1930 the figure had reached 1.5 million.[1] The 1910 Mexican Revolution sparked a large exodus of laborers to the Southwest but this "push" factor only coincided with "pull" forces in the United States. Economic development in the Southwest, principally in California, Arizona and Texas, was spurred by greater irrigation, extension of transportation systems and the demands of World War I. Unsettled by social and economic conditions in their homeland, Mexican laborers were attracted by better wages in the United States; unskilled occupations southwestern industries often paid common laborers five to ten times more than similar industries paid in México.

This influx of more than a million Mexican immigrants during 1910-1930 led to a confrontation between southwestern industries which needed casual labor and organized labor which opposed Mexican immigration for economic and racial reasons. During three different years, 1917, 1921 and 1924, Congress curtailed Oriental and European immigration. However, agriculture, transportation, and mining industries successfully lobbied to prevent restriction of Mexican immigration. Throughout this era, Mexican laborers alleviated labor shortages in unskilled and skilled occupations in the Southwest and also in some industries in the Midwest. Immigration from México and the response accorded to these newcomers has not been sufficiently examined. This essay is a small contribution to that task.

Beyond 1848

I

Historians generally recognize three major immigration movements to the United States. The first two immigration waves occurred between the years, 1815-1860 and 1860-1890, and were periods in which Germany, Ireland, and Great Britain contributed most heavily to the population growth of the country.[2] Mexican immigration was significant at the end of the third movement which occurred between 1890 and 1914. Heavy northward migration of Mexican laborers began with the construction of Mexican railroads connecting U.S. border towns with México City and greatly increased with the completion of México's National Railroad to the border in the 1880's. Although the United States Immigration Service kept only partial records of Mexican immigration in the last half of the nineteenth century, the national Census estimated that more than 50,000 Mexicans came to the United States between 1875 and 1900.[3]

Many of the Mexicanos recruited to work on the railroads during the 1880's settled in Los Angeles. Several California historians have estimated that the Mexican population in Los Angeles in 1887 numbered about 12,000, while another 15,000 were estimated to be residing in surrounding areas.[4] Chinese labor gangs built the extension of the Southern Pacific Railroad to Los Angeles, but when construction reached the San Fernando Valley, railroad supervisors recruited "Mexicans and Indians [to] join the work gangs."[5]

The completion of the Transcontinental railroad to Los Angeles gave birth to an economic boom. Between 1880 and 1890, the overall population of Los Angeles grew from 11,000 to more than 50,000 despite the exodus of thousands of residents after an economic recession in 1888. This population explosion created a dramatic change in the city's ethnic composition. According to one observer: "This boom made a permanent change in the city's character. The hybrid Mexican-American pueblo was no more."[6] For the first time, the Mexican population in Los Angeles became a numerical minority.

While Mexican immigration to the United States before 1900 was less than one percent of the total immigration, by 1900 the Mexican population in dozens of southwestern cities had doubled. The Mexican-born population of the United States in 1870, estimated at 42,435, increased to over 100,000 by 1900.[7] Ninety percent of the foreign-born Mexican population lived in three states: Texas, Arizona, and California. In 1900, Texas had the largest Mexican population, nearly 69.0 percent of the total, while 2.0 percent of the Mexican-born population lived in California.[8]

The Mexican population of California grew rapidly over the next thirty years and by 1930 had increased fourfold, giving California 15.2 percent of the total Mexican population in the United States.[9]

After 1900, most Mexicans entered the United States through Texas. Many, after having temporarily resided along the border, then traveled on to Arizona and California. In 1903, a Texas railroad official stated that Mexican immigrants had been recruited in El Paso for several years and railroad employers had substituted them for Italians and Blacks in the Southwest.[10] A few years later, a roadmaster working in Southern California reported that Mexicans had been employed in his division "four or five years and were displacing other laborers." He observed that he preferred them to other available laborers especially the Japanese.[11]

At the turn of the nineteenth century, nativists in California had raised the issue of the "yellow peril," and thereby unwittingly aided the demand for Mexican laborers. The issue was later well summarized by Charles A. Thomson, a San Francisco minister who wrote in 1926 :

> The Mexican is the preferred of all the cheap labor available to the Southwest. On Oriental labor, Chinese and Japanese and Hindu, the verdict has already been cast. California has swung our national jury to an almost unanimous vote.[12]

Racially, Mexican laborers were more acceptable in California than Japanese or Chinese laborers.

During the period 1900-1910, nearly 50,000 immigrants from México officially crossed the international line. Mexican immigration represented 0.6 percent of the total immigration to the United States during this period.[13] However, as one observer noted, they constituted one sixth of the section hands and extra gangs on the railroads in the Western division. Railroad companies took Mexican laborers to work as far north as Illinois and Colorado. Given the seasonal nature of some track work, the companies often paid the expenses of any worker who wished to return to México.[14] Thousands of Mexican laborers during this period traveled back and forth across the border, but an increasing number began to settle during the off-season in cities such as Los Angeles.

During the decade of the Mexican Revolution, 1910-1920, twice as many Mexicans entered the United States than in the previous decade. An analysis made in 1912 by journalist Samuel Bryan emphasized that "immigration from México was due to the expansion of [the transportation] industry, both in México and the United

States.[15] Moises González Navarro, a Mexican historian, wrote that the United States acted as a "safety valve" for México, for in times of political and social unrest thousands fled across the border into the United States.[16] Bryan explained Mexican migration in a similar manner, noting that Mexicans were pulled to the north by the expansion of industries, "drawing men from the farms and from the interior northward." This influx of immigrants, Bryan concluded, coincided with the economic expansion which took place in the southwestern United States.[17] The movement of immigrants to the border was facilitated by the use of the automobile and the railroad networks which connected the interior of México with the Southwest.

The railroad was the most common mode of transportation for the Mexican immigrant after 1910. Passage from central México to the U.S. border during the Revolution cost ten to fifteen dollars per person. In 1911 the average number of passenger miles traveled on Mexican railroads was 346, and by 1920 had increased to an average of 440 miles per passenger.[18] The increase in service and rail travel after the Revolution coincided with the general increase in Mexican immigration to the United States. Most of the immigrants going to California went by way of the Mexican border town of Juárez across from El Paso, Texas. Others also went by way of Nogales, Arizona and in the late 1920's through Calexico, California and Mexicali, Baja California.

Another popular means of transportation was the automobile. Many Mexican immigrants bought automobiles in border cities and then sold them or returned with them to the interior of México where United States automobiles were generally quite popular and always brought a good price. In one year alone, over five hundred Ford automobiles were taken back to México by returning Mexican laborers.[19] Automobile registration in México increased from over half a million in 1911 to over 8 million by 1920 and 17 1/2 million five years later, in 1925.[20] Frequently, immigrants bought automobiles in the United States in order to facilitate the migration of their members of their families, as did Ramón Lizárraga.

Lizárraga, a Mexican musician and an immigrant of the early twentieth century, utilized both the railroad and the automobile to emigrate to the United States. When Lizárraga first came to Los Angeles in 1903, he traveled by train. He returned to México in 1905 after having worked in Tucson and Los Angeles as a musician. In 1926, he again journeyed to Los Angeles by train, this time with enough money earned as a musician in México to enable him to purchase an automobile. He remained in the United States long enough to buy a "model T" Ford and returned shortly thereafter to México for his family. After selling his small farm in México, Mr.

and Mrs. Lizárraga and their children loaded all their personal belongings into the old Ford and headed once again for Los Angeles.[21]

II

Unlike the Lizárraga family, the greatest number of Mexican immigrants streamed through the border station at El Paso, Texas. On occasion, as many as one thousand individuals per day went through the humiliating process of hot baths, medical examination, and literacy tests in El Paso. Vera L. Sturges commented:

> Everything possible seems to be done to keep them clean and sanitary; but when five or six hundred steaming people, men, women, and children, are crowded into the room at one time, sanitation becomes a farce.[22]

Seldom did the Mexican laborers emigrate with more than one or two family members due to the cost of $18 per person for visas and consular fees. In the 1920's, between sixty-five or seventy percent of the Mexican immigrants were males, the majority of them single.[23] Those with large families often brought them across the border surreptitiously. Some immigrants frequently left their families at the border on the Mexican side while the father found suitable and stable employment which would enable him to return for his family. Some immigrants, unable to pay or frustrated by long delays, crossed by night with the aid of a coyote.[24]

Once the immigrants crossed the border, labor agents or enganchadores competed vigorously to recruit them. These agents often made extravagant promises to induce immigrants to sign labor contracts with the companies they represented. One immigrant, now living in Los Angeles, recalled his crossing more than fifty years ago. He reminisced:

> They [the Texas Rangers] helped us cross [the Rio Grande] because they wanted workers from México. The companies perhaps gave them some money for allowing us to cross. The next day we found work [at the mines]. We were standing near the office when we were asked to go to work right away. But they did not pay very much--10 cents per hour, but not 10 cents in money, rather they gave us chits and you took them to the [company] store and bought your groceries.[25]

Enganchadores recruited workers according to instructions given to them by various employers. Helen W. Walker, a social worker in Los Angeles, observed that it was not uncommon for the enganchadores and employment bureaus to use "unscrupulous methods" to recruit Mexican laborers, since "their object [was] to get as many men as possible."[26] The recruiters, Mrs. Walker found, gave "no guarantee of the length of employment" and rapid turnovers were common.[27] Some farmers in Texas instructed their agents not to hire Mexicans who came without their families, while other farmers preferred immigrants coming across to the United States for the first time.

Workers often signed up with one firm in order to receive transportation to more favorable areas of employment. Ramón Terrazas, a resident of Los Angeles since the 1920's, left El Paso along with several hundred fellow Mexican laborers. Upon reaching the Imperial Valley in California, Terrazas jumped from the train as it stopped and proceeded to look for work on his own.[28] In earlier years, some workers transported to an area left their jobs before completing their contracts. One farmer complained that he "lost an entire gang after paying $12.50 fare a head, before they reached the job, to which they had been sent."[29]

III

In 1911 and 1912, nearly eighty percent of all emigrants who left México went to the United States.[30] In those two years Mexican immigration records show that some 135,125 Mexican immigrants, most of them single males, crossed into the United States, and interestingly, almost as many returned to México at the end of the year.[31] In contrast, the United States Census data reported only 40,785 Mexican immigrants during the same period.[32] The Mexican figures are perhaps more reliable because all persons entering México had to register at the border or face charges of illegal entry, a serious crime during the Revolution. Illegal entrants to the United States, on the other hand, were merely deported. It seems obvious that large numbers of Mexicans entering the United States crossed illegally. Jay S. Stowell, a close observer of border affairs, estimated that as many as 75 percent of the Mexican immigrants entered illegally.[33]

As military activities intensified after the assassination of President Francisco Madero, movement across the border took on new and expanded dimensions. High loss of men through battle casualties and desertion plagued Mexican armies. The U.S. Department of Labor reported in 1914 that "approximately 8,000 panic-stricken aliens, mainly of the Mexican race, entered the United States at Eagle Pass, Texas within a few hours" after fleeing from the Federal forces "who were reported about to attack the town of Piedras Negras."[34] Countless hardships were related by immigrants who sought safety on the U.S. side of the border. The Los Angeles *Times* reported one story which was not at all typical of the refugees' experiences:

> Scores of women camp followers [of the civilian refugees] had lost their children in the scramble and were crying piteously in the corral proved for them on the American side. They were without clothing sufficient to protect them from the cold and were drenched from wading through the river. The scene of disorder was almost as bad on the American side as on the Mexican.[35]

During the years that many Mexicans fled to the United States as war refugees, thousands of others left because of social and economic disruptions. Unlike the seasonal laborers recruited by industry and agriculture, these refugees came from the middle and upper classes of México and intended to remain in the United States for a longer period. J. B. Gwin, an officer for the Red Cross, stated:

> The Mexican refugees have surprised all beholders with their healthy conditions, their quiet polite manners and especially with their failure to appear as half-starved, poverty-stricken people from a desolate land . . . They probably represent the best element there is in México today, the farmers and small businessman who have taken no part in the wars.[36]

Most refugees generally preferred to work in communities with Mexican settlements. Many Mexican immigrants stayed in the Southwest to work, rather than travel on to the Midwest, in order to remain close to México where many of them had left relatives. In the Southwest, the immigrant also had the advantage of finding more places where his language was spoken and his culture persisted.

Many of the refugees who entered the United States--sometimes only slightly ahead of the advancing Mexican armies--found themselves confined for days and even weeks in United States Army processing camps. Few labor agents visited these camps to bid for laborers thus giving the refugee camp immigrants limited employment options. In 1914 the Los Angeles *Times* reported that "the Mexican Federal soldiers . . . in the custody of the United States border patrol forces at Presidio, Texas [would] be transferred to Ft. Bliss and [would be] interned there indefinitely."[37] In the article entitled "Making Friends of Invaders," J. B. Gwin wrote: "the camp is growing smaller rapidly. Over fifty have left with their families to go on the `regancia' railroad work. Another forty have gone to the mines of New México.[38] Stories of the "invading hordes" constantly appeared in the Los Angeles *Times* during the years of the Mexican Revolution. Five thousand Mexican refugees crossed the "international Line," the *Times* reported one year, "enticed [by] Three Square Meals." The bill for feeding these refugees, the *Times* continued, would be sent to the Mexican government.[39]

IV

After the opening of the Panama Canal, boosters in California predicted "a large influx of South [sic] European immigrants by the way of the Panama Canal."[40] The boosters had hoped to replace Mexican laborers with Southern European immigrants. However, the outbreak of World War I crushed their hopes. Southwestern employers interested in inexpensive labor continued to send labor agents to México. "Each week five or six trains are run from Laredo," the Los Angeles *Times* stated in 1916, "carrying Mexicans who have been employed by labor agents, and similar shipments are being made from other border points." The demand for these laborers, concluded the *Times* "is so great that they are employed as fast as they cross the Rio Grande. Men, women and children are gathered up and placed upon the trains and shipped to the fields . . . "[41] The efforts of the labor agents in México proved to be very successful. In California, Mexican farm laborers had displaced other ethnic groups within a few years.

In 1917, the Immigration Restriction League pressured Congress to pass an immigration law over the objections of President Woodrow Wilson. The act doubled the head tax to $8.00 "and added chronic alcoholics, vagrants, and `persons of constitutional psychopathic inferiority' to the list of excluded classes."[42] Most significantly, the act required immigrants to pass a literacy test which restrictionists knew would curtail non-English speaking groups. For mining, agriculture and railroad interests, the law did two things: first, it cut off the supply of cheap European labor; second, it all but spelled an end to the surplus supply from México which had been activated after the outbreak of the Mexican Revolution. Railroad and agricultural interests lobbied in Congress for the exemption of Mexican labor from the Immigration Act of 1917 in order to insure once again the availability of cheap labor from México. Their efforts did not go unrewarded.

Acting as special interest groups, railroad, agriculture and mining companies employed several strategies in order to insure the continued availability of Mexican laborers. One plan of action called for frightening the public about food shortages; proponents of this plan argued that the curtailment of Mexican farm laborers would bring about a serious decline in food production. The Los Angeles *Times*, whose owner employed hundreds of Mexicans, sided with those who acknowledged a need for cheap labor. In 1917, the *Times* carried an article which warned of serious consequences due to the "exodus" of Mexicans from Texas: "The exodus has reached a serious phase, particularly as it relates to the growing of crops and attending of live stock interest upon many millions of acres upon the Texas border."[43]

A member of the California Fruit Growers' Exchange claimed in May, 1917, that unless prompt action was taken to mobilize farm labor in California, a serious shortage of workers would hamper the harvest of bumper crops in Southern California."[44] During the same week, the Los Angeles Chamber of Commerce sent a telegram to immigration Commissioner A. Caminetti in Washington requesting that Mexican laborers be excluded from Section 3 of the 1917 Immigration Act which denied admission to aliens who could not read the English language. In the opinion of growers in Los Angeles, the law seriously restricted the necessary supply of agricultural workers from México.[45]

Within six months of the passage of the Immigration Act of 1917, Congress yielded to the pressure exerted by southwestern industries and Congress yielded the decision to include Mexicans in the restrictive clauses. Congress allowed the United States Secretary of Labor to suspend the literacy test, the contract labor clause and head tax of the 1917 law. Interest groups that had argued for suspension actually wanted permission to tap the reserve labor pool available in México; they used as a pretext the existence of a labor shortage created by the outbreak of World War I.

Conditions in the United States during World War I made extensive immigration from México expedient. J. B. Gwin, an officer of the Red Cross, reported that after the Mexican Revolution of 1910, "the next impetus to immigration from México came as a result of the scarcity of laborers in the United States during the World War." Indeed almost twice as many Mexicans came during the period 1915-1919 than in 1911-1914.[46]

During the first World War Mexicans performed a valuable service to the United States and her allies. They manned railroads, helped construct new military bases and picked cotton used in gunpowder and clothing. Mexicans who worked in mines of the Southwest also helped to provide a steady flow of copper, lead, and other minerals needed in the war effort.

Thousands of Mexicans who entered the United States during the war years as temporary laborers remained after their six-month permission had expired. Of these remaining in California after the war, according to historian Robert G. Cleland, most of them settled in the Los Angeles metropolitan area, and by 1925 the former Spanish pueblo had become, next to México City itself, the largest Mexican community in the world.[47]

Those who used the war as a reason to hire Mexican laborers profited handsomely in return. Southwestern employers paid Mexican laborers low wages and provided them with poor housing. Vernon McCombs of the Home Council wrote in 1925:

> On the tuberculosis chart for the city [Los Angeles] there is a black cloud about the Plaza region. The causes are clear: low wages, seasonal employment, high rent, overcrowding, and inadequate nourishment. The average family has five members and the average house has two rooms, for which exorbitant rents are charged. In Los Angeles 28 percent of these Mexicans' homes have no running water 79 percent have no bathrooms, and 68 percent no inside toilets-many cases, six or eight families use a common toilet.[48]

Southwestern employers also violated the conditions of the immigration law under which Mexicans had been temporarily admitted. Mexican laborers were kept under employment longer than the government had sanctioned while the law clearly called for only temporary admission of Mexicans. The United States Secretary of Labor later extended the length of time allowed in the United States for Mexican workers involved in all forms of mining and all government construction work in the states within the southern department of the United States Army.[49] Abuses of these immigration restrictions frequently occurred, but violators generally escaped penalties.

However, the end of the war caused a surplus of Mexican workers in urban areas. Four million men at the rate of over 300,000 a month returned to civilian life after the signing of the Armistice on November 11, 1918.[50] The sudden return of so many men into civilian life put thousands of Mexican laborers out of work. Only in agriculture, transportation, and mining were Mexicans still in demand.

Moreover, successful pressure by interest groups in 1920 resulted in an extension of the "Exclusion Clause" of the 1917 Immigration Act, thus enabling a greater number of Mexican laborers to enter the United States. These workers, interest groups argued, were needed to keep pace with the increase in agricultural production. The cotton crop in California, for example, increased in value from $11,744 in 1909 to $9,237,182 ten years later. Arizona, whose irrigation works had been built by Mexican laborers, achieved even greater increases in cotton production, from an output valued at $730 in 1909 to $20,119,989 in 1919.[51]

Massive migration of southern Blacks to the North forced some southern and southwestern labor recruiters to go south of the border for workers. Midwestern states also began to rely more heavily on mexican labor and competed with southwestern states in recruiting Mexican workers. Aggressive recruitment of Mexicans to the sugar beet fields in Colorado exemplified this competition. In 1918, the United States Department of Labor cooperated with Colorado beet growers in developing a plan for securing Mexican laborers who were considered "admirably adapted to this work" according to a department spokesman.[52] In the fiscal year 1919, farmers recruited more than 10,000 of the 20,000 laborers admitted under the exclusion clause of the 1917 Immigration Act. Another 9,998 of these went to work on railroad maintenance.[53] According to United States officials, 50,852 Mexican immigrants entered this country between 1917-1920, and about half of them found employment with the railroads. While the law required these Mexicans to return to México within six months, nearly half of them remained, and in 1920, nearly 23,000 were still employed in the United States.[54]

V

After 1921, it became virtually impossible to hold back the influx of both legal and undocumented workers or "illegal aliens" from México. Gerald B. Breitigam, a journalist for The New York *Times*, reported in 1920, that since 1913 "more than five hundred thousand [had] entered the Southwest."[55] Another writer estimated that over a period of seven months in 1920, "more than one hundred thousand Mexicans . . . had crossed into the United States, relieving our farm labor shortage."[56]

Mexican immigrants came to the United States because they expected to find a more stable existence there and earn higher wages as well. The "higher wages have been effective stimulus," wrote sociology professor Emory Bogardus.[57] "Three dollars a day, for instance, in 1929, looked large to a Mexican accustomed to receiving the equivalent of fifty cents."[58] Economics professor Constantine Panunzio found that the average family income per year of one hundred non-migratory Mexican wage-earners' families was $1,337.35 for the year 1929-1930 in San Diego,

California.[59] In the mid-twenties, Bogardus, found that although wages varied greatly according to occupation and "to the types of Mexicans employed," the median wage appeared to range between $2.75 and $3.25 a day.[60] Some industries such as railroad and agriculture had high labor turnovers, despite relatively high wages, and working conditions which were far from suitable. The following corrido or ballad sung during the 1920's illustrates the disappointment over working conditions experienced by numerous Mexican laborers in the United States:

The Immigrants
Los Enganchadados -- ("The Hooked Ones")

On the 28th day of February,
That important day
When we left El Paso,
They took us out as contract labor.

We arrived on the first day
And on the second began to work.
With out picks in our hands
We set out tramping.

Some unloaded rails
And others unloaded ties,
And others of my companions
threw out thousands of curses.

Those who knew the work
Went repairing the jack
With sledge hammers and shovels
Throwing earth up the track.

Said Jesús, "El Coyote,"
As if he wanted to weep
"It would be better to be in Juárez
Even if we were without work,"

These verses were composed
by a poor Mexican
To spread the word about
The American system.[61]

Nonetheless, Mexican laborers served as the principal work force in the industrialization and development of agri-business in the Southwest. Without Mexican labor, high profits and large-scale expansion in industries, transportation and agri-business would have been impossible. The Commissioner General of Immigration in the United States understood the role of the Mexican laborers, stating that while "Mexican immigration was not very extensive . . . it played an important part in the labor supply of the Southwest." In fact, the Commissioner added, "much of the movement is made up of those whose coming and going is regulated by the demand for labor in the border states."[62] As has been shown, economic interests were able to successfully modify Immigration Laws in order to meet the demands for a source of cheap labor. However, vociferous and sharp opposition to Mexican immigration developed within the United States and México.

VI

The continuous flow of emigrants across the border during the Mexican Revolution was not always viewed favorably by the Mexican government. The *Christian Science Monitor* reported in 1920, "the Mexican government threatens to prevent by military force the exodus of workmen to the United States and . . . nevertheless hundreds leave daily because of the unsettled conditions of the country."[63] The great loss of life during the Revolution, a drop in the birth rate, and a need for laborers to help rebuild the nation prompted México to restrict emigration. Toward the end of the Revolution, at a time when U.S. laws favored the immigration of Mexicans, President Carranza "notified the [state] governments of Northern México that they must prevent the increasing exodus of laborers to the United States."[64] President Carranza had every reason to be alarmed; one report stated that a recruiter for a sugar-beet company from California had raided Carranza's army and returned to the United States with 1,400 Mexican soldiers.[65]

The Mexican government failed to keep citizens from leaving their villages and farms in México because the government could not provide jobs or political stability; something Mexicans hoped they would find in the United States. Nevertheless,

Mexican officials made various attempts to persuade Mexicans to stay home. Citizens were warned of the difficulties encountered in the United States by Mexicans. The Los Angeles *Times* commented in March of 1920 that the Mexican government had warned "the women not to leave México, stating that they would receive no protection from the American government, that justice would be denied them, and that they would become victims of mob violence if they went to the United States."[66] The *Times* stated that the exodus to the United States was causing alarm. Northern Mexican states sent news that there was "serious danger to numerous industries in Northern México through non-use and to large areas of farm land through lack of cultivation."[67] In March 1920, the Federal government instructed the governors of Northern México "to wage a publicity campaign to stop the emigration."[68] The campaign failed. Immigrants continued to cross into the United States, probably because conditions in México were still such that despite unfavorable publicity in the Mexican press, Mexicans preferred the risks of finding employment and housing in the United States to the hardships in México.

However, Mexicans did indeed encounter hardships in the United States: For example they, like most U.S. citizens, were adversely affected by the economic recession of 1921. But they survived and by the mid 1920's were working in midwestern cities that twenty years before had never seen a Mexican. Thousands of Mexican laborers had entered the industrial labor force in the Midwest by completely by-passing the border areas. Recruitment of Mexicans to the Midwest helped to draw them into urban areas of Illinois, Michigan, Kansas and Indiana. For example, by 1930, the Mexican population of Illinois numbered 28,906; Michigan listed 13,336, while Kansas had 19,150 and Indiana 9,642.[69] Important railroad connections from St. Louis and Kansas City to El Paso partially explained the movement of a large number of Mexicanos to those midwestern cities. In 1930, Kansas City, Missouri, and Kansas City, Kansas, both claimed Mexican communities of more than 5,000.[70] Edwin R. Brown, a Baptist minister from Los Angeles, California, commented on the movement of Mexicanos to the Midwest:

> During the past fifteen years of revolution [in México], no less than "five million Mexicans have come into the United States, and of these, some two million have returned to México. Each year now, from fifty to ninety thousand come north across the border so that today there are over three million Mexicans in the United States, scattered from the border northeast to Chicago and beyond.[71]

As Mexican immigration grew, however, opposition from various elements of U. S. society intensified.

The strongest opposition to unrestricted Mexican immigration came from organized labor. During the years before World War I when Mexican immigration amounted to less than one percent of the total immigration to the United States, organized labor all but ignored the influx of Mexican immigrants. In 1913, for example, the American Federation of Labor's (AFL) annual convention entertained a resolution by a San Diego labor organizer to solicit the membership of Mexican laborers in the area. These workers, the representative said, "are forced to work for wages below standard, thereby lowering the wages for all labor. Labor [in southern California] is mostly performed by workers of Mexican nationality." He urged the International Unions to admit Mexicans into their locals. The delegate also expressed a need for a Spanish speaking organizer to assist him in working with Mexicanos.[72]

In 1917, the AFL adopted the request of several of its delegates, including a Mexicano, C. A. Vargas, to work toward the organization of Mexican miners in the Southwest. Mexican miners already were organized in the Clifton-Morenci-Metcalf area in Arizona, with locals, 80, 84, and 86, representing more than five thousand men. The delegates urged the AFL leadership "to do everything in their power to organize the entire fourteen thousand Mexican miners" in Arizona, and throughout the Southwest.[73] The outbreak of World War I dealt a blow to the efforts of the AFL members supporting the recruitment of Mexicans into their locals. As more Mexicans crossed the border, organized labor changed its position toward Mexican workers. The AFL came to view Mexican workers more as competitors for jobs held by native Anglos than as potential union members.

When World War I broke out, Samuel Gompers, head of the AFL, became concerned over the thousands of Mexican workers being admitted to the United States to replace those workers engaged in combat. Harry W. Fox, a labor delegate to the AFL Annual Convention in 1919, perhaps best expressed Gompers' fear of Mexican immigration. Fox reported to the AFL Executive body that Mexicans in the sugar-beet industry not only held down wages, but "accepted employment in different lines of efforts [non-agricultural], to the detriment of labor standards."[74] The lowering of wages and the displacement of native labor were probably the main objections of the AFL to the admission of Mexican labor during the war. Gompers feared that Mexicans would not be content to remain in farm labor, and would soon enter semiskilled and skilled trades. Fox believed the movement of Mexicans into other employment was "detrimental to the best interest of the country."[75] The AFL

Executive body advised immigration officials to be careful to turn away those without proper permits. There was also a resolution introduced which criticized the use of Mexican laborers in construction crews at Fort Bliss, Texas. The delegate who brought up this resolution warned of the "necessity of employing red-blooded American citizens . . ," for he found the Mexicans "not only un-American in their ways, and non-union, but also aliens, owing their allegiance to another country."[76]

In addition to being seen as those who lower wages and displace native labor, Mexicans were also viewed as strike-breakers. For example, in the steel strike of 1919, steel companies in Chicago and Gary recruited labor from México. While it seems that some unwary Mexican workers became strike-breakers, they were but a small number and do not appear to have hindered union bargaining efforts. According to economist Paul S. Taylor, the number of Mexicans hired from 1916 to 1919 in the Chicago-Gary area was insignificant compared to the number of Southern Blacks.[77] In 1916, there were 18 Mexicans and 558 Blacks employed in the two major steel plants in the Chicago-Gary area. Three years later, during the nationwide steel strike, only 142 Mexicans and 2,699 Blacks worked in the two plants surveyed by Taylor in Gary, Indiana. By 1921, while organized labor pressed for the curtailment of European and Mexican immigrants, only 49 Mexicans and 1,375 Blacks labored in the previously mentioned steel mills.[78] Indeed Mexicans and Blacks suffered from the economic recession of that year, as well as from the successful campaign of organized labor to exclude them from industrial occupations.

Still, Mexican immigrants continued to arrive in large numbers. Their search for better work opportunities took them to states farther and farther away from the border. According to one observer, they were:

> probably recruited from the backway of the beet industry there are now about 8,000 Mexicans employed in various industries in Detroit. There are many in the automobile industry employed as unskilled laborers chiefly in the Ford Rough plant and the Briggs Mfg. Co. [sic] where parts are made for all cars.[79]

Organized labor was not the only sector of society to oppose large-scale Mexican immigration.

During the 1920's dozens of articles critical of the admission policies of the Immigration Service appeared in the United States. The concern voiced by those in opposition to Mexican immigration was typically expressed by *The Survey* of April 10, 1920:

> Amid wild gestures and mutual accusations between México City and Washington, Mexican laborers are leaving their own country for the United States in ever increasing numbers . . . They do not come singly but en masse, not from adjoining districts but often long distances. Whole villages emigrate together.[80]

This increase in Mexican immigration led restrictionists to organize vicious campaigns to end the unrestricted flow of Mexicans to the United States.

In 1920, President Warren Harding signed into law the Johnson Act, the first immigration quota law in U.S. history. This law limited the number of entrants admitted annually to three percent of the number of foreign born of that nationality already in the United States, according to the census of 1910. Mexicans, as well as Canadians and other immigrants from the Western Hemisphere, were protected from the Johnson Act through the efforts of strong special interest groups in the Southwest.

Those individuals favoring open Mexican immigration to the United States argued that it was relatively small compared to that of European nations. Mexicans represented less than 4.0 percent of the total immigration to the United States between 1911 to 1921.[81] Those who favored the exemption of the Mexican from the quota laws contended that Mexicans returned to México much like "homing pigeons." Others argued that the Mexican was less visible in the United States because he was geographically isolated and therefore did not present a racial problem to society. More than 90 percent of the Mexicanos lived in the three states of Texas, Arizona, and California, while the core of the Restrictionist movement was on the East Coast and concerned itself with non-nordic European groups such as italians, Jews, Slavs, and Greeks.

After the passage of the 1924 European Immigration Law, the question of Mexican immigration became more complex. Opponents of Mexican immigration became adamantly concerned about the failure of Congress to include the Mexican on the quota list. As the Restrictionists gathered strength, representatives from agriculture and railroad companies took an active role in defending the free flow of Mexican laborers into this country. A popular argument used by defenders of immigration from México rested on the premise that "White" men would not perform menial work. "White men" refused this work because of the "character of the toil, rather than the scale of wages."[82] Another supporter of Mexican labor added a somewhat contradictory statement when he argued: "We can't get good white labor at our common labor rate, 35 cents an hour."[83] In 1920, the Department of Labor conducted a survey to determine whether or not Mexican labor was in fact displacing

Anglo labor. The department hoped to settle the issue by submitting the following:

> Our investigation proves beyond a reasonable doubt that White men are averse to accepting and refuse to accept (as they have the right to do), employment as unskilled or common laborers . . .[84]

Other strong opponents of Mexican immigration included those who considered Mexicans non-assimilable or undesirable as an ethnic group. A statement by Congressman Albert Johnson in 1929 serves as a good example of this sentiment. Speaking before a group in New York, Congressman Johnson noted that "the time [had] come again when it [was] necessary for Congress to save California for Californians." To this statement, Roy Garis, writing in the *Saturday Evening Post*, added, "and the entire Southwest for Americans."[85] Remsen Crawford, expressed similar views when they said that "in various localities of the Southwest, there [was] almost perfect unanimity on the main point that these people can never be assimilated with white people.[86] A sociologist, W. Garnett argued against the introduction of Mexican laborers into Texas: "Negroes and Mexicans, of course, constitute our main non-assimilable population elements . . ." and would "bring racial complication to a section which heretofore [has] been blessed with freedom from this vexatious problem."[87] Other opponents of Mexican immigration warned the public of possible health problems, racial miscegenation, and displacement of Anglo workers.

Both organized labor and Restriction Leagues considered the exclusion of Mexicans from the quota laws a grave mistake. Kenneth L. Roberts, well known to *Saturday Evening Post* readers for his articles on European Immigration, voiced the concern of the Restriction Leagues. Roberts wrote that since the restriction of European immigrants, "the brown flood of Mexican peon immigration--the immigration of Mexican Indians and Mexican mestizos, or halfbreeds--has risen from year to year."[88] Aware of the congressional hearings regarding the admission of Mexicans into the United States, Roberts visited several cities to investigate the issue. In Los Angeles, Roberts reported, one can:

> see the endless streets crowded with the shacks of illiterate, disease, pauperized Mexicans, taking no interest whatever in the community, living constantly on the ragged edge of starvation, bringing countless numbers of American citizens into the world with the reckless prodigality of rabbits . . .[89]

Responses to Mexican Immigration

By the early 1920's organized labor's opposition to Mexican immigration had become unequivocal. Failing in its bid to have México included in the quota acts of 1921 and 1924, the AFL pursued the matter from another angle. Samuel Gompers, a long time "friend" of México, called upon leaders of the Confederación Regional Obrera Mexicana (CROM), México's largest labor union, to attend a meeting in Washington.[90] Gompers hoped that he could convince México to restrict the emigration of her citizens in a manner similar to the Gentlemen's Agreement of 1905 with Japan. Little came of the negotiations with México, and Mexican labor leaders often used the sessions to express disapproval of the treatment of Mexicanos in the United States. CROM leaders argued that Mexican workers often worked for lower wages than native Anglos because the AFL would not allow Mexicanos into their unions. After the death of Gompers, and the assassination of President Obregón in México, the two groups discontinued efforts to come to an understanding.[91]

VII

Immigrants have always played an important role in United States history, and Mexican immigrants have proven to be no exception. From the early 1880's, railroad companies employed Mexican laborers in construction and maintenance of railroad lines throughout the Southwest. At the turn of the century, the entrance of Mexicanos into the United States increased significantly, and so did the number of industries dependent upon their labor. Beginning in 1910, and continuing to 1930, social and economic dislocations in México drove thousands northward while even stronger economic factors associated with the expanding Southwest lured those emigrants into the United States. Immigration from south of the Rio Grande increased tremendously between 1900-1930 due to U.S. requirements for labor during the war years. This influx, however, did not come without some opposition. Organized labor accused Mexicanos of taking jobs from U.S. citizens. At the same time, other restrictionist organizations labeled Mexicans thriftless and prone to accept charity. Notwithstanding this opposition, Mexican laborers played an important role in the economic development of the Southwest. While debate in Washington D.C. over the restriction of immigration continued throughout the 1920's, perhaps a million Mexican immigrants entered the United States. Eventually not legislation but the economic depression after 1929 finally caused a marked decrease in Mexican immigration. By 1929 Mexicanos, moreover, had firmly established themselves in urban and rural communities throughout the Southwest and Midwest.

Notes

1. U.S. Bureau of the Census, *Fifteenth Census of the United States: 1930. Abstract of the Census* (Washington D.C.: U.S. Government Printing Office, 1932), pg. 130.
2. See for example, Maldwyn Allen Jones, *American Immigration* (Chicago: University of Chicago Press, 1960), Ch. 4 and 7; Robert A. Divine, *American Immigration Policy, 1924-1952* (New Haven: Yale University Press, 1967), Chapters 1-4.
3. U.S. Bureau of the Census, *Fifteenth Census*: 1930, pg. 130.
4. Carey McWilliams, *Southern California Country: An Island on the Land* (Santa Barbara: 1973), pg. 69, originally published in 1946; and Leonard Pitt, *The Decline of the Californios* (Berkeley: University of California Press, 1970) pg. 256.
5. Pitt, pg. 256.
6. WPA Writers Program, *Los Angeles: A Guide to the City and Its Environs* (New York: Hastings House Publishers, Inc., 1941) pg. 45
7. California Governor's Office, "Mexican Fact-Finding Committee," *Mexicans in California* (California State Printing Office, 1930), pg. 29.
8. Ibid., pg. 31.
9. Ibid.
10. Victor S. Clark, *Mexican Labor in the United States* (Washington, D.C.: U.S.Government Printing Office, 1908), pp. 477-478.
11. Ibid., pg. 478.
12. Charles A. Thomson, "The Man from Next Door," *Century Magazine*, Vol. 3 (January, 1926). pg. 279.
13. U.S. Bureau of the Census, *Fifteenth Census of the United States: 1930 Abstract of the Census, Population*, pg. 173.
14. Jeremiah W. Jenks, *The Immigration Problem* (New York: Funk, 1912), pg. 212.
15. Samuel Bryan, "Mexican Immigrants in the United States," *The Survey* (September, 1912), pg. 727.
16. Moises González Navarro, unpublished manuscript, 1973. (México D.F.:), pp. 735 and 738.
17. Samuel Bryan, "Mexican Immigrants," pg. 727.
18. México, Dirección General de Estadística, *Anuario Estadístico 1942* (México D.F., 1942), pp. 1054-1055; and Alfredo B. Cuéllar, *La situación financiera de los ferrocarriles nacionales de México con relación al trabajo* (México D.F.: 1935), pp. 42-45.

19. Manuel Gamio, *Mexican Immigration to the United States* (Chicago: University of Chicago Press, 1930), pg. 225.
20. México, *Anuario Estadistico* 1942, pp. 1081-1083.
21. Interview with Mr. Ramón Lizárraga, San Fernando, California, November, 1972.
22. Vera L. Sturges, "Mexican Immigrants," *The Survey* (July 2, 1921), pg. 470.
23. U.S. Bureau of the Census, *Fifteenth Census*: 1930, pg. 173.
24. Coyote: A person who engages in smuggling undocumented persons.
25. Interview with Mr. Valente S. Ramírez, December, 1972, in East Los Angeles, California.
26. Helen W. Walker, "Mexican Immigrants as Laborers," *Sociology and Social Research*, Vol. 13 (September, 1928), pg. 57.
27. Ibid.
28. Interview with Ramón Terrazas, August 1972.
29. Victor S. Clark, *Mexican Labor*, pg. 472.
30. México, *Censo general de la población*, resumen 1930 (México D.F., 1939), pp. 149-155.
31. Ibid., Table 44, "Entrada y salida, registradas en el país, durante el periodo 1908-1928," pg. 145.
32. U.S. Bureau of Immigration, *Annual Report of the Commissioner-General of Immigration to the Secretary of Labor, 1912-1913* (Washington D.C.: U.S. Government Printing Office, 1913), pp. 40, 54, and 92.
33. Jay S. Stowell, "The Danger of Unrestricted Mexican Immigration," *Current History* (August, 1938), pg. 763.
34. U.S. Bureau of Immigration, *Annual Report of the Commissioner-General of Immigration to the Secretary of Labor, 1914*, pg. 458.
35. Los Angeles *Times*, January 2, 1914.
36. J. B. Gwin, "Making Friends of Invaders," *The Survey*, Vol. 37 (March 3, 1917), pg. 621.
37. Los Angeles *Times*, January 13, 1914.
38. J. B. Gwin, "Making Friends of Invaders," pg. 622.
39. Los Angeles *Times*, January 17, 1914.
40. Henry Alvin Millis, *The Japanese Problem in the United States* (New York: Macmillan Company, 1915), pg. 124.
41. Los Angeles *Times*, September 18, 1916.
42. Maldwyn A. Jones, *American Immigration*, pp. 269-270.

43. Los Angeles *Times*, June 10, 1917.

44. Los Angeles *Times*, May 19, 1917.

45. Los Angeles *Times*, May 30, 1917.

46. J. B. Gwin, "Social Problems of Our Mexican Population," *Proceedings of The National Conference of Social Work: 1926.* pg. 328.

47. Robert Glass Cleland, *California in Our Time* (New York: Alfred A. Knoph, 1947), pp. 251-252.

48. Vernon McCombs, *From Over the Border: A Study of the Mexican in the United States* (New York, 1925), pg. 35.

49. U.S. Bureau of Immigration, *Annual Report of the Commissioner-General of Immigration to the Secretary of Labor, 1918*, pp. 692-693.

50. George Soule, *Prosperity Decade, From War to Depression: 1917-1929* (New York: Holt, Rinehart, & Winston, Inc., 1968), first published in 1947. See Chapter IV, "The Postwar Boom."

51. U.S. Bureau of the Census, *Fifteenth Census of the United States: 1930 Agriculture. Volume II, Part 3* (Washington D.C.: U.S. Government Printing Office, 1932), pg. 516; and U.S. Bureau of the Census, *Fifteenth Census: 1930*, pp. 674-675.

52. U.S. Bureau of Immigration, *Annual Report, 1918*, pg. 692.

53. U.S. Bureau of Immigration, *Annual Report of the Commissioner-General of Immigration, 1920*, pp. 7-8.

54. U.S. Congress, Hearings of the Senate Committee on Immigration, *Restriction of Western Hemisphere Immigration*, on S. 1296, S. 1437, S. 3019. 70th Congress, 1st Session, 1928, pp. 89-91 and 160; and U.S. Bureau of Immigration, *Annual Report*, 1920, pp. 7-8.

55. *The Literary Digest*, (July 17, 1920), pg. 53.

56. Ibid., pg. 39.

57. Emory Bogardus, *The Mexican in the United States* (Los Angeles: University of Southern California Press, 1934), pg. 39.

58. Ibid.

59. Constantine Panunzio, *How Mexicans Earn and Live* (Berkeley: University of Clifornia Press, 1933), pp. 14-15.

60. Emory Borgardus, "The Mexican Immigrant," *Journal of Applied Sociology*, Volume 2 (1926-1927), pg. 473.

61. Manuel Gamio, *Mexican Immigration to the United States* (Chicago: University of Chicago Press, 1930), pg. 84.

62. U.S. Bureau of Immigrant, *Annual Report of the Commissioner-General of*

Immigration, 1918-1919, pg. 61.

63. "Mexican Immigrant," *The Survey* (April 10, 1920), pg. 81.
64. G. Bromley Oxnam, *The Mexican in Los Angeles* (Los Angeles, 1920), pg. 21.
65. John R. Martínez, "Mexican Emigration to the United States, 1910-1930," (Ph.D. dissertation, University of California at Berkeley, 1957). See 1971 reprint, R and E Press (San Francisco, 1971) for quote, pg. 46.
66. Los Angeles *Times*, March 5, 1920.
67. Ibid.
68. John Martínez, pg. 48.
69. U.S. Bureau of the Census, *Fourteenth Census: 1920. Population, II* (Washington D.C.: U.S. Government Printing Office), pg. 731; and U.S. Bureau of the Census, *Fifteenth Census: 1930*, pp. 98-99.
70. U.S. Bureau of the Census, *Fifteenth Census: 1930*, pp. 98-99.
71. Edwin R. Brown, "The Challenge of Mexican Immigration," *The Missionary Review of the World*, Vol. 49, (March, 1926), pg. 192.
72. American Federation of Labor, *Proceedings of the 33rd Annual Convention*, 1913 (herein cited by date), pg. 164
73. AFL, Proceedings, 1917, pg. 264.
74. AFL, Proceedings, 1919, pg. 247
75. AFL, Proceedings, 1919, pg. 249.
76. AFL, Proceedings, 1919, pg. 242
77. Paul S. Taylor, "Some Aspects of Mexican Immigration," *Journal of Political Economy*, vol. 38 (October, 1930), pg. 614.
78. Ibid.
79. John McDowell, *A Study of Social and Economic Factors Relating to Spanish-Speaking People in the United States* (Home Missions Council, n.d.), pg. 15.
80. "Mexican Immigrants," pg. 81
81. Marion T. Bennett, *American Immigration Policies* (Washington: Public Affairs Press, 1963), pp. 61-62.
82. Gerge Marvin, "Monkey Wrenches in Mexican Machinery," *The Independent*, Vol. 120 (April 14, 1928), pg. 352.
83. Paul S. Taylor, *Mexican Labor in the United States*, Vol. VII, University of California Publications in Economics. (Berkeley: University of California Press, 1934), pg. 81; and Paul S. Taylor, "Monkey Wrenches in Mexican Machinery," pg. 352.
84. "Result of Admission of Mexican Laborers," *Monthly Labor Review* (November,

1920), pg. 1097.

85. Roy Garis, "The Mexicanization of American Business," *The Saturday Evening Post* (February 8, 1930), pg. 182.

86. Remsen Crawford, "The Menace of Mexican Immigration," *Current History* (February, 1930), pg. 904.

87. William Edward Garnett, "Immediate and Pressing Race Problems of Texas," *Proceedings of the Southwestern Political and Social Science Association* (Austin, 1925), pg. 35.

88. Kenneth L. Roberts, "Mexican or Ruin," *The Saturday Evening Post* (February 18, 1928), pg. 43.

89. Kenneth L. Roberts, "The Docile Mexican," *The Saturday Evening Post* (March 10, 1928), pg. 43.

90. Harvey A. Levenstein, *Labor Organizations in the United States and México* (Westport, Conn.: Greenwood Publishing Co., Inc., 1971), pg. 117.

91. Harvey A. Levenstein, "The AFL and Mexican Immigration in the 1920's: An Experiment in Labor Diplomacy," *Hispanic American Historical Review* (November, 1968), pg. 212.

During the Great Depression, the United States government sponsored a forced repatriation campaign aimed at Mexicans. Using various rationale, including their alleged illegal status, growing unemployment rates in the United States and the general antipathy toward the Mexican immigrant, the Mexican became the object of a forced return to Mexico. Abraham Hoffman enhances our vision of this era by placing return movements within the context of repatriation generally and restrictionist campaigns directed toward Mexican immigrants.

Closing America's Back Door
Abraham Hoffman

Throughout American history there are many examples of people who moved or were moved from one place to another, either on a voluntary basis or under compulsion. In the eighteenth century the Acadians were forcibly removed from Port Royal by the British; after the American Revolution, Tory sympathizers lost possessions and property. As settlers moved across the North American continent, dozens of Indian tribes lost their lands and were placed on reservations often far removed from the land their ancestors had known. Negroes who experienced the beneficence of the American Colonization Society "returned" to Africa to found the nation of Liberia. Mormons who endured the hostility of their neighbors were finally compelled to seek refuge in a Zion to the West. As part of the post-Civil War movement which brought thousands of people across the continent, displaced veterans left bankrupt farms and plantations in their search for new opportunities.

Events in our recent past show that population movements, involuntary or voluntary in their causation, still occur. The most notorious involuntary movement in recent years was the relocation of the Japanese-American population of the United States during World War II. On the other hand, voluntary movements are much more subtle and less sensational than blatant violations of constitutional rights. An example of the voluntary type of movement is repatriation.

Repatriation means a return to one's homeland--more than a return--a sending back. Repatriations carried out at different times have had different meanings, tailored for the occasion. This is especially true when applied to immigrants from Mexico who returned to their homeland. Writers dealing with Mexican repatriation have sometimes found it necessary to precede the word with "voluntary" or "forced," with quotation marks to distinguish the catalyst.[1]

Mexicans were not the only immigrant ethnic group to undergo repatriation. Although little has been written on the subject, other immigrants volunteered to return to their countries of origin to a degree that can be surprising to anyone who assumes that immigration to the United States was the culmination of a one-way dream. As many as four million immigrants, chiefly Englishmen, Germans, Greeks, Italians, and Poles, indicated their intention of going back to their homelands in the first two decades of the twentieth century. Between 1908 and 1922, 3,416,735 people classified as "aliens whose permanent residence has been in the United States who intend to reside permanently abroad" left the country.[2]

Inducements to Repatriate

Many aspects of the movement of Mexicans southward matched the return of European immigrants in motivation and circumstance, though with additional factors that should be noted. The closeness of the Mexican border, the convenience of railroad connections, and the nomadic nature of employment offered to Mexicans, promoted a two-way traffic across the border, as did the Mexican government's periodic announcements of agrarian reform programs. The chance to return to Mexico with relative ease to demonstrate the skills acquired and the possessions obtained, or to spend or invest the wealth earned, all contributed to a significant flow of Mexicans back to Mexico in the years preceding the depression.

Prominent agriculturists publicized the return of Mexicans to Mexico as part of the "cycle of migration" that occurred in a time of prosperity. Organized labor and opponents of unrestricted immigration, who noted the growth of the immigrant Mexican population in the United States, contested this viewpoint. The challenge of restrictionists affected the cycle of migration for Mexicans entering as well as leaving the United States. The fact that emigration from Mexico was abruptly reduced *before* the failure of the stock market deserves notice. Before the advent of the depression in 1929, attempts had been made to limit the number of Mexicans, particularly those classified as laborers, who were entering the United States.

Restrictionist Debates

Several recent studies have placed the movement for immigration restriction into historical perspective. Although the issue of a quota for Mexican immigration has been studied, it has not been described in any great detail. John Higham's *Strangers in the Land*, a study of American nativism from 1860 to 1925, presented a highly discerning examination of immigration and its restriction, but his book was concerned chiefly with immigration from Europe. Other books that included sections on immigration restriction for Mexico concentrated for the most part on congressional debates.[3] Nevertheless, a rich literature exists beyond 1924 that carries the argument on restriction to new heights (or depths) of polemical conviction, directed towards Mexicans.

Restrictionists included small farmers, progressives, labor unions, eugenicists, and racists, while large-scale growers of sugar beets, cotton, and vegetables, allied with railroads, chambers of commerce, and business associations generally favored unrestricted immigration. Both factions were prolific in their writings and verbose in their speeches, and both factions had politicians in their camps.

Passage of the Quota Act of 1924 had sealed off immigration from sections of Europe and Asia, but immigration from countries in the Western Hemisphere was not included in the law. With Mexico as the primary target, the American Federation of Labor, local governments with aliens on their relief rolls, and small farmers who felt they could not compete with growers who hired cheap Mexican labor, clamored to plug the hole in the law. They found a spokesman for their viewpoint in the House of Representatives, where John C. Box, a Democrat from east Texas, introduced one bill after another in successive sessions seeking to amend the Quota Act, only to see them die repeatedly in committee.

Box's initial effort was aired before the House Committee on Immigration and Naturalization during January and February 1926, but his bill ran into heavy opposition. Typical of the lobbyists who opposed immigration restriction was Samuel Parker Frisselle, a farmer owning five thousand acres of land in California. Frisselle's credentials included membership in the Fresno Chamber of Commerce, the California Development Association, and the California Federated Farm Bureau, all opposed to restriction. Frisselle declared that if the Box bill became law it would mean the end of agricultural development in the West. Crops grown there required large numbers of laborers to harvest them; white men would not or could not do the work, and the only source of labor came from Mexico.

Frisselle denied the existence of any established Mexican population in the San Joaquin Valley, believed the schools sufficient for the Mexican children, and, to questions regarding figures or statistics about the numbers of Mexicans, pleaded ignorance except to repeat that the Mexicans were "a transient population." He insisted, "We must have labor; the Mexican seems to be the only available source of supply, and we appeal to you to help us in the matter, imposing upon California the least possible burden."[4]

Other men took the stand to plead for unrestricted immigrant labor: farmers from

Minnesota, Arizona, Texas, and other states asserted the lack of desire by white men to do farm laborer work, and their dependence upon the Mexican. In addition, by drafting the bill to apply to all countries in the Western Hemisphere, the bill's authors invited even more arguments against its passage. Box's first attempt never got out of committee.

At his earliest opportunity Congressman Box reintroduced the bill, amid speculation on the chances of the bill's being passed, or even heard. The first hearing date was set for 1 February 1928, in the Senate committee, and the first House date was three weeks after that.

Long before this, however, lobbyists favoring unrestricted Mexican immigration laid plans to meet the challenge. On 5 October 1927, some three dozen men met in Los Angeles under the auspices of the Los Angeles Chamber of Commerce. Many members of southwestern business communities, representing agriculture, railroads, and industry, were present. So were Senator Samuel Shortridge and Congressman Joe Crail of California. Unanimous in their opposition to the latest Box bill, the group voted its sentiments into writing: "The agricultural interests through the border and mountain states are a unit opposing this bill, realizing that it will interrupt and embarrass agricultural production throughout these states." The men pledged that their "whole endeavor, therefore, should be to kill it if possible." A conference of businessmen at El Paso held in November strongly upheld this position.

Agitation on both sides developed as the hearing dates neared. George P. Clements, manager of the chamber's department of agriculture, busily drafted publicity, sending mimeographed copies of antirestriction propaganda to congressmen and senators. He stressed the point that since the Mexican was an alien he could be deported, whereas Negroes, Filipinos, and Puerto Ricans, if brought into the Southwest to do agricultural work, would be there to stay.

The proponents of restriction also made their preparations. The *Saturday Evening Post*, a strong partisan of restriction, timed a series of articles by novelist Kenneth L. Roberts to appear in January, February, and March of 1928, during the hearings in Washington. Roberts reviewed not only the recent history of immigration but also the rise of southwestern agriculture, and questioned whether "the economic value in the Southwest's proposal to provide hypothetical profits for some farmers and manufacturers in 1928" was worth "the expense of saddling all future Americans with a dismal and distressing race problem." *The Post* also strongly editorialized on 7 January 1928, that "Every consideration of prudence and sound policy indicates that Mexican immigration must be put under quota restrictions."

Meanwhile in Washington, the Senate opened its Hearings on Restriction of Western Hemisphere Immigration on 1 February 1928, with Congressman Box's counterpart, Senator William J. Harris of Georgia, introducing S. 1437, "A Bill to Subject Certain Immigrants, Born in Countries of the Western Hemisphere, to the Quota under the Immigration Laws," and several related bills.

Lobbyists representing agricultural interests in California, Arizona, Texas, New Mexico, Idaho, Wyoming, and Colorado, in addition to lobbyists from the railroad, cattle, and mining interests, were present. Only the Department of Labor favored the bill; the Departments of State, Agriculture, and Interior all presented spokesmen against it. Chester B. Moore of the Vegetable Growers of Imperial Valley and Ralph H. Taylor, executive secretary of the Agricultural Legislative Committee of California, representing, as Moore later put it, "practically every producing Cooperative Association in California and representing about 175,000 farmers, orchardists, grape growers, milk and poultry producers," led the campaign against restriction.

The opposition to the bills proved more than the restrictionist could handle. Although both Moore and Taylor were interrupted any number of times by House or Senate committee members, their testimony and the statements of the other lobbyists carried the day. In 1928 the bills again did not get out of committee. On 2 April 1928, lobbyist Moore wrote back to the Imperial Valley growers, expressing his jubilation at the victory:

We were informed on our arrival in Washington that our efforts to stop legislation at this session of Congress would prove useless, and we felt the Immigration Committees were going to vote the bills out. Due to the splendid cooperation of the various states and industries interested in opposition to such legislation, we were able to make considerable impression on the Committees.

The controversy continued as proponents and opponents of restricting Mexican immigration delivered speeches, wrote articles, and petitioned their representatives in state and federal government. Before such groups as the Pasadena Women's Civic League and later the Interdenominational Council in Spanish Speaking Work, meeting at Pomona College in November 1928, Clements warned of the dangers inherent in importing the "Porto Rican Negro" for field work, preferring the "man who had no idea of becoming a citizen or a menace," the Mexican. "Should the immigration quota be applied to Mexico?" he asked his audience, and followed it with his emphatic answer: "Most assuredly NOT!"

Each side filled magazines with articles that upheld its position while denouncing the other.[5] In the war of print the restrictionists predominated, as more articles favoring restriction appeared than did those which opposed it. The *Saturday Evening Post*, with its huge circulation totalling over 2.7 million, frequently editorialized against Mexican immigration. "Readers in the Southwest continue to bombard us with requests that we redouble our efforts to make Congress see the imperative necessity for putting Mexican immigration upon a quota basis, or for restricting it sharply by other means," went a typical example in the 22 June 1929 issue.

Some reasons for restrictions were ingenious. One professor at the University of California, S. J. Holmes, wrote in the May 1929 issue of *North American Review* that he believed the present *illegal* migration sufficient to meet American labor needs and reason enough why the legal entries should be restricted. Other writers continued to warn of the dangers of miscegenation, or of an inundation of people who could not be assimilated.[6] Still others repeated economic arguments and debated the relative need for and benefit from Mexican labor.[7] The American Federation of Labor, on the state and national level, annually passed resolutions calling for restriction of Mexican immigration, since Mexican workers so often proceeded from agricultural to nonagricultural occupations, and were sometimes employed as strikebreakers, as had happened during the 1919 steel strike.

The advent of the depression brought a new urgency to both factions. In May 1930, during the second session of the Seventy-first Congress, Box again entered his proposals, this time in two bills. And again, they failed to come to the House floor. A joint resolution issued in the third session proposed a total restriction on *all* immigrants for two years. This resolution passed the House but failed to clear the Senate.[8]

Renewed Enforcement

Further attempts at restriction through legislation were rendered superfluous by an important new development: Mexican laborers were no longer entering the United States. The victory that proponents of restriction finally achieved did not come to them by act of Congress. While restrictionist attempts to secure a quota for Mexico were defeated, a partial success was achieved when consular officers, on orders from the U.S. State Department, began enforcing provisions of the Immigration Act of 1917 which in effect denied entry to most Mexicans who applied for visas. At the same time, Congress passed a law making illegal entry a punishable crime.

President Hoover had endorsed these measures as a way of solving the problem without the passage of restriction legislation that might be insulting to the government of Mexico. These moves indicated that the years of lax enforcement of the immigration laws on the United States' southern border were coming to an end.

The 1917 Immigration Act had excluded illiterates and had required payment of an eight-dollar head tax. Companies and agriculturists had once evaded these requirements by securing exemptions, but by the late 1920s the reception for Mexican immigrants at the border stations had changed considerably. Lax enforcement had allowed thousands of Mexicans to enter illegally. Mexicans who had lacked the eight dollars--and after 1924, eighteen dollars, with the imposition of a ten dollar visa fee-- or for one reason or another had entered without applying through standard procedures, constituted a sizable if unknown quantity of Mexicans in the United States. There were also Mexicans living north of the border whose residence dated back to a time that preceded any regulations on border crossing procedure. "It is difficult, in fact impossible," stated the commissioner general of immigration in 1923, "to measure the illegal influx of Mexicans over the border, but everyone agrees that it is quite large."[9]

Besides the illegal entry of Mexicans, the Bureau of Immigration had to contend with the smuggling of Chinese, Japanese, and European aliens over the Mexican border, and French Canadians over the northern border. At this time of heavy border traffic, "bootlegging" came to refer to the smuggling of aliens as well as liquor.

The Border Patrol

No force existed to combat the widespread illegal entry until 1925, when Congress appropriated a million dollars for the creation of the Border Patrol. Handicapped at first by lack of uniforms, inadequate and unqualified personnel, and a high turnover rate, the Border Patrol, nevertheless, soon developed high standards of efficiency and morale. At first the patrol lacked sufficient officers and equipment; areas which required attention twenty-four hours a day were covered for eight at the most, if at all.

In 1926, with 472 men in the Border Patrol, Commissioner General of Immigration Harry E. Hull requested a force of 660; in 1927, with the force grown to 632 employees, he asked for at least 1,000. By mid-1928 the Border Patrol numbered 781 employees, of whom 700 were patrol inspectors. The service attracted veterans and men with a sense of dedication. By 1930 the Border Patrol had achieved a reputation for integrity and efficiency, with both its personnel and its appropriation almost double their original size.[10]

The work was dangerous. In the seven years following its creation, the Border Patrol captured over one hundred thousand illegal aliens, and over twenty-six hundred smugglers who had attempted to bring the aliens over the border. Of fifteen men killed while serving the Border Patrol, twelve met their deaths along the Mexican Border.[11] Despite the impressive record that was created in so short a time, the Border Patrol probably deterred few aliens from crossing illegally during the period when it lacked funds and personnel. Yet the rapidly expanding operations of the patrol helped serve notice that the United States intended to maintain the integrity of its borders.

Visa Refusals

A second key factor in the administrative restriction of Mexican immigration lay in the instructions issued to United States consular officers. Unlike the lax enforcement of earlier years, consular officers beginning in August 1928 denied visas to most Mexicans desiring entry into the United States. Three basic reasons were used as standards for rejection. The first was illiteracy; the second, a rigid interpretation of the "LPC"--the liable to become a public charge provision of the 1917 Immigration Act. If the consul decided that a visa applicant might become indigent in the United States the visa was refused, even if the applicant possessed funds at the time of his interview with the consul. The third reason for refusal centered on the issue of contract labor and placed the applicant in a dilemma. If he indicated an advance commitment for employment in the United States, his visa could be denied on the grounds that the commitment violated the provision forbidding the entry of contract labor (though following American entry into World War I this rule had often been waived); if he kept such a commitment a secret, his application might be denied anyway, with the consul invoking the LPC provision.

The effect of this new policy on legal entries was striking, as shown by Vice Consul E. F. Drumwright's report submitted to the State Department on 4 September 1931. Between 1923 and 1929 an average of 62,000 Mexicans a year had legally entered the United States. In the year the new visa policy was put into effect, the figure dropped to 40,013; and for the fiscal year ending 30 June 1930, the number had been cut to 11,801. Between 1 July 1930, and 30 June 1931, only 2,457 Mexican immigrants were granted visas, a reduction of 94 percent from the 1929 figure.

More significantly, after March 1930 no visas at all were issued to Mexicans who were common laborers, unless they had resided previously in the United States; and 40 Percent of the visas granted went to Mexicans who did not represent new immigration, but included people who were regularizing an illegal status or had lived in the United States previously as a legally entered alien.

Thus a border patrol increasing in size and efficiency, coupled with a strict policy on visa applications, provided a double deterrence to Mexicans who sought employment in the United States. Furthermore, according to the Act of 4 March 1929, aliens who entered the United States by illegal means subsequent to that date were guilty of a misdemeanor punishable by a year in prison or a fine up to one thousand dollars. Under the same act, the attempted return of a previously deported alien was a felony charge.[12]

As a result of these changes in policy, there was a brief period before the stock market crash during which Mexican labor was in short supply. Mexican migrant workers in California's Imperial Valley conducted a brief but unsuccessful strike for better working conditions and wages in May 1928. Texas, having served for years as a huge labor reservoir for other states to draw upon, in 1929 passed a law which placed a tax on companies which sought to recruit workers from within her boundaries.

The Great Depression

The public debate over a quota for Mexico reached its zenith at the end of the decade. As consular officers asserted that their scrutiny of visa applications had curtailed immigration, the Border Patrol continued to guard the boundaries with horses and automobiles. While Congressman Box and the restrictionist pursued their goal of a quota for Western Hemisphere countries, the stock market began its downward spiral in the autumn of 1929. The United States, accompanied by the rest of the world, entered the Great Depression.

Mexican workers in the United States were among the first to be dismissed from their jobs. During the first year of the depression, thousands of Mexicans were compelled to evaluate the position, achievements, and status they had attained by living and working in the United States. The limited employment opportunities, and the nature of the work offered to Mexicans, have already been noted. Working in the fields, Mexicans performed backbreaking tasks for their American employers. The seasonal nature of agricultural work made earning an adequate income an uncertain possibility. Growers expected Mexicans to answer their calls for labor and to put in a ten-hour day. Even in nonagricultural occupations, Mexicans earned low pay for long hours of work, in the face of the enmity of labor unions and small farmers.

Yet the differential in purchasing power made the sacrifices worthwhile. Tied to Mexico with bonds of birth, blood, and loyalty, many Mexicans spent years in the United States, periodically sending money back to their families and relatives in Mexico. In 1920, almost $9 million in postal money orders were remitted to Mexico; even during the agricultural depression of 1921, $4.5 million were sent. In 1928, before the depression, over $14 million in money orders were mailed back to Mexico. Individual amounts varied; some Mexicans remitted the full amount allowed by the post office, a limit of 207.25 pesos. Others might send as little as half a peso; still others sent nothing. Although some restrictionists claimed these remittances constituted a net loss to the United States, it was also pointed out that American industry and agriculture had benefitted greatly from the labor which the Mexicans performed for their earnings.[13]

Even as the Mexican immigrant had made his way to work in sugar beet fields and steel mills, his presence had provoked argument and hostility. In an age when neither the United States nor Mexico provided any meaningful supervision for laborers recruited by large companies, the Mexican worker might find himself stranded in a town whose mines had closed, or laid off during a slack period in railroad maintenance or harvesting. When this occurred, Anglo Americans were quick to complain about the presence of Mexicans on local relief rolls.

Where the English-speaking community on occasion offered active assistance, a lack of mutual understanding could occur. For example, in the spring of 1921, a period of unemployment in Fort Worth, Texas, the local Red Cross chapter noticed a large number of Mexican men in the bread lines. Anxious to do the right thing, the Red Cross offered beans to the Mexicans; unfortunately, since the Mexicans were mostly young single men, they were unable and unwilling to cook the beans, which had been given to them raw. The "bean line" was discontinued.

Some injustices and unfair practices were too much for a "docile Mexican" to tolerate. Occasionally remedies were available. California's State Commission of Immigration and Housing heard complaints from Mexicans regarding violations of contracts, fraud, interpretation of immigration laws, and wage disputes. The commission's complaint department reported that Mexicans more than any other nationality used its services, possibly because its clients could not afford to hire an attorney.

Mexico Beckons

The thought of returning to the homeland was apparently never far from the minds of most first generation Mexican immigrants. A return home prior to the depression meant short-term residents leaving after a season or two, or Mexicans who had been in the United States for years returning with material possessions and savings.

While the Mexican government endorsed a policy of repatriation from the time of Alvaro Obregón through the 1930s, the problems of Mexican politics prevented any organized program of repatriation from becoming fully implemented. Progress was made, however, in creating irrigation projects and constructing reservoirs. Projects in the states of Coahuila, Aguascalientes, Durango, Hidalgo, Chihuahua, Sonora, and elsewhere promised a revitalization of Mexican agriculture in the late 1920s and early 1930s.

Mexicans living in the United States were frequently invited to take part in the development of farmland in these projects. Announcements of both private and government-owned lands in Mexico being opened for purposes of agricultural development were made known to Mexicans in the United States through their local consulates. Although mention was occasionally made of donating land to destitute Mexicans who returned from the United States, most land offers required capital either for purchase or rental. An investment in seed, tools, and other necessities for farming meant that only Mexicans who were financially prepared to do so could accept the Mexican land offers of the 1920s.

Too often, however, American welfare agencies accepted these offers of land and employment at more than their face value. The idea that Mexicans were leaving the United States to partake of Mexico's offers of land became a rationale in which the departure was a positive act rather than one of possible embarrassment for welfare officials.

The movement of Mexicans southward was greatly accelerated by the depression. The first repatriates to return to Mexico during the winter 1929-1930 were not generally destitute, as can be seen by the many reports of *repatriados* returning with material possessions such as automobiles and furniture. Word of possible location on an agricultural colony established for repatriates by the Mexican government, desire to see family and relatives, the prospect of purchasing land in the homeland with money earned in the United States, and the Mexican government's periodic offer to indigents of free railroad transportation from the border to the interior were all factors in a Mexican immigrant's decision to return to Mexico.

The increased traffic southward was duly noted by the American consuls in the months following the crash and ensuing depression. Consul General William Dawson reported to the State Department in February 1930 that "over five thousand Mexicans, most of them possessed of some means," were gathered around San Antonio, Texas, and "preparing to return." The consul at Ciudad Juárez, W. P. Blocker, learned in August 1930 that the Mexican Migration Service had announced that a special train would deliver two thousand people at a time from the border to the interior of Mexico. This was the second such train in ten months, and it relieved Ciudad Juárez of an excess of population.

A year after the beginning of the depression, the numbers passing through the border stations were still on the increase. Robert Frazer, Dawson's successor as consul general, estimated that almost twenty-seven hundred repatriates had crossed through Nuevo Laredo in the first fifteen days of December 1930. With the start of 1931, consular dispatches continued to describe a torrent of people passing through their border stations, an amalgam of *repatriado* and deportee, with a growing percentage of them penniless and hungry. Ciudad Juárez's municipal government was feeding two hundred people a day. On a single day, 9 January 1931, eight hundred repatriates were counted entering Mexico through the ports of Nogales and Nuevo Laredo, divided among some two hundred automobiles.[14] Mexican border stations were swamped, and where an occasional special train had been sent to Ciudad Juárez or Nogales, the Mexican government now found it necessary to provide transportation on at least a weekly basis.

The American consul at Nuevo Laredo, R. F. Boyce, made a detailed analysis of the repatriates passing through his station and submitted his report to the State Department on 8 January 1931. He found Mexicans returning from a wide area in the United States, with Mexicans from Texas predominating, as might be expected from his location. Few of the repatriates were recording their departure with the American authorities, leading the consul to believe that "at least half and perhaps more of these repatriates were illegally in the United States." It may also have been that the repatriates did not expect to return, but planned on remaining in Mexico longer than six months. The consul observed that many *repatriados* were leaving "after many years residence in the United States. Nothing but an acute unemployment crisis could have forced them out of the United States. Nearly all have been without employment for several months and have come to Mexico because they see no indication of better conditions in the near future."

In fact, conditions were about to worsen considerably for the many thousands of Mexican immigrants who had not yet considered the idea of repatriation. Viewing the large number of aliens in the United States in a time of depression, the United States government commenced an active drive on aliens living illegally in the United States. While the federal government aimed its campaign at aliens in general, Mexican aliens-- those in the country legally as well as those who were deportable--were to find themselves prime targets for the Department of Labor's Bureau of Immigration.

Notes

Unless otherwise noted, material in this chapter is from General Records of the Department of State, Record Group 59, National Archives, Washington, D.C.; and the George P. Clements Papers, bundle 7, box 62, Department of Special Collections, University of California, Los Angeles, California.

1. Norman D. Humphrey, "Mexican Repatriation from Michigan," *Social Service Review* 15 (September 1941): 497; Samuel E. Wood, "California Migrants," *Sociology and Social Research* 24 (January-February 1940): 253; Donald Young, *Research Memorandum on Minority Peoples in the Depression*, pp. 42-43.

2. Saloutos, *They Remember America*, p. vii. U.S., Department of Labor, Bureau of Immigration, *Annual Report of the Commissioner General of Immigration*, 1923, p. 12. A fascinating study of the Back-to-Africa Movement between 1890 and 1910 has been written by Edwin S. Redkey, *Black Exodus: Black Nationalist and Back-to-Africa Movements, 1890-1910* (New Haven, 1969).

3. Maldwyn Allen Jones, *American Immigration*, pp. 290-93; Robert A. Divine, *American Immigration Policy*, 1924-1952, pp. 52-68.

4. U.S., Congress, House, Committee Immigration and Naturalization, *Hearings on Seasonal Agricultural Laborers from Mexico*, 69th Cong., 1st sess., 1925-1926, pp. 4-27, *passim*.

5. The antirestrictionist article by George Marvin, "Monkey Wrenches In Mexican Machinery," *Independent*, 14 April 1928, pp. 350-52, was rebutted by Richard L. Strout, "A Fence for the Rio Grande," *Indepdt.*, 2 June 1928, pp. 518-20. The pro-restriction articles by Kenneth L. Roberts in *Saturday Evening Post* were disputed by Charles C. Teague, president of the California Fruit Grower's Exchange, in "A Statement on Mexican Immigration," *Sat. Eve. Post*, 10 March 1928, pp. 169-70. Carleton Beals, "Mexico and the Harris Bill," *Nation*, 9 July 1930, pp. 51-52,

also opposed a quota for Mexico.

6. C. M. Goethe, "Other Aspects of the Problem," *Current History* 28 (August 1928): 766-68; idem, "Peons Need Not Apply," *World's Work* 59 (November 1930): 47-48; Remsen Crawford, "The Menace of Mexican Immigration," *Cur. Hist.* 31 (February 1930): 902-907; Chester Rowell, "Why Make Mexico an Exception?" *Survey*, 1 May 1931, p. 180.

7. Roy L. Garis, "The Mexicanization of American Business," *Saturday Evening Post*, 8 February 1930, p. 46; idem, "The Mexican Invasion," *ibid.*, 19 April 1930, pp. 43-44; Garet Garrett, "Government by Tumult," *ibid.*, 16 March 1930, pp. 43-44; Garet Garrett, "Government by Tumult," *ibid.*, 16 March 1929, pp. 14-15; Jay S. Stowell, "The Danger of Unrestricted Mexican Immigration," *Current History* 28 (August 1928): 763-66. Some more objectively written articles were McLean, "A Dyke Against Mexicans," *New Republic*, 14 August 1929, pp. 334-37; Gamio, "Migration and Planning," *Survey*, 1 May 1931, p.174; Bogardus, "The Mexican Immigrant and the Quota," *Sociology and Social Research* 12 (March-April 1928): 371-78; Thomson, "What of the Bracero?" *Survey*, 1 June 1925, pp. 290-91; Thomson, "Restriction of Mexican Immigration," *Journal of Applied Sociology* 11 (July-August 1927): 574-78; Glenn E. Hoover, "Our Mexican Immigrants," *Foreign Affairs* 8 (October 1929): 99-107; and Louis Bloch, "Facts about Mexican Immigration Before and Since the Quota Restriction Laws," *American Statistical Association Journal* 24 (March 1929): 50-60. See also the brief article by Galarza, "Without Benefit of Lobby," *Survey*, 1 May 1931, p. 181.

8. U.S., Congress, House, *Congressional Record*, 71st Cong., 3d sess., 1931, 74-74, pt. 7: 6744.

9. Bureau of Immigration, *Annual Report, 1923*, pp. 16-19.

10. *Ibid., 1925*, pp. 14-21; *1926*, pp. 16-18; *ibid., 1927*, pp. 16-19; *ibid., 1930*, pp. 34-44.

11. *Ibid., 1930*, p. 41; *ibid., 1931*, p. 60.

12. U.S., *Statutes at Large*, vol. 45, pt. I, chap 690, pp. 1551-52; editorial in *Nation*, 24 September 1930, pp. 309-10.

13. Gamio, *Quantitative Estimate, and Mexican Immigration to the U.S.*, pp. 30-31.

14. *La Opinión* (Los Angeles), 10 Jan 1931. See also issues of 11, 12, 13, 15, 19, 20, and 21 Jan. 1931.

The Congress of Mexican and Spanish-speaking People, organized in 1939 against the rising tide of discrimination, racial segregation, growing anti-immigrant sentiment and declines in the standard of living for working people, sought a nation-wide Latino-based advocacy organization that would represent the interests of Latinos in the United States. The organization's goals and agenda reveal the array of issues facing Latinos during the Great Depression and one of the responses to the crises facing the Latino community at this time. From this organization would come some of the first generation of Mexican American advocates: Luisa Moreno, Josefina Fierro de Bright, Eduardo Quevedo and others. It also "contributed to the deveopment of civil rights advocacy and philosophy among Mexican Americans. It influenced the direction of many organizations in the two decades following World War II."

Luisa Moreno and the 1939 Congress of Mexican and Spanish Speaking People
Albert Camarillo

By the turn of the century, the status of most Mexicans in the United States had been clearly stamped: they were a disenfranchised, poor working class population that had survived, though with great losses, the fifty year period of Americanization of their societies in the Southwest. Barely visible in the eyes of most Americans, Mexican descendants of the nineteenth century California *ranchos* were at best picturesque elements who provided local color for the state's growing towns and cities. In other areas of the region, Texas for example, most Mexicans lived in the southern sections of the state in a racially bifurcated society - one where often bitter racial attitudes persisted and where confrontational relations between Anglos and Mexicans were institutionalized and aptly represented in the actions of the Texas Rangers. Though longstanding racial attitudes prevented amalgamation of the two peoples, a certain racial co-existence had emerged by the late nineteenth century. This co-existence was shattered during the early twentieth century when hostile Anglo American attitudes towards Mexican's were rekindled as a result of mass immigration from Mexico.[1]

American attitudes were often ambivalent: Mexicans were needed as an important source of labor, but they were creating social and racial problems. When the volume of immigration increased dramatically after World War I, certain sectors of the American public began to Identify a "Mexican problem". Throughout the 1920s the problem was defined in several ways: Mexicans created health problems because of their low standard of living and overcrowded barrios; they were problems to educators because Mexican school children could not speak English, and when tested for IQs, large numbers were deemed "retarded or slow learners"; labor unionists characterized Mexicans as problems because they were "difficult" to organize and would work for wages considered intolerable by white workers; eugenists and immigration restrictionists saw them as potential diluters of American culture and as an unassimilable mass of foreigners.

These varying attitudes and descriptions of the so-called "Mexican problem" of the 1920s coalesced during the Great Depression. The Mexican problem changed its context during the first and worst years of the depression. What had been a multifaceted problem now became a single issue, one which the federal government - in conjunction with local public and private welfare agencies - posed as a question of "how to get the Mexican off relief"? Mexicans were a drain on welfare coffers, they claimed, and they took jobs away from unemployed American citizens. They were here as illegals, and according to many officials, including President Herbert Hoover, Mexicans were a chief source of the economic distress in the Southwest.[2]

The solution for dealing with the Mexican problem during the early 1930s was to deport them by any means necessary. Spearheaded by the Department of Labor, the Immigration Service, and local welfare and law enforcement agencies, a massive repatriation/deportation program aimed at Mexicans was conducted between 1931 and 1934. Many tactics-from devious scare tactics such as newspaper articles warning of immigration sweeps to offering of free one-way train travel to Mexico for those who would leave voluntarily-were employed. The result of these governmental efforts was the involuntary deportation and "forced voluntary" repatriation of nearly half a million Mexican immigrants as well as American citizens from the United States - the largest government initiated exodus in American history. More than anything else, the deportation of hundreds of thousands of Mexicans demonstrated vividly that they were "second class" citizens (for those who were born in the United States), they were an expendable group of foreign workers, and a social problem to be eliminated. Recalling their maltreatment in the U.S., many deported Mexicans could relate to the words repeated time after time in the following *corrido* or folk ballad.

> *Now I go to my country*
> *Where although at times they make war*
> *They will not run us from there.*
> *Goodbye, my good friends, You are all witness*
> *Of the bad payment they give us* [3].

Amid the chaos, despair, and trauma of the mass deportations during the early 1930s, Mexicans in the Southwest were attempting to defend themselves on another front - through labor unions. Mexican and other workers were involved in an unprecedented wave of rural agricultural, mining-related, and urban industrial strikes during the 1930s. Literally hundreds and hundreds of strikes occurred throughout the land. In the rural areas, strikes which paralyzed production in practically every major crop were ushered in by workers who banded together for self-protection. As the real "underdogs" of the American working class, farm workers unionized in part as a reaction to the repressive activities of the growers: significant wage reductions, deportation of workers and labor leaders, company stores which charged exorbitant rates for food and goods for which growers had a virtual monopoly, exploitation through the contract labor system, and armed guards and law enforcement agencies which meted out severe punishment to workers attempting to organize. All of these conditions facing Mexican farm workers led them to join labor unions in numbers never before imagined. It also led to the crushing defeat of their unions, deportation of many leaders, violence and bloodshed in the fields, and the reign of what Carey McWilliams appropriately labeled "farm fascism"[4].

For reasons similar to their counterparts in the rural farming and mining areas, urban Chicano workers joined unions in growing numbers during the 1930s as a way to deal with their worsening economic position. From the pecan shelling sheds of San Antonio to the strike by garment workers in Los Angeles to the fruit and vegetable packing sheds of San Jose-labor conflicts all of which involved predominantly women-Mexican workers unionized against wage cuts, work speed ups, and dictatorial management [5].

Organizations which played an instrumental role in the unionization of Mexican workers during this period were mutual aid associations. These organizations, known as *mutualistas*, not only provided rudimentary mutual assistance to members, but many of these organizations banded together to form the first rank and file Chicano labor organizations. Confederations of Mexican mutual aid associations, for example, provided the springboard for the development of one of the most active farm labor unions in California. Mutualistas and their various confederations later played crucial roles in the formation of the Congress of Mexican and Spanish Speaking People. Community and labor union organizations thus figured prominently in the development of civil rights advocacy for Mexican Americans [6].

The resistance that Mexican trade unionists faced during the 1930s and the deportations which affected the lives of hundreds of thousands of Mexican Americans during the Great Depression were part of an increasingly negative climate for Mexicans. It was an environment characterized by attitudes which reinforced the longstanding racial and class status of Mexicans in American society, one to which Chicanos during the 1930s fell victim. The barriers of racial segregation against Mexicans in the United States, especially in the Southwest where the great majority lived, were built higher and higher during the 1920s and 1930s. As more Mexicans entered the country during the first three decades of the century, more sectors of the dominant society became alarmed over their presence. Abundant evidence exists that documents an increase of institutionalized segregation against Mexicans. Throughout the Southwest, and in other regions where Mexicans were concentrated, segregative practices such as restricting Mexicans to certain sections of movie theaters or not allowing them to use public swimming pools, except on the day before the pool was drained and cleaned, were commonplace. More and more restaurants, barber shops, and other business establishments posted signs indicating "No Mexicans Allowed", "White Trade Only", "Este Baño es Solamente Para Americanos" (This Swimming Pool for Americans Only), and "No Negroes or Mexicans Permitted"[7].

De jure and de facto segregation of Mexican American school children in the public schools also reminded Mexican parents that their children were perceived as inferior to Anglo children and somehow were seen as a threat to the education of white students. One of the earliest successful court cases involving desegregation of minority school children in the nation did not involve blacks in the South, rather it involved Mexican children in Lemon Grove, San Diego County, California in 1931[8]. Mexicans were also commonly subject to residential segregation, as real estate covenants often restricted them and other racial minorities from living in most areas of cities by virtue of covenant clauses which stated "No portion of the herein described property shall ever be sold, conveyed, leased, occupied by, or rented to any person of any Asiatic or African race... nor to any person of the Mexican race[9].

The conditions which created institutional segregation against Mexicans and which led to repression of their labor activities and to mass deportations during the Great Depression made leaders of different Chicano organizations in the Southwest more determined than ever to do something about the increasing violation of their civil rights. Indeed, realization of the deteriorating condition of the status of Mexican Americans led to the first concerted drive to protect the group's civil rights all in an effort to achieve equality for Chicanos in American society. This realization among certain leaders reflected a self consciousness as Mexican Americans rather than Mexicans who eventually would return to Mexico. Among these leaders were persons on the left and extreme left who advocated for radical reform against a capitalistic society that benefitted from the exploitation of Mexicans, blacks, and other working class peoples. Others who assumed an identity as Mexican Americans, however, responded in more conservative directions and advocated assimilation-e.g., exclusive use of English, naturalization, and acquisition of American culture-as the only responsible way to achieve acceptance in American society. These two extremes manifested themselves organizationally in two very different groups-the Communist Party and the League of United Latin American Citizens [10].

Between these two extremes, however, is where most Mexican American leaders channeled their efforts for social reform. By the late 1930s, the Congress of Mexican and Spanish Speaking People galvanized many disparate groups and organizations around the banner of civil rights and equality for Latinos across the nation. Though common cause existed among the two million Spanish speaking people in the United States at the time, the idea to unite them belonged to a single person-Luisa Moreno.

Luisa Moreno and the congress' platform

Moreno's pivotal role in the formation of the Congreso has a unique and intriguing history. A Guatemalan citizen of well-to-do parents, Moreno, as a young woman, worked as a correspondent for a Guatemala City newspaper in Mexico City. She married an aspiring Mexican artist, a person who shared Moreno's career goal as a poet (she published her first book of poetry while in Mexico). Leaving her newspaper position in Mexico, Moreno and her husband decided to emigrate to the United States and headed for New York City to immerse themselves in their creative work. Moreno, now pregnant and unemployed, was unable to support herself as a poet (her husband was also unemployed), but she eventually found work in a garment factory in Spanish Harlem. Abandoned by her husband and left with an infant daughter to support, Moreno's work experience in the sweat shops of New York provided her first exposure to the condition of Latinos in the United States. Taken in by a group of Puerto Rican socialist workers and encouraged to help organize a labor union, Moreno began her long and illustrious labor union career during a strike initiated by the Needle Trades Workers Industrial Union in 1933. She was convinced that life as a labor organizer was the correct path for her, and her success among garment workers in New York attracted the attention of unionists from the American Federation of Labor who asked Moreno to join their efforts in organizing cigar workers in Florida. Enormously successful in organizing Italian and Cuban workers in several cities, but in disagreement with union leaders who would not support the workers' demands in negotiation with cigar factory owners, Moreno was reprimanded and transferred to Philadelphia and New York where she continued to organize cigar workers. Disgruntled with the AFL, she joined colleagues leaving the union in 1936 who formed the Congress of Industrial Organizations. As an organizer with the CIO, Moreno began to read about the plight of Mexican workers in the Southwest and in 1938 became deeply concerned with the CIO-led strike of Mexican pecan shellers in San Antonio directed by the affiliated United Cannery, Packing, and Allied Workers of America (UCAPAWA). She requested assignment to the San Antonio strike and for the next ten years established herself as one of the most effective organizers of Mexican labor in the country [11].

The strike of pecan shellers and the repression of their union efforts in San Antonio opened her eyes to something that sparked the idea of the Congreso. "You could not organize workers in the face of violence and terror", Moreno commented. Protection of the people's civil rights thus became top priority and, consequently, Moreno consulted with the president of UCAPAWA, Donald Henderson, and requested a leave-of-absence to attempt to organize a national, broad-based federation of Spanish speaking organizations - a civil rights group for Mexicans, Puerto Ricans, and Cubans which could serve as a launching pad for trade unionization among Latinos across the nation. With Henderson's support and encouragement, but without financial assistance from the union, Moreno set out to establish a network of local community, union, and other organizations willing to collaborate in a national association for the advancement of the rights of Spanish-speaking people [12].

Using some money she had saved, Moreno traveled throughout the Southwest visiting leaders of organizations and eliciting their support for a congress of Spanish-speaking people. Moreno soon realized the potential that existed to create an important civil rights organization. By early 1939, Moreno had canvassed the Southwest and had renewed her contacts with key leaders from the New York Puerto Rican community and with Cubans in Florida. She had planned the first Congress meeting for Albuquerque, New Mexico and delegates assembled in March. However, the local press was informed by the FBI that "communists and subversives" were plotting to hold a meeting on the University of New Mexico campus. The ensuing red baiting prevented many delegates, especially some local and state politicians who had promised their support, from attending. The Albuquerque meeting was canceled and Moreno immediately began plans for moving the Congress to Los Angeles in April [13].

Moreno, with the help of key California activists Eduardo Quevedo, Sr. and Josephine Fierro de Bright, convened a brilliantly successful first "National Congress of Mexican and Spanish Speaking People". The foundation was thus established for a civil rights crusade which the Congreso and its constituent groups embarked upon with great fervor and great expectations.

The Congreso was the first national organization to represent a broad base of the Spanish-speaking people in the United States, a fact acknowledged by *La Opinion,* one of the most widely read Spanish-language newspapers in the United States.

> *Con el objecto de hacer cristalizar los anhelos de unificacion latinoamericano, para prestar mayor proteccion a los intereses que afectan de origen mexicano y a los mexicanos en general que residen en Estados Unidos, el viernes se inaugurara el primer Congreso Mexicano e Hispano Americano en esta ciudad, con la asistencia de altos funcionarios del Estado de california* [14].

Delegates to the first Congress represented 136 local, state, and national organizations. Though the great majority were representatives from Mexican American community associations in California, Texas, Colorado, New Mexico, and Arizona, over 200,000 Puerto Ricans and other Latinos from New York were represented by a delegate from the Confederación Sociedades Hispanas. Membership in these organizations totaled 874,000. Moreover, the Confederación de Trabajadores from Mexico sent a delegate who represented one million workers south of the border. A diverse mix of ethnic, labor, and progressive organizations joined together during the three day meeting. Mexican mutual aid and cultural groups, state and local labor unions such as the Los Angeles County Workers, and progressive associations such as the Hollywood Anti-Nazi League and Women's Committee of the American League for Peace and Democracy were all actively involved. National organizations such as the CIO's UCAPAWA, International Longshoremen and Warehousemen's Union, and International Union of Mine, Mill and Smelter Workers also sent delegates. The Congress even attracted the support of California Governor Olsen, Governor Jones of Arizona, and, remarkably, that of conservative newspaper editor, Harry Chandler of the Los Angeles *Times*[15].

Most importantly, the first National Congress of Mexican and Spanish Speaking People crafted a platform and agenda that influenced Mexican American politics and civil rights efforts for more than a generation, even though the organization itself was short lived. The Congreso delegates, organized principally along working committee groups, fashioned their objectives from a progressive political orientation and concern for the civil liberties and rights of workers in a democratic state.

The complex and elaborate set of resolutions generated by the Congress delegates may be categorized in the following way: (1) issues involving civil rights and questions of racial and class discrimination; (2) political action and condemnation of legislation adversely affecting Latinos; (3) labor unionization; (4) health, education and welfare; (5) immigration and protection of the foreign born; and (6) international issues of concern to all Latin American people.

Perhaps the strongest statements issued by delegates were raised over the call for a Congressional investigation into the condition of Mexicans in the Southwest.

The conditions under which the Spanish-speaking people in the Southwest live are completely at variance with American standards - discrimination in the right of employment, differentials in wage payments, discrimination in relief, lack of cultural opportunities, lack of civil and political rights in many sections - in brief a condition under which in effect the Spanish-speaking people are denied the right of "liberty and the pursuit of happiness[16].

The Congreso's Committee on Discrimination and Civil Rights declared that the "Spanish-speaking people of the United States well recognize the fact that racial prejudice is caused by false theories of race supremacy based on biological and blood concepts and the low economic status of a racial group" and "the results of this discrimination is manifested daily by the experiences of over two million Spanish-speaking people..." The Committee proposed four courses of action to combat the problem of discrimination: to establish ethnic studies departments and programs in American universities and colleges focusing on the socioeconomic and political history of Spanish-speaking people in the Western Hemisphere; to censure public school textbooks which portray Spanish-speaking people as inferior; to encourage the teaching of Latin American history as an area of study comparable to the history of Europe; to educate the non-Spanish speaking people about the cultural and historical condition of the Spanish speaking in the U.S. so as to provide a better understanding between groups. Lastly, the Committee recommended the creation of a cultural school that would provide an authentic view of the historical and cultural background of Latinos [17].

Strategies to combat undesirable legislation and to improve the political clout of Spanish-speaking people also formed a fundamental part of the Congreso's platform. For example, the Congreso officially opposed all pending legislation regarding deportation of undocumented workers and laws such as the Criminal Syndicalist Act which had been used for years as a means to arrest leaders of labor unions and other alleged radical organizations. The Congress, emphasizing the point that "unification and progressive political action are important factors in forming the basis of effectively combating discrimination", went on record urging the "Mexican and Spanish-speaking people to judge... candidates [on what they] have done and are doing in the fight of the Spanish-American people against economic discrimination and for educational and cultural equality; and to endorse candidates only on the basis of their sincerity and devotion to the fundamental causes of the people, and not on the basis of nationality". The call for voter registration and participation "in all democratic-progressive" organizations was also made[18].

Reflecting the heavy influence of labor unions and the professional affiliation of Luisa Moreno with the CIO, it is not surprising that the Congreso's Committee on "Labor Unity" contributed so importantly to the overall platform of the organization. The delegates involved in this committee declared:

> *WHEREAS: The strongest unity of purpose for all workers is imperative in a world faced with slavery and concentration camps of fascism, and WHEREAS: The division that now exists in the American Labor Movement weakens the position of the workers whether organized or unorganized, and WHEREAS: A unified Labor Movement can best protect the interests of all American, Mexican and Spanish-speaking workers, and WHEREAS: The Trade Union Movement provides the most basic agency through which the Mexican and Spanish-speaking people become organized and receive the necessary education that will promote a unity of thought action and purpose, therefore BE IT RESOLVED: That the First Congress of the Mexican and Spanish-speaking People of the United States recommends to all Spanish-speaking peoples working in industry or agriculture to take immediate steps to affiliate with the union in their special field...*[19]

Delegates called for unity of Latino workers with the AFL and CIO and demanded that these two organizations publish newspapers in Spanish for its Spanish-speaking unionists and that any "important legislation affecting labor... be disseminated to the Spanish-speaking members". The Labor Unity Committee also passed a resolution stating that the first Congress was "opposed to any amendments to the Wagner [National] Labor Relations Act" which they believed was spearheaded in "a concerted drive on the part of reactionary forces which would detract from rather than strengthen the act..."[20]

The concern over the status of Latinos as workers went hand in hand with concern over their general health, education and welfare. Scattered throughout the resolutions drafted by various Congress working committees were statements and resolutions which, for example, called for greater Congressional support of relief administration appropriations which would help in the fight against the poverty "causing untold misery and suffering to millions of people". On the subject of health, the Congress stated that the need existed for better health care to those who could not afford such care and called for a program to meet the needs of its people: the passage of a National Health Bill and support for enabling acts making a National Health Bill applicable to all states by urging state legislators to memorialize Congress to pass the bill; passage of a California State Health Insurance Bill and similar legislation in every state; expansion of existing health care facilities at the local county and municipal levels; demands for the building of WPA or PWA health clinics in needy communities and neighborhoods.

In addition to concerns over the health of Latinos, the Congress also realized health could not be maintained without adequate housing and education. Delegates called, therefore, for passage of federal housing bills and for construction of federal housing projects in areas of greatest need. Congress delegates declared the following:

> "The problems of education among the Mexican people are really vital. Our struggle for more Mexican teachers in schools where there is a high percentage of Mexican children. Fight against segregation and inferior schools for our children. A real fight for "bi-lingual" classes for our children up to the eight [sic] grade so that they may not remain illiterate, and be able to learn both languages. Standardized schools for migratory workers. Adult education by Mexican teachers or Spanish-speaking teachers[21].

"The future of Spanish-speaking youth in the United States is of primary importance to the future betterment of all Spanish-speaking people", declared a committee which urged support of all youth programs initiated during the New Deal.

The first Congress of Mexican and Spanish Speaking People endorsed many resolutions and called for many plans of action, but none were as forcefully articulated as protection of the foreign born against abuses and discrimination. "Discrimination against the foreign born in the United States is on the increase", a committee reported, and "thousands of families face destruction thru the deportation of their breadwinners; many political and religious refugees are held for deportation..." Delegates stated that "numerous measures are pending in the national Congress, state and city bodies to deny jobs and relief to non-citizens for registration and fingerprinting and for wholesale deportation; tens of thousands are barred from citizenship by the high fees, red tape, educational requirements and discrimination". In response to these conditions confronting Mexicans in particular, the Congreso called for actions which would oppose deportation of the foreign born, reduce fees and educational requirements for citizenship, and restore immigration policies for admitting political and religious refugees [22].

Committee representatives were particularly concerned about naturalization and the Mexican immigrant. A committee reported that "about four million people, who entered this country in periods when immigration was encouraged, have been unable to obtain citizenship papers because of the high fees and red tape and are suffering economic discrimination and nearly all of them have been here longer than five years, and the majority came here before the Quota Laws of 1924". Members called for a set of specific recommendations to reform the naturalization statutes: that no person be denied naturalization due to race or political views, that fees be reduced, that the process of application. be shortened, and that all persons over twenty one years of age who have resided in the country more than five years be eligible for citizenship [23].

Though most of the issues which concerned the Congreso were domestic ones affecting Mexican and other Spanish-speaking people in the United States, international issues also were discussed. For example, the delegates condemned international fascism and applauded the efforts of the Lima, Peru conference for taking Roosevelt's Good Neighbor Policy to Central and South America. Another international issue surfaced over the expropriation of the Standard Oil Company holdings by the Mexican government in 1936; delegates pleaded for the United States to show restraint and not to intervene in Mexico, an action some delegates claimed was supported by "reactionary circles in the country"[24].

The Congress of Mexican and Spanish Speaking People, which represented a broad-based, grassroots effort to achieve civil rights for Mexicans, Puerto Ricans, and Cuban Americans, created an ambitious plan of action during its first meeting in Los Angeles in 1939 and in a second conference held later that same year. It was an organization dedicated to equality for Spanish-speaking people and one which was geared for action.

"Delegates to the three-day convention of the Mexican-Spanish American Congress had returned to their homes in the five states of the Southwest United States today", reported *People's World*, "committed to a program which included struggle against discrimination, alliance with progressive movements, and opposition to all attempts to attack American democratic institutions"[25]. Indeed, as the Congreso delegates disbanded, each affiliated organization pledged to return to their respective states and communities to establish a national network of "Comites Pro Congreso" for defense of Spanish-speaking peoples' civil rights. In fact, dozens of comites were created in California, Texas, New Mexico, and Illinois, and perhaps in other states, though no documents are available which cite where all Congreso chapters existed. The California initiative was the most active judging from comments by major participants. The activities of the two most able Congreso leaders in Los Angeles, Eduardo Quevedo, Sr. and Josephine Fierro de Bright, elected to the posts of National President and Executive Secretary respectively, ensured that California Mexican Americans would rally around the Congreso banner. Luisa Moreno left the job of grassroots organization to both Quevedo, and Fierro de Bright because her philosophy of organizing was to help initiate local efforts but to leave the long term work to local leaders [26].

Quevedo and Fierro de Bright at once began a drive to organize California Chicanos up and down the state and were successful in attracting the support of dozens of mutual aid and other community organizations. Other leaders embarked on organizing crusades throughout the Southwest and wherever Latinos were concentrated in large numbers.

By 1942 the Congress had built a network of state and local groups ready to work on the goals elaborated on during subsequent state conventions of the National Congress of Spanish Speaking People, particularly those held in California between December, 1939 and May, 1942. Several of the working committees continued to meet separately from the state conventions, and some, such as the Mexican Youth Committee, organized its own conferences. However, the entrance of the United States into the Second World War negatively affected the activities of the Congreso. Many of its most talented young leaders were inducted into the armed forces-many never returned from overseas. The war effort on the home front, which ushered Mexican women into the industrial labor force for the first time in large numbers, also disrupted the continuity among the Congreso rank and file membership[27].

However, many leaders of the Congreso-particularly those in California-continued to act on the agenda set forth in 1939. Luisa Moreno and Frank Lopez, for example, were Congreso representatives to the Fair Employment Practices Commission in California, advocating for the employment of Spanish-speaking workers in war-related industries[28]. Others directed their efforts toward investigation of civil rights offenses against Latinos, an activity reported in the *Ucapawa News* after California Governor Culbert L. Olsen appointed three Congress leaders to head an inquiry into the shooting and alleged suicide of two southern California Chicano teenagers. "Becoming a recognized force", the CIO union newspaper stated, "the

Spanish Speaking Peoples Congress is taking part in the state investigation of denial and violation of civil rights affecting California's important population of Mexican origin"[29]. Still others-including Josephine Fierro and Eduardo Quevedo-combatted police brutality in the celebrated Sleepy Lagoon case of 1942 and Zoot Suit Riots of 1943. Both also ran for political office, Quevedo as a candidate for California assemblyman from the 40th District in 1942 and later in 1945 as a candidate for the Los Angeles city council, while Fierro ran for a Congressional seat from the 51st district under the Independent Progressive Party ticket in 1951-both were unsuccessful in their bids for political office[30].

Any systematic attempts to achieve the objectives of the Congress were becoming increasingly more difficult as the war years progressed. To make matters worse, during and immediately following the war many Congreso leaders encountered an environment of anti-communism that pervaded California in particular. Consequently, leaders such as Luisa Moreno and Josephine Fierro de Bright and several leaders elsewhere were tagged as communists, red-baited, and were deported or were threatened with deportation as subversive illegal aliens during the late 1940s. In 1944, the Congress of Spanish-Speaking People was placed on a list together with approximately 150 other organizations and groups which were investigated by the California Committee on Un-American Activities and added to the list of alleged communist organizations that were identified on the loyalty oath affidavits for Los Angeles County employees. Later, in 1947, the Congress was labeled by the House Committee on Un-American Activities as a "Communist front" organization[31]. As the "red scare" developed into a national frenzy and without the guidance of its principal leaders, the Congreso became a defunct organization by the late 1940s.

Though the Congress did not exist more than a decade, it contributed tremendously to the development of civil rights advocacy and philosophy among Mexican Americans. It influenced the direction of many organizations in the two decades following World War II. Many leaders of the important post-war organizations in California in particular, such as the Community Service Organization (CSO), the Los Angeles Coordinating Council for Latin American Youth, the Asociación Nacional Mexico-Americano (ANMA was a civil rights organization with strong ties to progressive labor unions and advocated radical agendas for social reform), and the Mexican American Political Association (MAPA) were directed by persons who had been involved earlier in some way with the Congreso. Eduardo Quevedo Sr. continued his long time work among California Mexican Americans and directly applied many of the goals and objectives first articulated by the Congress in organizations such as the CCLAY and MAPA. Bert Corona was among the founding members of MAPA and played an instrumental role in ANMA. Ernesto Galarza was active in many organizations during the 1950s; and 1960s including MAPA, the Southwest Council of the La Raza (later named the National Council of La Raza). Luisa Moreno rose to prominence within the CIO leadership, serving as international vice-president of UCAPAWA and head of the California CIO Council before she resigned her positions in 1947 to defend herself against the criminal charges leveled at her by the federal government (she was imprisoned, stood trial, and deported in 1950 on charges of being a subversive illegal immigrant plotting to over throw the government). Josephine Fierro was an important participant in the Sleepy Lagoon Case and was among a handful of Mexican Americans who played a key role in ending the violence of the Zoot Suit Riots. These and a host of other key leaders of the "G.I. generation" in Texas, Arizona, New Mexico, Colorado, Illinois, and New York were all catalysts in the development of Latino organizations in the post-war era. Their political orientations were deeply affected by efforts during the late 1930s and 1940s to mold the Congress into the first national organization for Latino civil rights[32].

According to Beatrice Griffith, writing in 1948, the Congress was "the largest secular organization that has ever existed for Mexican Americans... It was a federation of organizations with a total membership estimated by some to be about sixty thousand persons in the Southwest". "On the whole", Griffith concluded in her pioneering work on Mexican Americans, "it was a broad people's campaign, backed at times by the Mexican government... [and] quite effective as long as it lasted"[33]. What Griffith did not realize was that the Congreso was an organization ahead of its own time in the advocacy for civil liberties, civil rights, and equality for Latinos in the United States. It was an organization that represented a pivotal turning point in the political adaptation of the Mexican American population and the development of Chicano groups advocating greater equality for Mexican Americans and other Latinos in the United States. And, most importantly, the Congress reflected a historical reality for Mexican and other Latinos in the United States that was significantly different from European immigrants and their offspring-a reality that created a different historical trajectory for Mexican Americans during the twentieth century. It was a reality, on the one hand, of an immigrant group searching for a better life in America and, on the other hand, an experience of a racial minority struggling for equality, opportunity, and justice under the law.

Notes

1. See, for example, the following: Ricardo Romo, "Responses to Mexican Immigration, 1910-1930", *Aztlan,* 6 (Summer 1975), pp. 173-94; Albert Camarillo, *Chicanos in California* (San Francisco: Boyd and Fraser Publishing Company, 1984), pp. 43-45. Studies that effectively describe the status of Mexican Americans in various states in the Southwest during the second half of the nineteenth century include: David J. Weber, *Foreigners in Their Native Land* (Albuquerque: University of New Mexico Press, 1973); Arnoldo De Leon, *The Tejano Community, 1836-1900* (Albuquerque: University of New Mexico Press, 1982) and *They Called Them Greasers: Anglo Attitudes Toward Mexicans in Texas, 1821-1900* (Austin: University of Texas Press, 1983); Griswold del Castillo, *The Los Angeles Barrio;* Garcia, *Desert Immigrant;* Camarillo, *Chicanos in a Changing Society;* Sheridan, *Los Tucsonenses.*
2. George Kiser and David Siberman. "Mexican Repatriation During the Great Depression", in George C. Kiser and Martha W. Kiser, eds., *Mexican Workers in the United States* (Albuquerque: University of New Mexico Press, 1979), pp. 45-56.
3. Quoted in Francisco Balderrama, in *Defense of La Raza - The Los Angeles Mexican Consulate and the Mexican Community, 1929-1936* (Tucson: University of Arizona Press, 1982), p. 28. See also, Abraham Hoffman, *Unwanted Mexican Americans During the Great Depression -Repatriation Pressures, 1929-1939* (Tucson: University of Arizona Press, 1974)
4. Carey McWilliams, *Factories in the Fields* (Boston: Little Brown, and Company, 1944); Cletus Daniel, *Bitter Harvest - A History of California Farmworkers, 1870-1941* (Berkeley and Los Angeles: University of California Press, 1982); Dick Meister and Ann Loftis, A *Long Time Coming - The Struggle to Unionize American Farm Workers* (New York: Macmillan, 1977).
5. Rodolfo Acuña, *Occupied America - A History of Chicanos* (New York: Harper and Row, 1981 second edition), pp. 234-44. See also, Mark Reisler, *By The Sweat of Their Brow: Mexican Immigrant Labor in the United States, 1900-1940* (Westport, Conn.: Greenwood Press, 1976).
6. Jose A. Hernandez, *Mutual Aid For Survival - The Case of Mexican Americans* (Malibar, Florida: Krieger Publishing Company, 1983), pp. 30-44, 75-83.
7. Alonzo S. Perales, *Are We Good Neighbors?* (1948; reprinted by Arno Press, 1974); Carey McWilliams, *North From Mexico* (1948; reprinted by Greenwood Press, 1968), pp. 206-26; Paul S. Taylor, *Mexican Labor in the United States,* especially the

volumes on the Imperial Valley and Dimmit County, Texas; Patricia Morgan, *The Shame of a Nation* (Los Angeles: n.p., 1954).

8. Thomas P. Carter, *Mexican Americans in School - A History of Educational Neglect;* Charles M. Wollenberg, *All Deliberate Speed - Segregation and Exclusion in California Schools, 1855-1975* (Berkeley and Los Angeles: University of California Press, 1976).

9. Vesta Penrod, "Civil Rights Problems of Mexican Americans in Southern California" (M.A. Thesis, Claremont Graduate School, 1948).

10. Mario Barrera, "The Evolution of Chicano Political Goals", *Sage Race Relations Abstracts,* 10:1 (February, 1985), pp. 10-15.

11. Interviews with Luisa Moreno, 1976, 1977, and 1979; interview with Josephine Fierro, 1977; interview with Bert Corona, 1977. For a summary of the pecan sellers' strike in San Antonio, see Acuña, *Occupied America, pp.* 234-36.

12. Ibid.

13. Camarillo, *Chicanos in California, pp.* 61-64. See also, Carlos Larralde, *Mexican American Movements and Leaders* (Los Alamitos, CA: Hwong Publishing Co., 1976), pp. 184-87.

14. April 27, 1939; see also, April 30, 1939.

15. First National Congress, "Digest of Procedings", file M224, Ernesto Galarza Collection, Department of Special Collections, Stanford University (herein cited as "Digest of Proceedings").

16. "Digest of Proceedings".

17. Interviews with Luisa Moreno, Josephine Fierro and Bert Corona.

18. "Digest of Proceedings".

19. *Ibid.*

20. *Ibid.*

21. *Ibid.*

22. *Ibid.*

23. *Ibid.*

25. See also the Los Angeles *Times*, (April 30, 1939).

26. Interviews with Luisa Moreno, Josephine Fierro, and Bert Corona

27. Ernesto Galarza Collection, file M224, Department of Special Collections, Stanford University.

28. John Anson Ford Collection, HLMs, Box 68, The Huntington Library.

29. *Ucapawa News*, December, 1939.

30. Acuña, *Occupied America*, pp. 337-38; Larralde, *Mexican American Movements and Leaders*, pp. 72-73; interview with Fierro.

31. John Anson Ford Collection, HLMs, Box 68, The Huntington Library; *House Report on Un-American Propaganda Activities*, Report No. 1311 (March 29, 1944); *California Special Committee (Dies Committee) on Un-American Propaganda Activities*, vol. 17 (September 27-29, 1944, October 3-5, 1944); *Hearings on Communist Infiltration of Motion Picture Industry*, 80th Congress (October 20-24, 27-30, 1947); House Document No. 137, *Subversive Organizations and Publications* (May 14, 1951).

32. Interviews with Moreno, Fierro, and Corona; Acuña, *Occupied America*, p. 168; Mario T. Garcia, "Mexican American Labor and the Left: The Asociación Nacional Mexico-Americana, 1949-54"; Camarillo, *Chicanos in California*, p. 64.

33. *American Me* (Boston: Houghton Mifflin Company, 1948), pp. 241-42. See also, John H. Burma, *Spanish Speaking Groups in the United States* (Durham, NC: Duke University Press, 1954), pp. 102-03; Miguel Tirado, "Mexican American Community Political Organization", *Aztlan*, 1:1 (Spring 1970), pp. 59-60. For examples of the political historiography about Mexican Americans, see the following: Armando Navarro, "The Evolution of Chicano Politics", *Aztlan*, 5:1, 5:2 (Spring and Fall 1974), p. 62; Alfredo Cuellar, "Perspective on Politics", in Joan W. Moore, ed., *Mexican Americans* (Englewood Cliffs, New Jersey: Prentice-Hall, Inc., 1970), p. 137; F. Chris Garcia, "Americans All: The Mexican American Generation and the Politics of Wartime Los Angeles, 1941-45", *Social Science Quarterly*, 65:2 June 1984), pp. 278-79; Richard A. Garcia, "The Mexican American Mind: A Product of the 1930s", in Mario T. Garcia, et al., *History, Culture and Society: Chicano Studies in the 1980s*, proceedings of the National Association for Chicano Studies (Ypsilanti, MI: Bilingual Press, 1983), pp. 67-68; Jose E. Limon, "El Primer Congreso Mexicanista de 1911: A Precursor to Contemporary Chicanismo", *Aztlan*, 5:1, 5:2 (Spring and Fall, 1974), pp. 85-118.

Richard A Garcia explores the emerging intellectual conflict between the "Los Ricos" and the emerging Mexican American mind in 1930s and 1940s San Antonio, Texas. The Mexican American community, under the leadership of the League of United Latin American Citizens, posed new challenges to the intellectual hegemony of the more Mexico-directed mentality of the Rico class. They stressed their Americanism, a cultural orientation which blended elements of the American and Mexican experiences, and sought a more aggressive civil rights agenda than the old Rico class.

The Mexican American Mind
Richard A. García

The intellectual history of Mexicans between 1929 and 1941 is best understood as the expression of a sociocultural crisis. It was a decade of an intellectual search for community by a rising middle class. The Mexican American mind emerged in the 1930s as a product of social differentiation, the crisis of the Depression, the Americanization role of such institutions as the family, the Catholic Church, and the educational system, the Mexican and American ethos of the city, the ideas and ideology of the exiled Mexican "Ricos" and the rise of the League of United Latin American Citizens (LULAC), as well as the relative absence of constant immigration.

The consciousness of a community is a difficult process to ascertain, but by examining the hegemonic position of the dominant social classes, there is some certainty, nevertheless, of determining when a new set of ideals, values, and opinions began to become predominant in a community. During the 1930s there began to emerge in San Antonio, Texas, a minute, bit viable Mexican middle class. The ideas and ideology of the social stratum were articulated by LULAC. This organization exhibited a new set of ideological tools from which to view the self and society. As a result of LULAC's the San Antonio Mexican community began to acquire a new set of ideas and values, in fact, a new sense of ethnicity which defined its forms of social, political, and intellectual life. This new zeitgeist of Mexican-Americanism, which differed from the idea of just being "Mexicano," although it varied from social stratum to social stratum, was by the 1930s and 1940s a cohesive collective cluster of ideas that permeated the extensive Mexican communities throughout the Southwest.

The development of the Mexican American mind, however, was in crisis during the 1930s in the Southwest, specifically in San Antonio, Texas, which is the focus of this paper. The emerging reality of this new mentality threatened the dominant cultural-intellectual hegemony of "Los Ricos," the exiled Mexican upper class of the community. This paper does not want to suggest that prior to the 1930s there were not any individuals who identified themselves as Mexican Americans, Latin

Americans, or Mexicano Tejanos. What is being suggested in this paper is that the 1930s was the period in which a whole community, in this case San Antonio, began to become aware of a new mentality--a Mexican American one--that was being advocated, programmed, and institutionalized by the voice of the developing middle class organization: the League of United Latin American Citizens. In order to fully understand the process of this intellectual development we must first focus on the development of the ethos of the city, the social differentiation within the Mexican community, the impact of the institutions on the Mexicans, and finally the ideas and ideology of "Los Ricos" and LULAC...

The very economic structure of San Antonio helped to divide the Mexicans economically into the working class and the lower middle class. The American workplace values were being fused with the Mexican cultural ones. The extent, of course, depended on the occupation. These different American occupations affected the Mexicans' lives by influencing the family's cultural and intellectual matrix. Moreover, because of the extensive Mexican population there had developed since the late nineteenth century an upper middle class of Mexican entrepreneurs and professionals that serviced the Mexican community with grocery stores, barber shops, furniture stores, drug stores, etc. This nascent class was strengthened by the middle class emigres during the great migration. Each of these classes had their own ideas and ideology, although they still were within the intellectual parameters of "el espíritu de la raza." Both American and Mexican intellectual and cultural traditions affected their daily lives.... In addition to the laboring class and the sectors of the middle class, there was also a very small number of approximately 100 families of exiled Mexican "Ricos" at the top of this socioeconomic pyramid by the 1930s. The upper middle class Mexicans, socially and culturally, were intertwined with "Los Ricos," and residentially "segregated" themselves in the Prospect Hill area of the West Side or in the San Pedro district, another enclave on the West Side. Others, like some of the "Ricos," moved outside of the "Mexican Quarter." But regardless of birthplace or residence, the employment situation was difficult during the thirties, although there were some Mexicans, such as the small shop owners, who managed to maintain their shops...

Although the culture and society of San Antonio's "Latin Quarter" was divided into three worlds—the laboring class, the middle class, and "Los Ricos"—they intersected on the issues of health, education, immigration and deportation, as well as politics. In these areas, many times, the two upper classes worked together to help the working class. However, the cultural hegemony was still held by "Los Ricos," although the "counter culture" of the Mexican American middle class was slowly rearing its head. But, regardless of the differences in culture, society, or class, the Mexicans in San Antonio faced the common problems of racism and discrimination. These were unwanted unifying factors that insidiously weaved their way into the core of the community. Like cancer, racism did not respect any class or status group. If nationalism was the positive unifying thread in the West Side, racism was the negative. Both kept Mexicans separated and segregated. If acculturation promised relief, racism did not. Mexicans became Americanized, but discrimination kept them, for the most part, Mexicans. The intellectual dilemma was clear; they were not quite Americans, but neither were they quite Mexicans. The synthesis was Mexican Americanism, although the "Ricos" tried to keep them on the Mexican side of the hyphen by asserting their intellectual role.

"Los Ricos" of San Antonio were a *comprador* class. For the most part, they had no economic or political base in San Antonio or throughout the Southwest. These exiled Mexicans always "faced South" toward Mexico and were more interested in the politics of Mexico and the rest of the world rather than in San Antonio. Yet, they still supported any improvement of the economic, the social or the political conditions for the Mexican in the United States, whether they were working class or middle class. In spite of these activities in San Antonio, these "Ricos," who included many of the political refugees who settled in San Antonio between 1908 and 1914 as well as many of the religious refugees who came in the 1920s, were persons, largely from Mexico's upper classes, [who] looked upon San Antonio more as a refuge than as a permanent home. Some of them left San Antonio as soon as conditions in Mexico permitted, but others remained."

This Mexican comprador class was exemplified by Ignacio E. Lozano and his newspaper, *La Prensa*. The newspaper was referred to as "un faro del pensamiento" (an intellectual light). Lozano was referred to at a banquet in 1937 as "the highest representative of Mexico" and a person who "ought to be an example for all Mexicans." These eulogies were from both the middle class Mexicans and "Los Ricos" who were trying to have Lozano elected as the president of the national organization *Alianza Hispano Americana*, which was headquartered in Arizona. This organization rivaled the LULACs and was more representative of Mexicans like "Los Ricos" who identified themselves more as Spanish (Hispanos) than as Mexicans. There were some middle class persons who aligned themselves closer to this sector of the population than to the growing Mexican American one in order not to be identified with the poor Mexicans. For the "Spanish" "Ricos" and the aspiring

Mexicano, Lozano was the "Champion of the Mexican People" and the "new Moses," as many referred to him...

"Los Ricos" felt that they were the "class people" (*gente decente*) that could return Mexico to normalcy, and that they were also the ones who could conserve the "spirit of La Raza" within the hearts of the Mexicans in the United States. Both "Los Ricos" and LULAC agreed on the preservation of this spirit, but LULAC and the middle class were adapting to the Americanization in their lives. The exiled businessmen and writers of *La Prensa*, however, always wanted to return to Mexico; they wanted La Patria. These "Ricos" were only building a feeling and a spirit in San Antonio. They were promoting a Mexican past and a tradition in which they hoped to envelop all the sectors of the West Side community. In juxtaposition, and not necessarily in constant conflict, was the middle class's everyday activities which were building a "new" sense of community. But, this "new order" was one of American traditions; it was a community based on the present not on the past. Change and time favored the Mexican American middle class since their dreams coincided with reality; the dreams of the "Ricos" did not. Nevertheless, the "Ricos" helped to maintain the Mexican cultural ethos that provided the continuity from the past to the present which the middle class used to support its ideological activities in the present while moving to the future.

This "spirit of La Raza" could best be maintained, the "Ricos" believed, through everyday cultural activities. Therefore, through the cultural activities which emanated from the Casino Social, through the sale of Mexican books, through the sale of Mexican music, and through the speaking and writing of its intellectuals, the "Ricos" of San Antonio continued to maintain the Mexican "spirit" and "soul"—La Cultura—despite the sea of acculturation. The "Ricos" were attempting to foster a "high culture" on the Mexicans of San Antonio and the Southwest. They were attempting to develop a sophisticated leadership and a *clase de gente decente*. Mexican leaders and the Mexican *élan vital*, the "Ricos" believed, could be built on the anvil of culture. For the "Ricos," artists were an integral part, if not the cornerstone, of Mexican culture. For the "Ricos" culture and politics were intertwined....

Unfortunately, "Los Ricos" always saw San Antonio through a nationalist ideology, rather than a class analysis. Mexicans, whether they were rich or poor, were Mexicans, according to "Los Ricos." LULAC, for "Los Ricos," was not the expression of an emerging class. It was just a different gestalt. Classes for "Los Ricos" did not exist. Consequently, their wish for a social and cultural homogeneity was idealistic, both for San Antonio and Mexico. They could not have just one culture and one society. Their ideology had no reality; in contrast, LULAC's ideology was based on the emerging reality of the 1930s.

The ideas and ideology of the League of United Latin American Citizens were the intellectual waves of the future for the Mexicans in San Antonio's West Side. It was the expression of a new consciousness; in fact, a new order. As the *LULAC News* stated:... in 1929, with the great social upheaval of the Depression just ahead, the Texas wind carried a whisper of hope to the most native of all Texas' sons, the Mexican Americans." Within the extensive Mexican community of "Los Ricos" there was forming a Mexican American mind. It was partially a product of the Mexican middle class' search for community during the 1920s and especially the 1930s. In 1939, J. Montiel Olvera, the compiler of the *Latin American Yearbook of San Antonio*, described this new mentality as one isolated from the intellectual roots that nourished it: the Anglo-American and the Hispano-American minds. This Mexican American mind flourished within the middle class of entrepreneurs: restaurateurs, bakers, barbers, shoestore owners, butchers, furniture store owners, gasoline station owners, jewelers, tailors, druggists, cleaner and laundry owners, and among the over 350 grocery store owners of the Mexican community as well as the small but significant number of professionals, doctors, and lawyers. It was from these Mexican citizens that a culturally cohesive and intellectually conscious Mexican American middle class developed. Their way of thinking and feeling—their lifestyle—was different from "Los Ricos" and "Los Pobres.". . . The consciousness of this small, but growing middle class was formulated and articulated by the LULAC members who sought, in general, "the promotion of the effective exercise of American citizenship, the cultural advancement of persons of Mexican ancestry, and the effacement of public school racial distinctions...."

The general basis for the "new consciousness" began in the nineteenth and twentieth centuries, but specifically it began in 1921 when the Order of the Sons of America was founded in San Antonio by a cadre of World War I veterans and other politically conscious individuals.... All were middle-class Mexicans. [John] Solís explained their effort in the following manner: "we didn't have anything [as Mexicans] in 1921[;] we decided to organize our people to try and better the condition of Mexican Americans here in San Antonio and Bexar County." The first year, according to Solís, thirty-seven people joined the organization whose general goal was "to develop better American citizens and urge education," and in October of 1921 the Order of the Sons of America, the first consciously Mexican American group, was chartered by the State of Texas. The other goals of the organization were also general, but straightforward: the achievement of economic, social, and racial equality with other Americans, the attainment of social and economic opportunity, and political power. The vehicles for achieving these goals were the Order of the Sons of America Councils that were established throughout Texas. The main membership requirement, because of their goals, was American citizenship. Also a major emphasis was placed on the members learning and speaking the English language....

With the closing of the "Roaring Twenties" two things became clear to these Mexicans who aspired to be Mexican Americans. They needed a very clear social and political program and they needed organizational unification. Therefore, in 1927, a call for a unification meeting of the major organizations—Order of the Sons of America, the Knights of America, the League of Latin American Citizens, and Los Caballeros de América—was issued. This call was made by Corpus Christi leader Ben Garza, the Head of Council IV of the Order of the Sons of America, the largest of the Mexican American organizations. The meeting, which was held at Harlingen, Texas, was the first of a series of meetings toward eventual unification. Such prominent San Antonio leaders as Alonzo S. Perales, Juan Solís, M. C. Gonzales, Maricio Machado, and James Tafolla attended. Three other major leaders attending were from South Texas, Ben Garza, J. T. Canales, and Luis Sáenz. These series of meetings finally culminated on February 17, 1929, at Obreros Hall. At this last major meeting, on May 18 and 19 of 1929, after much discussion, compromise, and argument, Ben Garza, the president of the sessions, and M. C. Gonzales, the secretary, announced that the League of United Latin American Citizens (LULAC) was now the single representative body of the Mexican American middle class. The acronym LULAC contained the central principles of the organization:

    L--For *Love* of country and fellowman
    U--For *Unity* of purpose
    L--For *Loyalty* to country and principles
    A--For *Advancement* of a people
    C--For *Citizenship*, true and unadulterated

With unification and a common philosophical goal—to make Mexicans into Mexican Americans—LULAC began immediately to spread and attempt to "uplift" cultural pride, increase the rate of American citizenship, and educationally advance the Mexican population to a new Mexican American consciousness throughout Texas, but especially in the San Antonio area. By 1933, LULAC chapters had spread from Texas to Arizona, New Mexico, Colorado, California and even the District of Columbus and other Eastern States. Wherever there was a Mexican middle class community, LULAC was embraced. Because the organization's growth by 1937 was in part due to the work of the women, the Texas LULAC leadership decided to give them equal leadership privileges and councils. However, their councils were to be composed solely of women. A dual organizational structure, therefore, was established. Mrs. F. I. Montemayor was elected the first woman to the LULAC general office. In addition to this women's section, LULAC established the Junior LULACs between 1938 and 1939 under the sponsorship of the adult councils. The LULAC leadership throughout the thirties sought to incorporate the whole Mexican family within the organizational structure....

Throughout the 1930s the LULACs were conscious that they had a historical-philosophical mission to accomplish. If the family, the church, the educational system, and the political arena were the institutional transmitters of change for the Mexican American generation, the LULAC members were the active bearers of change via ideas and ideology. In 1932 LULAC President M. C. Gonzales placed LULAC into historical perspective: "We are here on a mission. To make living conditions better for the coming and succeeding generations; not to accomplish that work is to fail in our duties." Then M. C. Gonzales underlined the LULAC's major task as the vehicle of the Mexican American generation of the 1930s. This task was the hegemonic confrontation with "Los Ricos" of San Antonio, who were only building a Mexican consciousness. "'Los Ricos' were never part of our [everyday] life," remembered Gonzales; "their newspaper, *La Prensa*, kept the image of Mexico alive, but never the welfare of Mexican American citizens of the United States or Texas." This role of "Los Ricos," however, was seen as useful by LULAC because it helped to preserve the "Spanish-Mexican culture." . . .

LULAC's "uplifting" mission was helped by the fact that by the thirties there were numerous towns and cities in the Southwest, including San Antonio, that already contained a population of Mexicans who were second- and third-generation American citizens. This generational situation was a drawback to "Los Ricos'" philosophy. These Mexicans were being changed by the institutions and their own decisions to change. Many times these native Mexican Americans welcomed their Mexican "relatives," but by the Depression decade they began to establish some social distance between themselves and the poor Mexicans. LULAC, as well as the community institutions, helped them form this distinctiveness....

In addition to pursuing this goal of material progress for all and bringing a new sense of dual consciousness, the San Antonio Mexican middle class led by LULAC sought specifically to eliminate racial prejudice, gain equality before the law, gain equal educational facilities, and gain equal political representation in local, state, and national politics. However, LULAC, as the conscious vehicle of the middle class mind, acknowledged that, as Weeks had noted, The greatest stumbling block in the way of accomplishing this end is the Mexican American himself, who possesses no clear conception of the significance of the privileges and duties of his American citizenship." In other words, LULAC had to first direct its activities to its own middle class before it could help the rest of the Mexican community. LULAC, therefore, sought to arouse the middle class "to a consciousness of that citizenship," Weeks wrote. LULAC also sought to educate the upper and middle class sectors in their political and civil rights and their obligations. Weeks observed that the LULAC members were the "intelligent class of Mexican Americans" and that they were not necessarily interested in the Mexican national nor the Mexican agricultural transient....

Thus, the "Mexican mind" during the 1930s was pitted against the Mexican American one. During this decade the "Ricos" sought to address themselves to *la epoca de la concordia*—the time of unification in Mexico. They sought to have "*los mejicanos de afuera* remember that they were Mexican and that they should return to work for Mexico." The LULACs, on the other hand, sought to address their search for community," also reminding the West Siders to remain Mexican, but to remember they were *mejicanos de adentro*, and thus their loyalties were to their present home, the United States. A LULAC leader forcefully responded to "Los Ricos'" cry of betrayal: The Mexicans [Los Ricos] say we're trying to Americanize, and get away from Mexican patriotism. We have to be American citizens [since we live in the United States] whether we want to or not." LULAC "faced North" and pursued the reality of their everyday existence In the United States; they looked toward the present and the future. "Los Ricos," however, always "faced South"; they remembered the past and wished to continue it. Regardless of their present exile in the United States, they continued to be Mexicans, from Mexico. Paul Taylor observing this hegemonic confrontation wrote "that if [community] dissensions were avoided, its [LULAC] program followed, and if its appeal to the working class succeeded, the Mexican-American mind would prevail." Taylor observed this, LULAC believed it, and most of the Mexican community, after a decade, accepted it. A continuing sense of cultural ethnicity rather than just a political and philosophical Americanization persisted with "astonishing tenacity" from 1929 through 1941 in the Mexican community....

. . . Mexican Americans did not seek to become assimilated. They sought a duality: Mexican in culture and social activity, but American in philosophy and politics. Within the latter role they sought to adhere to democratic ideals such as civic virtue, equality, right of education, and the right of citizenship. They sought to acquire the use of the English language, but maintain the right to Spanish. LULAC's ideals, intentions, and activities were beyond suspicion: they were for the community.

Mario García's study of the Asociación Nacional México-Americana offers a view of the issues and concerns of the Mexican American generation. Operating at a time of severe political repression, ANMA nonetheless militantly advocated for political unity among Mexican Americans with a strong working-class and union base. In many ways ANMA advocated political positions which challenged more conservative elements in their own community and American society in general. García's study also reveals striking similarities with Chicano goals two decades later.

Mexican American Labor and the Left: The Asociación Nacional México-Americana, 1949-1954

Mario T. García

The early development of the study of Chicano history during the late 1960s and early 1970s was accompanied by a strong emphasis on a radical tradition. Militant Chicano historians, as well as those in other disciplines, looked to a radical past to legitimize the emergence of a contemporary Chicano protest movement. Juan Gómez-Quiñones and other writers in *Aztlán*, for example, stressed the involvement of Mexican workers in labor conflicts during the early 20th century. In a study by Camarillo and Castillo, so-called "Mexican bandits" in 19th century California and elsewhere became "social bandits," and Chicano cultural heroes, such as Gregorio Cortez, were rediscovered in the early work of Américo Paredes. Gómez-Quiñones integrated the anarcho-syndicalist movement of Ricardo Flores Magón, especially during the Magonista exile in southern California at the time of the Mexican Revolution, into the Chicano radical tradition. In Rodolfo Acuña's *Occupied America*, Chicanos exemplified a colonized people fighting to liberate themselves from a system of internal colonialism. Such studies and others created an inspirational, albeit questionable, interpretation that assumed a direct link between the radicals of the past and those of the present.[1]

This attraction to a radical tradition is understandable given the militant temper of the late 1960s and early 1970s. Furthermore, what these studies lacked in original research was offset by a positive new orientation stressing, as anthropologist Octavio Romano urged in his classic essays in *El Grito* in 1967 and 1968, that Chicanos not only had a history, but one steeped in action and protest. Rather than being passive and accommodating, Chicanos struggled for freedom.[2]

Since the appearance of these early studies over 10 years ago, we have witnessed a more sophisticated Chicano historiography influenced by the radical tradition but also moderating it. Monographs such as those by Martínez, Camarillo, Griswold del Castillo, de León, Romo, and Balderrama, with their focus on Mexican communities in the United States involving generational, class, political, and cultural variables, suggest that these communities rather than being unidimensional, as proposed by the radical tradition, have instead been multidimensional. They have displayed various political tendencies and ideologies, including radicalism, liberalism, and conservatism. Such monographs further suggest the differences, as well as the similarities, from one historical period to another, something avoided by the radical tradition. It is the emergence of such diversity that has given recent Chicano historiography a distinct quality.[3]

Radicalism in the Chicano experience is one aspect of this diversity. That Chicanos have participated in radical and left movements in this country is indisputable. Besides the earlier works cited, other, more recent studies reveal this history. Emilio Zamora, for one, has noted the involvement of some Mexican Americans in Socialist Party activities in Texas. Victor Nelson-Cisneros and Vicki Ruiz have discovered that Mexican Americans, many of them women, had both rank-and-file and leadership roles in United Cannery, Packing, and Agricultural Workers of America (UCAPAWA). This leftist union, with a Communist Party orientation, successfully organized in the agricultural and canning industries of the Southwest during the 1930s and 1940s. Cletus Daniel, in the best study on agricultural radicalism in California, has similarly examined the relationship between the Communist party and Mexican farm workers. Douglas Monroy and Luis Arroyo have shown Mexican American activity in Los Angeles industrial unions that were led or strongly influenced by the Communist Party. And Acuña in his revised version of *Occupied America* has also introduced new information concerning Mexican American radical groups.[4] Yet although such research underscores a radical tradition, it needs to be complemented by an understanding that radicalism represents only one stratum in the ideological and political spectrum within Mexican communities in the United States.

II

Although the involvement of Mexican Americans in leftist unions and political organizations such as the Communist Party is beginning to be documented, almost nothing is known about specific, left-oriented Mexican American associations. This study is an attempt to fill this gap and concerns the Asociación Nacional

México-Americana (ANMA), which arose during the Cold War years of the 1940s and early 1950s, a period Acuña labels "the decade of defense" for Mexican Americans.[5]

ANMA was indirectly organized by the International Union of Mine, Mill, and Smelter Workers through its national headquarters in Denver, Colorado. This militant and progressive union traced its origins to the Western Federation of Miners and by the 1940s had organized many of the major mining and smelting regions of the West and Southwest. Some of its national officers suffered political persecution, especially during the 1950s, as alleged Communists. The CIO expelled the Union in 1950, along with several other progressive unions, on the charge of being Communist-dominated.[6] In New Mexico and Arizona, as well as in El Paso, the Mine, Mill, and Smelter union members consisted almost exclusively of Mexican Americans and Mexican nationals. The three El Paso locals, for example, by the early 1950s contained over 2,000 workers, almost all of Mexican descent, led by Mexican American officers. With such an ethnic composition, it appears that the International Union believed that ANMA could function as its political arm in the Mexican American communities of the Southwest.

Fifty delegates organized ANMA at a two-day meeting in Phoenix on February 12 and 13, 1949. They came, according to an ANMA history, from the sugar beet fields of Colorado, from the factories of Los Angeles, from the mines of New Mexico, and from the cotton fields of Arizona and Texas. They had assembled to establish an organization that would provide a "new voice" for Mexicans north of the border. ANMA was to represent "a national association for the protection of the civil, economic, and political rights of the Mexican people in the United States as well as for the expansion of their education, culture, and progress."[7] Any person or organization, regardless of citizenship, nationality, color, religion, or political affiliation, that was interested in the progress of "el pueblo mexicano," could join ANMA. These requirements contrasted with those of middle-class-oriented Mexican American organizations such as LULAC, which insisted on American citizenship for membership. ANMA was to be governed by its annual national convention and administered by an executive committee, a national committee, and a national office. The executive officer, a national president, would preside over the national convention and the meetings of both the executive and national committees.[8]

The objective conditions for the founding of ANMA are to be found in the particular plight of Mexican Americans and Mexican nationals during the postwar period. Despite certain economic improvements and gains in political and civil rights,

Mexicans in the United States still represented, according to ANMA, second-class citizens. ANMA recognized that racial minorities such as Mexicans and Blacks received special treatment in the form of greater economic insecurities, lower wages, inferior education, and suffered more than whites from recent rollbacks of New Deal welfare services. "What is even worse," ANMA proclaimed in 1952, "the Mexican people are objects of an accelerated program of discrimination, deportations, physical assaults, police brutality, and, at times, murder." In addition, they continued to be exposed to cultural discrimination and stereotyping as lazy, passive, and inferior people.[9]

ANMA concluded that the ascendance of political right-wing reaction in the country, made it imperative to organize all Mexicans into a national association for ethnic self-defense. This was no time for distinctions among the four to five million people of Mexican descent. ". . . (W)e are all united by the chord of language, culture, and lifestyle," ANMA stressed.[10] Believing that earlier attempts at organizing Mexicans had been characterized by false leaders and by betrayals, ANMA emphasized that Mexicans, despite standard stereotypes, could in fact be organized. "We should learn the lesson that labor unions learned when they started to organize," one ANMA leader noted, "that strength lies in unity."[11] ANMA hoped to be the vehicle for such unity especially among workers, intellectuals, youth, and professionals.[12]

In a period of three years, ANMA sponsored two national conventions: its founding convention in Los Angeles on October 14 and 15, 1950, and another in El Paso on July 12 and 13, 1952. Local chapters also sprang up in six regions: Arizona, northern California, southern California, Colorado, New Mexico, and Texas. These locals included Phoenix, Tucson, East Los Angeles, Denver, Albuquerque, El Paso, San Antonio, and Chicago. ANMA claimed further contacts in Utah, New York, San Diego. and Dallas. In 1950 it reported a membership of 4,000 in more than 30 locals.[13]

Ideologically, ANMA voiced radical views within the context of Mexican American politics. Its interpretation of Mexican American history, for example, had a different emphasis from that of LULAC. Whereas LULAC, through the influence of historians such as Carlos Castañeda, concentrated on the Hispanic roots in the Southwest as a way of convincing Anglos of the integral role Hispanics had played in American history and of their cultural contributions; ANMA focused on the conquest of northern Mexico by the United States in the mid-19th century. For

ANMA, Mexican American history had begun in violence, conquest, and the subjugation of the resident Mexican population.

Although not propounding what years later would be referred to as "internal colonialism," ANMA did emphasize the role of conquest. Because Mexicans had been annexed through force rather than voluntarily joining the United States, the Southwest possessed a culture and tradition quite different from the rest of the country. These differences had been recognized by the Treaty of Guadalupe Hidalgo ending the Mexican War in 1848 and promising to protect Mexicans' distinct culture and heritage. These guarantees, however, had not been fulfilled; arriving Anglos abused the Mexicans' culture, language, political rights, and economic holdings. Consequently, since 1848 Mexican Americans had been treated as an underclass of American citizens.

Such a legacy, moreover, continued into the 20th century when Southwestern economic concerns imported and exploited thousands of Mexican immigrant workers. Important as cheap labor during boom times, Mexicans also served as surplus labor and during the depressed 1930s faced unemployment, deportations, and forced repatriations. This historical experience, according to ANMA, had created much adversity for Mexicans in the United States. "This state of conditions has served to intimidate and oppress the Mexican worker throughout the Southwest," it concluded, "to force the Mexican to accept a low standard of life due to such exploitation and to impose on all other workers, especially in agriculture, to accept low wages due to the competition of Mexican labor."[14]

In addition, unlike other Mexican American civil rights organizations that stressed unity through citizenship as well as ethnic ties, ANMA emphasized unity through the fundamental working class nature of the Mexican population in the United States. Ninety-five percent of Mexicans north of the border were workers and ANMA believed this condition to be not only objective grounds for organization, but proof of the inescapable bonds between Mexican Americans and the union movement. Alfredo C. Montoya, ANMA's first president and an officer of the Mine, Mill, and Smelter Workers, observed in 1950 that recent gains by Mexican workers had been made possible through the assistance of Southwestern industrial unions. "With the help of the unions *el pueblo Mexicano* has eliminated many of the pre-existing wage distinctions [between Mexican and Anglo workers]," Montoya announced. "In many of the basic industries we have won the right to better jobs based on one's work and ability and at least (although not completely eliminated) we have broken the medieval control enjoyed by agriculture and mining interests over generations of Mexicans."

Just as the unions recognized that unorganized Mexicans only weakened the labor movement, Mexican workers realized that if the unions were destroyed they would also suffer. Montoya cautioned that he did not mean to imply that Mexicans should allow other groups to fight their battles for them, only Mexican Americans could achieve first-class citizenship for themselves. However, in their struggle, their natural allies were the unions.[15] ANMA did not proclaim what could be considered a revolutionary class position by calling on Mexican workers to overthrow capitalism and erect a socialist society. One could be indicted and sent to prison for espousing such views during the McCarthy period. Yet, it brought attention to the working class condition of most Mexicans, their class interests with other workers, and the exploitative nature of the class system in the Southwest. An economic elite exploited Mexicans as cheap labor and in turn amassed great profits. "The insufficient wages of the sugarbeet workers creates the vast wealth for corporations such as the Great Western Sugar Company that dominates the economic and political life of this state," one ANMA official in Colorado asserted.[16] ANMA believed, unlike such groups such as LULAC, that rectification of disparities in wealth and power could only be arrived at through a working class movement.

If ANMA recognized class in the formulation of its ideology, it also paid attention to the realities of race and culture. Mexicans were exploited as cheap labor and were oppressed as a distinct ethnic/racial community. ANMA in its short existence did not produce a sophisticated theory on race and class, but it did make it clear that Mexicans as well as Blacks faced double oppression. In a 1952 editorial, *Progreso,* ANMA's newspaper, commented that the Mexicans' participation in the class struggle had to contend directly with ethnic/racial segregation and discrimination. Such conditions aided in reducing the Mexicans' standard of living and forced them to accept hard, dirty, and cheap jobs.[17] Besides employment, Mexicans also faced discrimination in housing, education, political representation, and public services. Racism, according to ANMA, had become so pervasive and destructive that some Mexican Americans believed themselves inferior to Anglos and attempted to pass as "Spanish Americans" or "Nice Mexicans," as ANMA referred to them. These types of Mexican Americans either blamed other Mexicans for the existence of discrimination or else pretended it did not exist. ANMA observed, however, that few Mexicans, regardless of skin color and class background, successfully escaped prejudice. It recalled that even Edward Roybal, Los Angeles' only Mexican American city councilman, had been refused the sale of a home because he was of Mexican descent. ANMA further noted how the postwar housing boom permitted poor whites to purchase homes, but not Mexicans: "Today it is discovered that to be poor is not a great obstacle to buy a modest and decent house. But to be a Mexican is something else!"[18] "Why do such things exist?" ANMA queried. "It is not the fault of our people. Fault lies in discrimination-the discrimination which allows rich employers to pay us low wages and to divide us from other workers."[19] An exploitative class structure fueled racial/ethnic prejudice and discrimination. ANMA saw racism directly linked to a white ruling class and did not associate all whites, especially workers, with the perpetuation of such a system. ANMA would struggle alongside Anglo workers who also desired to eliminate racism. All workers would benefit from the elimination of an underclass of cheap labor.[20] To ANMA, both class and race had to be considered in developing a strategy for the liberation of Mexicans in the United States.

ANMA complemented these views by its discussion of culture. Deprived of an autonomous cultural development. Mexicans in the Southwest still possessed a distinct culture needing protection encouragement, and this uniqueness could be an objective basis for political organization. Employing a popular approach to culture, no doubt to distinguish it from the middle-class-oriented Mexican American organizations, ANMA promoted a form of cultural nationalism. It acknowledged the Mexicans' cultural heritage and praised efforts at cultural resistance.[21] Yet Mexican culture had come under more aggressive attack in the early 1950s. The Cold War and McCarthyism, in addition to bringing about violations of civil liberties and constitutional protections, created an irrational apprehension over anything considered "un-American." Consequently, Mexican Americans and Mexican nationals faced heightened cultural prejudice. "At the same time," *Progreso* warned in 1952,

> There is a subtle campaign, at times impudent, with the motive of desecrating our historical heritage, our culture and our language. All forms of the news media is being utilized to slandor [sic] and ridicule our people and our cultural institutions. At the same time there is a continual effort to negate, twist, and generally misrepresent our contemporary contributions as well as our historic economic and cultural ones in this country.[22]

ANMA observed that other ethnic groups whose families had arrived from Italy, Ireland, or Germany remained proud of their heritage. So too should Mexicans. One ANMA official declared,

We should understand and be proud of the rich culture of our ancestors and of Mexico-a culture of hard work, beautiful music, a culture that has produced the three greatest artists of the Americas-Orozco, Rivera, and Siqueiros. We know that Mexicans such as these are neither "sucios" (dirty), "flojos" (lazy), nor "estupidos" (stupid)-the usual untruthful characteristics generally attributed to Mexicans. ANMA struggles to preserve our culture and to promote dignity and pride in our nationality.[23]

Although ANMA favored cultural nationalism, it did not advance a theory of "nationhood" for Mexican Americans similar to that developed by the Communist Party for Blacks in the deep South. Rather, ANMA interpreted Mexican Americans more as a national minority, and stressed the integration of Mexican Americans through the acquisition of civil rights and the acceptance of a state of cultural pluralism whereby Mexican culture would be given due recognition in the United States.

In fighting for the rights of Mexican Americans, ANMA also encouraged an international consciousness, particularly with respect to Mexico and the rest of Latin America. It noted, for example, that the treatment of Mexicans in the United States represented a mirror reflecting United States attitudes and policies toward Latin America. If the United States treated Mexican Americans as second-class citizens, so too did it deal with Latin America as an inferior entity. Discounting particular differences, ANMA proposed that the relationship between Mexican Americans and Latin Americans was crucial and that the struggle for Mexican American liberation was linked with that of Latin America. ". . . (A)s long as this country takes unjust advantage of those people south of the Rio Bravo (Grande)," Alfredo Montoya concluded, "we shall never achieve what we are struggling for-first class citizenship."[24] Calling on Mexican Americans to shun the idea of a frontier between themselves and Mexico, ANMA proclaimed its defense of the rights of Mexican nationals in the United States and promised to develop ties of solidarity with Mexicans south of the Rio Grande.[25]

Domestically, ANMA advocated a united front. It opposed sectarianism and called for alliances with other Mexican American organizations subscribing to similar general principles and goals. A divided people would never alter their conditions, but united Mexican Americans could. "The situation and the times does not allow us the luxury of jealous, distrusts, and suspicions amongst us," Montoya appealed. "Such characteristics are almost semi-feudal vestiges which in the past have fatally damaged our cause. For this reason, our organization is ready to cooperate with others whose aim is to improve the lot of the Mexican people, and who believe in cooperation based on mutual respect and benefit."[26] ANMA, unlike middle-class-oriented Mexican American groups, also aspired to a united front with other oppressed peoples within the country, in particular Blacks and Jews. Mexican Americans represented only one of several minorities, who in some cases were worse off than Mexicans. The struggle and gains of one minority aided those of the rest.[27] "We should unite with Blacks who suffers similar conditions as our own, and in this way reinforce both groups," an ANMA official exhorted.[28] Such a coalition, including progressive labor unions, ANMA believed indispensable to the Mexican American cause.

In conformity with its ideology, ANMA developed a varied political program. First and foremost, due to the undeclared war in Korea, ANMA called on Mexican Americans to support the peace movement in the country. President Montoya, writing in 1952, observed that the Korean conflict represented a major setback for workers and minorities even though a majority of Mexican Americans and other Americans opposed the war. Not only was the war costing the lives of thousands of Mexican Americans out of all proportion to their numbers in the United States, but it also affected the well-being and rights of the Mexican American community. Montoya noted that attacks on Mexicans had increased since the beginning of the war in the form of police brutality, racial discrimination, the victimization of Mexicans through the use of the so called anti-subversive Smith and McCarran Acts, the loss of economic benefits through the application of the anti-labor Taft-Hartley Act, and the loss of social services for the poor, the aged, and the young. In addition, minority groups had to unjustly bear the costs of the war through excessive taxes, prices, and decreased wages.[29] Consequently, ANMA believed the war had to receive priority attention since it affected and magnified so many other problems. "The Mexican people not only deserve peace," *Progreso* stated, "but they need peace for their happiness and well-being." ANMA urged nations to resolve their problems through negotiations. "This is more sensible and civilized than killing millions of lives including those of our youth." As part of the struggle for basic rights, ANMA included the right to peace.[30]

With its emphasis on working-class solidarity, ANMA supported particular struggles of Mexican American workers in the Southwest. In 1952 it publicized the triumphs of Local 890 of the Mine, Mill, and Smelter Workers of Bayard, New Mexico, in its 15-month strike for improved wages and working conditions. The Bayard strike, of course, would be immortalized in the classic film *Salt of the Earth*.

The ANMA local in Denver, which had provided money and donations of clothes to the strikers, especially lauded the courageous role of the Mexican women who had taken over the picket lines after the workers had been barred from them.[31]

ANMA also called attention to the plight of migrant workers in Southwestern fields and supported a $1 an hour minimum wage for agricultural workers as well as a guaranteed annual wage.[32] As part of its concern for migrant labor, ANMA protested the bracero program whereby Mexico supplied field hands to American agriculture. ANMA considered the program to be a boon to agribusiness at the expense of both braceros and domestic farm workers. Braceros worked as peons, while Mexican American workers were forced to leave their homes in search of employment because they could not compete with cheaper bracero labor. ANMA advocated a suspension of the program and the involvement of both Mexican and U.S. labor unions in drafting an alternative solution to the need for agricultural labor in the Southwest.[33]

Finally, as part of its labor program, ANMA through its association with progressive labor unions encouraged unionism among Mexican Americans. Besides the Mine, Mill, and Smelter Workers, ANMA received support from such unions as the United Electrical Radio and Machine Workers of America, the National Union of Marine Cooks and Stewards, the International Longshoreman's and Warehouseman's Union, the Furniture Workers, Upholsterers and Wood Workers Union, and the Amalgamated Clothing Workers of America.[34]

The passage of anti-alien, anti-subversive, and anti-immigration laws in particular alarmed ANMA. In 1950 it officially protested the McCarran Act passed by the U.S. Congress. According to ANMA, such legislation, under the guise of controlling subversives, in fact aimed at destroying legitimate organizations such as labor unions working for peoples' rights. Anyone who protested against discrimination, police brutality, or injustices on the part of any governmental agency could now be accused of being a Communist and prosecuted under the McCarran Act. Minority groups would be especially vulnerable to unjust persecution.[35] Consequently, ANMA declared the McCarran Act to be a direct violation of the Bill of Rights.[36] As part of its 1952 platform, ANMA aided a successful campaign supporting four Mexicans in Santa Ana, California (the Sereno Case) who had been prosecuted as undesirable under the McCarran Act. ANMA further helped organize mass meetings against the Act, such as one in Los Angeles on March 13, 1952, attended by over 200 persons protesting the application of the McCarran Act to unfairly deport Mexican workers.[37]

Besides working conditions, ANMA sought other improvements in the quality of life for Mexican Americans. At least one ANMA local, for example, took up rent control as an issue.[38] The Lincoln Heights local in East Los Angeles was organized out of a struggle for improved housing.[39] In Denver, ANMA confronted local authorities regarding limited and segregated public housing for Mexican Americans.[40] Reflecting the increased educational aspirations of Mexican Americans, ANMA in Colorado questioned why less than 100 Mexican Americans attended all colleges and universities in that state. ANMA further observed that during the 1947-48 academic year only 78 Mexican American high school seniors could be found in Colorado. These conditions resulted not from lack of support for education by Mexican American parents, but from economic exploitation and discrimination that forced young Mexican American children to leave school at an early age to supplement the family income.[41]

Economic and social rights also needed to be complemented by effective political representation. ANMA thought it ironic that Mexican Americans were being asked to fight for democracy in Korea while being denied it in their own communities. The time had come for Mexican Americans to elect representatives from their own group rather than relying as in the past on politicians who had little or no interest in the problems of Mexican Americans. "This will reflect not only the revival of a civic consciousness," ANMA declared, "but a recognition that our progress is impossible without a voice and a vote within governing circles."[42] Responsible political representation, however, could only be achieved if Mexican Americans registered to vote and if they allied themselves with the labor movement and other minorities.[43]

This appeared to be happening and an encouraged ANMA noted in mid-1952 that in recent elections throughout the Southwest, Mexican Americans had not only voted in large numbers, but more Mexican Americans had run for office than ever before. These candidates conducted valiant, although mostly unsuccessful races, despite the fact that their opponents were in many cases supported by local chambers of commerce and other monied interests. The elections had revealed the potential political strength of Mexican Americans. "When the political power of five million Americans is freed from its bondage," ANMA promised, "then its voice will be heard."[44] In El Paso, ANMA organized a Poll Tax Committee to encourage Mexican Americans to pay their poll taxes and to use their vote to elect honest and capable representatives who would help alleviate problems associated with work, housing, health, and education.[45]

Youth work formed still another aspect of ANMA's political program. This was an especially important issue in light of continued cases of police harassment and brutality against young Mexican Americans. The Estrada Courts local in East Los Angeles, for example, had been organized is a result of an incident of police brutality.[46] Besides protecting against such injustices, ANMA attempted to organize youth as a way of preventing delinquency and of politicizing young people. Through its national youth director, it established ANMA youth clubs in at least two states. ANMA observed that young veterans in particular welcomed the opportunity for political work, since after returning from the battlefields they discovered that American society had little to offer them.[47]

Culturally, ANMA pursued a two-fold strategy. On the one hand, it attacked prevalent stereotypes of Mexicans, especially in the mass media. In its 1952 platform, ANMA announced a national campaign against the perversions of Mexican culture portrayed in the press, literature, radio, and television. It called particular attention to the Judy Canova radio show, which depicted Mexicans, through the character of "Pancho," as lazy and stupid.[48] Mexican Americans possessed a sense of humor, it being one of the few things enjoyed by poor people, and appreciated humor done in good taste, one ANMA official stated. However, the "humor" in the Canova show Mexican Americans could easily do without. "Behind the image of a stupid, lazy, and ignorant clown that is [Pancho]," Alfonso Sena of Colorado charged,

> there is a century of persecution and deprivation of our people. According to this humor our people should perform the most servile labor and receive the lowest wages. This humor sustains the poor health of many of our children, the terrible shacks where we are forced to live, the lack of educational opportunities, the brutality of the police toward our youth, the segregation and many other indignities that are forced upon us.[49]

It was not funny, Sena added, that more than 80 percent of the Mexicans in Denver labored in unskilled jobs and that the average family income of Mexican Americans in 1949 was only $1,840 compared to $1,930 for a Black family and $3,020 for an Anglo family. Nor was it funny that the average family income of a migrant family in Colorado only amounted to $1,424.[50]

To protest comedy at the expense of Mexicans, ANMA, along with certain allied labor unions, initiated a national economic boycott of the Colgate Palmolive Peet Company, Canova's sponsors. They asked the public to pressure radio stations airing the show and to boycott such products as Palmolive soap, Cashmere Bouquet soap, Colgate Shaving Cream, Super Suds, and Fab. "One of the principal objectives of ANMA is the defense of our people's dignity and the just representation of the real Mexican-*'el verdadero Mexicano*,'" the organization proclaimed, "and the true Mexican is the deprived and exploited worker who has maintained the railroads, labored in the fields, and built the cities. For the Mexican people, their low economic standing, the negation of their rights, and the ridicule which they are subject to are one and the same."[51] Two months later, *Progreso* reported that due to the boycott and protests, the Canova show had been canceled.[52] To prevent such stereotyping in the media, ANMA, at its second national convention in El Paso, adopted a resolution urging the employment of Mexican Americans in motion pictures, radio, and television. "We must fight for jobs for our people in all cultural and mass communications to which their talents entitle them," the resolution concluded.[53]

To present a more positive image of Mexicans and to promote ethnic pride, ANMA sponsored cultural programs. Through its national director of culture it encouraged locals to organize functions that would tap the talents of Mexican Americans. Cultural centers, it suggested, might be established by each local.[54] According to ANMA, music represented the art form that engaged most people and should therefore be concentrated on by the locals. "More than art, dance, and even literature," *Progreso* editorialized, "music occupies first place in our communities." Mexican music, of course, consisted of many types, including corridos, huapangos, and jarabes. Some Mexican music was really American music, having nothing to do with Mexican culture. Despite such variety, ANMA recommended that local directors of culture identify the most popular forms of music in their communities as well as those who performed them. Having done this, the locals could stage community concerts that would involve not only performances, but education through teaching the audiences the music and words of songs so they could directly participate. In addition to music, local cultural committees could arrange lectures on hygiene, art, the care of children, and on other ethnic cultures.[55]

As an example of what could be done in cultural work, ANMA's national culture committee organized a "Semana de Historia y Cultura Mexicana" in Los Angeles to coincide with the celebration of the 16th of September (Mexican Independence Day) in 1950. ANMA sponsored a number of musical variety shows at Croation Hall in Belvedere. These shows featured its own group of artists including singers, dancers, and musicians under the direction of Crescencio Ruiz, the national director of culture. Black and Jewish performers also participated. Evening shows highlighted a musical-slide presentation depicting the history of music and art in Mexico from pre-Columbian times to the present. Movies about Mexico were also part of the week-long festivities. Finally, the most important exhibition of Mexican American and Mexican art ever held in Los Angeles, according to *Progreso*, accompanied the ANMA program. Artists, including ANMA members, displayed nearly 150 pieces of art at Centro Soto-Michigan.[56]

The publication of *Progreso*, ANMA's national newspaper, also constituted part of ANMA's cultural agenda. Written primarily in Spanish in order to reach most Mexican nationals and Mexican Americans and to promote the Spanish language, ANMA did publish some articles in English. Indeed, ANMA acknowledged that a bilingual format was best because of the heterogeneity of the Mexican population in the United States and the cultural erosion and language discrimination faced by Mexican Americans. "Some say that Mexican Americans should know how to read Spanish," Dr. Edward Lamar, the national editor of *Progreso* wrote,

> We agree with that, unfortunately many do not. Many older people can read neither language because education was not available for them in their youth. They must depend upon their children to read the paper for them. Many of their sons and daughters speak both languages but have been taught to read only English and are often even penalized for speaking Spanish in school. ANMA must correct this condition; we must also recognize that it exists.[57]

Accepting English as a fact of life and not being dogmatic in its cultural nationalism, ANMA incorporated the values and benefits of bilingualism and biculturalism. "We all want to learn to use both languages well," Lamar insisted, "to appreciate the culture of others, to be in a position for better jobs in either the U.S. or Mexico, and to be ready to take our place in active leadership in our community."[58]

Although ANMA apparently did not have a specific program or commission on women, it appears that women played active and important roles in the organization. Isabel González, for example, was elected the first vice-president of ANMA in 1949. Other women in national offices included Florencia Lamar, who was national treasurer. In the locals, women held leadership positions, although none seem to have been elected presidents of their chapters.[59] Applauding the role of women in the "Salt of the Earth" strike, one male official impressed on ANMA members the need to recognize the potential leadership capacities of women. "We should accept them as leaders with all the respect they deserve," he stressed. "We should assist them to develop to their fullest potential as leaders of our organization, and we should recognize the marvelous contributions that Mexican women have made to ANMA."[60]

Desiring a united front, ANMA pursued contacts not only with labor unions, but with other community organizations. Alfredo Montoya, President of ANMA, and Mauricio Terrazas, southern California Regional Director, both participated in the short-lived American Council of Spanish-Speaking People headed by Dr. George I. Sánchez of the University of Texas.[61] No evidence exists, however, of any association with prominent but middle-class oriented Mexican American organizations such as LULAC and the American G.I. Forum. It is not unlikely that these staunchly anti-Communist groups shied away from the leftist ANMA. While ANMA's united front with prominent Mexican American civic organizations was limited and in some cases nonexistent, its contacts with left-oriented, non-Mexican American groups was not. Progressive collectives supporting ANMA included the Independent Progressive Party (which in 1948 ran former Vice-President Henry Wallace for President of the United States), the Los Angeles Committee for the Protection of the Foreign Born, the Civil Rights Congress, and the Jewish Peoples Fraternal Order of the International Workers Order.[62]

Because of its ideology and reform program, plus its affiliation with leftist organizations such as the Mine, Mill, and Smelter Workers, ANMA faced much harassment and political persecution as a so-called "red-front" group. At its 1952 national convention in El Paso, for example, one local newspaper announced the meetings with a headline reading: "Red Front Leaders Gather for Meeting." Interviewed by the *El Paso Herald-Post*, President Montoya denied that ANMA was allied with any Communist organization but was repeatedly questioned on whether ANMA supported the Korean War. In a biased statement intended to discredit ANMA, the *Herald-Post* wrote: "Montoya refused to give a 'yes' or 'no' answer as to whether or not he or his organization favors action against Red aggression in Korea." The newspaper also attempted to link ANMA with potential violence by reporting that the Chief of Police was "keeping his eye" on the convention. "We can't stop them from meeting," the Chief stated. "There is nothing we can do unless they start a disturbance. If there is any trouble we will put an end to it in a hurry."[63]

The *Herald-Post* further attacked ANMA for its criticism of Mexicans in the media, especially the comic strip characters "Little Pedro" and "Gordo." In an editorial entitled "Spreading Poison," the *Herald Post* dismissed ANMA's position as pure propaganda intended to breed hate and distrust in American institutions. "There's nothing harmful in roly-poly, good-natured Gordo, who brings admiring smiles to his readers. And Little Pedro is a smart chap who has a way of doing the unexpected." The newspaper concluded that ANMA's aim was simple: "Create class hatred, stir up trouble that can be used to enlist more fellow travelers-that's the object of such speeches."[64]

Two years later, the U.S. Attorney General listed ANMA as a subversive group as had been done with many other progressive organizations. Before the listing, ANMA had been accused without evidence of representing a front for the Communist Party during the El Paso trial of Mine, Mill, and Smelter organizer Clint Jencks. At the Jencks trial, Alfredo Montoya had also been charged with being a member of the Communist Party. Convicted of filing false non-Communist affidavits, Jencks was later acquitted partly on the grounds that witnesses who had testified against him had lied and were paid FBI informers.[65]

Faced with such charges and political pressures, ANMA defended itself by accusing its opponents of being antidemocratic and of wishing to destroy community organizations and labor unions that supported social improvements and constitutional protections for minorities and workers. ANMA recognized that in order to achieve these gains it had to also protect the right of protest and freedom of speech even though this might involve being a victim of red-baiting. ANMA also attacked efforts by local governments to pass anti-Communist ordinances requiring municipal and county employees as well as others to sign anti-Communist oaths or to register as Communist Party members. In Los Angeles it strongly applauded the courageous stand of Councilman Roybal who in 1950 voted along against such an ordinance passed by the city council. This ordinance was later declared to be unconstitutional.[66]

By the middle of the 1950s, ANMA appears to have ceased to function. Its demise is linked to the general persecution of the Left in the United States, commonly referred to as McCarthyism. Although pursuing a basic reform program and declaring its loyalty to the democratic principles of the U.S. Constitution, ANMA, along with many other similar progressive organizations, was perceived as a threat by a paranoid ruling circle and hence could not be allowed to function peacefully. ANMA's brief history, moreover, has to be seen in light of the political attacks on the Mine, Mill, and Smelter Workers, its chief patron. Although the Union survived, its own efforts to protect itself during the early 1950s must have detracted from the attention and support it could provide ANMA. Acuña also suggests that the demise of ANMA was linked to the shifting policies of the Communist Party during the 1950s.[67]

It is, of course, conceivable that ANMA's own internal program may have had something to do with its limited life. For example, it naively assumed that both

Mexican Americans and Mexican nationals in the United States held to a common identity and common interests. Its open alliance with labor unions and political groups regarded as "radical" may have underestimated the conservative nature of many Mexicans in the United States. The discovery of additional internal documents will, of course, shed light on this question. From what we know now, however, it would seem that external rather than internal pressures caused ANMA's decline. "The Chicano movement in the 1950s," Acuña correctly notes, "was in fact driven underground or forced to use calmer methods in order to counteract the highly undemocratic and unconstitutional pressures that existed during that time."[68]

Although we do not know the full extent of its influence and despite its demise, ANMA still represents perhaps the most important Mexican American leftist organization during the first half of the 20th century. In addition to its political program concentrating on the problems of working class Mexican Americans, ANMA was the only group that articulated a particular Mexican American leftist or radical political ideology. Although its program as a whole was limited to democratic reforms, due no doubt to its effort to achieve mass support and to the political persecution of Marxists at the time, ANMA nevertheless correctly stressed the working class conditions of most Mexicans in the United States and the exploitative class character of the American system. ANMA's attempt, moreover, at linking class, race, and culture in interpreting the Mexican American experience constitutes one of the first efforts to explore these fundamental themes by Mexican Americans. Finally, the history of ANMA is a testimony to the courage and dedication of those Mexican Americans who, by standing up for their rights as U.S. citizens and by refusing to be intimidated by the reactionary temper of the period, dared to challenge the contradictions of American society.

III

Beyond the discovery of a Chicano left in history is the issue of the extent and nature of its influence. This involves, for example, whether the relationship between Mexican Americans and the Left led to an ideology similar to that debated by Black Marxists during the 1930s. If so, did this ideology clashed with other dominant intellectual-political tendencies in the Mexican American communities, most notably, the political and cultural nationalism articulated by Mexican exile leaders and, by the 1930s, the Americanist ideology championed by LULAC and other middle-class-oriented Mexican American groups.

Beyond 1848

In addition to what already has been done in the historiography of the Chicano left, I would suggest the following points of departure for future work. First, it seems to me that the most important period for the study of the Mexican American left, aside from the recent past, includes the 1930s, 1940s, and 1950s. The most concerted activity among Mexican American leftists occurs during this time. The Great Depression of the 1930s not only created objective conditions for protest due to the increased hardships suffered by Mexicans in the United States, but it gave rise to a militant Communist Party that successfully organized among the unemployed, agricultural laborers, and industrial workers. Yet if radicalism marked one perimeter of this period, antidemocratic reaction marked the other, in the form of the Cold War and McCarthyism. As a result, the later stages of this period drove the Communist Party underground and weakened the leftist union movement. The years between 1930 and 1960 are therefore critical ones for evaluating the full extent of Mexican American participation in leftist politics and the influence of this activity within Mexican American communities.

From what we already know, let me advance what we will probably continue to discover. Although increased numbers of Mexican Americans and Mexican nationals joined leftist unions as well as the Communist Party, they concentrated primarily on basic economic, political, and civil rights for Mexican Americans within the context of the capitalist system. In so doing they did not effectively articulate a revolutionary political position aimed at successfully challenging what I interpret to be the dominant reformist tendency in Mexican American political circles, voiced by groups such as LULAC. Mexican American leftist leaders, although perceived as undesirable competitors by their middle-class counterparts, supplemented rather than superseded the reform movements of the period. This is not to suggest, however, that even had a revolutionary ideology been advanced it would have found fertile ground. Here I differ with Douglas Monroy's undocumented contention to the contrary.

One can make a case that both objective and subjective conditions for mass revolutionary consciousness among Mexicans in this country simply did not exist at that time. In this sense, Mexican American leftists, such as those in ANMA, represented true radicals in that they astutely understood the limitations of the conditions under which they worked and yet made the most of them in addressing the immediate interests of Mexican American workers. In any event, Mexican American leftist leaders found themselves too engaged in daily labor problems and in defending themselves against political persecution to develop an interpretation of Marxism/Leninism that might have challenged the hegemony of the reform

Americanism espoused and supported by many Mexican Americans, especially after World War II. The absence, moreover, of a leftist Mexican American intelligentsia--something that would not arise until the 1970s--hindered the birth of a specific leftist politics. By contrast, nonradical reformers had access to a small number of Mexican American intellectuals and writers such as Carlos Castañeda, George I. Sánchez, Alonso Perales, and Ignacio López, who presented a middle-class Mexican American world view. Only ANMA drafted a radical political platform, but even this was couched in reform language and limited by ANMA's brief existence.

Finally, it can be concluded that a Mexican American left emerged out of the 1930s, but it was one which focused more on reform than revolution. As a reform movement, the Mexican American left rather than being out of step with its time was very much a part of it. For reform and the achievement of the mythical "American Dream," not revolution, characterized the most politically active sectors of Mexican American communities between the 1930s and the early 1960s.

Notes

1. Juan Gómez-Quiñones. "The First Steps: Chicano Labor Conflict and Organizing 1900-1920," *Aztlán,* 3, 13-50; Ronald W. Lopez. "The El Monte Berry Strike of 1933, *Aztlán,* 1 (Spring 1970), 101-114. See special issue of *Aztlán* on labor history. especially Emilio Zamora Jr.. "Chicano Socialist Labor Activity in Texas. 1900-1920," 221-238; and Victor B. Nelson-Cisneros, "La clase trabajadora en Tejas. 1920-1940," 239-266. Also. see Albert Camarillo and Pedro Castillo, eds., *Furia y Muerte: Los Bandidos Chicanos* (Los Angeles: Chicano Studies Center. UCLA, 1972); Américo Paredes. *With his Pistol in his Hand: A Border Ballad and its Hero* (Austin: University of Texas Press. 1958); Gómez-Quiñones. *Sembradores: Ricardo Flores Magón Y El Partido Liberal Mexicano* (Los Angeles: Aztlán Publications. 1973); Rodolfo Acuña, *Occupied America: The Chicano Struggle Toward Liberation* (San Francisco: Canfield Press, 1972); José E. Limón, "El Primer Congreso Mexicanista de 1911: A Precursor to Contemporary Chicanismo, *Aztlán,* 5 (spring and fall 1974), 85-106.

2. See, for example, Octavio I. Romano, "Minorities, History, and the Cultural Mystique," *El Grito,* 1 (fall 1967), 5-11, and "The Historical and Intellectual Presence of Mexican-Americans," *El Grito,* 2 (winter 1969), 32-46.

3. Oscar J. Martínez, *Border Boom Town: Ciudad Juárez Since 1848* (Austin: University of Texas Press, 1978). Albert Camarillo, *Chicanos in a Changing Society:*

From Mexican Pueblos to American Barrios in Santa Barbara and Southern California, 1848-1930 (Cambridge: Harvard University Press, 1979). Richard Griswold del Castillo, *The Los Angeles Barrio: A Social History, 1848-1890* (Berkeley: University of California Press, 1980). Mario T. García, *Desert Immigrants: The Mexicans of El Paso, 1880-1920* (New Haven: Yale University Press, 1981). Arnoldo de León, *The Tejano Community, 1836-1900* (Albuquerque: University of New Mexico Press, 1982). Ricardo Romo, *East Los Angeles: History of a Barrio* (Austin: University of Texas Press, 1983). Francisco E. Balderrama, *In Defense of La Raza: The Los Angeles Mexican Consulate and the Mexican Community, 1929 to 1936* (Tucson: University of Arizona Press, 1982).

4. See Zamora, "Chicano Socialist Labor Activity," 221-238; Nelson-Cisneros, "La clase trabajadora," 239-266; Vicki Ruiz, "UCAPAWA and Mexican Women Workers" (Stanford, 1982); Cletus Daniel, *Bitter Harvest: A History of California Farmworkers, 1870-1941* (Berkeley: Univ. of California Press, 1982); Douglas Monroy, "Mexicans in Los Angeles, 1930-1941: On Ethnic Group Relations to Class Forces" (UCLA, 1978); Luis Arroyo, "Industrial Unionism and the Los Angeles Furniture Industry, 1918-1954" (UCLA, 1979); Acuña. *Occupied America*, revised ed., 1981.

5. Acuña, *Occupied America*, 213

6. Vernon Jensen. *Nonferrous Metals Industry Unionism*, 1932-1954 (Ithaca, NY: Cornell University Press. 1954).

7. See "Segunda Convención Nacional de la Asociación Nacional México-Americana." This and the other documents cited in the notes are in the author's possession.

8. Constitución de la Asociación Nacional México-Americana.

9. *Progreso*, June 1952, 2.

10. See document "Asociación Nacional México-Americana."

11. See Alfonso Sena, "Discurso Principal Conferencia Estatal de Colorado."

12. *Progreso*, December 1950, 1.

13. Ibid.; *Progreso*, October 1950, April 1950; "Convención Nacional Fundadora de ANMA," 6.

14. "Breve Historia del Pueblo Mexicano en E.U.," in *Progreso*, June 1952, 5-6. This history was taken from Isabel González, "Step-Children of a Nation" (American Committee for Protection of Foreign Born, 1947).

15. *Progreso*, October 1950, 2, 6.

16. Sena, "Discuro Principal."

17. *Progreso*, April 1952, 7.

18. Ibid., October 1950, 5.
19. Sena, "Discurso Principal."
20. Ibid.
21. *Progreso*, June 5-6.
22. Ibid., 2.
23. Sena, "Discurso Principal."
24. *Progreso*, December 1950, 2.
25. Ibid., 5.
26. Ibid., 2.
27. *Progreso*, June 1950, 8.
28. Sena, "Discurso Principal."
29. *Progreso*, April 1952, 4.
30. Ibid., 6.
31. Ibid., 1, 3; June 1952, 4.
32. Sena "Discurso Principal."
33. See document "Atención!" and *Progresso*, December 1950, 4.
34. See "Convención Nacional Fundadora" and "Segunda Convención."
35. *Progreso*, October 1950, 2.
36. Ibid., December 1950, 5.
37. Ibid., April 1952, 4, 6. For deportations of Mexicans under the McCarran Act, see also Acuña. *Occupied America,* 215-216.
38. *Progreso*, October 1950, 2.
39. Ibid., 4.
40. Ibid., June 1952, 4.
41. Sena, "Discurso Principal."
42. *Progreso*, April 1952, 1, 3.
43. Ibid.
44. Ibid., June 1952, 8.
45. See "Atención!" and press release, ANMA. El Paso, January 22, 1952.
46. *Progreso*, October 1950, 4.
47. Ibid., December 1950, 2.
48. Ibid., April 1952, 6.
49. Sena, "Discurso Principal."
50. Ibid.
51. *Progreso*, April 1952, 4.
52. Ibid., June 1952, 4.

53. *El Paso Herald-Post*, July 14, 1952, 1.
54. *Progreso*, December 1950, 4: April 1952, 8.
55. Ibid., June 1952, 3, 7.
56. Ibid., October 1950, 1, 5.
57. Ibid., December 1950, 3.
58. Ibid.
59. "Segunda Convención"; *Progreso*, December 1950, 3; April 1952, 8; June 1952, 6.
60. Sena "Discurso Principal."
61. *Progreso*, April 1952, 3.
62. See "Convención Nacional Fundadora" and "Segunda Convención."
63. *El Paso-Herald Post*, July 11, 1952, 1.
64. Ibid., 12.
65. Ibid., February 5, 1954, 1.
66. Ibid., October 1950, 4.
67. Acuña. statement to author.
68. Acuña, *Occupied America*, 213.
69. Douglas Monroy, "Anarquismo y Comunismo: Mexican Radicalism and the Communist Party in Los Angeles During the 1930s." *Labor History*, 24 (winter 1983), 34-59.

During the 1960s the collective image of the Southwest underwent a profound change. Chicanos rediscovered their ancient roots in Aztlán, (today's American Southwest) and launched numerous aggressive political movements to reclaim their political, economic and cultural rights. These movements, built upon the legacy of the Mexican American generation, were collectively called the Chicano Movement. Emerging from this movement were the leaders of the era: José Angel Gutiérrez, Rodolfo "Corky" Gonzalez, and Reies López Tijerina.

Aztlán Rediscovered
John R. Chávez

During the middle and late 1960s, the political situation in the United States developed into a crisis that permitted a resurgence of the image of the lost land. The myths of the Spanish Southwest and the American Southwest, which the Mexicans of the region had accepted for much of the twentieth century, were suddenly set aside. During that period when so many myths were being reexamined by U.S. society in general, many Mexican-Americans found it possible to challenge the images of themselves and their region that had been imposed by the Anglo majority. The shattering effect that the civil rights and the antiwar movements had on the Anglo self-image led many Mexican Americans to believe that their attempts to be like Anglos were against their own interests. They began to feel that perhaps they had more in common with blacks and even the Vietnamese than with the dominant Anglo-Americans. Reviewing their own socioeconomic position after two decades of "Americanization," Mexican-Americans found themselves lower even than blacks in income, housing, and education. Though they were not as discriminated against or segregated as blacks, Mexican-Americans realized that they had in no way become the equals of Anglos. In searching for the causes, the view that all "immigrant" groups initially experienced such problems seemed to explain less and less, for by 1960, 81 percent of Mexicans in the Southwest were United States-born. Furthermore, the condition of longtime residents in New Mexico and Texas was no better and often worse than that of other Mexican-Americans.[1]

The nationalist movements of such peoples as the Vietnamese and the Cubans inspired a significant number of Mexican-Americans to reexamine their own condition through history and conclude that they too had been the victims of U.S. imperialism. As a result, the nineteenth- and early twentieth century image of the Southwest as lost and of themselves as dispossessed reemerged from the collective unconscious of the region's Mexicans. As we have seen, that image had persisted, largely because of the intense Mexican nationalism that radiated from across the border, but in the 1960s it was reasserted and reshaped under the influence of contemporary ideas. Increasingly after World War II the former colonies of the world gained political independence and established nonwhite rule. Nonwhites sought to reestablish pride in their own racial backgrounds to combat the feelings of inferiority that colonialism had imposed. In the United States this phenomenon manifested itself in calls for black pride and black power, and also in cries for Chicano pride and Chicano power. The use of the term "Chicano," derived from *mexicano* and formerly used disparagingly in referring to lower-class Mexican-Americans, signified a renewed pride in the Indian and mestizo poor who had built so much of the Southwest during the Spanish and Anglo colonizations.[2] While investigating the past of their indigenous ancestors in the Southwest, activist Chicanos rediscovered the myth of Aztlán and adapted it to their own time.

After gaining independence from Spain and again after the revolution of 1910, Mexicans had turned to their ancient Indian past for inspiration. It is no surprise that Chicano activists did the same thing during the radical 1960s, especially given the example of contemporary nationalist movements. In the ancient myth of Aztlán, activists found a tie between their homeland and Mexican culture that antedated the Republic of Mexico, the Spanish exploration of the borderlands, and even Tenochtitlán (Mexico City) itself. As we have seen, ancient Aztec legends, recorded in the chronicles of the sixteenth and seventeenth centuries, recounted that before founding Tenochtitlán the Aztecs had journeyed from a wondrous place to the north called "Aztlán." Since this place of origin, according to some of the chroniclers, was located in what is now the Southwest, Chicano activists reapplied the term to the legion, reclaiming the land on the basis of their Indian ancestry. And although the preponderance of evidence indicates that the Aztlán of the Aztecs was actually within present Mexico, the activists' use of the term had merit. While the Aztlán whence the Aztecs departed for Tenochtitlán was probably in the present Mexican state of Nayarit, anthropological studies suggest that the distant ancestors of the Aztecs centuries prior to settling in Nayarit had inhabited and migrated through the Southwest. Thus, on the basis of Indian prehistory, Chicanos had a claim to the region, a claim stronger than any based only on the relatively brief history of Spanish settlement in the borderlands.

Since Aztlán had been the Aztec equivalent of Eden and Utopia, activists converted that ancient idealized landscape into an ideal of a modern homeland where they hoped to help fulfill their people's political, economic, and cultural destiny. Therefore, though "Aztlán" came to refer in a concrete sense to the Southwest, it also

Aztlán Rediscovered

applied to any place north of Mexico where Chicanos hoped to fulfill their collective aspirations. These aspirations in the 1960s, it turned out, were more or less the same hopes Southwest Mexicans had since the Treaty of Guadalupe Hidalgo. Chicanos sought bilingual/bicultural education, just representation in the government, justice in the courts, fair treatment from the police and the military, a decent standard of living, and ultimately that which controlled the possibilities of all their other aspirations—their share of the means of production, for this, intellectuals at least now believed, was what the Anglo conquest had fundamentally denied Southwest Mexicans. The northern homeland had been lost militarily and politically in the 1840s; the economic loss had come in subsequent decades with the usurpation of individually and communally owned lands that produced the wealth of the region. During Mexican rule the wealth of the land had been largely agricultural, but later the land of the Southwest had also given forth gold, silver, copper, coal, oil, uranium, and innumerable other products that enriched the Anglos but left Mexicans impoverished. In this respect, Chicanos increasingly saw a parallel between themselves and the native peoples of other colonized lands: all had been conquered, all had been reduced to menial labor, and all had been used to extract the natural bounty of their own land for the benefit of the conquerors.[3]

The Chicanos' historic loss of the economic power inherent in the land of the Southwest underlay the manifestations of militant nationalism that erupted in the late 1960s: the farm worker strikes in California, the land grant struggle in New Mexico, the revolt of the electorate in Crystal City, Texas, the school walkouts in Denver and Los Angeles, and the other major events of what came to be called the Chicano movement. Though these events exploded with suddenness, they were preceded by calmer yet significant developments in the previous decade that prepared a sizable number of Mexican-Americans for the move away from Americanization. As we have seen, the 1950s and early 1960s had been the nadir in the history of Mexican nationalism in the Southwest. But even though Mexican-American organizations had generally been weakened by the assimilation of potential members into the Anglo world, several new groups had managed to establish themselves during that time. The most important of these were the Mexican-American Political Association (MAPA) founded in California in 1959 and the Political Association of Spanish-Speaking Organizations (PASO or PASSO) founded in Arizona in 1960 and most influential in Texas.[4] These two differed from the League of United Latin American Citizens, the G. I. Forum, and other earlier groups because the new organizations believed in activating the political power of Mexican-Americans for the overall good of Mexican-

Americans. Earlier groups, more assimilationist in perspective, preferred a defensive posture, protecting the rights of Mexican-Americans in the name of all U.S. citizens. While the difference may seem subtle, the new emphasis on self-interest rather than universality prepared the way for the rebirth of Chicano nationalism.

It is not surprising that this change occurred in the closing years of the Eisenhower administration when the stress on Americanism was beginning to lose its force. The presidential campaign of John F. Kennedy, with its promise of a return to the principles of the New Deal and the Good Neighbor Policy, galvanized the Mexican-American community into political action. Kennedy's Catholicism, which seemed un-American to so many Anglos, was the critical link that allowed Mexican-Americans to identify with the candidate. Furthermore, Kennedy directly sought their vote with the result that MAPA and PASO members helped form the Viva Kennedy Clubs that won the Mexican-American vote for the Democrats, a vote that proved decisive in bringing victory to their candidate in the crucial state of Texas. With Kennedy's election Mexican-Americans looked forward to improved U.S. relations with Latin America and to better socioeconomic conditions at home.[5]

Even though the Kennedy administration was brief, the expectations of Mexican-Americans were met in several respects. During the Republican years U.S. relations with Latin America had generally been poor, but Mexican Americans, despite their strong ties with that part of the world and because they did not wish to be considered un-American, had protested little. Given the strong anticommunism of the period, they also thought it unpatriotic to support leftists such as those in Guatemala and Cuba. Mexican-Americans, therefore, welcomed Kennedy's Alliance for Progress, an attempt to improve conditions in Latin America with U.S. foreign aid. They felt that such a cooperative effort would lift Latin America out of poverty, furthering the cause of democracy and free enterprise against Cuban-style communism. The Alliance for Progress, like the Good Neighbor Policy, once again allowed Mexican Americans to feel more comfortable with their bicultural loyalties. Also, Kennedy's popularity in Mexico itself, resulting from his Catholicism and his demonstrated interest in the Latin American world, naturally pleased Mexican-Americans.

This popularity was evident in the summer of 1962 when Kennedy was well received by the populace of Mexico City during his visit. In his discussions with President Adolfo López Mateos, he agreed to expedite the settlement of a border dispute over a sliver of land known as El Chamizal, a small tract between El Paso and Ciudad Juárez. While only about 630 acres of underdeveloped land were involved, the dispute, caused by a shift in the course of the Rio Grande, had festered for nearly a century. The refusal of the United States to surrender the property, despite its having been awarded to Mexico by an arbitration commission in 1911, caused Mexicans to feel that their neighbor was still as imperialistic as in 1848. El Chamizal had become symbolic of all the land Mexico had lost to the North Americans. President Kennedy's decision to return the property was an intelligent exercise in goodwill because it made Mexicans and Mexican-Americans alike feel that they no longer need fear U.S. aggression. Kennedy's move was especially wise because it made North Americans appear less imperialistic at a time when the United States was carrying out a forceful policy against Fidel Castro's Cuba.[6]

Although Kennedy was able to do little to improve directly the condition of Mexican-Americans, his strong stand for the civil rights of minorities was appreciated. After Kennedy's assassination, Lyndon B. Johnson responded to the civil rights movement by promoting the social legislation that became known as the War on Poverty. Johnson's contact with Mexican-Americans, however, was limited, and they soon felt that their needs were being ignored by an administration which was more concerned with the increasingly volatile black communities. The riots that exploded in the black ghettos in the mid-1960s led the federal government to channel War on Poverty funds into these neighborhoods. Mexican -Americans, who had remained nonviolent despite deplorable conditions in the barrios, protested that the administration should also remember the needs of the quiet Spanish-speaking communities.[7] Shortly after the Watts riot of 1965, the major Mexican-American organizations of California (MAPA, LULAC, the CSO, and the G. I. Forum) sent President Johnson a joint resolution calling for aid to their communities.

This resolution was to be the last major Mexican-American statement couched in the terms of "Americanism." The organizations argued that since Mexican-Americans did not believe in or engage in civil disobedience or violent confrontation, they were good citizens, loyal to the democratic system, and should be included in antipoverty programs. The resolution reminded the President of the excellent military record of Mexican-Americans and of their contributions to the building of the American Southwest. Significantly, in mentioning their historical role in the Southwest, and despite their stress on Americanism, the Mexican-American organizations did not depict their people as immigrants in order to make them seem as "American" as any European ethnic group. The organizations proudly proclaimed their people's early presence in the Southwest, albeit in terms acceptable to the general public in 1965: "Over 150 years ago, Spanish-speaking Mexican-Americans stopped the Russian colonial advance and conquest from Siberia and Alaska, and preserved the Western portion of the United States for our country, which at that time consisted of thirteen colonies struggling for their existence, into which nation we and our predecessors became incorporated as loyal citizens and trustworthy participants in its democratic form of government...."[8]

The Mexican-American organizations were referring to Spain's eighteenth century efforts in California to prevent any encroachment on New Spain from Czarist Russia, which was advancing from the northwest. Reflecting the anticommunism of the Cold War period, the organizations interpreted the early settlement of the Southwest by the Spanish-speaking as historically significant because it prevented a potential Soviet presence on territory that would later become part of the United States. Though this interpretation was Americanist in that it portrayed the region as manifestly destined for democracy and the Union, it also revealed that some Mexican-Americans by then not only refused to see themselves as immigrants but declined to call themselves Spanish. Within a short while Chicano activists were to radicalize this image as they adopted the militant beliefs and tactics that the message to President Johnson had decried. Militants quickly learned the apparent lesson: if a minority group showed no signs of violence, it could expect little attention from U.S. society. Before long they also concluded that the War on Poverty, like the Alliance for Progress, was designed to prevent revolution, not to improve the conditions of the poor.[9]

During the very month that Johnson received the resolution of the California organizations, the quiet Mexican-American minority inaugurated the explosive Chicano movement. On 16 September (Mexican Independence Day) 1965, César Chávez's predominantly Mexican-American National Farm Workers Association (NFWA) voted to join a grape strike initiated in Delano, California, by the Filipino Agricultural Workers Organizing Committee (AWOC). Because of their greater numbers, Mexican-Americans soon dominated the strike and later controlled the United Farm Workers' Organizing Committee (UFWOC), which came into being as a result of the merger of the two original unions.[10] This strike was to lead to the first successful agricultural revolt by one of the poorest groups of Chicanos in the Southwest. Interestingly, this revolt was led by a man who believed in nonviolence, democracy, and religion; who had little faith in government programs; and who distrusted the very Chicano nationalism he inspired.

Chávez, whose grandfather was a "pioneer" in Arizona in the 1880s, was born near Yuma in 1927. "Our family farm was started three years before Arizona became a state," Chávez once remarked. "Yet, sometimes I get crank letters . . . telling me to 'go back' to Mexico!"[11] As a result of the depression the family's land was lost in 1939 because of unpaid taxes, and the Chávezes migrated to California where they became farm workers. After years of such work and a period in the navy, César Chávez joined the Community Service Organization which, though overwhelmingly Mexican-American in membership, stressed the acquisition and exercise of the rights of citizenship by the poor of all ethnic groups. This early influence later helped Chávez gain widespread support for the farm workers, even though it prevented him from becoming a true spokesman for Chicano nationalism. After ten years in the CSO, Chávez in 1962 decided to organize farm workers on his own when the CSO decided the task was beyond its range of activities.[12]

Shortly after the NFWA voted to strike, Chávez appealed to religious and civil rights groups for volunteers. By doing so, he converted a labor dispute into a social movement, and expanded his Mexican-American and Filipino base of support by including all others who wished to help. At the same time he nonetheless acknowledged that race was an issue in the strike. Chávez encouraged nationalism among the farm workers because he knew it could be a cohesive force against the Anglo growers who were accustomed to treating racial minorities as inferiors. Indeed, the Virgin of Guadalupe, the patroness of Mexico, became one of the chief nationalistic symbols used in the movement's demonstrations. Luis Valdez, playwright and propagandist for the farm workers, described her significance:

> The Virgin of Guadalupe was the first hint to farm workers that the pilgrimage to Sacramento in the spring of 1966] implied social revolution. During the Mexican Revolution, the peasant armies of Emiliano Zapata carried her standard, not only because they sought her divine protection, but because she symbolized the Mexico of the poor and humble. It was a simple Mexican Indian, Juan Diego, who first saw her in a vision at Guadalupe. Beautifully dark and Indian in feature, she was the New World version of the Mother of Christ. Even though some of her worshipers in Mexico still identify her with Tonatzin, an Aztec goddess, she is a Catholic saint of Indian creation—a Mexican. The people's response was immediate and reverent. They joined the march by the thousands, falling in line behind her standard.[13]

Thus, through the Virgin, Chávez and the Chicano workers linked their struggle to their aboriginal Mexican past.

Although the Mexican symbols used by the movement were generally associated with Mexico proper, Chávez was also aware of the Chicano farm workers' indigenous background in the Southwest. He had a personal interest in the history of the California missions and in their treatment of the Indians, the first farm workers. Chávez believed that though the missionaries had indeed used coercion on the Indians, they had saved them from far worse treatment at the hands of the secular authorities and the settlers. They had done this by making the missions sanctuaries where the Indians could work the land communally and by forcing the settlers to treat the Indians as human beings. As a result, Chávez once commented, "The Spanish began to marry the Indians . . .: they couldn't destroy them, so instead of wiping out a race, they made a new one."[14] The relative autonomy of the missions, politically and economically, together with the Franciscans' belief in the equality of all human souls, permitted the Indians a certain amount of security and even on occasion complete acceptance through intermarriage with the settlers. Like their Indian predecessors, twentieth-century farm workers, in Chávez's eyes, could only gain their rightful place in society if they believed in their own racial equality with other men and established themselves as an independent political and economic force capable of challenging the new owners of the land.

Chávez fully realized what the historic loss of the land had meant to the Indians and to their Mexican successors. The "Plan of Delano," a Mexican style proclamation stating the discontent of the farm workers and the aims of Chávez and his movement, reminded society of the oppression Southwest Mexicans had endured: "The Mexican race has sacrificed itself for the last hundred years. Our sweat and our blood have fallen on this land to make other men rich."[15] Chávez knew that the power of the Anglo growers rested on their ownership of the land, and he also realized that Chicanos and the other poor would ultimately achieve full equality only when they had recovered that land: "While . . . our adversaries . . . are the rich and the powerful and possess the land, we are not afraid.... We know that our cause is just, that history is a story of social revolution, and that the poor shall inherit the land." Though Chávez stated this belief publicly, he knew land reform was a distant ideal, and he was much too practical to make it a goal for his union. Despite this, the growers claimed that such statements, together with the symbols of Mexican nationalism, revealed Chávez to be communistic and un-American. One rancher remarked,

> Mr. Cesar Chavez is talking about raking over this stare—I don't like that. Too much "*Viva Zapata*" and down with the Caucasians, *la raza* [the Latin American racer, and all that. Mister Cesar Chavez is talking about n *revolucion*. Remember, California once belonged to Mexico, and he's saying, "Look, you dumb Mexicans, you lost it, now let's get it back!"[16]

Despite such distortions and in spite of his actual encouragement of nationalism, Chávez feared the divisive effects it could have within the movement. Since the growers were quick to exploit such divisiveness, he would not allow intolerance to split the ranks of his Chicano, Filipino, and liberal Anglo supporters. He was especially concerned that Chicanos not let their incipient nationalism get out of hand: "We oppose some of this La Raza business.... We know what it does. When La Raza means or implies racism, we don't support it. But if it means our struggle, our dignity, or our cultural roots, then we're for it." Because of this guarded attitude, however, Chávez could never become a fully committed advocate of Chicano nationalism. His struggle after all was economic, rather than cultural; his concerns were those of the poor as a whole, rather than more specifically Chicano issues, such as bilingual education. On the other hand, Chávez showed Chicanos that their cultural problems could not be solved by politics alone, since these problems were economic at their source:

> *Effective political power is never going to come, particularly to minority groups, unless they have economic power....*
>
> *I'm not advocating ... brown capitalism.... What I'm suggesting is a cooperative movement.*[17]

Such power lay in numbers and could best be harnessed if minority groups joined together with liberal Anglos in a broad interracial consumer movement.

During the grape strike, Chávez demonstrated how a cooperative movement could generate economic power, enough power to force the capitulation of the growers in 1970. His major weapon was a grape boycott extending beyond the Chicanos' Southwest, throughout the United States, and even into Europe. Since he had made the strike a moral and civil rights movement, many outsiders were willing to cooperate in the boycott. Within the UFWOC itself, as we have seen, Chávez made the workers understand that the struggle was for human equality, not merely for better wages and working conditions. As a result, in practical terms, the UFWOC itself became more a coöperative than a trade union: "It . . . developed for its members a death benefit plan; a cooperative grocery, drug store, and gas station; a credit union; a medical clinic; a social protest theater group ...; and a newspaper...." Such cooperative policies together with the nonviolent, mass protest methods of the civil rights movement (methods Mexican-Americans had earlier disdained to use) effectively countered such traditional grower tactics as the employment of strikebreakers from Mexico. After the grape growers agreed to sign contracts with the UFWOC in 1970, the farm-worker movement in the succeeding decades became an ongoing force as the union entered the lettuce fields, fought for the renewal of old contracts, and expanded to other parts of the nation. [18]

Beyond 1848

"Across the San Joaquin Valley," proclaimed the "Plan of Delano" in 1966, "across California, across the entire Southwest of the United States, wherever there are Mexican people, wherever there are farm workers, our movement is spreading like flames across a dry plain."[19] Within a short time the farm-worker front of the Chicano movement had indeed spread to Arizona and Texas, but, more important, other fronts of the movement had opened independently throughout the Southwest in other sectors of Chicano life. One of these fronts was the renewal of the land grant struggle in northern New Mexico. As we saw earlier, after the Treaty of Guadalupe Hidalgo, Mexicans in the Southwest were gradually deprived of their lands by an Anglo-American legal and economic system that constantly challenged land grants made under previous governments. In his investigation of problems resulting from the land grant issue during the 1960s, Peter Nabokov wrote that in northern New Mexico:

> *These ancestral holdings had originally been awarded to single people or to communities of at least ten village families. A man had his private home and a narrow rectangular plot which usually gave him access to river water. But the community's grazing and wood-gathering acreage, called ejido, was understood to be held commonly, and forever, a perpetual trust. A large percentage of the New Mexico ejido lands had been put in the public domain by the surveyors general of the period 1854-1880 because they recognized only claims made on behalf of individuals, not communities.*[20]

During the twentieth century much of this "public domain" was turned over to the Forest Service, which in turn was given the authority to lease the lands to private individuals and companies for the use and development of natural resources. Unfortunately for the long-settled small farmers of northern New Mexico, large out-of-state corporations, engaged in mining, logging, and tourism, received preferential treatment in their dealings with the Forest Service. The impoverished small farmers, on the other hand, were gradually denied their grazing rights by an agency that was unconcerned with and even hostile to their needs; in her study of the problem, Patricia Bell Blawis observed that "while logging firms contracted with the Forest Service for immense areas on their ancestral land, the grantees were forbidden to cut stove wood without a permit." Thus, according to Blawis, in the twentieth century the imperialism of the nineteenth continued surreptitiously: "The Forest Service is evidence of the colonial policy of the Federal government.... Through this Service, resources of the West are exploited by Washington, D.C. and its friends."[21] As we have seen, the native Mexicans had in the past reacted violently to this colonialism: between the 1880s and the late 1920s, for instance, at least two groups of nightriders, Las Gorras

Blancas and La Mano Negra, had burned buildings, torn down fences, and committed other such terrorist acts to protest the seizure of their lands.[22] During the late 1960s such violence flared again.

In 1963 the militant Alianza Federal de Mercedes (the Federal Land Grant Alliance—always popularly known as the Alianza, even though the official name changed several times) was incorporated under the direction of a dynamic leader named Reies López Tijerina. Tijerina, whose great-grandfather had been robbed of his land and killed by Anglos, was born in Texas in 1926; he lived and moved throughout the Southwest and beyond as a farm worker and later as a poor itinerant preacher. During these wanderings, he came to believe that the problems of his people had resulted from their loss of the land, for as he later stressed, "the ties of our culture with the land are indivisible."[23] As a consequence, he became interested in the land grant issue, spent a year studying the question in Mexico, and in 1960 settled in New Mexico where he felt there was the best hope of recovering the grants. After organizing many of the heirs into the Alianza, Tijerina unsuccessfully petitioned the U.S. government to investigate the land titles for violations of that portion of the Treaty of Guadalupe Hidalgo that guaranteed the property rights of Mexicans in the Southwest. He had also requested the Mexican government to look into the matter, but Mexico, having gradually become economically dependent on as well as ideologically aligned with the United States since the 1930s, had not and would not support any radical claims made by dissident Chicanos. Rebuffed in his efforts to get consideration through regular legal and political channels, Tijerina turned to civil disobedience.[24]

In October of 1966 Tijerina and other *aliancistas* occupied the Echo Amphitheater, a section of the Carson National Forest that had once been part of the land grant of San Joaquin del Río de Chama. Since the original Spanish and Mexican grants had permitted the villagers a good deal of autonomy, the *aliancistas* declared themselves the Republic of San Joaquin and elected as mayor a direct descendant of the original grantee. When several forest rangers attempted to interfere, they were detained by the "republic," tried for trespassing, and released on suspended sentences. By allowing this, Tijerina hoped to challenge the jurisdiction of the Forest Service over the land, thus forcing the land grant issue into the courts, possibly as far as the Supreme Court. Also, the declaration of autonomy would make public the Chicanos' need for self-determination, their need to escape a whole range of problems caused by their incorporation into U.S. society. Not least of these was the war in Vietnam, which even the traditionally patriotic *nuevomexicanos* were beginning to oppose:

"The people," as Tijerina had once remarked, "generally feel that our sons are being sent to Vietnam illegally, because many of these land grants are free city states and are independent." The "liberation" of the Echo Amphitheater had been a dangerous act, but as the increasingly radical Tijerina declared during the occupation: "Fidel Castro has what he has because of his guts. . . . Castro put the gringos off his island and we can do the same." Unfortunately for the Alianza, Tijerina would later serve two years in prison for assault on the rangers at the Echo Amphitheater; furthermore, the courts would refuse to admit discussion of the land grant issue. [25]

During May of 1967, according to Nabokov, "private northern landowners . . . began suffering from the traditional symptoms of unrest—selective cattle rustling, irrigation ditch and fence wreckage, shot-up water tanks, and arson." Although there was no evidence the Alianza had committed these acts, the authorities actually feared that guerrilla warfare might break out in northern New Mexico. When Tijerina revealed that his group planned to have a conference on June 3 at Coyote, a small town near the San Joaquin grant, the authorities anticipated another occupation and prevented the meeting by declaring it an unlawful assembly, blocking the roads to the town, and arresting any *aliancistas* who resisted. This proved to be a mistake, for it brought on the very violence the authorities had feared. Feeling that their right to free assembly had been violated, the *aliancistas* decided to make a citizen's arrest of the district attorney responsible for the police action. On June 5, in the most daring move of the contemporary Chicano movement, Tijerina and about twenty other armed *aliancistas* attacked the courthouse at the county seat at Tierra Amarilla. In the ensuing shoot-out two deputies were wounded, the courthouse was occupied, and the Coyote prisoners were freed. Finding that the district attorney was not present, the *aliancistas* then fled the town with two hostages.[26]

The reaction of the authorities brought the cause of the Alianza to the attention of the entire nation. Imagining "a new Cuba to the north," the state government in Santa Fe sent out four hundred National Guardsmen to join two hundred state troopers in an expedition into northern New Mexico that included the use of helicopters and two tanks.[27] After a few days Tijerina was captured and charged with various crimes connected with the raid, though he was subsequently released on bail. Once in the national spotlight, Tijerina elaborated on the issues and goals of the land grant struggle, issues that were important to Chicanos throughout the Southwest; "Not only the land has been stolen from the good and humble people," he commented, "but also their culture...." And he remarked, "A major point of contention is that we are being deprived of our language...." Tijerina also argued that in addition to property rights, the cultural rights of his people were guaranteed by the Treaty of Guadalupe Hidalgo. Once the guarantees of this treaty were honored and discrimination was ended, Indo-Hispanos, as Tijerina often called his people, would take their rightful place as intermediaries in the pluralistic Southwest:

> *We have forced by destiny to adopt two languages; we will be the future ambassadors and envoys to Latin America. At home, I believe that the Southwest is breeding a special kind of people that will bridge the color-gap between black and white.... [Moreover] We are the people the Indians call their "lost brothers."*[28]

While the many charges against him were being handled in the courts, Tijerina continued his activities with the Alianza and also participated in the interracial, antipoverty Poor People's March on Washington in 1968. In 1969, however, the Alianza was deprived of Tijerina's leadership when he was imprisoned for the Echo Amphitheater incident. Suffering from poor health, he was paroled in July 1971, but on condition that he no longer hold of lice in the Alianza. Deprived of his full leadership and lacking the organized economic power of an institution such as the United Farm Workers, the Alianza lost much of its drive, and not until 1979 was it able to convince the government to give even nominal reconsideration to the land grant issue.[29] Nonetheless, Tijerina and the Alianza did rejuvenate the ethnic pride of a good number of *nuevomexicanos*. Though many Hispanos considered Tijerina an outsider, many others joined his organization, and in doing so reaffirmed their ties to Mexico through reference to the Treaty of Guadalupe Hidalgo, and to their Indian ancestors through acceptance of the facts of *mestizaje* (Indo-Hispano intermarriage). In New Mexico no longer could "Spanish-Americans" easily deny their background. No longer could Spanish-American politicians, who had generally held a representative number of positions in government, ignore their economically depressed constituents without opposition from Chicano militants around the state—for increasingly among *nuevomexicanos* the image of the Spanish Southwest was giving way to the image of Aztlán.[30]

The person most responsible for the adoption of the term "Aztlán" by the rapidly spreading Chicano movement was Rodolfo "Corky" Gonzales, leader of the Chicano community in Denver, Colorado. In modern times the term was first applied to the Chicano homeland in 1962 by Jack D. Forbes, a Native American professor who argued that Mexicans were more truly an Indian than a mestizo people; his mimeographed manuscript, "The Mexican Heritage of Aztlán (the Southwest) to 1821," was distributed among Mexican-Americans in the Southwest during the early

1960s.[31] The term gained popularity, but was not universally accepted by the Chicano movement until, in the spring of 1969, the first Chicano national conference, in Denver, drafted "El plan espiritual de Aztlán," a document that declared the spiritual independence of the Chicano Southwest from the United States.[32] Paradoxically this sentiment was expressed in a city never legally within the confines of Mexico; however, like arguments for Puerto Rican independence presented in New York, this declaration from Denver signified the desire of a minority group for independence from the colonialism that had subjugated its native land and that continued to affect the individuals of the minority no matter where, they resided within the United States.

Born in Denver in 1928, Corky Gonzales was primarily a product of the urban barrios, even though he spent part of his youth working in the fields of southern Colorado. He managed to escape poverty by becoming a successful boxer. As a result of the popularity gained from this career, he became an influential figure in the barrios and was selected to head various antipoverty programs in the early 1960s. By 1965, however, he had become disenchanted with the antipoverty bureaucracy. He concluded earlier than other Chicanos that the War on Poverty was designed to pacify rather than truly help the poor. Had he read it, he would have agreed with a later comment made by a Chicano editor when government and foundation money poured into northern New Mexico in the aftermath of Tierra Amarilla:

> *They're trying to create Vendido power (sellout power) . . . trying to bring Vietnam to New Mexico and trying to create "leaders" the system can use as tools. But it hasn't worked with the Vietnamese and it's not going to work with Raza here in the United States.*

Disgusted with the strings attached to funds from the government and foundations, Gonzales organized the Crusade for Justice, a community self-help group. Through their own fund raising efforts, the members established a barrio service center, providing such assistance as child care, legal aid, housing and employment counseling, health care, and other services especially needed in poor urban areas. The Crusade was, moreover, outspoken in its concern for Chicano civil and cultural rights.[33]

More than Chávez and even more than Tijerina, Gonzales felt that nationalism was the force that would get Chicanos to help one another, and that the success of his Crusade exemplified the possibilities of self-determination. Although his participation in the Poor People's March of 1968 revealed his belief in the necessity of interracial cooperation, at heart he felt that Chicanos would have to help themselves and would do so if they became aware of their proud history as a people. Of Chicanos in his state, he once said, "Colorado belongs to our people, was named by our people, discovered by our people and worked by our people.... We preach self-respect ... to reclaim what is ours." Regarding the region as a whole, he commented, "Nationalism exists in the Southwest, but until now it hasn't been formed into an image people can see. Until now it has been a dream. It has been my job to create a reality out of the dream...." The Crusade was part of that reality and so was the Chicano Youth Liberation Conference, called by Gonzales to bring together Chicanos from throughout the nation, but especially from the cities, where 80 percent of all Chicanos lived. In Gonzales urban youth found a leader, unlike Chávez or Tijerina, who had successfully attempted concrete solutions to city problems. Consequently, 1,500 Chicanos from many different organizations attended the conference of this urban nationalist. [34]

As if in exhibit of the problems of urban Chicanos, the week before the conference riots broke out in the Denver barrios, resulting from events that began with a racist remark made by a teacher at a local high school. A student and community protest led to confrontation with police; according to Gonzales, "What took place... was a battle between the West Side 'liberation forces' and the 'occupying army.' The West Side won- police suffered some injuries and damage to equipment."[35] Although Gonzales opposed violence and tried to stop the rioting, he clearly felt the trouble was justified and was proud that Chicanos were capable of defending themselves against the government he believed had made internal colonies of the city's barrios. After the riots, the conference convened in an atmosphere permeated with nationalism and proclaimed the following in "El plan espiritual de Aztlán:"

> *"Conscious ... of the brutal "Gringo" invasion of our territories, we, the Chicano inhabitants and civilizers of the northern land of Aztlan, from whence came our forefathers, reclaiming the land of their birth.... We [who] do not recognize capricious frontiers on the bronze continent.... we declare the independence of our mestizo nation.* [36]

In that proclamation the Chicano delegates fully revived their people's traditional image of the Southwest and clarified it for their own time: the Southwest was the Chicano homeland, a land paradoxically settled by an indigenous people who were subsequently conquered. Furthermore, these people were now seen as native, not merely because their Spanish ancestors had settled the land hundreds of years before, but because their Indian ancestors had resided on the land thousands of years earlier, tying it permanently to Indian and mestizo Mexico.

With this image of the Southwest, the Chicano delegates established a context for a variety of demands that would gain impetus in the near future. Before long in the name of Aztlán and its people, activists would demand restitution from the United States for its conquest of the region and for its economic, political, and cultural oppression of the Southwest Mexican population. From the institutions of the United States, Chicanos would reject token representation and poverty programs with strings attached; from state and national institutions they would expect unrestricted compensation; over local institutions they would demand control. With such control, Chicanos hoped to establish bilingual/bicultural education, promote their own arts and customs, tax themselves, hire their own police, select their own juries, sit on their own draft boards, and especially found cooperatives to prevent further economic exploitation. Thus, the separatism at the conference, while expressing itself in the ideal of complete political independence from the United States, more importantly would promote the pragmatic goal of local autonomy. Gonzales' Crusade offered a practical example of how such autonomy might be gained. Another practical means, discussed at the conference, was the creation of a third party independent of Democrats and Republicans, especially in local elections. Many of these ideas found a national forum in the Chicano Youth Liberation Conference. This was Gonzales' major achievement. While his Crusade for Justice continued its work in Denver, as an organization it never spread far beyond that city. However, the delegates to the conference returned to their homes throughout the Southwest inspired by the urban nationalism that the Crusade exemplified.[37]

That the conference had articulated some of the major aspirations of the Chicano movement became evident in 1970 when Chicano activists put their beliefs into practice while seizing political control of Crystal City, Texas. Crystal City, a town of about 10,000 persons, was about 80 percent Mexican American, but was controlled by the Anglo population, as was the rest of heavily Mexican-American South Texas. Since most of the resident Mexican Americans were uneducated, often illiterate, immigrant workers, the Anglos were for decades able to manipulate the elections to ensure all-Anglo city governments. In his *Chicano Revolt in a Texas Town*, John Staples Shockley argued that a colonial situation existed between the two groups, a situation resulting from the gradual Anglo subjugation of the area during the violent times before 1930. In 1963, however, Crystal City's Mexicans out of their homes, caught the Anglos by surprise and elected a working-class Mexican American city government. That government administered the city well, but was unable to institute major reforms because the Anglos controlled the economy and the county tax structure. In a sense the old colonialism was replaced by a neocolonialism that allowed political but not economic independence. By 1965, moreover, the uneducated and inexperienced working-class councilmen had quarreled among themselves and were beaten at the polls by a sophisticated Anglo coalition that had coopted middle-class Mexican Americans.[38] Much like the Rhodesian government formed in 1979, the 1965 coalition government in Crystal City was composed of a "native" majority, but served the interests of the Anglo minority.

This form of neocolonialism, according to Shockley, continued in the town until 1969 when Jose Angel Gutiérrez, a Crystal City native, returned home from college to lead a new assault on Anglo power or, as he put it, "to begin Aztlán!"[39] Holding a master's degree in political science and thoroughly versed in the ideas and organizing methods of radical college movements, Gutiérrez converted an incident of discrimination in the schools into another electoral revolt. After organizing a third party called La Raza Unida, Gutiérrez's activists and working-class Chicanos seized the school board and city council from the Anglo and Mexican American coalition. Better equipped to govern than the leaders of the first revolt, La Raza Unida from the beginning used its new political power to the fullest to counteract continuing Anglo economic dominance. For example, the school system, which was one of the largest employers in the county, soon helped relieve Mexican American unemployment by dramatically increasing the number of the schools' nonprofessional positions. Also, the city government launched efforts to annex and tax a neighboring fruit packing plant, while La Raza Unida ran candidates for county offices that could be used to increase taxes on Anglo owned agricultural lands and oil properties, the area's chief means of production. Outside of government, the community organized cooperatives, Chicano businesses, and boycotts against hostile merchants. On the economic front, however, La Raza Unida was not nearly so successful as it was in instituting relevant educational programs, better police-community relations, improved public works, housing assistance, community health and legal services, and other projects directly affected by government.[40]

As the successes of Castro's Cuba promised to spread his revolution to the rest of Latin America, Anglos feared the successes of Crystal City would spread similar revolts throughout the Southwest. In fact, in the early 1970s La Raza Unida party was organized and fielded candidates throughout the region; but like Castro's revolution, Gutierrez's movement was contained. Although La Raza Unida won victories in other South Texas cities, in those cities it rarely achieved the firm position it won in Crystal City, and in areas outside Texas its successes were minimal despite much early enthusiasm. The reason for this was that the cohesive Chicano majority that existed in rural Crystal City was unique even in heavily Chicano South Texas. In the urban

Southwest, where most Chicanos lived, they were rarely majorities in their gerrymandering districts, and they were too numerous and divided to be readily organized electorates, especially once the Anglos intensified their co-optation tactics to counter the third-party threat.[41]

Just as its outward expansion was halted by the manipulative structures of U.S. politics, La Raza Unida's revolution within Crystal City was restricted by similar local structures designed to defend the economic status quo. In spite of his attacks on big business, Gutiérrez's power was too limited to implement thoroughly the socialism he believed was necessary.[42] What Crystal City showed Chicanos was that while they could gain a measure of local autonomy by their own nationalistic political efforts, they could not gain true self-determination without control of the local economy that provided their livelihoods. Since that economy was in the hands of businesses that operated on a national scale, only a national multiethnic movement to capture the federal government could ever secure true self-determination for individual minorities. This point was not lost on Chicano intellectuals, who were becoming increasingly radical, sometimes Marxist, as the Chicano movement progressed. In his *Occupied America* (1972), for example, Rodolfo Acuña wrote:

> *The only way the Chicanos of South Texas (or, for that matter, the United States) are going to realize self-determination is for the federal government to intervene and expropriate the land and means of production and give it to the barrios and colonias. The same principle must be applied internally that is applied when U.S. business is expropriated abroad.*[43]

Chicano intellectuals had found Gutiérrez's activities especially significant because he, being the most educated of the major Chicano leaders, had been the first to try putting radical "academic" theories into practice. The impact of a college graduate like Gutiérrez on the Chicano movement was also significant because he symbolized the importance to the movement of Chicano intellectuals and students generally. Indeed, in urban areas, students from high school through graduate school had been the major force behind the Chicano movement at least since 1968. In the spring of that year Chicanos in five East Los Angeles high schools walked out of classes to protest conditions in the schools that resulted in extremely high drop-out rates. This led, over the next few years, to a series of walk-outs in one city after another, as Chicano students and instructors throughout the Southwest demanded new schools, more sensitive teachers, and bilingual/bicultural education. Although Chicano student groups had been organized before 1968, the activism of that year put those groups into the forefront of the urban movement. In the colleges and universities of the Southwest, these groups successfully demanded Chicano studies and affirmative action programs, programs that would help produce the first group of Chicano college graduates committed to the cultural survival of their people. Even before they had graduated, these students became involved in off-campus groups to organize the poor and uneducated in the barrios and rural towns. These were the college people Gutiérrez symbolized.[44]

As time passed, campus groups that in 1967 had given themselves names such as the United Mexican American Students and the Mexican American Student Confederation became more militant. After many walk-outs and after Corky Gonzales's Chicano Youth Liberation Conference in 1969, most campus groups changed their names to El Movimiento Estudiantil Chicano de Aztlán (MECHA—The Chicano Student Movement of Aztlán), revealing their increasingly radical nationalism. At the Second Annual Chicano Youth Conference in the spring of 1970, representatives of student and other youth groups, reflecting their disenchantment with the United States, declared their opposition to the war in Vietnam. Many Chicanos were no longer proud of the fact that they, as a people, were once again dying in a U.S. war in disproportionately high numbers; moreover, they opposed dying in a war fought against a people they believed were victims of the same colonialism they themselves were experiencing. To demonstrate their opposition, a national Chicano antiwar rally was planned for August 1970 to be held in East Los Angeles, the barrio with the largest concentration of Mexican-Americans in the nation. Unfortunately, the rally became a riot when the police attempted to break up the demonstration and only succeeded in provoking the participants into the worst mass violence in East LA since 1943. For months thereafter violent protests erupted periodically, and the number of police on the streets of East LA visibly increased. Rarely had the colonial status of Chicanos seemed so evident.[45]

After 1970 the open confrontations of the previous five years became less frequent as the Chicano movement entered a period of consolidation. Having had many of its hopes and grievances dramatized, the Chicano community was gradually able to take advantage of the advances the movement had attained, especially in education and self-awareness. With a renewed pride in their culture, Chicano intellectuals set out to express a world view that had long been suppressed. That their image of the Southwest as Aztlán was an important part of that world view was clear from the titles of many of the publications that appeared as Chicano culture experienced a renewal in literature, art, and social thought. A scholarly quarterly entitled *Aztlán: Chicano Journal of the Social Sciences and the Arts* was first issued in 1970 by Aztlán Publications at the University of California, Los Angeles. A bibliography by Ernie Barrios published in 1971 bore the title *Bibliografia de Aztlán*. In 1973 Luis Valdez and Stan Steiner edited a work called *Aztlán: An Anthology of Mexican American Literature*. Two novels, *Peregrinos de Aztlán* (1974) by Miguel Mendez M. and *Heart of Aztlan* (1976) by Rudolfo A. Anaya, also carried the ancient name of the Southwest. As if to secure that name for posterity, *Aztlan: The Southwest and Its People*, a history for juveniles by Luis F. Hernández, was published in 1975.[46] Many other works with less obvious titles also reflected the rediscovered Chicano image of the Southwest. Among the most important was the already mentioned *Occupied America* (1972) by Rodolfo Acuña. In this history of Chicanos, Acuña interpreted the tradition of the lost northern homeland according to the modern theory of colonialism, a theory that made the image of Aztlán more meaningful to contemporary Chicanos.

Needless to say, not all Mexican-Americans accepted the image of Aztlán. Among the masses the images of the Spanish Southwest and the American Southwest continued to predominate during the 1970s, and into the 1980s, largely because these were still promoted by the educational system and the mass media. Through bicultural and Chicano studies programs, Chicano intellectuals worked to change this situation. However, a small group of Mexican Americans conversant with the affairs of their ethnic group refused to abandon borrowed images of the Southwest, usually because their lives had been formed within those images or because those views continued to help them accommodate themselves to the standards of Anglo society. Congressman Henry B. González of San Antonio, Texas, for example, had built his political career around the integrationist civil rights movement of the 1950s and early 1960s; as a result the nationalism of the Chicano movement struck him as nothing less than reverse racism. Since González accepted the integrationist melting pot ideal, he also perceived his region as the American Southwest, to which his parents, like European arrivals on the East Coast, had come to join the "nation of immigrants." Thus, in an address to Congress in 1969, he remarked:

> *As it happens my parents were born in Mexico and came to this country seeking safety.... It follows that I, and many other residents of my part of Texas and other Southwestern States—happen to be what is commonly referred to as Mexican-American.*

Since his background only "happened" to be Mexican, González could see little importance in notions such as Aztlán and vigorously opposed Chicano militancy.[47] Another knowledgeable individual who rejected the image of Aztlán was the

Franciscan man of letters Fray Angelico Chavez, a descendant of some of the original *nuevomexicano* settlers. Fray Angelico had spent more than twenty years writing poetry, essays, and history on the subject of New Mexico, always with the image of the Spanish Southwest in mind. Although he was too well informed to believe that *nuevomexicanos* were of pure Spanish descent, he nevertheless convinced himself that they were more Spanish than people south of the border and that Indian genes within the *nuevomexicano* population were largely confined to certain sections of the lower class.[48] Fray Angelico believed it was these lower-class people

> *who join the agrarian and urban Mexicans or Mexican-Americans in their social protests, and consequently like to be called "Chicanos" along with them.*
> *The true Spanish New Mexican castizo [Pure-blood] does not....*[49]

He made this comment in an informal history of his state called *My Penitente Land: Reflections on Spanish New Mexico* (1974), a work that revealed his complete fealty to the image of the Spanish Southwest.

Even though borrowed images of the Chicanos' place in the Southwest persisted, by the late 1970s some of the new group of educated Chicanos were in positions where they could reveal the image of Aztlán to the general public. For example, Tony Castro, a graduate of Baylor University, spent several years writing for various major newspapers around the country and was then hired in the late 1970s as a regular columnist for the conservative *Los Angeles Herald Examiner*. Devoting most of his columns and later his special reports to Chicano issues, Castro repeatedly exposed the generally conservative readership of that newspaper to the Chicano image of the Southwest:

> *The Chicano has been here since the founding of California and the Southwest. His pre-Columbian ancestors wandered here from the north, migrating farther south and establishing the great civilizations of the Maya, the Toltecs, the Aztecs....... [Yet] Mexican-Americans ... have been the conquered people, strangers in their own land.*[50]

Young professionals like Castro who were willing to argue for their people's rightful place in the Southwest and the United States were the most successful product of the 1960s movement. As we have seen, educational improvement had been a major goal of the movement; consequently during the 1970s education was the area where Chicanos made their greatest strides. With Chicano college enrollment having tripled by 1978 (despite a leveling off of progress by that time), more teachers, social workers, writers, social scientists, and others influenced by the nationalism of the 1960s were echoing that nationalism, albeit with caution, from new positions throughout the Southwest.[51]

Despite the emergence of this educated, nationalistic leadership, the progress of Chicanos as a whole was uneven in the 1970s and stagnant in the early 1980s. They continued to fit the description of a colonized people. In California, for example, where Chicanos were most heavily concentrated and where opportunities were often considered best, "Hispanics" over the age of twenty-five had completed high school at only 56 percent of the rate at which Anglos had gained the same level of schooling. And financially, the median Hispanic family income was only $16,140 or 71 percent of the equivalent white family income (1980 U.S. Census figures). While these figures did indicate some improvement over the 1960s, the gains were threatened by a backlash that persisted into the 1980s. Many of the educational and consequently the income gains of Chicanos had come as a result of affirmative action programs, compensatory programs that gave minorities preferential treatment in schooling and employment. These programs were attacked in the courts as reverse discrimination in case after case by Anglos who, though they failed to destroy the programs, managed to impede their effectiveness. Also, programs in Chicano studies and bilingual/bicultural education, while surviving, constantly met opposition from those who regarded them as contrary to the tradition of the nation of immigrants who learned English and forgot the old country. Given the fact that their educational and income gains were so recent, it is no surprise that Chicanos had accumulated little personal wealth and had made little progress toward recovering the means of production in their southwestern homeland.[52]

This continuing lack of economic power in the 1970s and 1980s caused Chicano gains in the political arena to be inconclusive at best. While U.S. presidents generally appointed an increasing number of Chicanos to positions in their administrations, these appointees usually found themselves beholden to their benefactors and isolated in government with little real power to help their people. Even those Chicanos elected to political office could rarely represent fully the interests of their people, since as politicians they generally owed their elections to the Anglo-controlled coalitions that funded their campaigns. In many cases, of course, the politicians themselves continued to be ideologically traditional. For example, in 1974 Arizona and New Mexico elected as governors conservative Raúl Castro and moderate Jerry Apodaca, the first southwestern governors of Mexican descent since Octaviano Larrazolo fifty years earlier. If traditional electoral politics had been the best way to the improvement of Chicano life, the election of two Mexican-American governors should have brought significant social change for Chicanos in those states, but this did not happen because the ideological frame of mind and the political structures within which the governors worked were developed to protect the status quo. As we have seen, even the radical La Raza Unida party often found the traditional structures impregnable. Without such a radical organizational base, individual Chicano politicians, regardless of any personal nationalism, found themselves coopted by a system that defended the Anglo owners of the means of production. Many newly educated Chicano leaders in other fields found themselves bound by the same strictures. Since their salaries were bestowed on them by the system they often opposed, nationalistic Chicanos could not easily put their more radical beliefs into practice. Thus, though new leaders were more conscious of the forces in control, they were not yet in a position to topple neocolonialism in the Southwest.[53]

This situation, however, failed to prevent Chicano nationalists from voicing their disapproval of the neocolonial practices of the United States. In Latin American affairs, for example, many Chicanos had long since become disillusioned with North American motives; President Johnson's armed intervention in the Dominican Republic in 1965 had shown the United States to be as imperialistic as eves. In 1973 North American cooperation in the over throw of a democratically elected Marxist government in Chile convinced more Chicanos that the United States was mote concerned with its economic interests than it was with democracy or social change in Latin America. In the early 1980s U.S. opposition to the new government of Nicaragua and to the leftist guerrillas of El Salvador caused renewed fears among Chicanos of possible U.S. military intervention in Central America.[54] As we have noted, Mexicans in the United States had always seen their fate as closely tied to that of other Latin Americans, and as a consequence a significant group now believed continuing neocolonialism in Latin America to mean continuing neocolonialism in the Southwest. Quite naturally, Chicanos were most concerned with relations between the United States and Mexico, relations which intellectuals now interpreted as between metropolis and "neocolony."

José Angel Gutiérrez in 1971 remarked concerning Chicanos and Mexico, "the Rio Grande never has separated us and never will."[55] During the 1970s and 1980s the growing dependence of Mexico on the United States would verify Gutiérrez's statement. Although the Mexican Revolution had been fought in part to free the country from foreign, specifically North American, economic domination, by 1978 the

United States was once again the major investor in and chief trading partner of Mexico. Similar to the situation during the Díaz dictatorship, the Mexican government was stable, but the economy was erratic—at times superficially prosperous, but ultimately deeply troubled. Unfortunately most of the wealth was once again accruing to foreign investors and to the few Mexicans belonging to the middle and upper classes. The masses, burdened by one of the highest birth rates in the world, continued their struggle with poverty and, as in the past, looked to the north for employment. The most important pattern in Chicano history during the 1970s and 1980s was the renewed migration of Mexicans into the Southwest. Composed almost entirely of undocumented workers, commonly called illegal aliens, this movement was the largest yet from Mexico. Though estimates of their number, based on apprehensions of the undocumented by the Immigration and Naturalization Service (INS), varied tremendously, the actual figure was undoubtedly in the millions.[56]

The arrival of so many undocumented workers presented problems for Chicanos; nevertheless, it could be argued that the migration was beneficial. As in previous migratory waves, the new arrivals competed with U.S. Mexicans for low-paying jobs and low-cost housing; they seemingly depressed wages and helped cause unemployment; they occasionally served as strikebreakers, and sometimes competed with Chicanos for aid from the government. Since the undocumented generally settled in the southwestern barrios, Chicanos not only bore the brunt of competition from the newcomers, but were also exposed to renewed Anglo-American xenophobia. With the appearance of so many un-Americanized newcomers, the Anglo notion that all people in the barrios were foreigners once again seemed plausible. As a result, harassment of Chicanos by INS agents increased, and some employers became more cautious about hiring anyone who looked Mexican since that person might be an undocumented worker. During the 1970s and 1980s, the illegal alien question, of all issues concerning Chicanos, was by far the most commonly discussed in the Anglo communications media. Though the undocumented were usually discussed in terms of a social problem, for example as an alleged tax burden on the citizenry, these terms usually hid a very real Anglo fear that the Southwest was being culturally and racially reconquered by Mexicans—a fear not entirely unfounded.[57]

"There is a distinct possibility," wrote one openly racist Anglo, "if the legal and illegal seepage of Mexican genes across the Rio Grande and the high Mexican-American birthrate continue at present levels, that Mexican Americans will regain their lost territories of Alta California and Texas . . .— not by violence or minority politics but simply by exercising squatters' rights."[58] In October of 1977, this fear of

Mexican invasion was so aroused by the media that the Ku Klux Klan announced it would conduct its own armed surveillance of the boundary to assist the undermanned Border Patrol in arresting illegal aliens. With the tacit approval of certain officials in the INS and of the San Diego (California) police, some Klan patrols were planned, but this activity ceased after strenuous protests from Chicano and other minority groups. Their nationalism having been revived during the 1960s, most U.S. Mexicans no longer disassociated themselves from their fellows across the border; they were no longer willing to stand by, as they had in the 1930s and 1950s, and watch Mexicans mistreated simply for lacking proper documents. Even though undocumented workers competed directly with Mexican-Americans, most Chicanos now felt their common national heritage outweighed their practical differences. Indeed, this feeling was strong enough that Chicano activists threatened to form their own armed patrols to counter the Klan's.[59]

That Chicanos had to some extent readopted their Mexican imagination was evident from the similarity of their image of the Southwest to the image of the region perceived by the undocumented. "Undocumented workers," reported Grace Halsell, author of *The Illegals,* "do not feel they commit a crime in traveling north from Mexico. They call it going to *el norte*. As far as the Southwest is concerned, 'we are the legals, the Anglos the illegals,' one Mexican said."[60] In spite of the artificial international boundary, many Chicanos now realized more than ever that both they and Mexicans belonged in the Southwest, and that the fate of Chicanos in that region would always be influenced by people from Mexico. Because of this, as long as Mexico existed in a neocolonial relationship with the United States, the Chicano barrios and hamlets in the Southwest would continue to be internal colonies of the United States. Deprived of a living by a Mexican economy profiting North American investors and a domestic elite, undocumented workers would continue to pour into the Southwest to provide capitalists with cheap labor and consumers with lower prices. Since the undocumented would continue to compete with Chicanos at the bottom of the economic ladder, Chicanos would continue to have a difficult time climbing out of poverty, especially given the cooptation, discrimination, and other forms of subjugation traditionally used in the Southwest to keep the Spanish-speaking colonized.[61]

In the past Mexican-Americans had at times supported efforts to seal the border against their competitors from Mexico, but after the 1960s many concluded that, besides being practically impossible, sealing the border would not eliminate domestic forms of subjugation and would only deprive the Mexican poor of desperately needed income. Many Chicanos concluded it was immoral to deny employment to the undocumented, especially when many were friends and relatives. For this season, in fact, some Chicanos by 1979 were quietly hoping for a completely open border. Journalist Richard Reeves noted:

> *I'm convinced that the real Chicano position on undocumented workers is total amnesty ..., and a totally open border.... No one will say that ...—but many people said things like this . . .: "We know where the undocumented workers are—they're sleeping on the couches in our living rooms. They're family and they're just thing to feed their families back home."*[62]

Moreover, the undocumented and other recently arrived Mexicans provided Chicanos with the best hope that their culture would survive in the Southwest. Because of the newcomers, Chicanos were forced to maintain their language and culture or suffer a breakdown in barrio communication.

In fact it was the new influx of people from Mexico, together with the emergence of an educated nationalistic leadership, that made Chicano activists in the late 1970s guardedly optimistic about the future, despite the obstacles set up by the dominant society.[63] Of course, they had no illusions that they were about to establish a politically independent Aztlán, nor did they then wish to do so. Several years earlier, this idea had been considered and rejected for obvious reasons. "Would a separate state be viable?" journalist Armando Rendón had asked in 1971. "My guess is that the United States Government would act very quickly to suppress Chicano efforts toward this end." While such a utopian course of action would never be permitted, by the late 1970s Chicano activists were optimistic that more practical social plans would have to be taken seriously by Anglo society, for that society could not continue to ignore the fastest growing minority group in the nation. Given the perpetually high Chicano and Mexican birth rates, Chicano voting strength was growing by the year; if the newly nationalistic leadership ever organized that power, Anglo supremacy throughout the Southwest would be challenged as it had been in Crystal City. Faced with such a possibility, Anglos would have to make concessions because, as columnist Tony Castro commented, "The Mexican-American in the Southwest today is like a Palestinian in the Middle East. An accommodation has to be made."[64]

The analogy with the Palestinians had some merit because, being a dispossessed group, Chicanos continued to have the potential for violent rebellion. That potential became a reality on May 7, 1978, when Houston Chicanos rioted in response to news that city policemen responsible for the death of a young Chicano the previous year had received light sentences for their crime. The Houston riot served as a warning that if Chicano optimism about the 1980s were to become disillusionment that decade could see more violence than had the late 1960s. The analogy with the Palestinians was appropriate in at least one other way—in the mid-1970s the fate of Chicanos began to be influenced by oil. At that time a major oil discovery was made in southern Mexico, and though there was a good deal of controversy concerning its exact size, speculation that the discovery might equal the reserves of Saudi Arabia caused everyone involved to reconsider the relations between the United States and Mexico, and consequently the relations between Anglo-Americans and persons of Mexican descent.[65]

In the late 1970s some North American businessmen began to consider the advantages of a common market including the United States and Mexico, a common market that, according to Carey McWilliams, would "permit the free movement across their borders not only of all commodities—particularly oil and gas—but also of people." In their need for petroleum, some North Americans were beginning to consider the idea that the boundary between the Southwest and Mexico might indeed be artificial. In return for increased supplies of energy, North Americans were beginning to think about legalizing the seemingly inevitable migration of Mexicans into the Southwest.[66] Such a concession to the Chicano image of the region, while not eliminating the neocolonial status of the Mexican and Chicano masses, would certainly improve their condition by providing economic opportunities for the former, and numerical and cultural strength to the latter. The thought of this is what made Chicano activists optimistic about the future of Aztlán. While such concessions would not end neocolonialism in the Southwest, they would permit Chicanos to entrench themselves until revolutionary changes in the general society of the United States could allow true self-determination.

However, the guarded optimism of the late 1970s decreased as the 1980s proceeded. In the United States the backlash of the former decade increased with the introduction of conservative federal policies on such matters as the enforcement of civil rights laws; moreover, the economic position of minorities suffered during a period of recession and slowed government spending. Declining petroleum prices left Mexico unable to repay huge loans secured with its oil discoveries, and this development stifled idealistic hopes of a common market between the two nations and of swift progress toward equality between Anglos and Chicanos in the Southwest. Significant recovery of control in the region, the myth of Aztlán, seemed as far off as ever. As a result, for the foreseeable future, the Chicanos' image of the land as lost, and of themselves as dispossessed, would continue to have credibility.[67]

Beyond 1848

Notes

1. Leo Grebler, Joan W. Moore, and Ralph C. Guzmán, *The Mexican-American People: The Nation's Second Largest Minority* (New York: Macmillan Co., Free Press, 1970), pp. 29, 143, 185, 25 1.
2. Edward Murguía, *Assimilation, Colonialism and the Mexican American People*, Mexican American Monograph Series, no. 1 (Austin: Center for Mexican American Studies, University of Texas, 1975), pp. 1, 62; Frantz Fanon, *Black Skin, White Masks*, trans. Charles Lam Markmann (New York: Grove Press, Evergreen Black Cat, 1968), pp. 223-32 passim; Albert Memmi, *The Colonizer and the Colonized*, trans. Howard Greenfeld, with an Introduction by Jean-Paul Sartre (Boston: Beacon Press, 1967), pp. 145-53 passim; and Fernando Peñalosa, *Chicano Sociolinguistics: A Brief Introduction*, Series in Sociolinguistics (Rowley, Mass.: Newbury House Publishers, 1980),
   pp. 2-3.
3. Gilberto López y Rivas, *Los Chicanos: Una minoría nacional explotada*, Temas de Actualidad, 3rd ed. (Mexico City: Editorial Nuestro Tiempo, 1979), pp. 107- 14, 148; and Mario Barrera, *Race and Class in the Southwest: A Theory of Racial Inequality* (Notre Dame, Ind.: University of Notre Dame Press, 1979), pp. 218-19.
4. Matt S. Meier and Feliciano Rivera, *The Chicanos: A History of Mexican Americans*, American Century Series (New York: Farrar, Straus & Giroux, Hill & Wang, 1972), pp. 247-50.
5. Ibid.
6. Gladys Gregory, "The Chamizal Settlement: A View from El Paso," *Southwestern Studies* 1 (Summer 1963):4-5; and Sheldon B. Liss, *A Century of Disagreement: The Chamizal Conflict*, 1864-1964 (Washington, D.C.: University Press and Latin American Institute, 1965), pp. 104-7.
7. Rodolfo Acuña, *Occupied America: The Chicano's Struggle Toward Liberation* (San Francisco: Harper & Row, Canfield Press, 1972), pp. 225-26.
8. Eduardo Quevedo et al., "Open Resolution Directed to the President of the United States and Executive Departments and Agencies, by National Hispanic and Mexican-American Organizations on Civil Disobedience and Riot Investigations," in "The History of Political Organizations among Mexican-Americans in Los Angeles Since the Second World War," by Kaye Lynn Briegel (Master's thesis, University of Southern California, 1967),
   p. 64.
9. Acuña, p. 225.
10. Meier and Rivera, pp. 260-61.
11. Quoted in Jacques E. Levy, *Cesar Chavez: Autobiography of La Causa* (New York: W. W. Norton & Co., 1975), p. 8.
12. Ibid., pp. 42, 84, 98, 144-45.
13. Quoted in Peter Matthiessen, *Sal Si Puedes: Cesar Chavez and the New American Revolution*, rev. ed. (New York: Random House, 1973), pp. 128-29; see also Levy, pp. 196-98.
14. Quoted in Matthiessen, p. 300.
15. [Luis Valdez], "The Plan of Delano," in *Aztlan: An Anthology of Mexican American Literature*, ed. Luis Valdez and Stan Steiner, Marc Corporation Books (New York: Alfred A. Knopf, 1972), p. 198.
16. Quoted in Matthiessen, pp. 347, 73.
17. Quoted in Levy, pp. 123, 537; see also Matthiessen, pp. 108-10, 143-45,179.
18. Meier and Rivera, pp. 261-62, 269; see also *Albuquerque Journal*, 7 June 1980.

19. Valdez, "The Plan," p. 201.

20. Peter Nabokov, *Tijerina and the Courthouse Raid* (Albuquerque: University of New Mexico Press, 1969), p. 27; cf. Roxanne Dunbar Ortiz, *Roots of Resistance: Land Tenure in New Mexico, 1680-1980*, {Monograph no. 10] (Los Angeles: Chicano Studies Research Center Publications and American Indian Studies Center, University of California, 1980), pp. 45-47, 96-97.

21. Patricia Bell Blawis, *Tijerina and the Land Grants: Mexican Americans in Struggle for Their Heritage* (New York: International Publishers Co., New World Paperbacks, 1971), pp. 41, 43.

22. Nancie L. González, *The Spanish-Americans of New Mexico: A Heritage of Pride*, rev. and enl. ed. (Albuquerque: University of New Mexico Press, 1969), p. 90, and Robert J. Rosenbaum, *Mexicano Resistance in the Southwest: "The Sacred Right of Self Preservation,"* The Dan Danciger Publication Series (Austin: University of Texas Press, 1981), pp. 118-24, 139.

23. Quoted in Blawis, p. 26.

24. Nabokov, pp. 194, 204, 211.

25. Quoted in Nabokov, pp. 19, 227; see Blawis, pp. 56- 60.

26. Nabokov, pp. 28, 66, 74, 82-88; and Reies Lopez Tijerina, *Mi lucha por la tierra*, with a Prologue by Jorge A. Bustamante, Vida y Pensamiento de México (Mexico City: Fondo de Cultura Económica, 1978),
pp. 152-56.

27. Alfonso Sánchez, quoted in Nabokov, p. 185; and Meier and Rivera, p. 271.

28. Quoted in Blawis, pp. 146, 139-40. For further comment on the relationship between Chicanos and Native Americans, see Rudolph O. de la Garza, Z. Anthony Kruszewski, and Tomás A. Arciniega, comps., *Chicanos and Native Americans: The Territorial Minorities* (Englewood Cliffs, N.J.: Prentice-Hall, Spectrum Books, 1973), p. 4; Jack D. Forbes, *Aztecas del Norte: The Chicanos of Aztlán* (Greenwich, Conn.: Fawcett Publications, Premier Books, 1973), pp. 178-205; and Armando B. Rendón, *Chicano Manifesto* (New York: Macmillan Co., 1971), pp. 294-95, 297.

29. Meier and Rivera, pp. 273-74; *Albuquerque Journal*, 16 March 1979.

30. F. Chris Garcia, "Manitos and Chicanos in New Mexico Politics," in *La Causa Politica: A Chicano Politics Reader*, ed. F. Chris García (Notre Dame, Ind.: University of Notre Dame Press, 1974), pp. 271-80.

31. Forbes, p. 17.

32. "The Spiritual Manifesto of Aztlán," in *Literatura Chicana: Texto y Contexto/Chicano Literature: Text and Context*, ed. Antonia Castañeda Shular, Tomás Ybarra-Frausto, and Joseph Sommers (Englewood Cliffs, N.J.: Prentice Hall, 1972), p. 84.

33. *El Papel* (Albuquerque), April 1970, quoted in Blawis, p. 175; Stan Steiner, "The Poet in the Boxing Ring," in García, *La Causa Politica*, pp. 323-25; and Meier and Rivera, pp. 274-75.

34. Quoted in Steiner, p. 326; see also Mario Barrera, Carlos Muñoz, and Charles Ornelas, "The Barrio as an Internal Colony," in García, *La Causa Politica*, p. 282; and Meier and Rivera, p. 276.

35. Quoted in Steiner, p. 329.

36. "The Spiritual Manifesto," p.84.

37. See Richard Santillán, *La Raza Unida*, Chicano Politics (Los Angeles: Tlaquilo Publications, 1973), pp. 19-24; and Denver Post, 11 September 1977.

38. John Staples Shockley, *Chicano Revolt in a Texas Town* (Notre Dame, Ind.: University of Notre Dame Press, 1974), pp. 3-4, 79.

39. José Angel Gutiérrez, "Aztlan: Chicano Revolt in the Winter Garden," *La Raza* 1, no. 4 [1971],

n. pag.

40. Shockley, pp. 162, 200-205.

41. Santillán, p. 16; Tony Castro, *Chicano Power: The Emergence of Mexican America* (New York: Saturday Review Press/E. P. Dutton & Co., 1974), pp. 181-82; Shockley, pp. 2 14- 16, 225; and *San Antonio Express,* 3 October 1980.

42. Ibid., 9 March 1975.

43. Acuña, p. 236.

44. Ibid., pp. 227-29; and Meier and Rivera, *p.* 252.

45. Acuña, pp. 229, 258-60.

46. Ernie Barrios, *Bibliografia de Aztlan: An Annotated Chicano Bibliography* (San Diego, Calif.: Centro de Estudios Chicanos Publications, San Diego State College, 1971); Luis Valdez and Stan Steiner, eds., *Aztlan: An Anthology of Mexican American Literature,* Marc Corporation Books (New *York:* Alfred A. Knopf, 1972); Miguel Méndez M., *Peregrinos de Aztlán: Literature Chicana (novela)* (Tucson, Ariz.: Editorial Peregrinos, 1974); Rudolfo A. Anaya, *Heart of Aztlan* (Berkeley, Calif.: Editorial Justa Publications, 1976); and Luis F. Hernández, *Aztlan: The Southwest and its People* (Rochelle Park, N.J.: Hayden Book Co., 1975).

47. Henry B. González, "An Attack on Chicano Militants," in *A Documentary History of the Mexican Americans,* ed. Wayne Moquin with Charles Van Doren, with an Introduction by Feliciano Rivera (New York: Praeger Publishers, 1971), pp. 358-59; see also Richard Rodríguez, *Hunger of Memory: The Education of Richard Rodriguez, an Autobiography,* Bantam Windstone Books (New York: Bantam Books, 1983), pp. 157-60.

48. Fray Angélico Chávez, *My Penitente Land: Reflections on Spanish New Mexico* (Albuquerque: University of New Mexico Press, 1974), pp. 223, 200-202; cf. Gonzalez, *The Spanish-Americans, pp.* 26-27.

49. Chávez, p. 270.

50. *Los Angeles Herald Examiner,* 8 October 1978, 24 July 1983.

51. Lorenzo Middleton, "Colleges Urged to Alter Tests, Grading for Benefit of Minority Group Students: A Ford Foundation Commission Endorses a System to Admit students Based on Potential," *Chronicle of Higher Education* 23 (3 February 1982): 1,10.

52. *La Red/The Net* (Ann Arbor, Mich.), June 1982; see also *Los Angeles Times,* 1 August 1983; and Tom Mathews with Diane Camper, "The Hard Cases Coming," *Newsweek,* 10 July 1978, p. 32.

53. Arizona Republic (Phoenix), 5 January 1975; and Shockley, pp. 218-19.

54. *La opinión* (Los Angeles), 21 August 1983; and *Los Angeles Times,* 24 July 1983; also resolutions against the violence and intervention in Central America were issued by the Association of Mexican American Educators (14 November 1981), the California Association for Bilingual Education (12 March 1982), and the National Association for Chicano Studies (25-27 March 1982).

55. Quoted in Shockley, p. 226.

56. *Arizona Republic,* 25 July 1978; Grace Halsell, *The Illegals,* John L. Hochmann Books (New York: Stein & Day, 1978), pp. 211-12; and George W. Grayson, *The Politics of Mexican Oil,* Pitt Latin American Series (Pittsburgh, Pa.: University of Pittsburgh Press, 1980), p. 161.

57. See Griffin Smith, Jr., "The Mexican Americans: A People on the Move," *National Geographic,* June 1980, pp. 794-96; and Kurt Anderson, "'The New Ellis Island': Immigrants from All Over Change the Beat, Bop and Character of Los Angeles," *Time,* 13 June 1983, pp. 22-24.

58. Wilmot Robertson, *The Dispossessed Majority*, 2nd rev. ed. (Cape Canaveral, Fla.: Howard Allen, 1976), p. 196; cf. letters to the editor in *Herald Examiner, 19* September 1977, and in *UCLA Monthly*, March-April 1979.

59. *Herald Examiner,* 21-22 October 1977.

60. Grace Halsell, "Who Are the Real Illegals in California?" *Herald Examiner,* 26 July 1978; see also *Los Angeles Times,* 19 August 1979.

61. Shockley, p. 226; and Barrera, pp. 128, 103, 197.

62. Richard Reeves, "Mexican America: Frito Bandito Is Dead—Mexico's Oil Is Giving Chicanos New Power," *Esquire,* 2-16 January 1979, pp.8,10.

63. See Jonathan Kirsch, "Chicano Power: There Is One Inevitable Fact—by 1990 California Will Become America's First Third World State," *New West,* 11 September 1978, pp. 35-40.

64. Rendón, p. 309; and *Herald Examiner,* 20 May 1979.

65. *Young Socialist (New* York), July-August 1978; *Los Angeles Times,* 18 May 1979; and Grayson, p. 225.

66. Carey McWilliams, "A Way Out of the Energy Squeeze?" *Los Angeles Times,* 8 April 1979; cf. Grayson, p. 230.

67. Cheryl M. Fields, "Administration Moves to Ease Federal Anti-bias Regulations: Critics Charge That White House Efforts Will Weaken Affirmative Action," *Chronicle of Higher Education* 23 (2 September 1981): 1, 21; and B. Nissen, "Mexico: Hard Times for an Oil Giant," Newsweek, 12 July 1982, p. 51.

Richard Griswold del Castillo provides a focus on contemporary conditions and issues affecting Latinos and Chicanos during the past decade. Included is a discussion of demographic trends, increasing socio-economic diversity among Latinos and the growing underclass. Griswold also includes a review of the growing political influence of Latinos and their impact on American popular culture. In addition, Griswold explores bilingual education issues, movements against undocumented immigrants and the growing visibility of Chicanos and Latinos in the arts.

Latinos and the "New Immigrants," Since 1975
Richard Griswold del Castillo

In the summer of 1983 the *Los Angeles Times* published a series of articles examining the Mexican American experience in that city. In one feature article, the reporters explored the problem of preferences for ethnic labels and found a lack of unanimity about what Chicanos/Latinos/Hispanics/Mexican Americans/Mexicanos wanted to call themselves. Generally, the native born preferred the label "Mexican-American," followed by "Latino." The term "Hispanic" was third in preference. Mexican immigrants favored the term "Mexicano," also followed by "Latino." While a plurality could agree on the term "Latino" only a small minority (four percent) agreed that the term "Chicano" fit them.[1]

In the 1980s, "Latino" replaced "Chicano" as a term that most people could agree upon. "Hispanic," enjoyed popularity among the middle class but provoked sharp criticism from others who were sensitive to the Indian and mestizo backgrounds of most Mexican Americans. The occasional confusion and debate over terminology led to the use of a more neutral term "Latino." The *L.A. Times* poll indicated something of the increasing complexity of the city's population. It demonstrated changes in self perception, away from a parochial ethnic identity ("Chicano") towards a more pan-Latin American identity ("Latino"). "Latino" referred to a national Spanish speaking community, with a majority of Mexican ancestry but including large populations of Central and South Americans. The Latino communities extended to the Cuban American enclaves in Florida and the Puerto Ricans in New York and Chicago. More and more Chicanos recognized the cultural and linguistic bonds they shared with the hundreds of thousands of Latin American immigrants who had been flooding the city and the nation. Thus the waves of immigration to the U.S. from Central America and Latin America was bringing about a shift in ethnic self identification.

In the 1980s, a dramatic demographic explosion in the Spanish speaking population, fueled by a new wave of immigration from Latin America and Mexico, underlay the increased visibility of Latino culture. This so-called, "New Immigration" produced ambivalent reactions from the Anglo American mainstream. Elements of Latino culture gained nation-wide popularity but Latino immigrants became the targets of discrimination and rejection. This chapter will examine how new waves of immigration from Latin America affected the cultural and economic context of Mexican American history through the 1990s.

Demographic and Economic Shifts

Between 1975 and 1989 more than eight million immigrants entered the United States legally. About a third of these, three million, were Latin Americans and Mexico's share was about one million. More Asian than Latin American legal immigrants entered the U.S. during this period. If we were to include the migration of Puerto Ricans to the mainland (not officially counted as immigration) and the entry of estimated millions of undocumented Mexican and Central American immigrants, the number of entrants from Latin America undoubtedly was the largest group.

Rubén Rumbault, in his 1991 study, noted that this "new immigration" from underdeveloped regions of the world (Asia and Latin America) was changing the culture of ethnic America. "The American ethnic mosaic is being fundamentally altered, and ethnicity itself being redefined and its new images redefined in the popular media and reflected in myriad and often surprising ways. Immigrants from a score of nationalities are told that they are all "Hispanic," while far more diverse groups, from India and Laos, China and the Philippines--are lumped together as 'Asians.'"[2]

Latin American immigration contributed to a dramatic increase in the Latino population of the United States. A very high Latino birth rate, the highest of any ethnic group in the United States, contributed to this demographic surge as well. Between 1980 and 1988 the Latino population grew from 14.6 millon to 19.4 million, an increase of thirty-four percent compared with only a seven percent increase in the general population. Latin American immigration counted for at least two million of the increase. Another two million could be accounted for by undocumented immigrants who were settlers rather than sojourners, leaving a million explained by the excess of births to deaths. Of almost twenty million Latinos in the United States in 1988, those of Mexican descent accounted for sixty-two percent of the total. Puerto Ricans were about thirteen percent of the mainland Latinos and Cuban Americans were five percent; twelve percent of the total came from Central and South America and the remaining eight percent were counted as "Other Hispanics."[3]

The 1990 Census showed that the proportion of Mexican immigrants within the larger Latino population declined during the 1980s. This could be explained by the relative large flow of immigrants from Central and South America. For example, California by 1990 had become the most populous state in the union with 29,760,000 people and about one fourth of these were Latino. About thirty-eight percent of the Los Angeles County's population and twenty percent of San Diego County's were Latino. Projecting a steady high rate of growth, demographers have estimated that the Latino population would reach thirty million by the year 2000. In some states, such as California and Texas, the projected increase would, by the year 2010, make the Latinos almost half their population. Projections were that, by the year 2060, Latinos would become the nation's largest ethnic or racial group.[4]

The use of the word "Latino" to describe immigrant and non-immigrant Spanish speaking populations, created a false notion of unity. Not all Latinos regarded the new immigrants as brothers to be welcomed into the community. The attitudes of Mexican Americans towards this new immigration varied according to socio-economic class, education, and generational status. A survey conducted by a research group at Pan American University in South Texas in 1984, disclosed that the more affluent and educated Mexican Americans believed that undocumented immigrants were taking unfair advantage of social services, particularly public education. They did not regard job competition as serious a problem as did the working class Mexican Americans. Overall Mexican Americans regardless of socioeconomic class did not think that this immigration from Latin America was having a negative impact on their lives. The more acculturated and educated Mexican Americans, however, supported stricter immigration controls.[5] Rudolfo de la Garza, a leading analyst of Chicano political opinion regarding Mexico and Mexican immigration, concluded that while Chicanos were "the principal group openly defending the Mexican position on the issue of undocumented workers," there was still "historical antipathy between Chicanos and Mexicans."[6] Another study by Christine Sierra pointed out the diversity of Mexican American responses to proposals for immigration restriction. Native born Latinos were much more likely to support employer sanctions and stricter enforcement measures than foreign born Latinos. When compared to other racial and ethnic groups, however, the native born Latinos tended to be less supportive of strict immigration controls.[7] Apart from these few studies researchers knew very little about the relationship between Mexican Americans and Mexican immigrants in the 1980s. Impressionistic evidence, gathered from school yards and the work place suggested an ambivalent relationship characterized by antagonism and competition along with a shared language and racial background. Certainly more acculturated Mexican Americans continued to be intermediaries between the *recien llegado* (recently arrived immigrant) and the larger society and economy. Bilingual and bicultural Mexican Americans worked as the bosses, supervisors and contractors managing (and exploiting) monolingual Spanish speaking Latino immigrants.

A Growing Underclass

The new flood of immigration from Latin America had long term consequences for the economy of the United States. Between 1980 and 1987 one fifth of the nation's employment growth was because of increased Latino employment, especially of Latino women. In the 1980s Latinos were the nation's fastest growing work force. The non-Latino work force grew by ten percent but the number of Latino workers increased by forty percent. The inflow of Mexican and Latin American immigrants who sought out jobs at the bottom of the American occupational ladder fueled most of this occupational increase. Latino women had a much higher rate of employment gain than men, almost a fifty percent growth rate in the period, two and a half times that of the growth rate for non-Latino women.

Despite the growing numbers of Latinos entering the work force, Latino unemployment caused by technological innovation, job competition by new immigrants, and business failures, remained about one and a half times above that of the general population but below that of African Americans. Unemployment varied according to national origin: Cuban Americans had the lowest rate of unemployment, about five percent, and Puerto Ricans and Mexicans had the highest, about ten percent. Meanwhile the unemployment rate for Anglo Americans ranged from six to nine percent. In terms of occupational mobility for all Latinos there was no significant change in their status during the 1980s. The vast majority remained in the lower paid skilled and unskilled blue collar jobs. Although Latino women entered the mid-level sales and technical occupations faster than did Latino men, more than half of all employed Latino men continued to work in blue collar jobs.[8]

Scholars noted that most of the new Latin American immigrants who entered the U.S. came from the employed and skilled working classes in their countries of origin. The middle class Cuban refugees who arrived after 1959 followed this pattern, with heavy representation in the professional middle classes. (The Cuban immigrants (*Marielitos*) who arrived in the late 1970s, however did not). Nevertheless, in comparison to the relatively affluent U.S. working class, the immigrants entered at the bottom of the American socio-economic pyramid. Native born Latinos who were U.S. citizens such as a majority of the Puerto Ricans in New York, Chicanos in the inner city barrios, Hispanos in New Mexico's small towns, and Tejanos in South Texas also endured high rates of poverty and educational underachievement.

While immigration continued at a high level, the federal government cut social services funding. Latino poverty, school drop outs, and unemployment rose. By 1990, Latinos were collectively even worse off than they had been in 1980. At the beginning of 1980, thirteen percent of Latino families lived below the poverty line. By the end of the decade, the number rose to more than sixteen percent. Meanwhile, the Latino median income adjusted for inflation declined from $23,088 to $21,759. Thus, the Latino experience became more polarized with some success stories but many more tales of human tragedy and defeat.

The Latino Middle Class

Not all Latinos were impoverished immigrants or blue collar workers. During the late 1970s and 1980s one of the fastest growing economic groups in the United States was the Latino middle and upper classes. Affluent Latinos, those having annual incomes of more than $50,000 a year, grew from 191,000 in 1972 to 638,000, an increase of 234 percent. Most of the expansion during the 1980s came from the growth of the Latino middle class (with incomes between $50,000 and $100,000). The proportion of Latino families living in affluence grew from seven percent of all households in 1972 to eleven percent in 1988, surpassing the proportion of middle class blacks (which was ten percent in 1988) but remaining below the proportion of Anglo Americans' twenty three percent). The low average income of all Latinos tended to mask the growth of this small but important group.

Like most well-off Americans, most Latino affluent families had two or more paychecks to support their life-styles. Unlike the Anglo American middle class the Latino families tended to be younger, have more children and have less education than their Anglo counter parts (only twenty nine percent of the Latino middle class had a college degree vs. fifty percent for Anglo Americans). More Latino affluent lived in metropolitan areas than was true for Anglos. Those cities having the largest Latino middle class segments in 1989 were Honolulu, Hawaii (twenty five percent), Washington D.C. (twenty four percent), Detroit (eighteen percent), San Francisco (fifteen percent), San Jose, California (fifteen percent), Orange County (fourteen percent)[9] In the 1980s this group's growth provided an important resource for the mobilization of a new kind of politics. Culturally, this group would be supporters of a more mainstream approach to Latino music and art.

Advertising agencies and corporate managers discovered the "Hispanic Market" in the 1980s. They generated a good deal of survey research to plumb the buying habits of Latinos and how they could best exploit this fast growing group. The collective buying power of Latinos grew to over $171 billion in 1989, increasing at ten percent per year. Businesses began to expand their portion of products in the Spanish language, using Latino images. This created new opportunities for Latino marketing firms and models, especially in the major Southwestern metropolitan areas.[10] The expanded economic clout of Latinos provided Latino political groups with additional weight as they pushed for expanded hiring of Latinos within key companies. In 1985, for example, six national Latino groups led by the

League of United Latin American Citizens (LULAC) and the American G.I. Forum signed an agreement with the Adolf Coors Corporation. After a ten year boycott of Coors by Chicano activists because of its anti-union, anti-Mexican policies, Coors agreed to a minimum hiring level of Latinos and committed its company to invest in the Latino community in proportion to its increase in sales.[11]

Some governmental officials and businessmen labeled the 1980s "The Decade of the Hispanic," sounding an optimistic note based on the growing economic and political power of Latinos. Despite the affluence of the Latino middle class, the final record of this decade proved to be mixed concerning the overall progress for all. Latino society perhaps became more differentiated with regards to education, socio-economic status, upward mobility and acculturation.

Latino Politics

Obviously there was an important political motive for the widespread adoption of the terms "Hispanic" and "Latino," particularly among the middle classes. These terms allowed Latino politicians and middle class organizations to claim that they represented a much larger national constituency than if they remained identified with ethnic nationalism. In the 1980s scores of Hispanic and Latino political caucuses, professional associations and business groups organized as political pressure groups. In the U.S. Congress and in the state governments of Florida, California, Arizona, New Mexico and Texas, Latino legislators formed lobbies and caucuses to push for agendas that would benefit their constituencies.

Two of the most active Latino organizations in this period were the Mexican American Legal Defense and Education Fund (MALDEF) and the Southwest Voter Registration Project (SWVRP). Together, they began many legal actions to attack impediments to Latino electoral victories. Their attack on the at-large district election system was a strategy that would have profound political consequences. The at-large election system was a structure that forced candidates in local district elections to win their election at-large or in city-wide contests. This political practice handicapped Latino candidates who had limited resources for city-wide campaigns and who lacked political appeal outside their ethnic districts. In the 1980s, both MALDEF and SWVRP won hundreds of court victories overturning the at-large electoral system. They won by proving in court that this system discriminated against Latinos who were protected under the Voting Rights Acts of 1965, 1975 and 1982.

Another front in the political battle for fair representation was the struggle over redistricting. For decades, Latinos had been victims of gerrymandered electoral districts. Historically, Anglo American incumbents of both parties had diluted the Latino voting block to create "safe" districts and insure their reelection. Redistricting occurred every ten years, after the federal census, to readjust election districts to reflect population shifts. In 1981, Latino organizations through out the Southwestern states, spearheaded by MALDEF and SWVRP, launched major efforts to challenge redistricting procedures and overcome Latino political fragmentation. Other Latino groups such as the Puerto Rican Legal Defense and Education Fund (PRLDEF) in New York and the Hispanic Coalition on Reapportionment (HCR) in Michigan and Pennsylvania also lobbied the state reapportionment commissions and presented their own reapportionment plans. Richard Santillan in his analysis of the politics of the redistricting struggles in 1981, argued that hard won victories in creating Latino electoral districts led to significant Latino electoral gains during the rest of the decade.[12] Benefiting from the civil rights struggles of the previous decades and the victories against gerrymandering and at-large elections reenergized political strategies. Latino political organizations had unparalleled success in the 1980s in electing officials. The SWVRP's work in registering new Latino voters was important in many of these electoral victories. The decade saw the election of Latino mayors in Denver (Federico Peña), San Antonio (Henry Cisneros) and Miami (Xavier Suárez) and Latino governors in New Mexico (Toney Anaya) and Florida (Bob Martínez). The voters elected hundreds of other Latinos to local and state offices, primarily in the Southwest. There were enough Latino elected officials to form a national organization, NALEO (National Association of Latino Elected and Appointed Officials), which issued annual status reports on the growing electoral strength of Latinos. In 1987, NALEO reported that there were 3,317 elected Latino officials in the United States, a number double the number in 1980.[13] The four southwestern border states, California, Arizona, New Mexico and Texas had the majority of elected Latinos but Florida, New York and the Mid-West also voted in substantial numbers.

The preponderance of Latinos won elections at the local level, serving on school boards, county offices and city councils. While Hispanic women were underrepresented in public offices, a higher proportion of Latinas were elected (eighteen percent) than was true for women in the general population (twelve percent). Most of the Latino officeholders in the 1980s had first entered electoral politics in that decade but they were not, as a group, particularly young, having an average age of about forty-four years. Most Latino elected officials in this decade were native born citizens (ninety percent). These new leaders represented ethnic constituencies, districts of more than fifty-five percent Latino in population, but the new office holders also appealed to a broader spectrum of non-ethnic voters by their articulation of issues.[14]

Representing this new Latino political leadership were people like Gloria Molina, Henry Cisneros, and Xavier Suárez. They were highly educated, committed, and articulate leaders who had a broad appeal while retaining the solid support of voters within their ethnic communities.

Gloria Molina was a crusading Chicana in East Los Angeles who won her first election in 1982 in an Assembly race against Richard Polanco, who was a well entrenched establishment politician. Daughter of a California farm worker, she lived in the East Los Angeles barrio and had gotten grass roots political experience during the Chicano movement in the 1960s. In the state Assembly Molina fought long and hard against the construction of a state prison in her district. She ultimately succeeded by organizing a myriad of local groups and embarrassing the Latino politicos who had supported the prison in hopes of political favors. She ran unsuccessfully against Richard Alatorre in a 1986 Los Angeles City Council race but the next year she won a stunning victory in being elected to a newly created Los Angeles councilmanic seat. In 1991 she ran against her arch enemy Richard Alatorre for the Los Angeles County Board of Supervisors. She won that election with majority support of both men and women, Anglos and Latinos. This was the first time in more than 100 years that the voters had elected a Latino to this powerful office. Most observers predicted that from here she was in an ideal position to enter national politics.

Gloria Molina rose to prominence because of her passionate advocacy of women's rights and issues of community development. As an outsider to both the Anglo dominated political establishment and the old boy network of Chicano officials, she represented a populist and feminist approach to Latino politics who appealed to a wide variety of middle class non-ethnic voters.[15]

Henry Cisneros, a young professor of Public Administration, came much more from a conservative political background. Born in San Antonio, Texas, Cisneros descended from an old-line elite family who had immigrated during the Mexican Revolution. Cisneros attended a Catholic high school and Texas A & M, later earning two master's degrees and a doctorate degree from Ivy League universities. When he returned to Texas he worked as a professor at the University of Texas in San Antonio until he won election to the City Council in 1975 as part of a multi-ethnic coalition. His youthful optimism and charismatic style along with his management training and fiscal conservatism made him a favorite of the San Antonio Anglo middle class. Also he appealed to the working class Chicanos of San Antonio who identified with his success. He won reelection as a mayor of the city in 1981 with support of Anglos and a huge majority (ninety-four percent) of the Chicano vote. His ability to move in elite circles and his adept manipulation of complex issues made him an unusually attractive figure to national politicians. In 1983 President Reagan appointed him to the National Bipartisan Commission on Central America. He ultimately endorsed a report that justified the administration's policy. His conservative economic philosophy did not antagonize his Chicano and Mexicano constituency since he also lobbied for more jobs and education. In 1989 Cisneros decided not to run again for mayor, citing personal economic hardships in continuing. In the 1990s he devoted himself to building a Latino controlled financial management corporation called The Cisneros Group.

Xavier Suárez was a Cuban born, naturalized citizen who, in 1985, was elected mayor of the largest Latino majority city in the United States, Miami, Florida. Suárez was the ninth of 14 children from a middle class Cuban family. His father had been an engineer and a college dean. After the Cuban Revolution his family fled to the U.S. and settled in Washington D.C. Reportedly, Suárez learned English in only two months. He went on to earn a degree in mechanical engineering, a master's degree in Public Administration and a law degree from Harvard. Moving to Miami he joined a law firm and soon got involved in local politics. With the support of wealthy Cuban bankers, he ran several times unsuccessfully for a seat on the Miami City Commission. In 1983 he ran against Maurice Ferré, the Puerto Rican born incumbent mayor who had been in office for 12 years. Ferré was supported by a coalition of Anglo, Black and Cuban voters. Ferré won that election but in the process alienated key members of his coalition. In the next election, Suárez succeeded in knocking off Ferré. The tone of Miami politics changed from its traditional anti-communist Cuban orientation towards local issues like drugs and unemployment. Along with Florida governor Bob Martínez and a host of other Cuban Americans who rose to local political office in the 1980s, Suárez represents a new generation of Latino leadership outside the four Southwestern states.[16]

Despite these success stories and optimistic trends, Latinos remain underrepresented at all levels of government. In California, for example, where Latinos comprise more than twenty percent of the population, less than two percent of the federal, state and county officials were Latino. In Texas where more than twenty percent of the total population are Latino, in 1983 they were less than six percent of the local municipal elected officials. The same kind of inequity continues to exist in every other Southwestern state with the possible exception of New Mexico.

Education

The existing educational system was one of the most important ways that immigrant and native born Latinos could escape the cycle of poverty and marginalization. There continued to be a devastating school drop out rate in public schools and relatively low numbers of Latinos attended and graduated from college. In the 1980s, white Americans "discovered" the educational problem as nation-wide reading and math scores declined for all groups. Several best selling books criticized the secondary schools and colleges' failure to teach basic literacy and numeracy. A well publicized government study stated that the failures of the educational system was placing our nation at risk.[17]

Chicanos and Mexican immigrants had been "at risk" for many decades. The influx of hundreds of thousands of new immigrants made the educational system's failure more visible. Long charged with the task of mainstreaming or "Americanizing" immigrants, the public schools proved unequal to the task as larger and larger numbers of Latino children failed to keep up with their Anglo American peers.

An example was the Los Angeles City School System. Perhaps one of the most multi-racial, multi-ethnic school systems in the nation, about half of the students were foreign-born in 1980. The largest contingent of the foreign-born, about 80 percent, were Mexican immigrant children, followed by Central American and Asian born students. Between 1970 and 1980 the Latino school population in Los Angeles had doubled to 267,000 students while white enrollment fell to 120,729. By 1990 the school population exceeded 300,000 Latinos while black and Anglo school enrollment continued to decline. Concentrated in segregated regions of the city, the Latino students had a school drop out rate of forty-eight percent. This compared with a national drop out rate (in 1980) of forty-five percent for Mexican Americans, twenty-eight percent for blacks and seventeen percent for whites.[18]

The educational environment in other school districts having large numbers of Latinos was not much better. In Texas a long tradition of segregation that led to the inequitable funding of non-white schools aggravated the high drop out rate. In Texas the poorest school districts were invariably Latino or black. Yet they were the districts saddled with the highest property tax rates and the lowest allocation of state funding. In 1973, the Supreme Court had ruled in *San Antonio School District v. Rodriguez* that this inequity did not violate the constitution. The problem of unequal funding continued to plague Texas' Latino school districts and resulted in increasing educational neglect for Latinos.[19]

In addition, legal discrimination against Mexican children continued. In 1975, the Texas state legislature added a statute to the Education Code declaring that only children of U.S. citizens and legal aliens could receive free public education. Many school districts subsequently began charging up to $1000 a year tuition to children of undocumented workers. In 1977, the Mexican American Legal Defense and Education Fund (MALDEF) filed a law suit to challenge this policy. In *Doe v. Plyler* MALDEF argued that the state's policy was unconstitutional, violating the 14th Amendment that states that no state shall "deny to any person . . . the equal protection of the laws" of the United States. Further, they argued that the Federal government, not the state, was responsible for enforcing immigration laws. In 1980, MALDEF won their case on appeal thus setting a precedent for the educational rights of undocumented immigrants.[20]

Educational experts were much better at describing the dimensions of the problem than at constructing remedies. Educators knew that there were many reasons for the high drop out rate for Latinos. The most important were related to the income and educational backgrounds of the parents, the recency of immigration and exclusive use of Spanish at home, and the characteristics of the school itself--class size, school facilities, and teacher motivation and training. The actual reasons for Latinos quitting school before graduation varied tremendously ranging from pregnancy to boredom, but almost all drop outs were below their grade level in reading and writing skills. This educational lag most often appeared by the third grade indicating that the most important remedies for the problem (primarily intensive tutoring in reading and writing skills) were to be addressed at the grammar school level.

Since the 1960s Chicano educators had argued in favor of reform of the elementary school system, in particular, through the institutionalization of bilingual education. Bilingual advocates argued that it was most important to teach Spanish-speaking students how to read in their native language first, and then, once students had mastered reading skills, it would be easier to teach them how to read in English. By using Spanish as the language of instruction in the grammar schools to teach native Spanish-speakers, teachers would be able to reinforce the family cultural values of immigrant children and create a more positive learning environment for the teaching of English and other subjects. Almost all Latino immigrant families wanted their children to learn English since it was obvious to them that this skill was important in getting a job.[21]

The bilingual advocates had support from the Supreme Court when the *Lau v. Nichols* decision in 1972 directed the schools to address the needs of the non-English-Speaking students. The Lau decision allowed school districts to determine the methods to be used in fulfilling this mandate. For the next twenty years a wide variety of bilingual programs arose (not only Spanish-English but also dealing with Asian languages) funded by local, state and federal funds. The funds however were never sufficient to meet the demand. Moreover, President Ronald Reagan's administration cut federal funding for bilingual education by a third. Experts estimated that by the end of the 1980s less than three percent of the Latino school age population had bilingual education programs.

Yet there was evidence that bilingual programs were having success in easing the transition from Spanish to English and in preventing drop outs. A 1984 Department of

Education study, for example, tracked 2,000 Spanish speaking grammar school children over four years and found that they achieved skills at the same level as their English speaking peers. The study confirmed that bilingual programs, if managed correctly, were one way of combating the school's failure to educate. Other studies concluded that bilingual programs improved the self concept and cognitive functioning of students. Truly bilingual students outperformed their Spanish speaking peers who had been left to "sink or swim."[22]

Despite these successes, the modest diffusion of programs with the avowed aim to mainstream immigrant children, bilingual education came under attack. Many whites feared the implications of the massive immigration flooding the U.S. from so-called Third World countries. Nativists worried about the decline of "all-American" values that they linked to the school's failure linguistically to assimilate foreigners. Bilingual education and its assumptions of multicultural equity bothered those who feared the "balkanization" of American culture. In 1975, the U.S. Congress amended the Voting Rights Act to require that electoral information and ballots be multilingual. This provoked criticism from conservatives who argued that American citizens should be able to understand English in order to vote.

In 1978 Emmy Shafer was unable to communicate with any of the Spanish speaking clerks in the Dade County (Florida) administrative offices. In protest, she organized a local initiative that succeeded in making it illegal to translate official signs into a language other than English. This was the beginning of the English-Only movement, a conservative backlash against bilingual education, and Spanish speaking Latinos.

In 1982 Senator S.I. Hayakawa (R., Calif.) proposed a constitutional amendment to make English the official language of the United States. When Congress defeated his proposal, Hayakawa formed a private organization called U.S. English to implement English-Only laws through initiative procedures and lobbying state legislatures. U.S. English claimed a membership of over 300,000 and engaged in fund rasing and mass mailings to promote their cause. Eventually, more than seventeen states voted referendums to make English the official language. The states with the largest Chicano and Mexican immigrant populations, California and Texas, both passed English-only laws. New Mexico, with its long tradition of Spanish language and culture, passed instead an "English Plus" law stating that "Proficiency on the part of our citizens in more than one language is to the economic and cultural benefit of our State and Nation."[23]

The English-Only movement attracted nativists and members of the radical right and generated a good deal of patriotic and linguistic xenophobia. One nativist, Richard Viguerie mailed a letter to more than 240,000 homes asking for the repeal of federal bilingual education legislation. Included with his letter was a Mexican peso with the message, "I know the peso is worthless in the U.S. but I enclosed it to make an important point about a billion-dollar U.S. government program that's worthless too. It's called the Bilingual Education Act."[24]

Immigration and Nativist Response

The growing tide of immigrant workers flowing into the U.S. during the 1970s and 1980s led to intense debates over cultural and economic consequences. A large portion of the immigrant influx came as undocumented workers. In 1983, for example, the INS apprehended more than a million illegal entrants from Mexico. This represented only a small fraction of those who actually crossed in that year and was equal to the total number of legal entrants from Mexico during the decade of the 1980s.[25] The daily apprehension of thousands of these "illegal aliens" raised the specter of a nation unable to control its borders. In 1977 President Jimmy Carter asked Congress to consider drafting a new immigration law that would impose sanctions on employers for knowingly hiring undocumented workers and bolster the police powers of the Border Patrol. Included in his message was the suggestion that the Congress also draft a program to grant amnesty to undocumented immigrants already residing in the U.S. These basic points, employer sanctions, expanded enforcement and amnesty became the substance of several immigration bills later introduced into Congress.

The most long-lived proposal was the Simpson-Mazzoli bill, introduced in 1982. The Simpson-Mazzoli bill proposed a fine of $10,000 for employers who hired "illegal aliens" and would have granted amnesty to long term residents. Additionally the bill proposed a bracero-like guest worker program (H-2 Program) to import seasonal workers from Mexico and the Caribbean in case of a labor shortages. Special interests emerged in the debates in Congress over this bill. S. I. Hayakawa (R., Calif.) sought to attach an "English as the official language" provision to the bill. Labor unions generally supported the sanctions' provisions but were wary of the H-2 Program. Latino human rights groups opposed the penalty provisions fearing that they would be used by employers to justify their discrimination against Latino citizen. Church groups and those against U.S. support for the escalating war in Central America opposed the bill fearing the massive deportation of the thousands of Central American refugees who had fled to the U.S. to escape political terrorism. Other Latino groups were divided. The American G.I. Forum supported the idea of immigration restriction and increased support for the border patrol and they were opposed by groups like the San Diego based Committee for Chicano Rights. MALDEF supported immigration reform but opposed many of the provisions of the Simpson-Mazzoli bill. The League of United Latin American Citizens (LULAC), a conservative middle class organization, voted to boycott the Democratic Party's convention in 1984 unless the delegates voted to oppose the Simpson-Mazzoli bill.[26] The "Latino Lobby," composed of the leaders of the National Council for La Raza, LULAC, MALDEF, and the United Farm Workers Union opposed different aspects of the immigration proposal. They worked in coalition with other immigrant rights groups to advance their interests.[27]

Eventually, legislators introduced alternative bills to meet the objections of the various lobbies. The result was the passage in 1986 of the Immigration Reform and Control Act (IRCA). This law provided for employer sanctions, a strengthened border patrol, a guest worker program and amnesty for undocumented workers who arrived before 1982. It also had provisions to review the implementation of the law to see the extent of violation of the rights of Latino citizens and Central American refugees.

A surge in nativist attitudes accompanied the long debate over various provision in the immigration bills. Community spokespersons portrayed Mexican and Central American immigrants as a threat to "the American way of life." They believed that the immigrants were responsible for rising crime rates, disease, unemployment, rising welfare costs, moral decay and decline in the quality of life. Despite a large body of social scientific studies that contradicted these assertions, a kind of paranoia regarding immigrants swept the country. The Democratic governor of Colorado, Richard Lamm, coauthored *The Immigration Time Bomb* and argued that the U.S. should curtail immigration from Latin America because it was undermining the nation's economy, corrupting American values and fragmenting the social fabric of the country.[28] In San Diego, California, Tom Metzger reorganized the Ku Klux Klan as the White Aryan Resistance. They distributed hate literature in high schools and public meetings warning Mexicans to go back or face violent consequences. Attacks against undocumented immigrants grew in number, not only by local racists, but by Border Patrol officers who had a war zone mentality. Sadly many of the attacks also came from Chicano and Mexican thieves (some of them Mexican officials) who preyed on the undocumented crossers. In the 1980s, the U.S. Mexican border region became the most dangerous terrain in America as every year hundreds of undocumented immigrants were robbed, beaten, raped and killed as they tried to cross.

Despite the anti-immigrant rhetoric, the U.S. increasingly needed immigrant labor in order to keep as economy prosperous. The *Wall Street Journal* in 1976 had said that ". . .illegals may well be providing the margin of survival for entire sectors of the economy." By 1985 the *New York Times* reported that respected economists believed that "illegal immigrants" had become the backbone of the economy.[29] Demographers, like Leo Estrada at UCLA, warned that the nation faced a severe labor shortage in the 1990s, particularly in the blue collar occupations, as the general population grew older and had less children. A work force augmented by immigration was the only way that the U.S. could continue to be competitive in a world economy. Undocumented and legal immigration from Mexico and Latin America provided the surplus labor that employers could use to lower their operating costs and expand production. The money spent and taxes paid by the "new immigrants" in turn created more jobs and helped fund social services. David Hayes-Bautista, for example, found that in California the population of working younger Latinos, including immigrants, was increasingly responsible for supporting social programs for the aged Anglos.[30] Other researchers found that those areas of the country that had the greatest economic growth and the least unemployment were the same areas that had substantial immigration. James Cockcroft's book *Outlaws in the Promised Land* (1986) reviewed the literature on the economic impact of Latin American immigration during the first half of the 1980s. He concluded, "In general, U.S. citizens benefit disproportionately from not just the migrants' labor and consumption but all the tax and benefit program checkoffs paid by immigrant workers."[31]

One of the effects of the debates over immigration restriction in the 1980s was to educate millions of U.S. Latinos about the importance of this "new immigration" to their political and cultural survival. Latinos joined Central American refugee support groups like CISPES (Committee In Support of the People of El Salvador) and included demands for amnesty for Central American refugees along with demands for police reform and Affirmative Action programs. MALDEF and The SWVRP targeted immigrant communities for future citizenship and voter registration drives. The generally anti-Mexican tenor of the debates in Congress mobilized many middle-class Latino organizations to take a stand in favor of immigrant rights.

Maturation of Latino Arts

The demographic, economic and political prominence of the Latino during the 1980s provided a context for a florescence and maturation in the performing and visual arts. Generally speaking, Latino artists joined the mainstream. Bolstered by the new creative energies coming from the Cuban, Puerto Rican and Latin American cultures, Mexican American creative artists enjoyed a new popularity. One important aspect in "the boom" in Latino visual and performing arts was the growth of a Latino market. For the first time it was possible for many Latino artists to earn a living from their work by selling their art to other Latinos. The main impetus in the change in Latino arts, however, came from the artists themselves who made a conscious choice to expand beyond the barrio and movement audiences to gain acceptance and recognition from the larger society.

Perhaps the most dramatic evidence of the emergence of Latino culture was in the film industry. After having Hollywood's exclusion of Latinos from producing and directing major productions for decades, the 1980s saw the exhibition of major motion pictures written, directed, or starring Latinos based on Latino themes. Perhaps the most artistically powerful statement tying the immigration to Latinos was the movie *El Norte* (1983), a moving saga about a Guatemalan brother and sister and their adventures in fleeing through Mexico to the U.S. Produced and directed by Gregory Nava, a Chicano, and staring a well-known Mexican actor, Pedro Arisméndez, the film made powerful statement about the tragedies experienced by Latino immigrants in the U.S. It also highlighted the competitive and exploitative relationship between the Chicano and the newly arrived immigrant. *El Norte* had limited distribution. The first in a series of box office hits was *La Bamba* (1987) written and directed by Luis Valdez about the life and tragic death of Ritchie Valens, a popular rock and roll star of the 1950s. Earning more than fifty five million dollars, the film showed Hollywood that Latino themes could sell. Next, Cheech Marin stared in the movie *Born in East L.A.* (1987) a comedy with serious undertones about Mexican immigrants and their relationship to Latinos. This also was a modest financial success. In 1988 Hollywood produced three major films starring Latinos and developing Mexican American cultural themes. Robert Redford with Moctezuma Esparza did *The Milagro Bean Field War* with a large Latino cast and starring Rubén Blades, a well-known Latino recording artist. Ramon Menendez directed *Stand and Deliver*, staring Edward James Olmos, based on the true story of a successful barrio high school math teacher and Raul Julia starred in the film *Romero*, a moving account of the life and assassination of Archbishop Romero in El Salvador. In 1989 other films emerged to capture a portion of the market. Raul Julia and Sonia Braga (Brazil) starred with Richard Dryfus in *Moon Over Parador*, a satire about a Latin American dictatorship and Jimmy Smitts with Jane Fonda starred in Carlos Fuentes' *Old Gringo,* a story set during the Mexican Revolution.

    A consequence of these and other films being produced in the 1980s was the promotion of new Latino film stars, many of who had been languishing in stereotypical minor roles. One of the most promising of these was Edward James Olmos, who had grown up in East Los Angeles of Mexican immigrant parents. After several number of small parts in television series, Olmos was "discovered" by Luis Valdez who cast him as the Pachuco in the 1978 play *Zoot Suit*. For his acting, Olmos won a Tony nomination and a Los Angeles Drama Critics Circle award and this led to his being cast in supporting roles in the films *Wolfen* (1981) and *Blade Runner* (1982). Olmos had a commitment to accept only roles that presented positive images of Latinos. His most important films in this regard were *The Ballad of Gregorio Cortez* (1982), a drama based on Américo Paredes' book, and *Stand and Deliver* (1988). He accepted of the role of Lieutenant Martin Castillo on the popular television series *Miami Vice* in 1984 only after promises that he would have creative control of the character. By the end of the decade, Olmos had established his own production company with the goal of making Latino movies that were artistically powerful and as well as socially responsible.

In the area of music, a growing Latino population meant more of a domestic market for Latino sounds, but the non-ethnic mainstream also picked up on the beat. Latino groups and artists sought to find a popular audience by mixing and crossing over. The Miami Sound Machine sold 1.25 million albums with their pop salsa rhythms. Los Lobos, an East L.A. Chicano group, provided the music for the hit movies *La Bamba* and *Salsa* and sold millions of albums of their unique blend of rock and roll, Tex-Mex, and Mexican corridos. Rubén Blades, the Panama-born recording artist, made his first album in English, *Nothing But the Truth*, keeping the rhythm and style but reaching the non-Latino audience. Linda Ronstadt, from the Tucson-Sonora Ronstadt family, had a big hit with her *Canciones de Mi Padre*, ballads sung in Spanish with the Mariachi Vargas de Tecalitán from Mexico.[32]

While retaining an ethnic tone and message Latino films and music appealed to large mixed audiences. The same tendencies were true for the performing arts. Perhaps the best example of this was the play *Zoot Suit* (1978), the first Chicano play to be performed on mainstream stages in Los Angeles and New York City. Written and directed by Luis Valdez, *Zoot Suit* was based on the Sleepy Lagoon incident in 1943. Incorporating music and dance of the 1940s, *Zoot Suit* had a social-political message but was entertaining as well. It was immensely popular in Los Angeles, running forty six weeks and having an audience of over 400,000. It was less so in New York, perhaps because of their lack of familiarity with Chicano culture. This play and subsequent ones by Valdez like, *I Don't Have to Show You No Stinking Badges*, and *Corridos* sought to entertain larger audiences while remaining faithful to Mexican and Chicano ideals.

Aside from Valdez, several Chicano playwrights contributed their talents to producing an authentic Chicano theater that could be appreciated by non-Latinos. Carlos Morton wrote a series of plays and won the Hispanic Playwrights Festival Award, New York Shakespeare Festival. Rubén Sierra wrote *La Raza Pura o Racial, Racial (The Pure Race or Racial, Racial)* and with Jorge Huerta, *I Am Celso*, Fausto Avedaño wrote *El Corrido de California* and Estela Portillo Trambely *Sor Juana* and *Blacklight*, the latter winning second place in the American Theatre Festival in New York.

Jorge Huerta established the nation's first Master's in Theater Arts specializing in Hispanic/Latino theater at the University of California in San Diego. Besides training a cadre of professional actors, directors and playwrights, he worked with the local Old Globe Theater and San Diego Repertory Theater to produce original Chicano productions and productions of noted Latin American playwrights.

Nicolás Kanellos, a literary critic and historian, aptly summarized the state of Chicano theater in the 1980s:

> "[T]he days of teatro as an arm of revolutionary nationalism are over. The revolutionary aims of the movement have resulted in modest reforms and certain accommodations. Luis Valdez now sits on the California Arts Council. Many other teatro and former teatro people are members of local arts agencies and boards throughout the Southwest. Former teatristas are now professors of drama, authors, and editors of scholarly books and journals on Chicano literature and theater."

If Chicano literature did not produce a best seller or a poet laureate during this era it was not for lack of talent or productivity. The big publishing houses, located in New York, remained impervious to the literary merits of Latinos. The national appeal of Latino works had yet to be proven. A major breakthorugh, however, occurred in 1989 with the publication of the *The Mambo Kings Play Songs of Love* (1989) by Oscar Hijuelos, a Cuban American resident of New York City. Hijuelos' book won the Pulitzer Prize for literature and became a best seller for Harper Row Publishers. It was a lyrical and sorrowful story of a couple of Cuban musicians in New York during the 1940s and 1950s as they became part of the Latin music boom of that era. Hijuelos' passionate and rich style evoked a barrage of sensual images that captured people's imagination. Concurrent with the success of this book, Gabriel Garcia Marquez (Colombia) and Octavio Paz (Mexico) won Nobel Prizes for their literature and this sparked a surge in English language translations of their works.

Despite this modest Latino "boom" in literature, most Chicano writers did not have large commercial success. Many may have eschewed it. Most Chicano writers were university professors whose orientation tended to be away from the marketplace. Most of the well known Chicano fiction writers of the previous decade continued to publish short stories and novels but there emerged a new group of writers. Nash Candelaria wrote a triology based on New Mexico's history. *Memories of the Alhambra* (1977), *Not by the Sword* (1982) and *Inheritance of Strangers* (1985) tracing the history of José Rafa's family through 400 years. The main themes of the Rafa trilogy were conquest, conflict and identity while underscoring the Chicano's links to universal humanity. Arturo Islas created *The Rain God: A Desert Tale* in 1984 as a historical-autobiographical novel set in El Paso and Lionel García wrote *Leaving Home* in 1985 about a Latino baseball pitcher in the 1930s and 1940s and *A Shroud in the Family* in 1987 about a Tejano searching for his identity in family relations.

Latinas also made important contributions to the development of fiction. Gloria Anzaldua wrote *This Bridge Called My Back* and *Borderlands/Fronteras* (1987) exploring issues of sexual and cultural politics. Irene Beltrán produced *Across the Great River* (1987), dealing with the experiences of an undocumented immigrant family as seen through the eyes of a young girl. Denise Chávez, in *Face of an Angel* (1990), wrote about the survival strategies of a career waitress and Ana Castillo's *Sapagonia* (1990) reflected on the meaning of being a Mestizo in the Americas. There were many collections of short stories written by Latinas published by the two most prominent Latino editorial houses, Arte Publico Press and Bilingual Review Press.

Modern Chicano literature continued to be intensely personal. The most controversial, and so best selling, autobiography of the 1980s was *The Hunger of Memory* (1982) by Richard Rodríguez. This book, more than any other, perhaps, challenged the values of the Chicano movement. In the book Rodríguez described his alienation from the main Chicano activists and his willingness to abandon the Mexican culture and embrace Anglo American values. His book was about language and the importance of learning a public language (English) rather than preserving a private one (Spanish). He attacked bilingual education, Affirmative Action and ethnic politics. Praised by the Anglo American critics for his literary style and power, *The Hunger of Memory* came under attack by Chicano intellectuals because of its conservative message. Rodríguez wrote several essays that appeared in national magazines, and he narrated television documentaries on Mexican culture. Because of his literary skill he became, ironically, the most well-known Chicano writer in the U.S.

Writing for a smaller audience, Chicano poets turned away from didactic political messages and became more introspective. A major development in these years was the emergence of an energetic group of Chicana and Latina poets. Bernice Zamora published *Restless Serpents* (1976) that explored the contradictory and conflictive feelings about being a woman in a male dominated culture. Zamora linked Chicana poetry to American literary works, with frequent alusions to the mainstream tradition. Alma Villanueva wrote *Bloodroot* and *Poems* in 1977 and *Mother, May I?* in 1978, poetry that was intensely personal and confident, powerfully asserting female sexual superiority and creative power while emphasizing her identity as a woman rather than as a Latina. Another prominent Chicana poet of these years was Lorna Dee Cervantez who wrote *Emplumada* (1981), a complex array of feminist poems that developed themes springing from barrio life.[34]

The most prolific and widely-acclaimed poet in the 1980s, however, was Gary Soto. Born in the San Joaquin Valley, Soto's poems moved away from the overt political declamations of the Chicano movement years and explored personal themes using vivid and evocative language. Critics acclaimed his first collection *The Elements of San Joaquin* (1977) as a masterpiece that captured the essence of rural landscapes and people. *The Tale of Sunlight* (1978) was more psychological in character and *Father is a Pillow Tied to a Broom* (1980) evoked more somber and sorrowful tones. *Where Sparrows Work Hard* (1981) and *Black Hair* (1985) and *Who Will Know Us, New Poems* (1990) were all major advances in the use of language. Soto won national and international prizes for his work. His collection of short stories, *Living Up the Street* (1985), about his childhood in Fresno, California, won the National Book Award.

Latino visual artists had somewhat more success than fiction writers in gaining national recognition for their work. The diversity of artistic expression multiplied and mural art declined as the dominating form for Chicanos. In 1987, a national touring exhibition of Latino artists, "Hispanic Art in the United States: Thirty Contemporary Painters and Sculptors," showcased the rich imagery and vitality of modern Latino artists of diverse Latin American backgrounds. Another national touring exhibition, opening in 1990, "CARA: Chicano Art Resistance and Affirmation" interpreted the Chicano art movement (1965-1975) within a larger historical and cultural framework. Another historical retrospective organized by the Bronx Museum in 1990 was "The Latin American Spirit: Art and Artists in the United States, 1920-1970" that focused on the international influences of Latin American art and artists in the United States. These shows, and many other locally organized art exhibits, publicized the emergence of new talent and energies and challenged the conservative dominions of the American art academy. In 1991, the Mexican government organized a major historical and contemporary touring exhibit of visual art entitled "Mexico Splendors of Thirty Centuries." This exhibit made the public even more aware than ever of the traditions of Latino art.

The main aesthetic directions of Chicano art in the 1980s was towards the private and away from the public. Artists sought commercial success in creating canvas paintings not public murals. A host of new talent sold their work in galleries in Los Angeles, Austin, San Francisco and San Diego. As art collectors began to bid thousands for works by artists such as John Valadez, Luis Jimenez, Carmen Lomas Garza, and Carlos Almaraz, Chicanos graduated from the streets to the salons.

Conclusions

Immigration from Latin America and a dramatic growth in the Latino population shaped the years following the decline of the heightened political sensibilities of the Chicano movement (1965-1975). The economic, linguistic and national diversity of the U.S. Spanish speaking population expanded. The new immigrants filled an important niche in American economy and, at the same time, the general Latino population became more economically polarized. The middle and upper class Latino classes grew. So too did the Latino underclass. The new wave of immigration led to new political activities. MALDEF and the SWVRP made an intense effort to enlarge Latino representation within the existing political system. Instead of demonstrations they used the courts and the ballot boxes. Latino immigration provoked a nativist backlash that resulted in a new immigration law in 1987 that promised to "cure" the problems attributed to the newcomers. The conservative political and social tone of the Reagan years had its reflection in Latino politics. Large national organizations made deals with multinational corporations to help fund their activities. With some notable exceptions, Latino politicans increasingly joined the mainstream and eschewed radical ethnic approaches. The Chicano renaissance of the 1960s and 1970s became a Latino "boom" in the 1980s.

Mainstream America became more aware of the rich cultural expressions of Latino artists in the movies and music. The mood of the 1980s was to commercialize ethnicity and seek ways of selling it. Meanwhile a fundamental contradiction remained between the underclass of working class Latino immigrants and native born and the growing Hispanic middle classes.

Notes

1. The series was reprinted as *Southern California's Latino Community* (Los Angeles: Times Mirror Co., 1983). See Frank Sotomayor's, "A Box Full of Ethnic Labels," p. 27-28.
2. Rubén Rumbaut, "Passages to America: Perspectives on the New Immigration," in *America at Century's End: American Society in Transition* by Alan Wolfe, ed. (Berkeley: University of California, 1991).
3. *La Red/The Net*, Vol. 2, no. 2 (1989), p. 20.
4. "U.S. Hispanic Population: The Year 2080," *Hispanic Business,* 9:3 (March 1987), 50.
5. Lawrence W. Miller, Jerry L. Polinard, and Robert D, Wrinkle, "Attitudes Toward Undocumented Workers: The Mexican American Perspective," *Social Science Quarterly*, 65, no. 2 (June 1984): 483-493.
6. Rudolfo O. de la Garza, "Chicanos and U.S. Foreign Policy: The Future of Chicano-Mexican Relations," *Mexican-U.S. Relations: Conflict and Convergence*, Carlos Vásquez and Manuel García y Griego, eds. (Los Angeles: UCLA Chicano Studies Reseach Center and UCLA Latin American Center Publications, 1983), pp. 401-403.
7. Christine Marie Sierra, "Latinos and the 'New Immigration': Responses from the Mexican American Community," *Renato Rosaldo Lecture Series 3: 1985-1986* ed. Ignacio García

(Tucson: Mexican American Studies and Research Center, University of Arizona, 1987), pp. 42-55.

8. Peter Cattan, "The Growing Presence of Hispanics in the U.S. Work Force," *Monthly Labor Review* (August 1988), pp. 9-13.

9. William O'Hare, "The Rise of the Hispanic Affluence," *American Demographics*, Vol. 12 (August 1990) pp. 40-43.

10. George Swisshelm, "U.S. Hispanics Move to Rediscover their Ethnic Roots," *Television/Radio Age* Vol. 36 (July 1989): A1-A47.

11. Tom Díaz, "Coors Get on Board Hispanic Trend," *Nuestro* (January/February 1985), pp. 12-18.

12. Richard Santillan, "The Latino Community in State and Congressional Redistricting, 1961-1985," *Journal of Hispanic Policy*, Vol. 1, no. 1 (1985), pp. 52-65.

13. Harry P. Pachon, "Overview of Hispanic Elected Officials in 1987," *1987 National Roster of Hispanic Elected Officials* ed. by National Association of Latino Elected and Appointed Officials (Washington D.C.: NALEO Education Fund, 1987).

14. Harry P. Pachon, "Overview of Hispanic Elected Officials in 1987," *1987 National Roster of Hispanic Elected Officials* ed. by National Association of Latino Elected and Appointed Officials (Washington D.C.: NALEO Education Fund, 1987), pp. xv-xxiv.

15. *Los Angeles Times*, February 20, 1991, A18.

16. *Nuestro*, Jan./Feb. 1986, pp. 15-17.

17. See National Commission on Excellence in Education, *A Nation at Risk: The Imperative for Educational Reform* (Washington D.C., April 1983); also Erick Hirsh, Cultural Literacy: *What Every American Needs to Know* (Boston: Houghton Mifflin, 1987); Charles Sykes, *Profscam: Professors and the Demise of Higher Education* (Washington D.C.: Regnery Coteway, 1988).

18. Thomas Muller and Thomas J. Sepenshade et. al., *The Fourth Wave: California's Newest Immigrants* (Washington D.C.: The Urban Institute, 1985), pp. 80, 82.

19. Rudolfo Acuña, *Occupied America: A History of Chicanos* (New York: Harper & Row Publishers, 1988), pp. 389-90.

20. *MALDEF Newsletter*, Vol. X, No. 4 (Fall 1980): 1:1.

21. For an excellent discussion of drop outs and educational statistics see selected essays in Pastora San Juan Cafferty and William C. McCready, *Hispanics in the United States: A New Social Agenda* (New Brunswick, New Jersey: Transaction Books, 1985).

22. Pastora San Juan Cafferty, "Language and Social Assimilation," in *Hispanics in the United States: A New Social Agenda*, pp. 102-4; describes the evaluation of bilingual

programs. For a more recent study see "Bilingual Students Held to Do Well," *Los Angeles Times,* February 12, 1991: 1:2.

23. Mark R. Halton, "Legislating Assimilation: The English-Only Movement," *The Christian Century,* Vol. 106 (November 29, 1989), p. 1119.

24. Raul Yzaguirre, "The Perils of Pandora: An Examination of the English-Only Movement," *Journal of Hispanic Policy,* Vol. 2 (1986-1987), p. 5.

25. David Reimers, *Still the Golden Door: The Third World Comes to America* (New York: Columbia University Press, 1985), p. 203.

26. James D. Cockcroft, *Outlaws in the Promised Land: Mexican Immigrant Workers and America's Future* (New York: Grove Press, 1986), pp. 218-227.

27. Christine Marie Sierra, "Latinos and the 'New Immigration': Responses from the Mexican American Community," p. 51.

28. Richard D. Lamm and Gary Imhoff, *The Immigration Time Bomb: The Fragmenting of America* (New York: Truman Talley Books, 1986).

29. Cited in Cockcroft, p. 130.

30. David E. Hayes-Bautista, Werner O. Schinek and Jorge Chapa, "Young Latinos in an Aging American Society," *Social Policy,* Vol. 15, no. 1 (1984): 49-52.

31. Ibid., p. 135.

32. "A Surging New Spirit," *Time Magazine,* July 11, 1988, pp. 46-76.

33. Quoted in Shirley and Shirley, p. 88.

34. Carl Shirley and Paula Shirley, Understanding Chicano Literature (Columbia: University of South Carolina Press, 1988), pp. 41-48. This book has a fine bibliography of surveys and original works in Chicano literature.

Key Terms and
Discussion Questions

Photo courtesy of César A. González

Key Terms and Discussion Questions

The Psycho-Historical and Socioeconomic Development of the Chicano Community in the United States
Rodolfo Alvarez

Key Terms

land and souls
heterogenous society
Benito Juarez
Creation Generation
Mexican American Generation
"psychic security"

homogenous society
"cooperative experience"
"revolutionary experience"
Migrant Generation
Chicano Generation
push and pull factors

Discussion Questions

1. What two factors does Alvarez consider in his definition of a generation?

2. The English-inspired expansionists sought land. The Spanish sought *land and souls*. Discuss the difference.

3. What was the "cooperative experience?" The revolutionary experience?"

4. Why does Alvarez refer to the first generation as the Creation Generation?

5. What are the various reasons why Alvarez refers to the Mexicans immigrants as migrants?

6. According to Alvarez, the Mexican American Generation achieved a sense of "psychic security." What is meant by this and why was this a false sense of complacency?

7. In what ways did the Chicano Generation challenge the assumptions of the Mexican American Generation. What did they mean by self-definition?

Key Terms and Discussion Questions

The Treaty of Guadalupe Hidalgo

Discussion Questions

1. Discuss the significance of Article V.

2. What does Article VIII assert with regard to the citizenship of Mexicans who remained in the acquired territories?

3. What were the important historical precedents established by Article VIII with regard to citizenship rights for Chicanos?

4. What does Article X (prior to its omission) assert in terms of ownership of Spanish and Mexican land grants?

Key Terms and Discussion Questions

The Protocol of Querétaro

Discussion Questions

1. Why was the Statement of Protocol necessary?

2. What does the Protocol assert with regard to the legal ownership of Spanish and Mexican land grants?

The U. S. Courts and the Treaty
Richard Griswold del Castillo

Key Terms

Mintern v. Bower et al.
Asociación de Reclamantes
United States v. Moreno
Botiller v. Domínguez
Cessna v. United States et al.
Article X

Palmer v. United States
Reies López Tijerina
McKinney v. Saviego
Tenorio v. Tenorio
Texas Mexican Rail Road v. Locke

Discussion Questions

1. In what ways did the courts interpret the treaty liberally during the 1848-1889 period?

2. In what ways was the conservative interpretation of the treaty evident during the 1889-1930 period?

3. What was the significance of the *Botiller v. Dominguez* Supreme Court decision?

4. How did Reies López Tijerina use the treaty?

Key Terms and Discussion Questions

The Lost Land
John R. Chávez

Key Terms

californios	*nuevomexicanos*
El Clamor Público	*El Horizonte*
Francisco P. Ramírez	Juan N. Cortina
Foreign Miners' Tax Law of 1850	Miguel Antonio Otero I
Tiburcio Vásquez	Miguel A. Otero II
Land Law of 1851	Casimiro Barela
El bejareño	Francisco Perea

Discussion Questions

1. What were the various impacts of the California gold rush on the *californios*?

2. What was the Land Law of 1851? What impact did it have on the *californio* land base?

3. Why did numerous *nuevomexicanos* oppose statehood in 1889?

4. Why was Miguel A. Otero considered a progressive?

5. How did Casimiro Barela reflect the interests of the traditionalists?

Key Terms and Discussion Questions

Race and Class in a Southwestern City: The Mexican Community of Tucson, 1854-1941
Thomas E. Sheridan

Key Terms

Alianza Hispano-Americana
Tucsonenses
"institutionalized subordination"
"geographic dualization"

Ramón Soto
Lingua franca
mutualistas
La Liga Protectora Latina

Discussion Questions

1. Discuss the Mexican contribution to the early settlement and development of southern Arizona.

2. How did the arrival of the railroad in 1880 alter the southern Arizona economy?

3. How did the Tucson occupational structure reveal the subordination of the Mexican working class?

4. What does Sheridan mean by "institutionalized subordination?"

5. How did residence patterns reveal subordination?

6. Discuss the various methods utilized by Mexicans to resist subordination.

Key Terms and Discussion Questions

Las Gorras Blancas:
A Secret Gathering of Fence Cutters
Robert J. Rosenbaum

Key Terms

mayordomo de acequia	*Los Ricos*
pastores	*los pobres*
jefe politico	Nestor Montoya
Lorenzo Marquez	Antonchico Grant
Governor Prince	Las Vegas Grant
Juan José Montoya	*El Partido del Pueblo Unido*
La Voz del Pueblo	Knights of Labor

Discussion Questions

1. What were some of the features of early New Mexican pastoral life?

2. What were the various functions of *Los Ricos, los pobres* and *jefes politicos*?

3. How were New Mexican and American concepts of upward mobility distinct?

4. What were the issues which led to the early formation of Las Gorras Blancas?

5. Discuss the role of Juan José Herrera in the formation of Las Gorras Blancas.

6. In what ways did Las Gorras Blancas and the Knights of Labor correspond in goals and methods?

7. In what ways did Las Gorras Blancas build upon a sense of ethnic and class identification?

Key Terms and Discussion Questions

An Essay on Understanding the Work Experience of Mexicans in Southern California, 1900-1939
Douglas Monroy

Discussion Questions

1. What are the various factors which account for employment instability for Mexican workers during this time?

2. Why were urban industrial occupations more attractive to Mexican workers?

Beyond 1848

3. In what ways did urban industrial occupations disrupt the traditional Mexican family unit?

4. In what ways did urban industrial occupations often produce generational conflicts?

Key Terms and Discussion Questions

Responses to Mexican Immigration, 1910-1930
Ricardo Romo

Key Terms

1917 Immigration Act
Restriction League

enganchadores

Discussion Questions

1. Discuss the role played by Mexican labor in the growth of Southwestern agriculture and industry.

2. Why did Congress exclude Mexican immigration from provisions of the 1917 Immigration Act?

3. What measures did the Mexican government take in an attempt to stem the flow of immigration to the United States?

4. In general, why did organized labor oppose Mexican immigration at this time?

Key Terms and Discussion Questions

Closing America's Back Door
Abraham Hoffman

Key Terms

Repatriation
1917 Immigration Act
repatriados

Quota Act of 1924
"LPC"

Discussion Questions

1. Why did some U.S. interests favor the restriction of Mexican immigration?

2. Which interest groups opposed the restriction of Mexican immigration? Why?

3. What methods were utilized to encourage Mexicans to voluntarily return to Mexico?

4. How did the Mexican government attempt to accommodate the *repatriados*?

Key Terms and Discussion Questions

Luisa Moreno and the 1939 Congress of Mexican and Spanish Speaking People
Albert Camarillo

Key Terms

"Mexican problem"
mutualistas
Luisa Moreno
Eduardo Quevedo
Congress of Mexican and Spanish Speaking People
Good Neighbor Policy
Mexican American Political Association (MAPA)

repatriation/deportation
Great Depression
UCAPAWA
Josefina Fierro de Bright
Criminal Syndicalist Act
Community Service Organizationn (CSO)

Discussion Questions

1. In what ways were American attitudes toward Mexicans "ambivalent?"

2. What was the so-called "Mexican problem" and what was the solution for it?

3. What are some of the examples of institutionalized segregation of Mexicans?

4. What were some of the resolutions passed by the Congress?

5. In what ways was the Congress concerned about worker's issues?

6. How was the Congrreso concerned about immigrant rights?

7. How did the Congreso contribute to civil rights and Mexican American advocacy?

Key Terms and Discussion Questions

The Mexican American Mind
Richard A. García

Key Terms

League of United Latin American Citizens (LULAC)
La Prensa
J. Montiel Olvera
Ben Garza

"Los Ricos"
Alianza Hispanoamericana
Juan Solís

Discussion Questions

1. How did the economic structure of San Antonio help to divide Mexicans economically?

2. In what ways did "Los Ricos" "face south"?

3. In what ways were the ideas and ideologies of LULAC different from those of "Los Ricos"?

4. Why was the 1927 founding of LULAC pivotal in the formation of the Mexican American mind?

5. What were some of the aspirations and goals of the LULAC organization?

6. How were LULAC's objectives distinct from "Los Ricos"?

Mexican American Labor and the Left:
The Asociación Nacional México-Americana, 1949-1954
Mario Garcia

Key Terms

Progreso
McCarren Act

Alfredo C. Montoya
McCarthyism

Discussion Questions

1. How did ANMA's version of Mexican American history differ from LULAC's?

2. How did ANMA analyze race and class issues?

3. How did ANMA encourage internationalism?

4. In what ways did ANMA promote the preservation of Mexican culture?

5. In what ways was ANMA the target of harassment and political persecution?

Key Terms and Discussion Questions

Aztlán Rediscovered
John R. Chávez

Key Terms

Aztlán
Mexican American Political Association (MAPA)
Virgen of Guadalupe
National Farm Workers Association (NFWA)
Agricultural Workers Organizing Committee (AWOC)
United Farm Workers Organizing Committee (UFWOC)
Chicano Youth Liberation Conference
Alianza Federal de Mercedes (Alianza)
MECHA
Political Association of Spanish-Speaking Organizations (PASSO)
El Chamizal
César Chávez
Plan of Delano
Reies López Tijerina
La Raza Unida Party
Rodolfo Acuña
José Angel Gutiérrez
El Plan Espiritual de Aztlán
Armando Rendón

Discussion Questions

1. Explain the origins of the term Chicano.

2. In what ways did "Aztlán" embody the homeland to Chicanos?

3. What are the major events which comprised the late 1960s Chicano movement?

4. How did César Chávez's movement embody some of the ideals of the Chicano movement?

5. What were the goals and objectives of the Alianza movement?

6. What did "nationalism" mean to Corky Gonzales?

7. Discuss some of the successes of La Raza Unida party.

8. Discuss why the Chicano Youth Liberation Conferences were significant to the Chicano movement.

Latinos and the "New Immigrants," Since 1975
Richard Griswold del Castillo

Key Terms

Southwest Voter Registration Project (SWVRP)
Mexican American Legal Defense and Education Fund (MALDEF)
National Association of Latino Elected and Appointed Officials (NALEO)
San Antonio School District v. Rodríguez
Gloria Molina
Xavier Suárez
Toney Anaya
Simpson-Mazzoli bill
Henry Cisneros
Federico Peña
Latino
Chicano
U. S. English
Doe v. Plyler
Bob Martínez
Lau v. Nichols
Immigration Reform and Control Act (IRCA)

Discussion Questions

1. What variables impacted on the way resident Chicanos responded to the new immigration?

2. In what ways were Latinos viewed as a market for commercial products?

3. Name and discuss two impediments to Latino electoral progress?

4. In what ways have Latinos influenced the direction of modern American popular culture?

INDEX

A
Abeyta, José, 42
Across the Great River, 263
Agricultural Workers Organizing Committee (AWOC), 218
Alatorre, Richard, 252
Alianza Hispano-Americana, 71, 86, 183
Alianza Federal de Mercedes Libres, 44, 223-225
Amaya, Amos, 43
American Federation of Labor, 147, 151, 154, 167
Anzaldua, Gloria, 263
Arisa v. New Mexico and Arizona Railroad, 37, 46
Armory Park, Tucson, 79
Arroyo, Luís, 192, 210
Asociación Nacional México-Americana (ANMA), 191-212
Asociación de Reclamantes, 47
Aztlán, 24, 68, 69, 120, 122, 124, 177, 179, 191, 209, 213, 214, 225-229, 231-233, 238, 239, 240-242

B
Ballad of Gregorio Cortez, The, 260
Balli, Alberto, 43
Barela, Casimiro, 66, 70
Barrio Anita, Tucson, 80
Barrio Libre, Tucson, 80
Barrio Sin Nombre, Tucson, 80
Bilingual Education Act, 257
Black Hair, 264
Bloodroot and Poems, 263
Board of Land Commissioners, 35
Bogardus, Emory, 135, 146
Border Patrol, 14, 131, 155-157, 237, 257, 258
Born in East L.A., 260
Box, John C., 151
bracero, 162, 200, 257
Braga, Sonia, 260
Breitigam, Gerald B., 135
Bryan, Samuel, 127, 144
Bufkin, Don, 79, 89

C
California Land Act (Land Law of 1851), 36, 55
California Land Commission, 41
California Powderworks v. Davis, 37, 46
Californios, 49-53, 55, 68, 90, 144
Camarillo, Albert, 68, 114, 122, 163, 177, 209
Cananea, 87
Canciones de mi Padre, 261
Candelaria, Nash, 262
Carrillo, Leopoldo, 74
Chávez, César, 218-221
Chávez, Denise, 263
Chicano Youth Liberation Conference, 227, 228, 231
Chicano Generation, 19, 20, 22-25
Chihuahua (Mexico), 74, 159
Cisneros, Henry, 251, 252
Civil War, The 33, 34, 58, 64

Clark, Victor S., 144, 145
Clements, George P., 152, 161
Commissioner General of Immigration, 137, 155, 161
Communist Party, 124, 167, 192, 198, 206, 208, 212
Community Service Organization (CSO), 175, 217, 219
Congress of Industrial Organizations (CIO), 113
Consul General William Dawson, 160
Cooperative Association in California, 153
"cooperative experience," 5
corridos, 54, 101, 120, 203, 261
Cortez, Gregorio, 191, 260
Cortina, Juan N., 58, 69
Court of Private Land Claims, 38
Crawford, Remsen, 142, 148, 162
Creation Generation, 7, 11, 17, 20, 22-25,
Crocker, Charles, 74
Crusade for Justice, 226, 228

D

de la Garza, Rudolfo, 247
De la Guerra, Pablo, 68
Department of the Interior, 42
Department of Indian Affairs, 36
deportee, 160
Doe v. Plyler, 254

E

Educational Subordination, 81

El Partido del Pueblo Unido, 100, 103
El Norte, 237, 260
El Clamor Público, 52, 55, 56, 68
El Convento, 80
El Chamizal, 216, 217
El Grito, 191, 209
El Plan Espiritual de Aztlán, 226, 227
Elías, Perfecto, 85
employment vulnerability, 113
Emplumada, 263
Enganchadores, 129, 130
Esparza, Moctezuma, 260
Estrada, Leo, 258
Ethnic Enclavement, 78, 80, 81
European Immigration Law of 1924, 141

F

Face of an Angel, 263
Father is a Pillow Tied to a Broom, 264
Fierro de Bright, Josefina, 163
Fonda, Jane, 260
Foreign Miners' Tax Law of 1850, 53
Fox, Harry W., 139
Frazer, Robert, 160

G

G.I. Forum, 205, 250, 257
Gadsden, James, 72
Gadsden Purchase, 60, 73-75, 78, 82, 85
Galarza, Ernesto, 176, 178

Gamio, Manuel, 124, 145, 146
García, Lionel, 262
Garza, Ben, 186
Gómez-Quiñones, Juan, 68
Gompers, Samuel, 139, 143
Gonzales, Rodolfo "Corky", 225-228
González Navarro, Moises, 128, 144
González, Senator Henry B., 232
Good Neighbor Policy, 173, 216
Great Depression, 40, 77, 149, 157, 163, 164, 166, 167, 208
Griswold del Castillo, Richard, 27, 33, 69, 113, 114, 122, 245
Gutiérrez, José Angel, 213, 235, 214, 229-231

H

Harding, President Warren, 141
Heart of Aztlan, 232, 242
Hermosillo (Mexico), 54, 72
Hijuelos, Oscar, 262
Huerta, Jorge, 261
Hull, Harry E., 155
Hunger of Memory, The, 263

I

I Am Celso, 261
Immigration Act of 1917, 132, 133-135, 155
Immigration Restriction League, 132
Inheritance of Strangers, 262
Institutionalized Subordination, 77, 78
Internal Colonialism, 191, 195

International Union of Mine, Mill and Smelter Workers, 169
Islas, Arturo, 262

J

Jencks, Clint 206
Jim Crow, 78
Johnson, Albert, 142
Johnson Act, 141
Juarez, Benito, 4

K

Kennedy, John F., 216
Knights of Labor, 98-100, 106
Ku Klux Klan, 237, 258

L

La Bamba, 260, 261
la calle Meyer (Tucson), 80
Lamar, Dr. Edward, 204
La Mano Negra, 223
land and souls, 4
Land Law of 1851 (CA), 36, 55
La Raza Unida Party, 229, 235, 241
Las Gorras Blancas, 91, 92, 98-100, 102, 104, 106, 223
La Prensa, 183, 184, 187
La Voz del Pueblo, 99
League of United Latin American Citizens (LULAC), 86, 167, 181,182, 184-188, 193, 194, 196, 205, 207, 208, 215, 217, 250, 257, 258
Leaving Home, 262
Legarra, Joaquín, 85

Lewis, Oscar, 84, 120, 124
Liga Protectora Latina, 86
Living Up the Street, 264
Lockhart v. Johnson, 37, 46
López Tijerina, Reies, 44, 213, 223
Los Lobos, 261
Los Ricos, 182-185, 187, 188
Lumber and Sawmill Workers Local, 117

M

McCarran Act, 200, 211
McCarthyism, 197, 206, 208
McKinney v. Saviego, 36, 39, 45-47
Madero, Francisco, 130
Marin, Cheech, 260
Marquez, Lorenzo, 92
Martínez, Bob, 251, 253
Memories of the Alhambra, 262
Menlo Park, 80
mestizo, 4, 5, 214, 225, 227, 245, 263
Metzger, Tom, 258
Mexican American Generation, 14-16, 19, 20, 22-24, 179, 187, 191, 213
Mexican American Legal Defense and Education Fund (MALDEF), 254, 255, 257-259, 265, 266
Mexican American Political Association (MAPA), 175, 176, 215-217
Mexican Revolution, 87, 125, 127, 132, 133, 137, 191, 252, 260
Migrant Generation, 9, 11-13, 15-19, 24

Mintern v. Bower, 35
Molina, Gloria, 252
Monroy, Douglas, 113, 122, 124, 192, 210, 212
Montoya, Juan José, 202
Montoya, Alfredo C., 195
Moon Over Parador, 260
Moore, Chester B. 153
Moreno, Luisa, 163, 167, 171, 174-176, 178
Morton, Carlos, 261
Mother, May I?, 263
Movimiento Estudiantil Chicano de Aztlán (MECHA), 231
Moynihan, Daniel, 84
Murieta, Joaquín, 54, 55

N

National Association of Latino Elected and Appointed Officials (NALEO), 251, 266
National Farm Workers Association (NFWA), 218, 219
Nava, Gregory, 260
Nepomuceno Seguín, Juan, 57, 69
New Deal, 40, 172, 194, 216
Not by the Sword, 262
Nuevomexicanos, 49, 60, 61, 63-66, 223, 225, 233

O

Occupied America, 69, 90, 177-179, 191, 192, 209-212, 230, 232, 240, 266
Ochoa, Estevan, 74, 85
Old Gringo, 260

Index

Olmos, Edward James, 260
Outlaws in the Promised Land, 259, 267

P
Pacheco, Nabor, 85
Padre Island, 43
Palmer v. United States, 35, 46
Panama Canal, 132
Panunzio, Constantine, 135, 146
Papagos, 72
Parker Frisselle, Samuel, 151
Paz, Octavio, 262
"pecking order", 75
Peña, Federico, 251
Perales, Alonso, 209
Perea, Francisco, 64
Philips v. Mound City, 35
Pimas, 72
Pitt River Tribe et al. v. United States, 42, 47
Plan of Delano, 220, 222, 240
Plessy v. Ferguson, 33
Polanco, Richard, 252
Portillo Trambely, Estela, 261
Progreso, 196, 197, 199, 203, 204, 210-212
Protocol of Querétaro, 31-32, 34, 35, 38

Q
Quevedo, Eduardo, 163, 169, 174, 175, 240
Quota Act of 1924, 151

R
Ramírez, Francisco, 52, 55
recien llegado, 247
Red Cross, 131, 133, 158
repatriados, 159, 160
Restless Serpents, 263
Restriction Leagues, 142
"revolutionary experience," 6
Riggins, Rachel, 83
Rio Grande, 12, 27, 39-41, 47, 58, 59, 61, 62, 94, 124, 124, 132, 143, 161, 198, 217, 235, 236
Roberts, Kenneth L., 142, 148, 152, 161
Rodríguez, Richard, 242
Romano, Octavio, 191
Romero, 260
Ronstadt, Linda, 261
Rose, Superintendent C.E., 81
Roybal, Edward, 196
Royce, Josiah, 53, 54, 68
Ruiz, Vicki, 192, 210

S
Salt of the Earth, 199, 204
Samaniego, Mariano, 74, 85
San Antonio, 57, 58, 63, 69, 160, 165, 168, 178, 181-188, 194, 232, 242, 251, 252, 254
Sánchez, George I., 205, 209
Santa Cruz River, 72
Santillan, Richard, 252, 266
Sapagonia, 263
Scott, Dred, 34
Sevilleta de la Joya Grant, 41
Shafer, Emmy, 256

Shoshonean Indians, 41
Sierra, Christine, 247
Sleepy Lagoon, 175, 176, 261
Sor Juana, 261
Smitts, Jimmy, 260
Sociedad Amigos Unidos, 86
Sociedad Mutualista Porfirio Díaz, 86
Solís, Juan, 186
Soto, Gary, 263
South Meyer Street (Tucson), 80
Southern Pacific Railroad, 74, 79, 126
Southwest Voter Registration Project, 250
Stand and Deliver, 260
Stowell, Jay S., 130, 145, 162
Strangers in the Land, 57, 150
Sturges, Vera L., 129, 145
Summa Corporation v. California, 41

T

Taylor, Paul S., 123, 140, 147, 177
Taylor, Ralph H., 153
tejanos, 43, 57-60, 182, 248
Tenorio v. Tenorio, 41, 46, 47
Terrazas, Mauricio, 205
Texas Mexican Railroad v. Locke, 39
Texas Rangers, 14, 163
This Bridge Called My Back and Borderlands, 263
Thomson, Charles A., 127, 144
Townsend et al. v. Greeley, 35, 46

Treaty of Guadalupe Hidalgo, 3, 27, 31, 33-45, 50, 55, 67, 195, 215, 222, 223, 225
    Article V, 27-28
    Article VIII, 29, 34, 36, 42, 43, 46
    Article IX, 29, 31, 42
    Article X, 30, 31, 35, 38
Tubac, 72
Tucsonenses, 71, 73-75, 78, 79, 85, 90, 177

U

United Cannery, Packing, and Agricultural Workers of America (UCAPAWA), 168, 169, 174, 176, 178, 192, 210
United Farm Workers Organizing Committee (UFWOC), 218, 221
United States Department of Labor, 130
United States Immigration Service, 126
United States Supreme Court, 34, 38, 39
United States v. Lucero, 36, 46
United States v. Moreno, 35
United States v. Reading, 35, 46
United States v. Sandoval, 37, 46

V

Valdez, Luis, 69, 219, 232, 240, 242, 260-262
Valens, Ritchie, 260
Vallejo, Mariano, 50, 56
Vásquez, Tiburcio, 54, 55
Velasco, Carlos, 86

Index

Viguerie, Richard, 256
Villanueva, Alma, 263

W

Walker, Helen W., 130, 145
Wallace, Henry, 205
Western Federation of Miners, 87, 193
Where Sparrows Work Hard, 264
Who Will Know Us, New Poems, 264
Wilson, President Woodrow, 132
World War I, 125, 132, 133, 139, 156, 163, 185

Z

Zamora, Bernice, 263
Zoot Suit, 260, 261
Zoot Suit Riots, 175, 176

Contributors

Rodolfo Alvarez is professor of Sociology at the University of California, Los Angeles.

Albert Camarillo is professor of history at Stanford. He received his Ph.D. from UCLA and has since published six books and over a dozen articles dealing with the experiences of Mexican Americans and other racial and immigrant groups in American cities. In addition to his teaching and research, he has held numerous administrative positions. He is currently the director of the newly established Center for Comparative Studies in Race and Ethnicity.

John R. Chávez is an associate professor of history at Southern Methodist University. He did his undergraduate work at California State University, Los Angeles and received his Ph.D from the University of Michigan. He has written several articles and a book, *The Lost Land: The Chicano Image of the Southwest*, that was nominated for a Pulitzer Prize. A second book, *Eastside Landmark: A History of the East Los Angeles Community Union* is forthcoming.

Mario T. García is professor of History and Chicano Studies at the University of California, Santa Barbara. He received his Ph.D. from the University of California, San Diego. His publications include *Desert Immigrants: The Mexicans of El Paso, 1880-1929* (Yale University Press, 1981); *Mexican Americans: Leadership, Ideology, and Identity, 1930-1960* (Yale University Press, 1989); *Memories of Chicano History: The Life and Narrative of Bert Corona*, and *Ruben Salazar, Border Correspondent* (University of California Press, 1995). His awards include a Guggenheim fellowship in 1992-93.

Richard García is an American intellectual and cultural historian with specialties in ethnic history and cultural studies. He is author of *Rise of the Mexican American Middle Class, San Antonio, 1929-1941* (1941), *Cesar Chavez: A Triumph of Spirit* (co-authored with Richard Griswold del Castillo) (1995) and *Notable Latino Leaders* (1997) co-authored with Matt Meier et al. He is professor of Ethnic Studies at California State University, Hayward.

Richard Griswold del Castillo is a Professor of Mexican American Studies at San Diego State University. He received his Ph.D. in History, with an emphasis on Chicano and U.S. history, from the University of California, Los Angeles. He has served as a consultant for a variety of film and publication projects and is active in promoting the inclusion of Chicano history within the school curriculum. He is the author of three major books: *The Los Angeles Barrio* (UC Press, 1980), *La Familia: Chicano Urban Families in the Southwest* (Notre Dame, 1984) and *The Treaty of Guadalupe Hidalgo* (University of Oklahoma Press, 1990). Currently he is collaborating on a biography of Cesar Chavez as well as a college level textbook history of Chicanos.

Abraham Hoffman is the author of *Unwanted Mexican Americans in the Great Depression*.

Douglas Monroy is Associate Professor of History and W.M. Keck Foundation Director of the Hulbert Center for Southwest Studies at The Colorado College. A native of Los Angeles and a graduate of UCLA he presently lives in Colorado Springs with his two children. Author of *Thrown among Strangers: The Making of Mexican Culture in Frontier California* (University of California Press, 1990), an Organization of American Historians prize winner, he is presently at work on a book about twentieth century Mexican Southern California.

Ricardo Romo is currently Professor of History at the University of Texas at Austin. He received his Ph.D. in History from the University of California, San Diego and is author of *East Los Angeles: History of a Barrio*.

Robert J. Rosenbaum received his Ph.D. in American History from the University of Texas at Austin. He is now a Special Assistant to the Commissioner of the Texas General Land Office. He is author of *Mexican Americans in Texas* and *Mexicano Resistance in the Southwest: "The Sacred Right of Self-Preservation."*

Thomas E. Sheridan is Associate Curator of Ethnohistory at the Arizona State Museum in Tucson. Dr. Sheridan received his Ph.D. in anthropology from the University of Arizona. His books include *Los Tucsonenses: The Mexican Community in Tucson, 1854-1941* and *Where the Dove Calls: The Political Ecology of a Peasant Corporate Community in Northwestern Mexico*. He is past director of the Mexican Heritage Project at the Arizona Historical Society and is currently completing a history of Arizona.